In loving memory of my parents

NETWORK SECURITY AND MANAGEMENT

THIRD EDITION

Brijendra Singh
Professor of Computer Science
Department of Computer Science
University of Lucknow
Lucknow

PHI Learning Private Limited
Delhi-110092
2022

₹ 795.00

NETWORK SECURITY AND MANAGEMENT, Third Edition
Brijendra Singh

ISBN-978-81-203-4497-6 (Print Book)
ISBN-978-93-5443-523-2 (e-Book)

Published by Asoke K. Ghosh, PHI Learning Private Limited, Rimjhim House, 111, Patparganj Industrial Estate, Delhi-110092 and Printed by Syndicate Binders, A-20, Hosiery Complex, Noida, Phase-II Extension, Noida-201305 (N.C.R. Delhi).

Contents

Preface

The positive response to the second edition of the book from students and academics encouraged me to come out with this third edition. In this edition, all chapters have been revised and updated and two new chapters have been added.

The term 'security' brings to mind all sorts of issues that refer to data protection and prevention of unauthorized access. Furthermore, there is no single definition of the term 'network security.' What is important are the assets that an organization deems crucial for successful operations and how to keep that safe. Once all the data are collected on items and/or services that are important, only then can a security policy be developed and implemented. Security policies do not come in generic flavours. Once the needs are determined, an organization can start building on security policies, modeled after existing implementations, but the policies will need to be tweaked and modified to fit the specifics of the organization.

The goal of network management is to provide users with a quality of service. To meet this goal, network services plan involve strategic and tactical planning of engineering, operations and maintenance of the network.

The field of network security and management is constantly undergoing changes in technology, applications and hence the need for continually changing skills set on the part of academics. Though this book is primarily designed as a one-semester course on Network Security and Management for students of computer science and engineering, information technology, computer application streams, it is equally suitable for professional audience.

The book is organized into eighteen chapters.

Chapter 1 introduces the concepts and basic vocabulary of network security and management, and explains the need for network security. It also describes the principles of security and management, and quality of good networks.

Chapter 2 mainly deals with organizational policy and security. It includes the information policy, security policy, physical security, social engineering and building a security plan.

Chapter 3 discusses security infrastructure, which includes infrastructure components, goals of security infrastructure and security models.

Chapter 4 provides a concise survey of the cryptographic algorithms and protocols underlying network security applications, including encryption methods, cryptographic algorithms, secret key and public key cryptography, message digest and security mechanisms.

Chapter 5 introduces network fundamentals with a brief history and outline of the applications in the field of computer networks.

Chapter 6 deals with hardware and software security, which includes smart cards, biometrics, virtual private networks, trusted operating systems, pretty good privacy and security protocols.

Chapter 7 begins by describing the introduction to databases, and discusses various issues on database security. It also discusses a vendor-specific security, and data warehouse control and security.

Chapter 8 dwells on information system security.

Chapter 9 describes the intrusion detection systems. Chapter 10 covers the fundamental concepts on network security, security services and firewalls.

Chapter 11 deals mainly with wireless security, which includes WAP security and security issues with WTLS. Chapter 12 describes the Web Security. Chapter 13 begins by describing the goals of network management and proceeds to examine network management standards, network management models, the infrastructure for network management and simple network management protocols.

Chapters 14 and 15 discuss various issues of security management, risk management and incident management. Chapter 15 covers security and law, which includes IT Act, 2000, Indian Contract Act, 1872, Indian Penal Code, Indian Copyright Act and Consumer Protection Act, 1986.

Chapter 17 describes the Internet governance and electronic mail policies for organizations. Chapter 18 covers Internet Banking Systems, which includes security problems, methodology for security and schematic flow of Internet Banking.

Questions and answers have been included at the end of the book with a view to helping the readers increase their understanding of the subject.

I thank Prof. M.K. Misra, Vice Chancellar, University of Lucknow, for fostering the excellent academic atmosphere at University of Lucknow which enabled me to write this book.

I express my deepest sense of regards to Prof. Ram Prakash Singh, Vice Chancellor, University of Lucknow, Lucknow; Prof. S.K. Ghosh, J.K. Institute of Applied Physics and Technology, University of Allahabad, Allahabad; Prof. Promod Chandra P. Bhatt, IIIT Bangalore; Prof. Deepak B. Phatak, IIT Bombay; Prof. C.R. Muthukrishnan, IIT Madras; Prof. L.M. Patnaik, IISc Bangalore; Prof. N.N. Jani, Saurashtra University, Rajkot; Prof. S. Kuppuswami, Pondicherry University, Pondicherry; Prof. M.P. Jaiswal, MDI Gurgaon; Prof. B.V.R. Reddy, I.P. University Delhi; Prof. A. Toll, University of Applied Science, Dresden, Germany; and Prof. Gopal Gupta, Monash University, Australia for their valuable guidance and suggestions.

I thank Prof. D.P. Dube, Institute for Development and Research in Banking Technology, Hyderabad, for contributing the chapter on Security of Internet Banking System. Many people have directly or indirectly contributed to the development of the book. Though I am unable to express my gratitude to each one of them individually, I remain grateful to all of them.

I greatly appreciate the efforts and cooperation of all the members of PHI Learning, in bringing out this book.

I thank my daughters Boentika and Sadhika for graciously accepting my absence from them during writing of this book. Finally, I owe a debt of gratitude to my wife for the constant support she lent me throughout the course of this endeavour.

Brijendra Singh

CHAPTER 1

Introduction

Chapter Outline

Computers are an integral part of everyday operations. Organizations depend on them. A computer system failure will have a critical impact on the organization. Potential vulnerabilities are computer system that could undermine operations, must therefore, be minimized or eliminated. Today the cost to business of stolen, misused, or altered information can be high, especially if real or purported damages to customers can be raced back to mismanagement. That is why you must value your information resources within the context of your business goals and constraints.

The objective of security management is to eliminate or minimize computer vulnerability to destruction, modification, or disclosure. If a security plan is to be effective, top management must be fully convinced of the need to take counteractive steps. To assess the seriousness of a computer breakdown or loss of data, each business has to evaluate threats to the company, the potential losses if the threats are realized, and the time and cost that will be necessary to recover from any breach in security.

Computer security itself is a term that has many meanings and related terms. Computer security entails the methods used to ensure a system is secure. Subjects such as authentication and access controls must be addressed in a broad terms of computer security. Seldom in today's world are computers not connected to other computers in networks. This then introduces the term network security to refer to the protection of the multiple computers and other devices that are connected together. Related to these two terms are two others, information security and information assurance, which place the focus of the security process not on the hardware and software being used, no on the data that is processed by them. Assurance also introduces another concept, that of the availability of the systems and information when we want them.

Security problems are as follows:

- Sixty years ago, very few people had access to computer system or network, and securing them was relatively an easy matter.
- There are many different ways to attack computers and networks to take advantage of what has made shopping, banking, investment, and leisure pursuits a simple matter of "dragging and clicking" for many people.
- The different types of electronic crime fall into two main categories: crimes in which the computer was the target of the attack, and incidents in which the computer was a means of perpetrating a criminal act.
- There are a number of different threats to security, including viruses and worms, intruders, insiders, criminal organizations, terrorists, and information warfare conducted by foreign countries.
- The biggest change that has occurred in security over the last forty years has been the change in the computing environment from large mainframes to a highly interconnected network of much smaller systems.
- One significant trend observed over the last several years has been the increase in the number of non-affiliated intruders as opposed to attacks by organized "hacking groups", criminal organizations, or nations.

1.1 WHY NETWORK SECURITY IS NEEDED

On September 11, 2001, terrorists seized control of four airplanes. Three were flown into buildings and the fourth crashed, with catastrophic loss of life. In the after month, the security and reliability of many aspects of society drew renewed scrutiny. One of these aspects was the widespread use of computers and their interconnecting networks. The issue is not new. In 1988, approximately 5,000 computers throughout the Internet were rendered unusable within 4 hours by a program called "*worm*". While the spread, and the effects, of this program alarmed computer scientists, most people were not worried because the worm did not affect their lives on their ability to do their jobs. In 1993, more users of computer systems were altered to such dangers when a set of programs called sniffers were placed on many computers run by network services providers and recorded login names and passwords.

Almost daily we read about computer and network viruses either about new attacks or the dangers of more potent viruses that are difficult to track and stop. We are strongly encouraged to install antivirus software if we own a computer. You may have experienced an attack on the Internet, during which you were not able to access your favorites websites for several hours. Most corporations have experienced one or more outages because of viruses or denial-of-service attacks, although they are often loathe to report the attacks, sometimes out of embarrassment.

This increase in terrorist attacks on the general population, as well as on specific segments of our society's infrastructure, comes at a time when large and small organizations of all types are becoming increasingly dependent on networks to carry on their activities. Networks have become assets like computers, data information. Without these assets most organizations find it impossible to conduct business. Communications with customers, suppliers, employees and other organizations are handled primarily through networks. The loss of the network communications channel could effectively cripple an organization. No longer can a business be operated without having access to information and reliable communication system. The network asset must be protected like other assets and surrounded with proper controls and the appropriate security. No wonder there is such a strong interest in the subjects of network and computer security. Organizational leaders and employees in all segments want to know what they can do to safeguard networks, their computers, and their livelihoods.

It is virtually impossible to eliminate all network security problems. Solutions that work well today may not provide adequate protection tomorrow because technology continues to advance. Determined, creative and unscrupulous people find ways to bypass or work around even the most stringent network security measures. We can minimize the risk of major network security incident, however, by making it extremely difficult expensive, or both to break through an organizations security defenses.

1.2 MANAGEMENT PRINCIPLES

"Network Security Policy'' is management's statement of the importance of their commitment to network security. The policy needs to describe in general terms what will be done, but does not deal with the way the protection is to be achieved. Writing the policy is complex because, in reality, it is normally a part of a broader document: the organizations information security policy. The network security policy needs to clearly state management's position about the importance of network security and the items that are to be protected. Management must understand that there is no such thing as a perfectly secure network. Furthermore, network security is a constantly moving target because of the advances in technology and the creativity of people who would like to break into a network of its attached computers. Measures put in place of minimize security risks today will need to be upgraded in the future and upgrades usually have a price attached, for which management will have to pay.

Management, at all levels, needs to support the policy and periodically reinforce it with employees in various ways. IT and network staff may need to install additional hardware, software and procedures to perform automated security checking. For a company to adequately manage information security on the network, it must have the following:

- A network security policy clearly defines the reasons why security is important to the company.
- Clearly defined roles and responsibilities to ensure that all aspects of security are performed.
- A security implementation plan that describes the steps needed to implement the policy.
- An effective implementation of appropriate security hardware and software.
- A plan to deal with any security breaches that do occur.
- A management review process to periodically ensure that the security policies and standards are adequate, effective and are being enforced.

1.3 SECURITY PRINCIPLES

There are many branches of security. If you consider the field of security as a hierarchy, you have "security" at the root and many branches leading outward from that, For example, national security, information security, and economic security may be considered subsets of the entire discipline of security.

In this book, we are considering network security, which is a subset of information security, as shown in Figure 1.1.

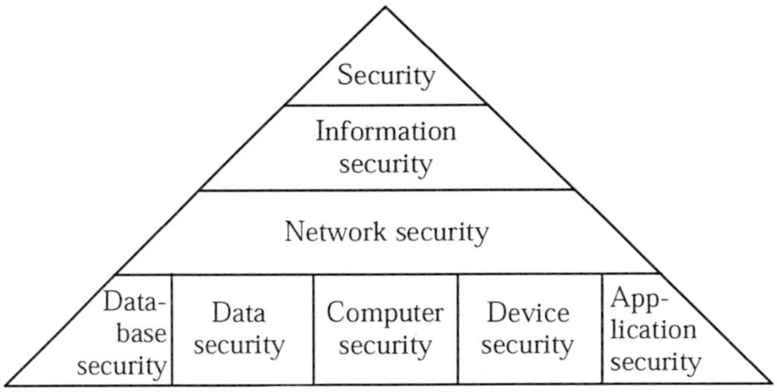

Figure 1.1 The hierarchy of security specializations.

The field of security is concerned with protecting general assets.

Information security is concerned with protecting information and information resources, such as books faxes, computer data, and voice communication; Network security, is concerned with protecting data, hardware, and software on a computer network.

For many years, the focus of security was on prevention. If we could prevent somebody from gaining access to our computer systems and networks then we assured that we had obtained security. Protection was thus equated with prevention. It was wrong concept.

Every security technique and technology fall into at least one of the three elements: prevention, detection and response. Security equation can be represented as:

Protection = Prevention + (Detection + Response)

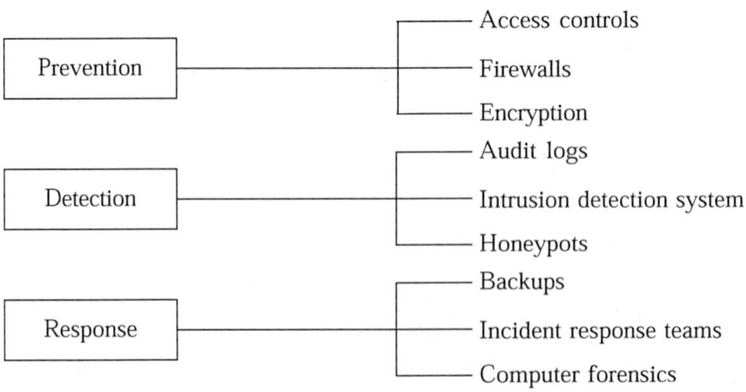

There are three ways an organization can choose to address the protection of its networks: ignore security issues, provide host security and approach security at a network level. The last two hosts and network security, have prevention as well as detection and response components.

If an organization decides to ignore security, I have chosen to utilize the minimal amount of security that is provided with its workstations, servers, and devices. No additional security measures will be implemented. Each "out of the box" system has certain security settings that can be configured they should be. To actually protect an entire network, however, requires work in addition to the few protection mechanisms that come with systems by default.

Host security takes a granular view of security by focusing on protecting each computer and device individually instead of addressing protection of the network as a whole. When host security is used, each computer is relied upon to protect itself. If an organization devices to implement only host security and does not include network security, there is a high probability of introducing or overlooking vulnerabilities. Most environments are filled with different operating systems (Windows, UNIX, Linux), different versions of those operating systems, and different types of installed applications. Each operating system has security configurations that differ from other systems and different versions of the same operating system may in fact have variations between them. Ensuring that every computer is "locked down" to the same degree as every other system in the environment can be overwhelming and often results in an unsuccessful and frustrating effort.

Host security is important and should always be addressed. Security, however, should not stop there, as host security is a complementary process to be combined with network security. If individual host computers have vulnerabilities embodied within them, then network security can provide another layer of protection that will hopefully stop any intruders getting into the environment. In some smaller environments, host security by itself may be an option, but as systems becomes connected into networks, security should include the actual network itself. In network security, an emphasis is placed on controlling access to internal computers from external entities. This control can be through device such as routers, firewalls, authentication hardware and software, encryption and Intrusion Detection Systems (IDSs).

1.4 NETWORK MANAGEMENT

Managing corporate network is becoming harder as such networks become larger and more complex. When we talk about network management, it includes not only the components that transport information in the network, but also systems that generate the traffic in the network. What use in a computer network if there are no systems in the network to provide service to the users? The system could be client hosts, or database servers or file servers, or mail servers. In the client/server environment the network control is no longer centralized, but distributed.

Network management can be defined as OAM and P (Operations, Administration, Maintenance and Provisioning) of network and services. The operations group is concerned with daily operations in providing network services. Network administration is concerned with establishing and administering the overall goals, policies and procedures of network management. The installation and maintenance group handles functions that include both installation and repairs of facilities and equipment. Provisioning involves network planning, and circuit provisioning, traditionally handled by the engineering or provisioning department.

The goal of the network management is to ensure that the users of a network receive the information technology services with the quality of service that they expect.

- Network Operations
  - Fault management/service restoration
  - Configuration management
  - Performance management
  - Security management
  - Accounting management
  - Reports management
  - Inventory management
  - Data gathering and analysis
- Network Provisioning
  - Planning
  - Design
- Network Maintenance
  - Fault management
  - Trouble ticket administration
  - Network installation
  - Network repairs
  - Facilities installation and maintenance
  - Routine network tests

1.5 SECURITY ATTACKS

How serious is a particular attack type, is depends on two things, how the attack is carried out and what damage is done to the compromised system. An attacker being able to see code on his machine is probably the most serious kind of attack for a home user. For an e-commerce company, a denial-of-service (DoS) attack or information leakage may be of more immediate concern. Each vulnerability that can lead to compromise can be traced to a particular category, or class of attack. The properties of each class give you a rough feel for how serious an attack in that class is, as well as how hard it is to defend against.

We examine seven categorized attack types. These seven attack types are the general criteria used to classify security issues.

- Denial-of-service (DoS)
- Information leakage
- Regular file access
- Misinformation
- Special file/database access
- Remote arbitrary code executing
- Elevation of privileges

1.5.1 Denial-of-Service (DoS)

What is a denial-of-service (DoS) attack? A DoS attack takes place when availability to a resource is intentionally blocked or degraded by an attacker. In other words, the attack impedes the availability of the resource to its regular authorized users. These types of attacks can occur through one of two vectors: either on the local system, or remotely from access a network. The attack may concentrate on degrading processes, degrading storage capability destroying files to render the resource unusable or shutting down parts of the system or processes.

1.5.2 Information Leakage

Information leakage can be likened to leaky pipes. Whenever something comes out, it is almost always undesirable and results in some sort of damage. Information leakage is typically an abused resource that precludes attack. In the same way that military Generals rely on information from reconnaissance troops that have penetrated enemy lines to observe the type of weapons, manpower, supplies and other resources possessed by the enemy, attackers enter the network to perform the same tasks, gathering information about programs, operating systems, and network design on the target network.

1.5.3 Regular File Access

Regular file access can give an attacker several different means from which to launch an attack. Regular file access may allow an attacker to gain access to sensitive information, such as the usernames or passwords of users on a system. Regular file access could also lead to an attacker gaining access to other files in other ways, such as changing the permissions or ownership of file, or through a symbolic link attack.

1.5.4 Misinformation

The concept of misinformation can present itself in many ways. Let's go back to the military scenario. Suppose that guards are posted at various observation points in the field, and one of them observes the enemy's reconnaissance team. The guard alerts seniors, who send out their own reconnaissance team to find out exactly whop is spying on them.

Now, you can guess that the enemy General has already thought about this scenario. Equally likely, he has also considered his options. He could wide all of his troops and make it appear as if nobody is there. But what if somebody saw may forces entering the area, would be his next thought. And if the other side was to end a "recon" team to scope out his position and strength, discovering his army greater than theirs, they would likely either fortify their position, or move to different position where they would be more difficult to attack, or where they could not be found.

Therefore, he wants to make his forces seem like less of a threat than they really are. He hides his heavy weapons, and the greater part of his infantry while allowing visibility of only a small portion of his force. This is the same idea behind misinformation.

1.5.5 Special File/Database Access

Methods used to gain access to a system are through special files and database access. These types of files, although different in structure and function, exist on all systems and all platforms. From an NT system to Sun Enterprise 15,000 to a Unisys Mainframe, these files are common amongst all platforms.

1.5.6 Remote Arbitrary Code Execution

Remote code execution is one of the most commonly used methods of exploiting systems. Several noteworthy attacks on high profile websites have been due to the ability to execute arbitrary code remotely. Remote arbitrary code is serious in nature because it often does not require authentication, and therefore, may be exploited by anybody.

Returning to the military scenario, suppose the enemy General's reconnaissance troops are able to slip past the other side's guards. They can then sit and map the other's position and return to the General with camp coordinates, as well as the coordinates of things within the opposing side's camp.

The General can then pass this information to his Fire Support Officer and the Fire Support Officer can launch several artillery strikes to soften up the opponents's targets. Suppose that the enemy knows about the technology behind the artillery of the General's army and has the capability to remotely take control of the coordinates inputs of the General's artillery pieces, the enemy would then be able to turn its own artillary on the General's army.

This type of control is exactly the type of control an attacker can give by executing arbitrary code remotely. If the attacker can execute arbitrary code through a service on the system, the attacker can use the service against the system, with power similar to that of using an army's own artillery against them.

1.5.7 Elevation of Privileges

Of all attacks launched, elevation of privileges is certainly the most common. An elevation of privileges occurs when user against access to resources that were not authorized previously. These resources may be anything from remote access to a system to administrative access on a host.

1.6 QUALITIES OF A GOOD NETWORK

Computer networks must respond to many needs. These needs often collide. The conflicts start with the fundamental incompatibility of access and security needs. You must protect your most important information. At the same time, though, it does no good to have all this well-secured information, if no one can make use of it. The need for security will always conflict with the need for access.

To meet the organization's information needs, a network must have qualities like these:

- Network should work together
- Their operations should be transparent to users
- They must provide remote access
- They must maintain peak performance.

While meeting all these demands for open access, a network must also meet the organization's security needs. The important are:

- Confidentiality
- Reliability
- Integrity.

A network should not allow anyone to see confidential information without authorization. This requires a reliable way to identify users. It also requires that you set up a system like the government's security clearances. Only certain people should have access to certain kinds of information your salary, to name the first and best examples.

Of all the sad words of tongue and pen, some of the saddest must be, "The computer is down". To put it simply, a secure network must work right. Ideally, it will always work right. That won't happen in practice, of course, but, beware of arbitrary goals that encourage you to stop short of your best. If your goal is to make the system work right 98.6% of the time, you will tend to relax and pat yourself on the back once you have achieved that statistics. In the spirit of continuous improvement, you should then be shooting for 98.7%. Never stop trying to do better.

An employee should always has access to accurate timely information. That should indicate all the information that is needed to do the job well. Since an important element of security is to protect the system's integrity, security, measures must include features like validation systems to screen out errors, both deliberate and accidental.

The modern approach to quality and reliability concerns excellence. Excellence when the network is designed, excellence when the network is made, excellence as the network is used, and excellence throughout its lifetime. Good quality network requires an appropriate combination of statistical, engineering, management and motivational efforts.

REVIEW QUESTIONS

1.1 Define computer security and its importance. Justify that computer failure will have a critical impact on the organization.

1.2 Why network security is needed and how to maintain?

1.3 Why security management is needed? Explain why management, at all levels, needs to support the policy and periodically reinforce it with employers in various ways.

1.4 Why network security policy is important?

1.5 Explain management principles with respect to network security of particular organization.

1.6 Discuss security principles. Explain the hierarchy of security specializations.

1.7 How is it possible for organization to protect network of organization?

1.8 Why host security is important?

1.9 What is the role of network management? How to control network operation?

1.10 What is the importance of network provisioning? how it will select the network management?

1.11 Explain the importance of network maintenance and how will you justify that it is a part of network management?

1.12 Explain security attacks.

1.13 What is a denial-of-service attack?

1.14 Write short notes on:

(a) Information leakage

(b) Regular file access

1.15 What is the difference between information leakage and misinformation?

1.16 Explain remote arbitrary code execution.

1.17 Explain elevation of privileges.

1.18 Describe qualities of good network. Justify that the need for security will always conflict with the need for across.

CHAPTER 2

Organizational Policy and Security

Chapter Outline

Today the cost to businesses of stolen, misused, or altered information can be high, especially if real or purported damages to customers can be traced back to mismanagement. That is why you must value your information resources within the context of your business goal and constraints.

The objective of security management is to eliminate or minimize computer vulnerability to destruction modification, or disclosure. A good manager will know the types and forms of information generated and how the information is used in the business before planning, and how to manage it.

Policy provides the rules that governs how systems should be configured and how employees of an organization should act in normal circumstances and react during unusual circumstances. Policy defines how security should be implemented. This includes the proper configurations on computer systems and networks as well as physical security measures. Policy will define the proper mechanisms to use to protect information and systems.

However, the technical aspects of security are not the only things that are defined by the policy. Policy also defines how employees should perform certain security-related duties such as the administration of users. Policy also defines how employees are expected to behave when using computer systems that belong to the organization.

Security policies can generally be subdivided into many categories, depending on their evidence and scope. Often, the following broad categories are used, along with other that may apply in specific circumstances:

- *Computer systems and networks:* These policies apply generally to system and network administrators who are responsible for designing, implementing and supporting computers and networks. These policies tell the administrators what types of technology to use, how and where network controls should be placed, and what business requirements pertain to product selection. Examples include password and/or authentication mechanisms, system level protection such as antivirus and desktop firewall software, hardware firewalls, and network segmentation. The policies tell the administrators what the company expects from each of these categories.

- *Personal management:* These policies apply to individual employees. In general, they apply to all employees of the company without exception, so they will be consistent across the enterprise. These policies tell the employees how to conduct their everyday business in a secure fashion. Examples include password management, handling of sensitive or confidential information, and dealing with social engineering. The policies tell the employees what the company expects of them in each of these areas.
- *Physical security:* These policies typically apply to the facilities, and somewhat peripherally to system and network administrators. They define what types of physical security controls are to be used. Examples include visual surveillance, door entry mechanisms and audible alarms. The policies tell the managers and staff responsible for physical security what protections should be employed to safeguard physical assets and people.

The security policy tells its audience what must be done. It does not address how these things should be done—that falls under the domain of implementation, which must be kept completely separate from the policy itself. Figure 2.1 gives an indication of the organizations in a typical company that would need to read the security policy.

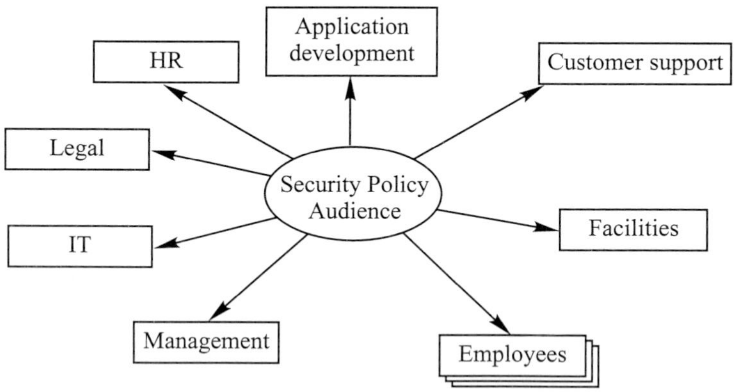

Figure 2.1 Security policy audience.

The topics covered by the security policy follow from the business requirements, which, in general, should have been previously identified by senior management so the policy will support the business process. The topics included in a security policy vary from organization to organization. Figure 2.2 demonstrates the process required to create an effective security policy. First, business requirements must be clearly defined so the policy will be relevant to the business environments. Also, the scope of the policy must be classified so the affected parties can be consulted during its development. The business requirements definition and the scope definition should be part of the management and planning (initial) phase of any

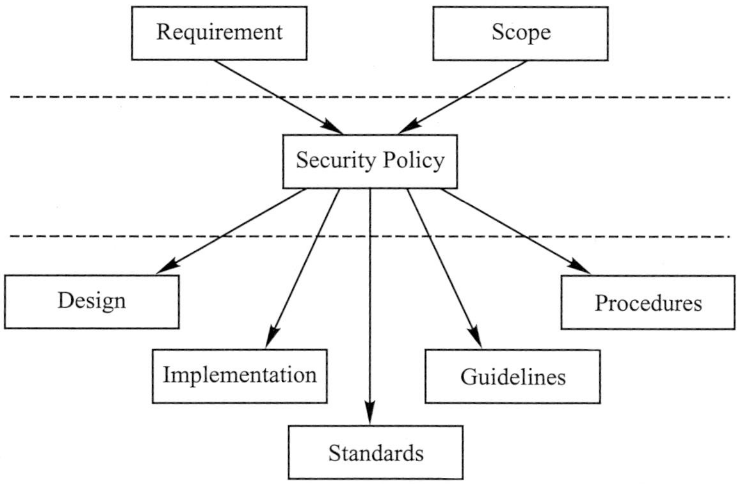

Figure 2.2 The security policy's place in a hierarchy of implementation.

implementation, which is why they are grouped together in the top section. Next, the security policy is documented, based on the business requirements. Once the security policy is in place, management decisions can be made with regard to the design and implementation of network technologies and controls. Security policy development should follow requirements and scope definition, and this process is shown in the middle section. After the security policy is put in place, procedures, standards and guidelines can also be produced to direct the use and management of those technologies and controls. This represents the implementation phase in lower grouping.

2.1 SECURITY POLICIES, STANDARDS AND GUIDELINES

An important part of any organization's approach to implementing security are the policies, standards, procedures and guidelines that are established to detail what users and administrators should be doing to maintain the security of the systems and network. Collectively, these documents provide the guidance needed to determine how security will be implemented in the organizations. Given this guidance, the specific technology and security mechanisms required can be planned for:

Policies are high-level, broad statements of what the organization wants to accomplish. They are made by management when laying out the organizations position on some issue.

Standards are mandatory elements regarding the implementation of a policy. They are accepted specifications providing specific details on how a policy is to be enforced.

Guidelines are recommendations relating to a policy.

Procedures are the step-by-step instructions on how to implement policies in the organization.

The constant monitoring of the network and the periodic review of the relevant documents are part of the process that is the operational model. When applied to policies, this process results in what is known as the policy life cycle. This operational process roughly consists of four steps:

- Plan
- Implement
- Monitor
- Evaluate.

The first step is to plan for security in your organization. In this step, you develop the policies, procedures, and guidelines that will be implemented and design the security components that will protect your network.

In second step, implement the plans and next you monitor to ensure that both the hardware and software as well as the policies, procedures and guidelines are effective in securing your systems. Finally, you evaluate the effectiveness of the security measures you have in place. After evaluating your security posture, you begin again with step one, this time adjusting the security mechanisms you have in place, and then continue with this cyclic process.

2.2 INFORMATION POLICY

The information policy defines what sensitive information is within the organization and how that information should be protected. This policy should be constructed to cover all information within the organization. Each employee is responsible for protecting sensitive information that comes into employee's possession. Information can be in the form of paper records or electronic files. The policy must take both into account.

An information policy must address how sensitive information is transmitted. Information can be transmitted in a number of ways (e-mail, regular mail, fax, and so on), and the policy should address each of them. For sensitive information sent through mail, the policy should specify encryption of the file (if attachments) or the body of the message. If the hardcopies of the information are to be sent some method that requires a signed receipt is appropriate. When document is to be faxed, it is appropriate to require a phone call to receiving party and for the sender to request the receiver to wait by the fax machine for the document. This will prevent the document from sitting on the receiving fax machine for an extended period of time.

Information of different types need to be secured in different ways. Therefore, a classification system is needed, whereby information is classified, a policy is laid down on how to handle information according to its class and security mechanisms are enforced on systems handling information accordingly.

Here, a classification system is proposed which has four classes based on information. The lowest **Class 1** is the least sensitive and the highest **Class 4** is for the most important information/processes.

Concepts:

- All data has an owner.
- The data or process owner must classify the information into one of the security levels depending on legal obligations, costs, corporate into policy and business needs.

- If the owner is not sure at what level data should be classified, use level 3.
- The owner must declare who is allowed to access the data.
- The owner is responsible for this data and must secure it or have it secured (e.g. via a security administrator) according to its classification.
- All documents should be classified and the classification level should be written on at least the title page.

Once the data on a system has been classified to one of the following levels, then that system should be installed to conform to all directives for that class and classes below. Each level is a superset of the previous level. For example, if a system is classified as Class 3, then the system must follow the directives of Class 1, 2, and 3.

If a system contains data or more than one sensitivity class, it must be classified according to that needed for the most confidential data on the system.

Class 1: Public/non-classified information

Data on these systems could be made public without any implications for the company (i.e. the data is not confidential). Data integrity is not vital. Loss of service due to malicious attacks is an acceptable danger.

Examples: Test services without confidential data, certain public information services, product brochures widely distributed, data available in the public domain anyway.

Class 2: Internal information

External access to this data is to be prevented, but should this data become public, the consequences are not critical (e.g. the company may be publicly embarrassed). Internal access is selective. Data integrity is important but not vital.

Examples of this type of data are found in development groups (where no live data is present), certain production public services, certain customer data, "normal" working documents and project/meeting protocols, telephone books.

Class 3: Confidential information

Data in this class is confidential within the company and protected from external access. If such data were to be accessed by unauthorized persons, it could influence the company's operational effectiveness, cause an important financial loss, provide a significant gain to a competitor or cause a major drop in customer confidence. Data integrity is vital.

Examples: Datacenters normally maintain this level of security. Salaries, personnel data, accounting data, passwords, information on corporate security weaknesses, very confidential customer data and confidential contracts.

Class 4: Secret information

Unauthorized external or internal access to this data would be critical to the company. Data integrity is vital. The number of people with access to this data should be very small. Very strict rules must be adhered to in the usage of this data.

Examples: Military data, secret contracts.

The security required of a system depends on what information it processes, for what purposes. The information and information processing functions should have sensitivity and availability labels (be classified), so that the security needs to the system can be specified.

The security needs of the system may concentrate on availability, confidentiality or integrity, for example:

- A system may not contain confidential data, but it must be available 24 hours a day so it has low-data sensitivity, but high-availability requirements. High-availability systems always require better confidentiality to prevent "denial-of-service" attacks.
- For other systems confidentiality (i.e. non-disclosure of information) is more important than integrity (modification of information), for others the reverse is true.

Systems need to be broken down into components and the security of each component analyzed. When a user access data, he passes through a variety of possible security controls, or components. Some of these controls are physical, some organizational and some are computer-based. The following is one way of representing the components/controls involved as shown in Figure 2.3.

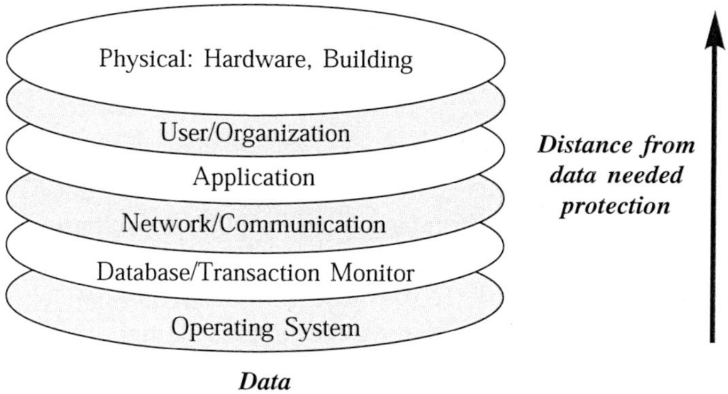

Figure 2.3 Security of various components of system.

For data to be secured *each of the different layers (security components) from physical to operating system need to be correctly configured and monitored.* It is not enough to simply secure the physical access for example, because access via the network may also be possible.

In using a model of this kind, it is possible to breakdown the measures needed to protect a system (or data) into subsystems which correspond to real-life software/hardware/human entities.

2.3 SECURITY POLICY

The security policy defines the technical requirement for security on computer systems and network equipments. It defines how a system or network administrator should configure a system with regard to security. This configuration will also affect users and some of the requirements stated in the policy should be communicated to the general user community. The primary responsibility for the implementation of this policy falls on the system and network administrators with the backing of management.

The security policy should define the requirements to be implemented by each system. However, the policy itself should not define specific configurations for different operating systems. This should be provided in the specific configuration procedures.

The security policy should define how users will be identified. Generally, this means that the security policy should either define a standard for user IDs or point to a system administration procedure that defines that standard.

The security policy should define the standard requirement for access controls to be placed on electronic files. Two requirements should be defined; the mechanism that is required and the default requirement for new files.

The audit section of the security policy should define the types of events to be audited on all systems. Normally, security policies require the following events to be audited.

- Logins
- Logouts
- Failed access to files or system objects
- Remote access (successful and failed)
- Privileged actions (those performed by administrators both successes and failures)
- System events (such as shutdowns and reboots) Each event should also capture the following information:
  - — User ID
  - — Date and time
  - — Process ID (if there is one)
  - — Action performed
  - — Success or failure of the event.

The security policy should specify how long the audit records should be kept and how they should stored. If possible, the security policy should also define how the audit records should be reviewed and examined, including how often.

Permanent network connections are those that comes into the organization over some type of permanent communication line. The security policy should define the type of security device to be used on such connection. Most often, a firewall is the appropriate device. Just specifying the type of device does not specify the appropriate level of protection. The security policy should define a basic network access control policy, should define a basic network access control policy to be implemented on the device as well as a procedure for requesting and granting access that is not part of the standard configuration.

Often, organizations allow employees to access internal system from external locations. The security policy should specify the mechanisms to use when this type of access is to be granted. It is appropriate to specify that all communications should be protected by encryption and point to the section on encryption or specifies on the type of encryption. Since the access is from the outside, it is also appropriate to specify a strong authentication mechanism. The security policy should also establish the procedure for allowing employees to gain authentication for such access.

The security policy should define acceptable encryption algorithms for use within the organization and point back to the information policy to show the appropriate algorithms to protect sensitive information. There is no reason for the security policy to specify only one algorithm. The security policy should also specify the required procedures for key management.

The security policy should specify where security programs that look for malicious code (such as viruses, root kits, backdoors) are to be placed. Appropriate locations include file servers, desktop systems, and electronic mail servers. The security policy should specify the requirements for such security programs. This may include a requirement for such security programs to examine specific file types and top check files when they are opened or on a scheduled basis. The policy should also require updates of the signatures for such security programs on a periodic basis such as monthly.

Detailed security configurations for various operating systems, network devices, and other telecommunication equipment should be placed in appendices or separate configuration procedures. This allows these detailed documents to be modified as necessary without changing the organization's security policy.

2.4 PHYSICAL SECURITY

Physical security consists of all mechanisms used to ensure that physical access to the computer systems and networks is restricted to only authorized users. The purpose of the physical access controls is the same as that of computer and network access controls—you want to restrict access to those who are authorized to have it.

The physical security of the organization's building is a key component of information security. The examination of physical security measures should include the physical access controls to the site as well as of sensitive areas within the site. For example, the data centre should have separate physical access controls from the buildings as a whole. At a minimum, access to the data centre must be strictly limited. When examining the physical security measures, determine the following:

- The type of physical protections to the suite, buildings, office space, paper records, and data centre.
- Who holds keys to what doors?
- What critical areas exist in the site or building aside from the data centre and what is so important about these areas?

You should also examine the location of communication lines within the building and the place where the communication lines enter the building. These are places where networks taps may be placed so all such locations should be included in the sensitive or critical areas list. There are also sites that may be subject to outage based solely on where they are located.

Physical security also includes the power of environmental controls, and fire suppression systems used with the data centre. Gather the following information about these systems:

- How power is supplied to the site and data centre?
- What types of UPS are in place and how long the existing UPS will keep system up?
- Which systems are connected to UPS?
- Who will be notified if the power fails and the UPS taken over?
- What environmental controls are attached to the UPS and what type of environmental controls are in place in the data centre?
- Who will be notified if the environmental controls fail?
- What type of fire suppression system is in place in the data centre?

2.5 SOCIAL ENGINEERING

Social engineering is the process of convincing an authorized individual to provide confidential information or access to an unauthorized individual. Social engineering takes advantage of what continually turns out to be the weakest point in our security perimeter—the humans Kevin Mitnick, a convicted cyber criminal turned security consultant, once stated "Don't rely on network safeguards and firewalls to protect your information." Look to your most vulnerable spot. You will usually find that vulnerability lies in your people.

The goal of social engineering is to gradually obtain the pieces of information necessary to make it to the next step. This is done repeatedly until the ultimate goal is reached. If social engineering is such an effective means of gaining unauthorized access to data and information; how can it be stopped? The most effective means is through the training and education of users, administrators, and security personnel. All employees should be instructed in the techniques that attackers might use and trained to recognize when a social engineering attack is being attempted. One important aspect of this training is for employees to recognize the type of information that should be protected and also how seemingly important information may be combined with other pieces of information to potentially divulge sensitive information. This is known as data aggregation.

2.6 SECURITY PROCEDURES

The best physical and technical methods are of little value if your employees do not use them properly. More important you can use procedural methods to conduct your overall business operations. At the same time, you can minimize the degree to which security measures interface with full, productive use of your computers.

Procedural security is a set of management and supervisory controls. It includes rules for the use of computers and data, and ways to detect unauthorized use.

- Data input
- Data processing

- Program development
- Output
- Communication
- Storage.

Procedural security covers the entire range of computer operations, it becomes an integral part of your business. You will consider it when hiring employees. Many operating controls will be based on security considerations. Auditing and supervisory techniques will be designed with security in mind. You can establish a secure computer system and back it up with adequate check and balances, as an everyday management activity.

Most procedural security measures are based on two established principles:

- Make each employee personally accountable.
- Make sure that it take more than one person to commit a fraudulent act.

If a sensitive transaction is being made, you should be able to identify the person responsible and hold that employee personally responsible for the results.

A good procedural security program should include:

- A written policy that spells out employee's responsibilities, provides a means to detect violations, and has enough management control to make sure it is properly implemented.
- Management controls to make sure the policies are observed, make sure they keep up with the development of your computer systems.
- Control over processes of computer use, and access to programs and data.
- Regular tests of your security system, to make sure it is adequate and employees are observing the proper procedure.
- A standard procedure to deal with anyone caught missing the system. This can range from minor disciplinary action to criminal changes if necessary. Be ready to take this action even if it might mean had publicity for the company.
- Constant communication, management officials and members of the technical staff should stay in touch to discuss security needs and problems.

2.7 BUILDING A SECURITY PLAN

The basic goals of a network security system are pretty much like the security goals for any kind of computer system.

- To protect information from accidental destruction or modification.
- To protect information from deliberate destruction or modification.
- Make sure the data is available to authorized users, when they need it and in a form they can use.

To secure a networked system, you will need nearly as much diplomatic sense as technical know-how. For example, you will have to influence people in client department. People over whom you have no particular authority. You will find yourself in many situations where you must build alliances in support of a working security plan. One of the most effective alliances you can form is with Human Resources. There are many ways HR can help you.

- Helping you identify the key managers in each client department.
- Devising professional surveys and other means to learn about employees; current attitudes towards security.
- Helping to set up and conduct interviews with department managers and employees.
- Planning and delivering training programs to support the security program.

Your main objective is to determine just where the organization's security might need improvement. Many employees also have useful ideas about security problems in their areas of responsibility and may even have some suggestions for solving them. You can present a case to top management, pointing to specific problems and offering legitimate solutions.

Areas to examine in the preliminary assessment

- Enterprise–wide systems that carry sensitive information but may be lacking in security. Electronic mail systems are common examples.
- Applications and networks that see heavy use in day-to-day operations. These busy services are the most likely to carry information that should be protected.
- Danger spots where data might be altered or lost during transmission. For example, a large transmission of engineering drawing may overload the capacity of a local area network.
- Network components that need physical protection. These can include servers and wiring hubs.
- Ensuring security policies and practices. Assess how well they respond to identified needs and how well they are observed.
- Prevailing employees attitudes about security.

Sometimes knowing what employees think can give you significant clues to the major challenges you face. You can ask questions like these determine employee's sentiments and their levels of security awareness.

- What do you understand about computer security?
- How do you feel about present security practices? Are they effective? Do they interface with your doing your job?
- What do you do in your job to protect sensitive information?

2.7.1 Elements of Security Plan

Your completed security plan should have two major sections:

1. A risk assessment.
2. Strategies to deal with identified risks.

These strategies fall into several categories:

- Procedural tactics like revised security policies.
- Physical protection, to prevent direct access to important resources.
- Technical security, which includes both hardware and software techniques.

A good way to access your risks is to examine the kind of data you handle. Ask questions like these:

- What kind of data do you maintain?
- For what purposes does the organization use it?
- What would the organization lose if the data were lost or stolen?

If your budget is limited and whose is not, it makes sense to concentrate your effort on the threats that are most serious to your organization. Once you have countered the most serious threats, additional spending will be less cost-effective.

2.7.2 Network Security Planning

A full-scale security plan, is a complex document that can take a large toll on your time and energy. Not everyone writes a complex new plan from scratch. Not everyone has to.

The only time you need to go through the full process of analysis and justification is if you decide not to follow the prevailing standard. For example, should you decide a particular risk is too small, and its solution too expensive to be used in your organization, you should be prepared to defend that judgement. Be equally prepared, should you believe your unique situation dictates a higher than normal degree of security.

First level security: The need is so universal nearly everyone will use them.

Second level security: These are used less universally, but they are still familiar, standardized and well-accepted. Someone who proposes one of these controls should demonstrate that the risk is worth the effort, but the selection of the strategy itself is more or less automatic.

Third level security: Here, both the risks and the responses are truly unique to your situation. Anyone who makes a proposal at this level should be prepared to strongly justify both the needs and the response.

Table 2.1 illustrates how first level security works. It starts with a list of standard security techniques that represent the element of first level security.

Table 2.1 List of first level security controls

Item	*Class*
Administrator computer access control	Procedural/technical
Backup data files and programs	Procedural/technical
Comply with laws and regulations	Procedural
Allow for contingency recovery-equipment replacement	Disaster control
Create a disaster recovery plan	Disaster control
Encrypt the password file	Technical
Establish computer security management committee	Procedural
Establish passwords for network access	Procedural/technical and physical
Isolate sensitive production jobs	Procedural/technical
Log user trouble cells	Procedural/technical
Minimize the no. of copies of sensitive data files and reports	Procedural
Minimize traffic and access to work areas	Physical
Place employees identification on work products	Procedural
Place physical security of remote network node	Physical
Network activity records	Procedural
Restrict the display of sensitive information	Technical
Validation data input	Technical

You should plan to adopt these measures unless you have a specific reason not to do so. Also listed are the types of security measures into which each measure falls: Physical, procedural, technical or disaster control. Some measures include elements of more than one type.

Table 2.2 illustrates how second level security works. There are standard tactics you can use when conditions indicate. The table includes some conditions under which you would normally consider them.

Table 2.2 List of second level security controls

Item	*Use When*	*Class*
Appoint a computer security officer	You have enough computer resources to justify the position	Procedural/physical
Control access to loading locks	You want to maintain strict control overall access	Physical
Encrypt data	You need the highest degree of protection	Technical
Generate passwords automatically	There are many people with access to the network	Technical
Monitor computer use	You want to ensure that only employees have access	Procedural

(*Contd.*)

Table 2.2 List of second level security controls (*Contd.*)

Item	*Use When*	*Class*
Provide alternative power supply	You need a high degree of reliability	Disaster control
Provide for dynamic password. Changes by users.	There may be frequent interruptions in the network node use	Technical
Provide for identification and trust worthiness of couriers	You use couriers to carry sensitive information	Physical/procedural
Provide terminal identifiers	You need a high level of security at individual access points	Technical
Separate test and production systems	You have a large system of linked networks	Technical
Sign agreements with remote users	You want to control remote access	Procedural

The process of building network security has seven basic steps:

Step 1: Determine the scope of the review (start by identifying, at least in broad strokes the people and facilities that will be involved in the security plan)

Step 2: Identify existing security controls.

Step 3: List additional control techniques.

Step 4: See what preliminary list of first level security controls.

Step 5: Build a preliminary list of first level security controls.

Step 6: Identify and address the remaining risks.

Step 7: Prepare a management proposal based on network security planning.

2.8 IMPLEMENTING A SECURITY POLICY

The security policy is a living document. This means it is not written once and left unchanged for years. The policy should be regularly updated in response to changing business conditions, technologies, customer requirements, and so on. Some form of document version control technology may be helpful in managing this lifecycle process.

In order to communicate the security policy, it is best to keep it online or in a place where its audience will be able to review and understand changes as they are approved and implemented. Some companies use an intranet web site to communicate this security policy, so employees can easily reference it throughout the work day.

Once the security policy is in place, well established, and in a position to dictate daily company operations, an audit may be performed by outside agencies or internal departments. An audit compares existing practices to the intentions of the policy. Having an unbiased third-party perspective can be helpful in isolating weaknesses or problems with the policy and its enforcement—this requires a disinterested party (not the security organization or the IT department) to perform the audit. Audits can be performed as often as needed-monthly, quarterly, yearly, or at some other interval. Security policy compliance should be audited at least once a year, because longer perods may allow for substantial deviation between the policy and the operations.

REVIEW QUESTIONS

2.1 Explain objective of security management. What is the difference between policy and standard?

2.2 Why policies, standards and guidelines are important for any organization to implement the security? Explain the various categories of security policies.

2.3 What are the steps in operational process?

2.4 Explain information policy. Why it is important for any organization?

2.5 What is the difference between information policy and security policy?

2.6 Describe physical security. Justify that physical security is the key component of information security.

2.7 Explain environment control. Is it a part of physical security, Why?

2.8 What is the purpose of social engineering with respect to security of organization?

2.9 Why security procedures should be implemented? Is it a part of management?

2.10 What are the important steps to build a security plan? Explain various elements of security plan.

2.11 What is the difference between first level security and second level security?

2.12 What are the steps used in the process of building network security?

CHAPTER 3

Security Infrastructure

Chapter Outline

Infrastructure security begins with the actual design of the infrastructure itself. The proper use of the right components not only improves performance but also improves security. Today, a computing environment is not isolated from its network components. The network components are part of the overall computing environment and have become an essential aspect of a total computing environment. From routers, switches and cables that connect the devices. As the firewalls and gateways that manage communication from the network design to the protocol employed all of these items have essential roles, from both performance and security standpoints.

Before we dive into design principles, we must first understand some basic definitions and components of our security design. What is a security infrastructure? The response to that question may be many different things to many people, but let's try to boil its meaning down into one comprehensive thought. A security infrastructure should provide a synergistic use of many components of its architecture, organized in such a manner as to improve the overall security posture beyond any single component. Using this definition, we can infer many things about the design and a nature of a security infrastructure.

Employing a firewall, however excellent your security policy may be, does not constitute a security infrastructure if does not work in conjunction with other components of your architecture. Because this firewall, for example, does not interact with other aspects of your security infrastructure, it is security component and not part of the security infrastructure.

Security failures can occur in two ways. First, a failure can allow unauthorized users access to resources and data they are not authorized to use, compromising information security. Second, a failure can prevent an authorized user from access to resources and data overlooked, but it can be as serious as the first. The primary goal of network infrastructure security is to allow all authorized use and deny all unauthorized use of resources.

3.1 INFRASTRUCTURE COMPONENTS

The major components of a security infrastructure can be defined as belonging to one of four categories. These categories are:

- Networks
- Platform
- Physical
- Process.

3.1.1 Network Category

The network category encompasses firewalls, routers, and switches, remote access devices (such as VPNs, and dial-up modem banks) and network-based ID systems that add some security features to the overall design. These components are used to monitor, filter and/or restrict traffic as seen either by their network interfaces or as defined logic in software.

3.1.2 Platform Category

The platform category encompasses the server and client side software (such as underlying operating system and security applications controls). Devices that perform some electronic operation such as smart cards and readers hardware token-producing cards, and hardware-based encryption devices fit into this platform category. Application-level access controls, such as soft-taken producing programs, digital certificates, host-based ID intrusion detection and analysis, virus detection and event accounting and analysis. These security functions are used to protect the application that resides within these major infrastructure boundaries.

3.1.3 Physical Components

The physical components of a security infrastructure include standard door keys and locks, key cards, identification badges security cameras, motion sensors audible and visual alarms, cages, fences, security guards and systems. Biometric components fit into this category as well and include hand geometry readers, facial geometry cameras, and retinal-scan cameras. The typical intent of these biometric components is to identify and authenticate users via the nature and purpose of their hardware design. Network cabling and backup power devices such as UPS systems and diesel generators fit into this category as well. The primary goal of a physical security component is to keep unauthorized persons out and keep infrastructure components supplied with power and network connectivity.

3.1.4 Process Category

The process category includes corporate security policy and procedural documentation that governs the creation, use, storage and disposal of corporate data, as well as the systems and networks on which that data resides. The purpose of a corporate security policy is to define the scope of protection for corporate assets and suggest or require a specific protection mechanism for those assets. Corporate security procedures, a component of the corporate security policies document, are utilized to guide employee actions in particular circumstances.

3.2 GOALS OF SECURITY INFRASTRUCTURE

The primary goal of a security infrastructure design in the protection of corporate assets. The way we protect these assets is by the proper deployment of security components into an organized and cohesive security infrastructure. Assets may include hardware, software, network components and intellectual property. The controls applied in a protection of these assets should be in line with your corporate security goals as well as your corporate security policy documentation. Though only the protection of data is mentioned, it is implied that in protecting the data and ensuring its availability, the underlying systems and networks are also protected.

Depending upon your chosen data classification scheme, each of the following data protection goals should be approximately represented and weighted accordingly:

- Data confidentiality
- Data integrity
- Data availability.

When designing a security infrastructure, target your applications for the best results. Your applications are the closest things to your data as they process, exchange, and store your data. By deciding that your design goals will address data confidentiality, data integrity, and data availability, you will discover that you are securing not only your applications, but your enterprise as well.

3.2.1 Data Confidentiality

The purpose of confidentiality is to ensure that only those individuals who have the authority to view a piece of information may do so. No unauthorized individual should ever be able to view data they are not entitled to. In other words, confidentiality is the protection of transmitted data from passive attacks. With respect to the release of message contents, several levels of protection can be identified. The broadcast service protects all users data transmitted between two users over a period of time. For example, if a virtual circuit is set up between two systems, this broad protection would prevent the release of any user data transmitted over the virtual circuit. Narrower forms of this service can also be defined, including the protection of a single message or even specific fields within a message. These refinements are less useful than the broad approach and may even be more complex and expensive to implement. The other aspect of confidentiality is the protection of traffic. This requires that an attack not be able to observe the source and destination, frequency, length, or other characteristics of the traffic on a communication facility.

3.2.2 Data Integrity

Integrity is a related concept but deals with the generation and modification of data. Only authorized individuals should ever be able to create or change (or delete) information. In other words, data integrity is concerned with the protection of any unauthorized alteration or destruction of data. The primary focus of this goal, then, is the accuracy and legitimacy of the data.

A common solution for providing data integrity involves the use of common encryption strategies (such as Internet Protocol Security) that use such a checksum strategy to ensure that the data sent equals the data that was received. In protecting data from corruption or destruction, the solution can be as simple as the use of antivirus programs or as complicated as the deployment of critical path storage solutions, clustered highly available firewalls, and company-wide acceptance of change management practices.

3.2.3 Data Availability

The goal of availability is to ensure that the data or the system itself, is available for use when the authorized user wants it. A variety of attacks can result in the loss of or reduction in availability. Some of these attacks are amenable to automated counter measures, such as authentication and encryption, whereas others require some sort of physical action to prevent or recover from loss of availability of elements of a distributed system.

3.3 DESIGN GUIDELINES

The first and arguably most important design guidelines to follow is to ensure that your corporate security policies and procedures are in line with your present business objectives. If they are not, then steps should be taken to implement the necessary changes to these policies and procedures prior to designing and building a security infrastructure. Without the full acceptance and support of such corporate guidelines from executive management, your security design cannot fully reach its potential and in fact may fail due to the lack of both written guidelines and managerial support.

When policies and procedures are in line with present business practices, so it is the time to design the infrastructure security services that will directly support the stated guidelines and requirements.

These services include:

- Authentication
- Authorization

- Accounting
- Physical access controls
- Logical access controls.

3.3.1 Authentication

Authentication is the process of binding a specific ID to a specific computer connection. The authentication of authorized users prevents unauthorized users from gaining access to corporate information systems. The use of authentication mechanism can also prevent authorized users from accessing information that they are not authorized to view. Currently, passwords remain the primary authentication mechanism for internal system access. If passwords are to be used the following are recommended as best practices.

- *Password length:* Passwords should be a minimum of eight characters in length.
- *Password change frequency:* Passwords should not be more than 60 days old. In addition, passwords should not be changed for one day after a password change.
- *Password history:* The last ten passwords should not be reused.
- *Password content:* Passwords should not be made up of only letters but instead include letters, numbers and special punctuation characters. The system should enforce these restrictions when the passwords are changed.

Passwords should always be stored in encrypted form, and the encrypted passwords should not be accessible to normal users.

For extremely sensitive system or information, passwords may not provide sufficient protection. In these cases, dynamic passwords or some form of two authentication should be used. Keep in mind that authentication includes some combination of three things:

- Something a person knows, like a password
- Something a person has, like an access card
- Something a person is, like a fingerprint.

Two factors authentication is used to counter the weakness that each type of authentication information has. For example, passwords may be written down and thus discovered. Access cards may be stolen, and biometrics tend to be expensive and require controlled or trusted access between the user and the machine.

All organization systems should be configured to start a screen server to remove information from the screen and require re-authentication if the user is away from the computer for longer than ten minutes. If employees were to leave a computer logged into the network and unattended, an intruder would be able to use that computer as if he was the employee unless some form of re-authentication were required.

3.3.2 Authorization

Authorization is the process of permitting or denying access to a specific resource. Once identity is confirmed via authentication, specific actions can be authorized or denied. Many types of authorization schemes are used, but the purpose is the same: determine whether a given user who has been identified has permissions for a particular object or resource being requested. This functionality is frequently part of the operating system and is transparent to users.

The separation of tasks, from identification to authentication to authorization, has several advantages. There are many methods to perform each task, and on many systems several methods are concurrently present for each task. Separation of these tasks into individual elements allows combinations of implementations to all work together.

Authentication is a process of verifying properly presented credentials; the source of the credentials is not a relevant item. You can authenticate users and computer processes (ID carried by script), the concept of authentication and implementation is identical. Different forms of authorization can be implemented, based on the resource being requested such as database access or router admin access.

Any system or resource, be it hardware (router, workstation) or software component (database system) that requires authorization can use its own authorization method once authentication for a connection has been resolved for it. This makes for efficient and consistent application of these principles.

3.3.3 Accounting

Accounting refers to the logging and monitoring of actions, events and subsequent alerts that result from a satisfied condition. Most operating systems can be configured to produce accounting logs used to alert administrators of various system-generated events. The most prevalent operating system log utilities are syslog (used on UNIX-based systems) and Ntevent log (used on Microsoft NT-based systems). The satisfied condition may simply be a UNIX syslog or Microsoft NT event log setting of WARNING that produces WARNING–level messages (or of a higher significance) in its log file. However, the condition may be as complex as correlating and collaborating several non-contiguous events from different agent sources across the corporation such that the resultant alert means something of importance. Regardless of complexity, accounting results can provide us with the following:

- Operating system usage details
- Application usage details
- Internet, Extranet, or Intranet network connectivity
- Data for forensic analysis
- Data for trending analysis
- Data for report generation.

Each of these results is valuable to a corporation for many reasons. In addition to providing performance forecasts and trending analysis, events can be used to as certain one's security profile and to identify existent or potential threats. Operating system events can be used to notify security staff members of failed logon attempts, attempts to gain root or administrator access, and whether file systems have been mounted for export to name a few.

The timeliness of events is just as important as the scope that the events cover. What value is there in monitoring security events from your operating system, key applications, and the traffic on the segment when an administrator only manually reviews these events logs once per week. Chances are that by the time your administrator gets around to reviewing these events logs, he or she will be looking at the piece of history, both the hacker, and any traces of their exploits, may be long gone, possibly except for Trojan or two they left behind to siphon critical data out at will.

In this Internet age of point and click, everything happens quickly. Even novice hackers are well-prepared to target your corporate assets with potentially dozens of hacker tools. By reaping the benefits of expert hackers, these novices (or script kiddies) with their tailored hacker tool sets can week havoc like the best of them.

3.3.4 Physical Access Controls

Physical access controls pertain to the elements of your security infrastructure that typically work in conjunction with one another to reduce the effects of abuses by humans and acts of God. Physical controls are as much operational as they are physical.

Common physical access controls include standard keys, key cards, smart cards, identification badges, security cameras, motion sensors, audible and visual alarms, doors, locks, cages, fences, signage, security guards and system or device labels. The way these elements are put into use determines the quality of your physical access control strategy. Operational procedures, as defined in your corporate security policies and procedures documentation, should define how specific classifications of data and underlying systems are protected. These procedures should also state which actions are taken to notify appropriate personnel in the event of a disaster, define appropriate forensic procedures as they apply so the importance of data affected, and state how associated risks may be mitigated.

In addition to reducing the risk, or effects of a security breach, disruption of service must also be factored into your physical protection strategy. Disruption of service strategies typically includes a mixture of proper component placement of physical security infrastructure components is as important as redundancy for several reasons.

3.3.5 Logical Access Controls

Logical access controls probably receive the most limelight of all the security infrastructure control availability. These controls consist of firewalls, routers, switches, VPNs, and application-level controls put in place to restrict both system and network use. Logical access controls sometimes utilize authentication and authorization information to make a determination as to whether access will be granted or denied. Other times, these decisions are made based upon either the port or protocol being used. Logical access controls can be applied in a variety of ways to restrict system or network use.

3.4 SECURITY MODELS

An important issue when designing the software that will operate and control, secure computer systems and networks is the security model that the system or network will be based upon. The security model will implement the security policy that has been chosen and enforce those characteristics deemed most important by the system designers. For example, if confidentiality is considered paramount, the model should make certain no data is disclosed to unauthorized individuals. A model enforcing confidentiality may allow unauthorized individuals to modify or delete data as this would not violate the tenets of the model since the true values for the data would still remain confidential. Of course, this model may not be appropriate for all environments. In some instances, the unauthorized modification of data may be considered a more serious issue than its unauthorized disclosure. In such cases, the model would be responsible for enforcing the integrity of the data instead of its confidentiality. Choosing the model to base the design on its critical if you want to ensure that the resulting system accurately enforces the security policy desired.

3.4.1 Bell–La Padula Confidentiality Model

The Bell and La Padula model is a formal description of the allowable paths of information flow in a secure system. This model's goal is to identify allowable communication when maintaining security requirements for systems concurrently handling data at different sensitivity levels.

This model was especially useful in designing multilevel security systems that implemented the military's hierarchical security scheme which included levels of classification such as unclassified confidential, secret and top secret. Similar classification schemes can be used in industry, where classifications might include publicly releasable, proprietary and company confidential.

We are interested in secure information flows because they describe acceptable connections between subjects and objects of different levels of sensitivity. One purpose for security-level analysis is to enable us to construct systems that can perform concurrent computation on data at two different sensitivity levels. For example, we may want to use one machine for top secret and confidential data at the same time. The programs processing top-secret data would be prevented from leaking top-secret data to the confidential data, and the confidential users would be prevented from accessing the top-secret data. Thus, the Bell–La model is useful as the basis for the design of systems that handle data of multiple sensitivities.

3.4.2 Biba Integrity Model

In the Biba model, instead of security classifications, integrity levels are used. A principle of integrity levels in that data with a higher integrity level is believed to be more accurable or reliable than data of a lower integrity level. Integrity levels indicate the level of "trust" that can be placed in information at the different levels. Integrity levels differ from security levels in another way—they limit the modification of information as opposed to the flow of information.

The Bell–La Padula model applies only to secrecy of information. The model identifies paths that could had to inappropriate disclosure of information. However, the integrity of data is important too. Biba constructed a model for preventing inappropriate modification of data.

Suppose Paul is known to be untruthful. If Paul can create or modify a document, other people should distrust the truth of the statement in that document. Thus, untrusted subject who has write access to an object reduces the integrity of that object. Similarly, people are rightfully sceptical of a report based on unsound evidence. The low integrity of a source object implies low integrity for any object based on the source object.

This model addresses the integrity issues that the Bell–La Padula model ignores. However, in doing so, the Biba model ignores secrecy. Secrecy-based security systems have been much more fully studied than have integrity-based systems. The current trend is to join secrecy and integrity concerns in security systems, although no widely-accepted formal models' achieve this compromise.

3.4.3 Clark-Wilson Security Model

The Bell–La Padula model was developed in the early 1970s but was found to be insufficient for all environments. As an alternative, Biba studied the integrity issue and developed the Biba security model in the late 1980s that led to the Clark–Wilson security model, which also places its emphasis on integrity rather than confidentiality.

The Clark–Wilson security model takes an entirely different approach than the Biba and Bell–La Padula models, using transactions as the basis for its rules. It defines two levels of integrity only, constrained data items (CDI) and unconstrained data items (UDI). The model then defines two types of processes: integrity verification process, which ensure that CDI data meet integrity constraints (to ensure the system is in valid state) and transformation process, which change the state of data from one valid state to another. Data in this model cannot be modified directly by a user, it must be changed by rusted transformation processes, access to which can be restricted (thus, restricting the ability of a user to perform certain activities). It is useful to return to the banking account balance used earlier to describe the need for integrity-based models. In the Clark–Wilson model, the account balance would be a CDI because its integrity is a critical function for the bank. A client color preferences for their checkbook is not a critical function and would be considered a UDI (Unconstrained Data Item). Since the integrity of account balances is of extreme importance changes to a person's balances is of extreme importance. Changes to a person's balance must be accomplished through the use of a transformation process. Ensuring that the balance is correct would be the duty of an integrity verification processes. Only certain employees of the bank should have the ability to modify an individuals accounts. So, we can control this by limiting the number of individuals who have the authority to execute transformation processes that result in account modification. Certain very critical functions may actually be split into multiples transformation processes to enforce another important principle, separation of duties.

This limits the authority of any one individual so that more number of individuals will be required for certain critical functions.

The Clark–Wilson security model is an integrity-based model designed to limit the processes an individual may perform as well as require that critical data be modified only through specific transformation processes.

REVIEW QUESTIONS

3.1 Briefly describe security infrastructure.

3.2 Discuss the infrastructure components with respect to various categories such as network, plateform, physical and process.

3.3 What are the infrastructure components belong to network category?

3.4 What are the infrastructure components belong to platform category?

3.5 Physical components, why so important as a part of infrastructure components?

3.6 What is the goal of security infrastructure?

3.7 Explain data integrity and its importance in goals of security infrastructure.

3.8 Explain data availability and its importance in goals of security infrastructure.

3.9 Explain data confidentiality and its importance in goals of security infrastrucutre.

3.10 Why design guidelines should be followed. Justify that design of infrastructure security services such as authentication, authorization, etc. will directly support the stated guidelines and requirements.

3.11 What does the authentication?

3.12 Explain password length and password change frequency.

3.13 Explain authorization and why it is important?

3.14 What does the accounting mean?

3.15 Is it important to control physical access, why?

3.16 Explain logical access control.

3.17 What is the difference between physical access control and logical access control?

3.18 Describe Bell-La Padula confidentiality model and explain its goal.

3.19 Explain Biba integrity model.

3.20 Explain Clark-Wilson security model. How it is different from Biba and Bell-La Padula models.

CHAPTER 4

Cryptography

Chapter Outline

Cryptography (secret writing) is the strongest tool for controlling against many kinds of security threats. Well-distinguished data cannot be read, modified, or fabricated easily. Cryptography is rooted in higher mathematics; group and field theory, computation complexity and even real analysis, not to mention probability and statistics. Fortunately, it is not necessary to understand the underlying mathematics to be able to use cryptography.

We begin this chapter by brief history of cryptography. An evidence of the oldest known secret writing was found in the form of a clay table having inscriptions dating back to 4000 years. It was found from a small town Menet Khufu on the bank of Nile River. An unknown scribe describing the living style of his master had written this in hieroglyph form. It was installed on the tomb of a noble man Khnamoteb. In this inscription some uncommon and unusual symbols were used most probably to show the ingenuity of the scribe. This alternation could be treated as an aspect of secret writing and it could be described as the oldest written evidence of cryptographic methods.

During the same period, the people of Egypt wrote epitaphs using unintelligible symbols with the hope that common people would spend more time to decipher them, and thus, appreciated the skill of the scribes; the evidence of use of cryptography is some form in Mesopotamia has been noted in the form cuneiform table found on the banks of river Tigris. This tablet contains some uncommon cuneiform signs describing a method of making clay pots. The intention of the scribe seems to be hide the formula from others.

The civilization of Babylon is the oldest and the Babylonians also used some unusual cuneiform signs in dating their tablets, which were called colophons. The colophons developed in Iraq were transformed to numbers. Such an inscription during back to 130 BC found in Iraq contained the message: "Paliah 21 50 10 40 pa ......", which actually meant—one who worships Anu-u-An-tu (Gods) would not remove it. Here, 21 represents Anu, 50 represents U and so on. Such replacement of normal words, phrases or sentences by some symbols is what is called Code now. Thus, these colophons could be called one of the oldest codes used in ancient time.

As far as India is concerned, evidence-establishing use of cryptographic methods during olden days are available in the history. The book Arthshasthra by Kautilya has described the importance of secret communication at many places. Other books such as "Lalit Vistara" and "Kamasutra" have descriptions of different arts of writings and communicating through symbolic movement of eye's and gestures. "Subhasha" and "Nirbhasha" were such gestures prevalent in old days. The sign language used by hearing impaired persons, developed in India, could also be thought of as a form of cryptography.

Another historical evidence of use of cryptographic method goes back to 500 BC when soldiers of Sparta used a device known as sky-tale. It consisted of a simple wooden cylinder on which a strip was wrapped around in spiral form and the message was written top to down columnwise. This trip when unwrapped consisted of whole message but the alphabets dislocated making the message unreadable. For reading the plain message one had to wrap it again on the cylinder of the same dimension and read it. This would be thought of an ancient version of today's transposition cipher. Early history of modern cryptography centers around a lots of developments in the military domain.

4.1 TERMINOLOGY AND BACKGROUND

Consider the steps involved in sending messages from a sender S, to a recipient R. If S entrusts the message to T, who then delivers it to R. T then becomes transmission medium. If an outsider, O, wants to access the message (to read, change or even destroy it) we call O an interceptor or intruder. Any time after S transmits it via T, the message is vulnerable to exploitation, and O might try to access the message in any of the following ways:

- *Block it:* By preventing its reaching R, thereby affecting the availability of the message.
- *Intercept it:* By reading or listening to the message, thereby affecting the confidentiality of the message.
- *Modify it:* By signing the message and changing it in some way, affecting the message integrity.
- *Fabricate:* An authenticate-looking message, arranging for it to be delivered as if it came from S, thereby also affecting the integrity of the message.

As you can see, a message is vulnerabilities reflect the four possible security failures. Fortunately, encryption is a technique that can address all these problems. Encryption, probably the most fundamental building block of secure computing, is a means of maintaining secure data in an insecure environment.

Terminology

Ciphertext: The encrypted form of a message is known as ciphertext or scrambled message produced as output. It depends on the plaintext and the secret key. For a given message, two different keys will produce two different ciphertexts.

Cryptanalysis: The process of attempting to discover the plaintext or key is known as cryptanalysis.

Cryptology: The art of devising ciphers (cryptography) and breaking them (cryptanalysis) is collectively known as cryptology.

Cryptosystem: The cryptosystem involves a set of rules for how to encrypt the plaintext and how to decrypt the ciphertext.

Decryption: The process of changing the ciphertext into plaintext.

Description algorithm: This is essentially the encryption algorithm run in reverse. It takes the ciphertext and same secret key and produces the original plaintext.

Encryption: The process of changing the plaintext into ciphertext.

Encryption algorithm: The encryption algorithm performs various substitutions and transformations on the plaintext.

Plaintext: The original form of a message is known as plaintext.

Cryptographic systems are characterized along three independent dimensions

(i) *The type of operations used for transforming plaintext to ciphertext. All encryption algorithms are based on two general principles:* substitution, in which each element in the plaintext (bit, letter, group of bits or letters) is mapped into another element, and transposition, in which elements in the plaintext are rearranged. The fundamental requirement is that no information be lost (that is, that all operations are reversible). Most systems, referred to as product systems, involve multiple stages of substitutions and transpositions.

(ii) *The number of key used:* If both the sender and the receiver use the same key, the system is referred to as symmetric, single-key, secret-key, or conventional encryption. If the sender and the receiver each use a different key, the system is referred to as asymmetric, two-key, or public-key encryption.

(iii) *The way in which the plaintext is processed:* A block cipher processes the input one block of elements at a time, producing an output block for each input block. A stream cipher processes the input elements continuously, producing output one element at a time, as it goes along.

4.1.1 Encryption Algorithms

The cryptosystem involves a set of rules for how to encrypt the plaintext and how to decrypt the ciphertext. The encryption and decryption rules are called algorithms, often use a device called a key, denoted by K, so that the resulting ciphertext depends on the original plaintext message, the algorithm, and the key value. We write this dependence as C = E (K, P), where C is ciphertext and P is plaintext. Essentially, E is a set of encryption algorithms

Sometimes the encryption and decryption keys are same so P = D (K, E (K, P)). This form is called symmetric encryption because D and E are mirror image processes. At other times, encryption and encryption keys come in pairs. Then, a decryption key, K_D, inverts the encryption of K_E, so that P = D (K_D, E (K_E, P)). Encryption algorithms of this form are called asymmetric because converting C back to P involves a series of steps and a key that are different from the steps and key of E. The difference between symmetric and asymmetric encryption is shown in Figure 4.1.

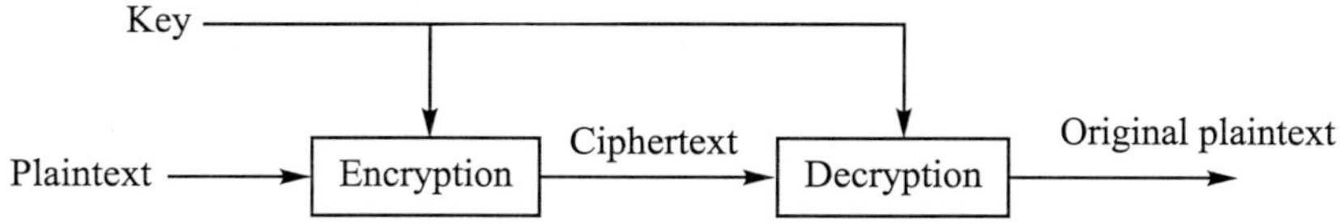

(a) Symmetric cryptosystem

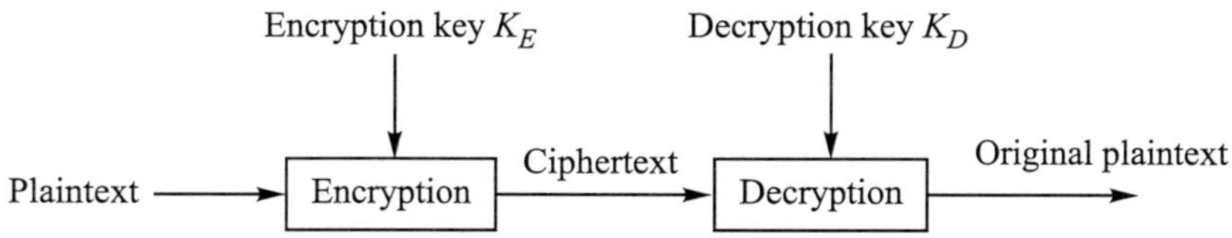

(b) Asymmetric cryptosystem

Figure 4.1 Encryption with keys.

A key gives us flexibility in using an encryption scheme. We can create different encryptions of one plaintext message just by changing the key. Moreover, using a key provides additional security. If the encryption algorithm should fall into the interceptor's hands, future messages can still be kept secret because the interceptor will not know the key value. An encryption scheme that does not require the use of a key is called a keyless cipher.

4.1.2 Cryptanalysis

The process of attempting to discover the plaintext or key is known as cryptanalysis. The strategy used by the cryptanalyst depends on the nature of the encryption scheme and the information available to the cryptanalyst.

Cryptanalyst can do any or all of six different things:

(i) Attempt to break a single message.

(ii) Attempt to recognize patterns in encrypted messages, to be able to break subsequent ones by applying a straight forward decryption algorithm.

(iii) Attempt to infer some meaning without even breaking the encryption, such as noticing an unusual frequency of communication or determining something by whether the communication was short or long.

(iv) Attempt to deduce the key, in order to break subsequent messages easily.

(v) Attempt to find weaknesses in the implementation or environment of use encryption.

(vi) Attempt to find general weaknesses in an encryption algorithm without necessarily having intercepted any messages.

An analyst works with a variety of pieces of information: encrypted messages, known encryption algorithms, intercepted plaintext, data items known or suspected to be in a cipher-text message, mathematical or statistical tools and techniques, properties of languages, computers, and plenty of ingenuity and luck. Each piece of evidence can provide a clue, and the analyst puts the clues together to try to form a large picture of a message's meaning in the context of how the encryption is done. Remember that there are no rules. An interceptor can use any means available to tease out the meaning of the message.

4.2 DATA ENCRYPTION METHODS

Encryption methods have been divided into two categories:

1. Substitution ciphers
2. Transposition ciphers.

4.2.1 Substitution Ciphers

In a substitution cipher each letter or group of letters is replaced by another letter or group. One of the oldest known ciphers is the Caesar Cipher, attribute to Julius Caesar. In this method a becomes D, b becomes E, and c becomes F, ... and z becomes C.

For example, attack becomes DWWDFN. In examples, plaintext will be given in lower case letters and ciphertext in upper case letters.

A slight generalization of the Caesar Cipher allows the Ciphertext alphabet to be shifted by P letters, instead of always 3. In this case K becomes a key to the general method of circularly shifted alphabets.

The next improvement is to have each of the symbols in the plaintext, say the 26 letters for simplicity, map on to some other letter.
For example

Plaintext: a b c d e f g h i j k l m n o p q r s t u v w x y z

Ciphertext: Q W E R T Y U I O P A S D F G H J K L Z X C V B N M

This general system is called Monoalphabetic substitution, with the key being the 26-letter string corresponding to the full alphabet. For the key above, the plaintext "attack" would be transferred into the cipher text "QZZQEA". At first glance this might appear to be safe system because although the cryptanalyst knows the general symbol (letter for letter substitution), he does not know which of the 26! = 4×10^{26} possible keys is in use. In contrast with Caesar Cipher, trying all of them is not a promising approach. Even at 1μ sec, per solution, computer would take $(10)^{13}$ years to try all the keys.

4.2.2 Transposition Ciphers

Substitution Ciphers preserve the order of the plain text symbols but disguise (to make sound different from normal) them. Transposition ciphers, in contrast, reorder the letters but do not disguise them.

The cipher is keys by a word not containing any repeated letters. In this example BOENTIKA is the key. The purpose of the key is to number the columns, column 1 being under the key letter closest to the start of the alphabet and so on. The plaintext is written horizontally in a row. The ciphertext is read out by columns, starting with the column whose key letter is the lowest.

B	O	E	N	T	I	K	A
2	7	3	6	8	4	5	1
p	l	e	a	s	e	t	r
a	n	s	f	e	r	t	e
n	t	h	o	u	s	a	n
d	r	u	p	e	e	s	t
o	m	y	s	w	i	s	s
b	a	n	k	a	c	c	o
u	n	t	s	e	v	e	n
t	w	o	s	e	v	e	n
2	7	3	6	8	4	5	1

Plaintext: Please transfer ten thousand rupees to my Swiss bank account, seven two seven

Ciphertext: R E N T S O N N P A N D O B U T E S H U Y N T O E R S E
I C V V T T A S S C E E A F O P S K S S L N T R M A N W
S E U E W A E E

4.3 CRYPTOGRAPHIC ALGORITHMS

Broadly speaking, there are three types of cryptographic algorithms; secret key algorithms, public key algorithms, and hashing algorithms. Secret key algorithms are symmetric in the sense that both participants in the communication share a single key. Figure 4.2 illustrates the use of secret key encryption to transmit data over another wise insecure channel. DES (Data Encryption Standards) is the best known example of a secret key encryption function, while IDEA (International Data Encryption Algorithm) is another.

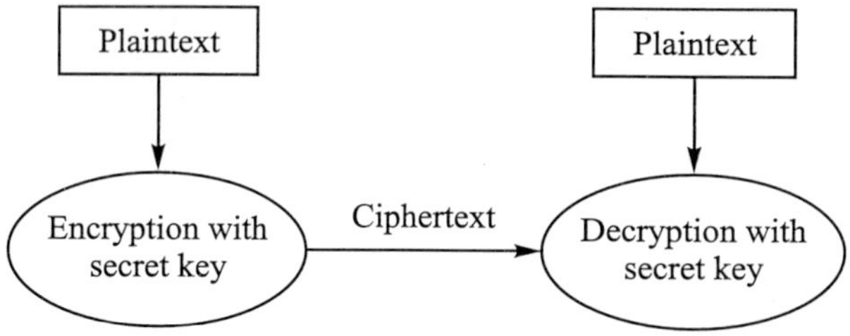

Figure 4.2 Secret key encryption.

In contrast to a pair of participants sharing a single secret key, public key cryptography involves each participant having a private key that is shared with no one else and a public key that is published so everyone knows it. To send a secure message to this participant, you encrypt the message using the widely known public key. The participant then decrypts the message using his or her private key. This scenario is depicted in Figure 4.3. RSA—named after its inventors, Rivest, Shamir and Adleman—is the best-known public key encryption algorithm.

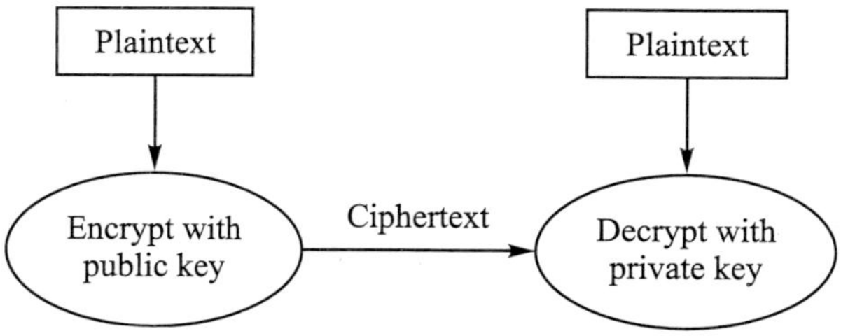

Figure 4.3 Public key encryption.

The third type of cryptography algorithm is called a hash or message digest function. Unlike the proceeding two types of algorithms, cryptographic hash functions typically don't involve the use of keys. Instead, the idea is to map a potentially large message into a small fixed-length number, analogous to the way a regular hash function maps values from a large space into values from a small space.

The best way to think of cryptographic hash function is that it computes a cryptographic checksum over a message. That is just as a regular checksum protects the receiver from accidental changes to the message, a cryptographic checksum protects the receiver from malicious changes to the message. This is because all cryptographic hash algorithms are carefully selected to be one-way functions—given a cryptographic checksum for a message, it is virtually impossible to figure out what message produced that checksum. Said another way, it is not computationally feasible to find two messages that hash to the same cryptography checksum. The relevance of this property is that if you are given a checksum for a message (along with the message), and you are able to compute exactly the same checksum for that message, then it is highly likely that this message produced the checksum you were given.

The most widely used cryptographic checksum algorithm is Message Digest Version 5 (MD5). An important property of MD5, in addition to those properties outlined in the previous paragraph, is that it is much more efficient to compute than either DES or RSA.

To reemphasize, cryptography algorithms like DES, RSA and MD5 are just building blocks from which a secure system can be constructed. Figure 4.4 gives a simple taxonomy that illustrates this point. In looking at these services and building blocks, we should consider the following question: How did the participants get the various keys in the first place? This is the key distribution problem, one of the central problems in security.

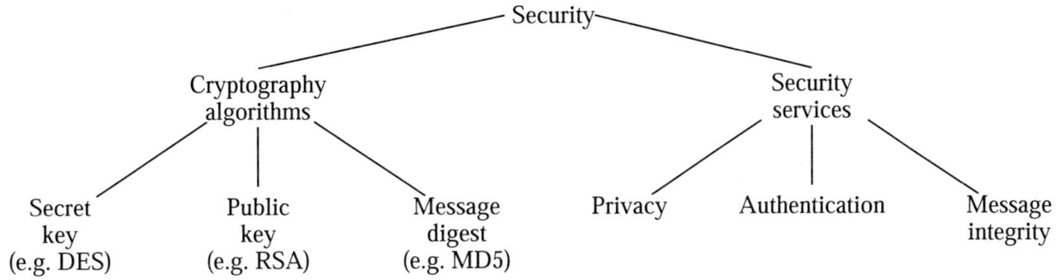

Figure 4.4 Taxonomy of network security.

4.4 SECRET KEY CRYPTOGRAPHY

The present is the era of digital communication, where the alphabet {0,1}. Different codes such as Murry, ASCII etc. are used to convert content in the form of text or speech or image or multimedia into a sequence of binary bits. For speech communication, coding techniques such as PCM, CVSD, RELP etc. are used. Similarly different protocols in binary domain have emerged for compressing and transmitting information. In secret key (Private key) cryptography, the key is a shared secret between the communicating parties. Three broad classes of cipher in use are:

(i) Stream ciphers
(ii) Block ciphers
(iii) Code-book ciphers

4.4.1 Stream Ciphers

The concepts of pseudorandom sequence generators and noise-producing electronic mechanisms are primary importance in this class. The encryption method is based on simple XOR of binary bits. The operation looks quite simple but is highly non-linear. A stream cipher encrypts one bit at a time as shown in Figure 4.5.

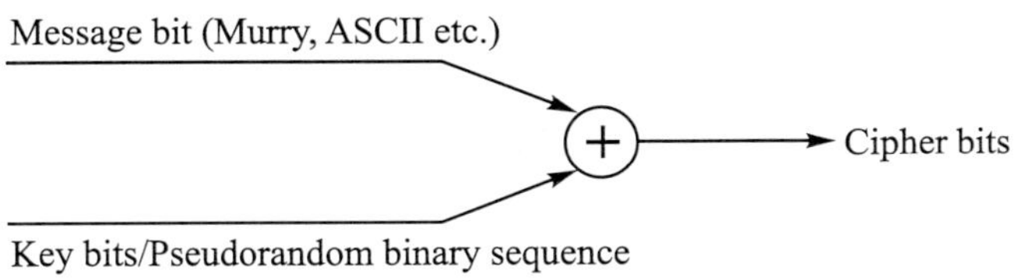

Figure 4.5 A stream cipher encrypts.

The key sequence is generated based on highly complex mathematical algorithms. Linear congruence generators, linear feedback shift register (LFSR) based on primitive polynomials and combinations of several such LFSR using different linear and non-linear logic provide very high levels of complexity. Clock control, Geffe, stop-and-go etc. are some examples of shift register-based sequence generators. In fact a very large class of such generators has been developed through non-linear logics. The generators which provide correlation immune sequences are preferred so that attacks on ciphers-based on auto-correlation, cross-correlation are not feasible.

A number of variations are in vogue, where apart from XOR some other operations such as block–permuting, bit-expansion are also performed to ensure better confusion and diffusion of bits (that is the bits are intermixed well even after replacements). Sometimes, the encryption operations are also performed at byte levels.

4.4.2 Block Ciphers

As the name suggests, in a block cipher a block of bits/characters/bytes are taken at a time and encrypted. In the category of classical cryptosystems, Hill cipher is a block cipher since a block cipher of 'n' letters of the message are encrypted at a time. Similarly, the transposition is also a block cipher since a block of 'n' letters is reshuffled at a time.

In 1972, the National Bureau of Standards (NBS), USA, now the National Institute of Standards and Technology (NIST) initiated a program to develop a single cryptographic algorithm that could be certified as a standard and could be used in different cryptographic equipments. In May 1973, NBS issued a public request for proposals for National Standard Cipher Algorithm specifying a series of design criteria. Within this project, the Data Encryption Standard (DES) was developed by NBS/IBM and was adopted as a standard.

DES Algorithm

The symmetric systems provide a two-way channel to their uses: A and B share a secret key, and they can both encrypt information to send to the other as well as decrypt information from the other. The symmetry of this situation is a major advantage. As long as the key remains secret, the system also provides authentication, proof that a message received was not fabricated by someone other than the declared sender. Authenticity is ensured because only the legitimate sender can produce a massage that will decrypt properly with the shared key. DES is a system developed for the U.S. government for use by the general public. It has been officially accepted as a cryptographic standard.

The DES algorithm is a careful and complex combination of two fundamental building blocks of encryption: substitution and transposition.

The algorithm derives its strength from repeated application of these two techniques, one on top of the other, for a total of 16 cycles. DES encrypts a 64-bit block of plaintext using a 64-bit key. The key actually contains only 56 usable bits—the last bit of each of the 8 bytes in the key is a parity bit for that byte, Also, messages larger than 64 bits can be encrypted using DES, as described:

DES has three distinct phases:

- The 64 bits in the block are permuted (shuffled).
- Sixteen rounds of an identical operation are applied to the resulting data and the key.
- The inverse of the original permutation is applied to the result.

DES belongs to a class of block ciphers termed as substitution—permutation network (SP networks). The operations can be viewed as a complex generalization of the classical substitution and transposition ciphers. DES operates on a 64-bit block of bits (Plaintext converted to bits or any data). After an initial permutation (IP), the block is broken into two halves, the right-half and the left-half, each 32 bits long. Then there are 16 rounds of identical operations involving bit expansion, a substitution table look-up (S-box), bit compression and permutation. Each of these operations is parameterized by the round key bits, which are generated by expanding the initial 64-bit input key. After the sixteenth round the right and left halves are swapped and joined for a final permutation, which is the inverse of the initial permutation.

With advancement in the processing speed of computer and also due to developments in cryptanalysis methods. DES is not thought to be secure enough now.

How can symmetric algorithms such as DES be made more secure? Theoretically, there are two ways: either the key length needs to be increased or the number of rounds in the encryption process needs to be increased. Both of these solutions tend to increase the processing power required to encrypt and decrypt data and slow down the encryption/decryption speed because of the increased number of mathematical operations required. Examples of modified DES include 3–DES.

Triple DES (3DES)

Triple DES is a variant of DES. Depending on the specific variant, it uses either two or three keys instead of the single key that DES uses. It also spins through the DES algorithm three times via what's called multiple encryption.

Multiple encryption can be performed in several different ways. The simplest method of multiple encryption is just to stack algorithms on top of each other. Taking plaintext, encrypting it with DES, then encrypting the first ciphertext with a third key. In reality, this technique is less effective than the technique that 3DES uses, which is to encrypt with one key, then decrypt with a second, and then encrypt with a third, as shown in Figure 4.6.

This greatly increases the number of attempts needed to retrieve the key, and this is a significant enhancement of security. The additional security comes with a price, tough, it can take up to three times as long to compute 3DES as it does to compute DES. However, the advances in memory and processing power in today's electronics should make this problem irrelevant in all devices except for very small low power handhelds.

The only weakness of 3DES are the ones that already exist in DES, and due to the use of different keys in the same algorithm, affecting a longer key length by adding the first key space to the second key space, and the greater resistance to brute forcing, 3DES as less actual weakness. 3DES is a good interim step before the new encryption standards, AES (Advanced Encryption Standard), is fully implemented.

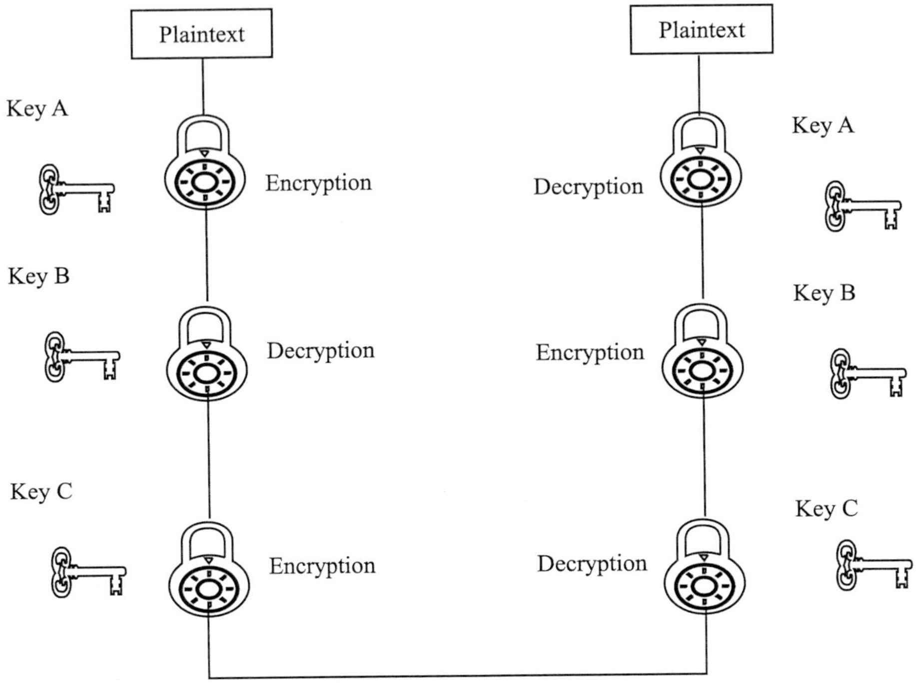

Figure 4.6 Triple DES.

Advanced Encryption Standard (AES)

In January 1997, NIST called for cryptographers top develop a new encryption system. As with the call for candidates from which DES was selected, NIST made several important restrictions. The algorithms had to be:

- Unclassified
- Publicity disclosed
- Availability of royalty—free for use worldwide
- Symmetric block cipher algorithms, for blocks of 128 bits
- Usable with key sizes of 128, 192 and 256 bits.

In August 1998, fifteen algorithms were chosen from among those submitted; in August 1999, the field of candidates was narrowed to five finalists. The fire then underwent expensive public and private scrutiny. The final selection was made on the basis of not only security but also of cost and efficiency of operation and case of implementation in software. The winning algorithm, submitted by two Dutch Cryptographers, was Rijndael (RINE DAHL). The algorithm's name is derived from the creator's names Vincent Rijmen and Joan Daemen.

Rijndael is a fast algorithm that can be implemented easily on simple processors. Although it has strong mathematical foundation, it primarily uses substitution, transposition, and the shift, exclusive OR, and addition operations. Like DES, AES uses repeat cycles. There are 9, 11, or

13 cycles for keys of 128, 192 and 256 bits, respectively. In Rijndael, the cycles are called "*rounds*". Each cycle consists of four steps:

1. Byte substitution
2. Shift row
3. Mix column
4. Add subkey.

The characteristics of DES and AES are compared in Table 4.1

Table 4.1 Comparison of DES and AES

	DES	*AES*
Date	1976	1999
Block size	64 bits	128 bits
Key length	56 bits (effective length)	128, 192, 256 bits
Encryption primitives	Substitution, permutation	Substitution, shift, bit mixing
Cryptographic primitives	Confusion, diffusion	Confusion, diffusion
Design	Open	Open
Design rationable	Closed	Open
Selection process	Secret	Secret, but accepted open public comment
Source	IBM, enhanced NSA	Independent Dutch cryptographers

At present, AES seems to be a significant improvement over DES, and it can be improved in a natural way if necessary.

The International Data Encryption Algorithm (IDEA)

The International Data Encryption Algorithm (IDEA) is symmetric block cipher developed by Xuejia Lai and James Massey of the Swiss Federal Institute of Technology in 1991. It uses a 128-bit key. IDEA differs markedly from DES both in the round function and in the sub key generation function. For the round function, IDEA does not use S-boxes. Rather, IDEA relies on three different mathematical operations: XOR, binary addition of 16-bit integers, and binary multiplication of 16-bit integers, These functions are combined in such a way as to produce a complex transformation that is very difficult to analyze and hence very difficult to crypt-analyze. The sub key generation algorithm relies solely on the use of circular shifts but uses these in a complex way to generate a total of six subkeys for each of the eight rounds of IDEA. IDEA is used in *PGP* (as one alternative) as well as in a number of commercial products.

CAST—128

CAST is a design produced for symmetric encryption algorithms developed in 1997 by Carlisle Adams and Stafford Tavares of Entrust Technologies. One specific algorithm developed as part of the CAST project is CAST—128, defined in RFC 2144, which makes use of a key size that varies from 40 bits to 128 bits in 8-bit increments. CAST is the result of a long process of research and development and has benefited from extensive review by cryptologists. It is beginning to be used in a number of products, including PGP.

CAST uses fixed S-boxes, but ones that are considerably larger than those used in DES. These S-boxes were carefully designed to be very nonlinear and resistant to cryptanalysis. The subkey-generation process used in CAST—128 is different from that employed in other conventional block encryption algorithms described in the literature. The CAST designers were connected to make subkeys as resistant to known cryptanalytic attacks as possible and felt that the use of highly nonlinear S-boxes to generate the subkeys from the main key provided this strength. Another interesting feature of CAST—128 is that the round function, *F*, differs from round to round, again adding to cryptanalytic strength.

Some of the principal characteristics of conventional Encryption Algorithms are compared in Table 4.2.

Table 4.2 Conventional encryption algorithm

Algorithm	*Key size*	*Number of Rounds*	*Mathematical Operations*	*Applications*
DES	56 bits	16	XOR, fixed *S*-boxes	SET, Kerberos
Triple DES	112 or 168 bits	48	XOR, fixed S-boxes	Financial key management, PGP, S/MIME
IDEA	128 bits	8	XOR, addition, multiplication	PGP
CAST-128	40 to 128 bits	16	Addition, substraction, XOR, rotation, fixed S-boxes	PGP

4.4.3 Code-book Ciphers

Apart from the above electronic and digital cipher system, codes are still being used for secret communication. A code is a lookup table where letters/words/phrases or even sentences are expressed by some symbols or groups of alphanumeric characters or numbers. For example, Morse code represents all 26 alphabets by some combination of dots and dashes. Telegraphic codes are decimal digits for sending standard messages such as greetings. Murray and ASCII are binary codes for alphanumeric alphabets. For secrecy purpose such code assignments or code tables are made very carefully to foil any statistical attack on ciphers.

In case of Chinese traffic, there are around 10,000 characters/groups and each of these is represented by some number between 0000 and 9999. The code book is prepared and distributed to users. Thus a message of the form.

2341340043781123434400008989125687230000 ....

May be a coded Chinese message.

Similar codes are also in use for other regional languages. Frequent change of the code-table and physical security of the code-book are essential. In practice, the code-table contains one to many correspondences. That means one letter/words/phrase is represented by more than one code in a cipher. It is also possible that at one place a word say cold may be represented by just one code say 3209, whereas at the other location this word may be coded as c-o-l-d using four codes, one corresponding to each other.

Though the code-books are thought to be very safe, a compromise needs immediate replacement. Further, in that case the adversary would be able to read all old ciphers, which would have been encoded on that code-book. To provide further security, the concept of superencipherment is also adopted. A random sequence of numbers (0-9) is selected and added to the coded message digit-by-digit module 10 (which means without carry). The process is illustrated below.

Plain-coded message:	2341	3400	4378	1123	4343	0000	8989	1256	8723	0000
Key sources:	2567	3873	4565	6791	0091	5634	5678	1349	0089	9834
Cipher:	4808	6273	8833	7814	4325	5634	3557	2595	8702	9834

For deciphering, one has to subtract the key from the cipher without carry and then consult the code-book. The key sequence may be generated randomly on-line by the communicating machines in a synchronous mode or may be exchanged before hand by means of some key-books.

Apart from numerical codes, there are many other ways to generate ones own codes. For many language, the codes can be designed in the form of bigrams alphanumeric characters. In such case, a word like attack may be represented as AS E4 5R 45 QW 09, where AS is the code for the letter a and so on. Clearly, in this case superencipherment as described above is not applicable but further security may be provided in many other ways. For example, the coded message can be read out on secure-radio or secure-telephone. Or else, it could be converted to binary form, modulated and sent on any digital channel. Encryption on this coded binary message could also be applied before communicating.

4.5 PUBLIC KEY CRYPTOGRAPHY

In all the cryptographic methods described above, the basic principles involved was that the decryption-key was same as (or easily computable from) the encryption-key. Such methods come under the class of symmetric key cryptography. The previous section discussed such methods.

Figure 4.7 shows the basic public key or asymmetric encryption operation. As you can see, both the sender or receiver of the information must have a key. The keys are related to each other (hence they are called a key pair), but they are different. The relationship between the keys is such that information encrypted by K1 can only be decrypted by K2. If K2 encrypts the information, it can only be decrypted by K1.

In 1976, Diffie and Hellman came up with a brilliant concept where different keys could be used for encryption and decryption, which are not easily derivable from each other. Thus the concept of public key cryptography (PKC) came into existence.

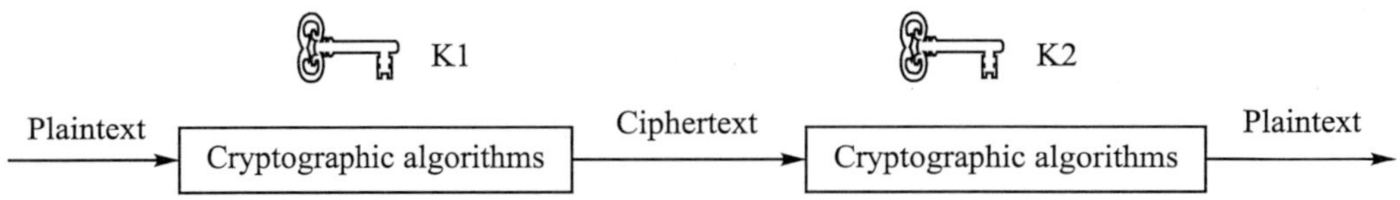

Figure 4.7 Public key encryption.

In public key cryptography (PKC), there is a pair of keys per user—one known only to the user (Private key), and the other key made public, like a telephone number (Public key). The enciphering and deciphering algorithms are public and use the public and private keys respectively. For encryption, the public key of identified recipient is used for encrypting the message. The recipient uses his private key to decrypt and read the message. A remarkable feature of the public key cryptography is that the public and private keys can be used for either operation. This provides the interesting mechanisms of digital signature on the message. Any one can verify this digital signature by decrypting with the public key of signer. In practice, additional mechanisms for providing, integrity, authenticity and trust are required. These are provided by the public key infrastructure. In India, a progressive legislation in the form of the IT act has been put in place by the government.

A well known public key-encryption-algorithm due to Rivest, Shamir and Adleman (RSA is widely used in the context of digital signatures.

4.5.1 Diffie-Hellman Algorithm

Whitefield Diffie and Martin Hellman developed this public key encryption system in 1976. The Diffie-Hellman system was developed to solve the problem of key distribution for private key encryption systems. The idea was to allow a secure method of agreeing on a private key without the expense of sending the key through another method. Therefore, they needed a secure way of deciding on a private key using the same method of communication that they were trying to protect. Diffie-Hellman cannot be used to encrypt or decrypt information.

The Diffie-Hellman algorithm works like this:

(a) Assume we have two people who need to communicate securely and then need to agree on an encryption key.

(b) P1 and P2 agree on two large integers a and b such that $1 < a < b$.

(c) P1 then chooses a random number i and computes $I = a^i \bmod b$; P1 sends I to P2.

(d) P2 then chooses a random number j and computes $J = a^j \bmod b$; P2 sends J to P1 ("mod" means remainder. For example, 12 mod 10 is 2. Two is the remainder that is left when 12 is divided by 10).

(e) P1 computes $k1 = J^i \bmod b$.

(f) P2 computes $k2 = I^j \bmod b$.

(g) We have $k1 = k2 = a^{ij} \bmod b$ and then k1 and k2 are the secret keys to use for the other transmission.

If someone is listening to the traffic on the wire, they will know *a*, *b*, I and J, however, *i* and *j* remain secret. The security of the system depends on the difficulty of finding *i* given I = a^i mod *b*. This problem is called the discrete algorithm problem and is considered to be a hard problem (that is, computationally infeasible with today's computer equipment) when the numbers are very large. Therefore, *a* and *b* must be chosen with care.

For example, *b* and (*b*-1)/2 should both be prime numbers and at least 512 bits in length. A better choice would be at least 1024 bits in length. The Diffie-Hellman key exchange is used by many security systems to exchange secret keys to use for additional traffic. The one weakness in the Diffie-Hellman system is that it is susceptible to a man-in-the-middle attack as shown in Figure 4.8. If an attacker could place his system in the path of traffic between P1 and

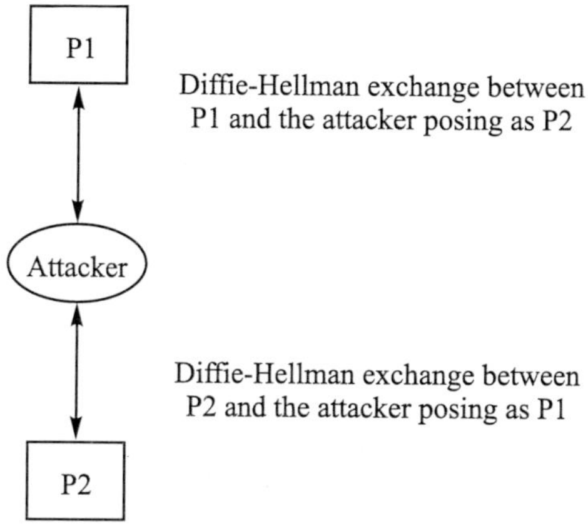

Figure 4.8 Diffie-Hellman system—a man-in-the-middle attack.

P2 and intercept all of the communication, the attacker could then act like P2 when talking to P1 and P2 when talking to P2. Thus, the key exchange would be between P1 and the attacker and P2 and the attacker. However, this type of attack requires significant resources and is very unlikely to occur in real world.

4.5.2 RSA Algorithm

The Rivest-Shamir-Adelman (RSA) cryptosystem is a public key system. Based on an underlying hard problem and named after its three inventors. This algorithm was introduced in 1978.

RSA is a public-key encryption/decryption algorithm and is much slower than DES. The key length is variable and the block size is also variable. A typical key length is 512 bits. RSA uses a public-key and private-key, and uses the fact that large numbers are extremely difficult to factorize.

The two keys used in RSA, *d* and *e*, are used for decryption and encryption. They are actually interchangeable; either can be chosen as a public key but, having chosen one, you must keep the other one private. For simplicity, we call the encryption key e and the decryption key d. Also because of the nature of the RSA algorithm, the keys can be applied in either order:

$$P = E\ (D(P)) = D\ (E(P))$$

(You can think of E and D as two complementary functions each of which "undoes" the other).

Any plaintext block P is encrypted as P^e mod n. Because the exponentiation is performed mod n, factoring P^e to uncover the encrypted plain text is difficult. However, the decrypting key d is carefully chosen so that $(P^e)^d$ mod n = P. Thus, the legitimate receiver who knows d simply computer $(P^e)^d$ mod n = P. and recovers P without having to factor P^e.

The RSA algorithm was two keys, d and e, which works in pairs, for decryption and encryption, respectively. A plaintext message P is encrypted to ciphertext C by

$$C = P^e \bmod n$$

The plaintext is recovered by

$$P = C^d \bmod n$$

Because of symmetry in modular arithmetic, encryption and decryption are mutually inverses and commutative. Therefore,

$$P = C^d \bmod n = (P^e)^d \bmod n$$

$$(P^d)e \bmod n$$

This relationship means that one can apply the encrypting transformation and the decrypting one, or the decrypting one followed by the encrypting one.

The encryption algorithm is based on the underlying problem for factoring large numbers. So far, nobody has found a short cut or easy way to factor large numbers in a finite set called a field. Because the problem has been open for many years, most cryptographers consider this problem a solid base for a secure cryptosystem.

4.6 MESSAGE DIGEST

Any telecommunications engineer is familiar with the cyclic Redundancy check (CRC) method of deselecting errors in digital transmission. It involves calculating a chicksum based on the data in the frame or packet at the sending end and transmitting it along with the data. The CRC, also known as checksum, is computed at the receiving end and matched against the received checksum to ensure that the packet has not been corrupted. An analogous principle is used in validating the integrity of the message. To ensure that the message has not been tempered with between sender and the receiver, a cryptographic CRC is added to the message. It is desired using a cryptographic hash algorithm called message digest (MD).

SHA (Secure Hash Algorithm)

SHA was developed in 1993 by the National Institute of Standards and Technology (NIST) and National Security Agency (NSA). It was designed as the algorithm to be used for secure hashing in the US Digital Signature Standard. (Hashing functions are one of the most commonly used encryption methods. A hash is a special mathematical function that performs one-way encryption).

SHA is modeled on the MD4 algorithm and implements fixes in that algorithm discovered by the NSA. It creates message digests 160 bits long that then can be used by the Digital Signature Algorithm (DSA), which can then compute the signature of the message. This is computationally simpler, as the message digest is typically much smaller than the actual message.

Smaller message = less work

MD5 was developed in 1991 and is structured after MD4 but additional security to overcome the problem MD4. Therefore, it is very similar to the MD4 algorithm, only slightly slower and more secure.

Secure has functions should create a checksum of at least 128 bits. The two most common secure has functions are MD5, which produces a 128-bit checksum, and SHA, which produces a 160-bit checksum.

A hash function can be called secure if:

(a) The function is one-way. In other words, the function creates a checksum from the information, but you can not create the information from the checksum.

(b) It is very difficult to construct two piece of information that provide the same checksum when run through the function.

Implementation and Performance

DES and MD5 are several orders of magnitude faster than RSA when implemented in software. On a state-of-the-art processor, for example, DES processes data at a rate of roughly 100 Mbps and MD5 at approximately 600 Mbps, while RSA runs at only 100 kbps. In practice, people don't think about RSA performance in terms of throughput rates because it doesn't make sense to run RSA on a data message. Instead, we typically talk about RSA in terms of the number of values per second it can sign and verify, respectively. On today's processors, RSA can sign approximately 100 1024-bit values per second and verify approximately 2000 1024-bit values per second.

When implemented in hardware, that is, by custom VLSI chip, it has been reported that DES and MD5 can achieve rates measured in gigabits per second, whereas RSA rates are still measured in kilobits per second. This is why DES and MD5 are the more likely of the three algorithms to be implemented in hardware on a given computer—even when implemented in hardware, RSA is still too slow to be of any practical use in encrypting data messages. Instead, RSA is typically used to encrypt very small amounts of data, such as secret key. Security protocols then use these RSA-protected secrets in conjunction with DES and MD5, possibly implemented in hardware, to provide message privacy and integrity.

4.7 DIGITAL SIGNATURES

A digital signature or digital signature scheme is a mathematical scheme for demonstrating the authenticity of a digital message or document. A valid digital signature gives a recipient reason to believe that the message was created by a known sender, and that it was not altered in transit. Digital signatures are commonly used for software distribution, financial transactions, and in other cases where it is important to detect forgery and tempering.

In order to understand how to transfer funds electronically person to another, it is also equally important to understand how this transaction is handled in the conventional, paper mode:

- A cheque is a tangible object authorizing a financial transaction.
- The signature on the cheque confirms authenticity since (presumably) only the legitimate signer can produce that signature.
- In the case of an alleged forget, a third party can be called in to judge authenticity.
- Once a cheque is cashed, it is cancelled so that it cannot be reused.
- The paper cheque is not alterable. Or, most forms of alteration are easily detected.

Transaction business by cheque depends on tangible objects in a prescribed form. But tangible objects do not exist for transactions on computers. Therefore, authorizing payments by computer requires a different model.

A digital signature scheme typically consists of three algorithms:

(i) A key generation algorithm that selects a private key uniformly at random from a set of possible private keys. The algorithm outputs the private key and a corresponding public key.

(ii) A signing algorithm that, given a message and a private key, produces a signature.

(iii) A signature verifying algorithm that, given a message, public key, and a signature either accepts or rejects the messages claim to authenticity.

Two main properties are required. First, a signature generated from a fixed message and fixed private key should verify the authenticity of that message by using the corresponding public key. Secondly, it should be computationally infeasible to generate a valid signature for a party who does not possess the private key.

A digital signature is an authentication mechanism that enables the creator of a message to attach a code that acts as a signature. The signature guarantees the source and integrity of the transmitted message. A message can be digitally signed by a system by including a header, a body, and a signature as part of the message. These components are described as follows:

- The header describes the identity of the sender.
- The body contains the message to be sent.
- The signature contains a computed checksum of the message contents, encrypted with the secret key of the sender.

The receiver can decrypt the checksum using the sender's public key and ensure the checksum matches a computed checksum of the transmitted message. The checksum process provides a sum for a group of items in the message, which is used for error checking.

The risk of the message forgery is an important reason to use a digital signature. Forged messages can be used to provide false information about a person or some event. Message forgery can also occur on the Internet if someone wants to smear another person or an organization. Another issue related to this subject is called message repudiation or denial that a message was transmitted.

4.8 SECURITY MECHANISMS

Cryptographic algorithms are just one piece of the picture when it comes to provide security in a network. The use of cryptographic algorithms grows everyday as more and more information becomes digitally encoded or put online. All of this data needs to be secured, and the best current way to do that has been encryption.

We have looked at the algorithms, we will now consider some of the tasks they accomplish and things that they are best-suited for. Security is typically defined as a product of five components; confidentiality, integrity, availability, authentication and nonrepudiation. Encryption can address four of these five components with confidentiality, integrity, nonrepudiation and authentication.

Confidentiality is what is typically thought about when the term security comes up. Confidentiality is the ability to keep some piece of data a secret. In the digital world, confidentiality is something that encryption excels at providing. There are two uses of confidentiality; on stored data and on transmitted data. In both cases, symmetric encryption is favored because of its speed and because some asymmetric algorithms can significantly increase the size of the object being encrypted. In the case of stored item, there is typically no need to have a public key, as the item is being encrypted to protect it from others. In the case of transmitted data, the typical case is to use public key cryptography to exchange the secret key, and then to use symmetric cryptography to ensure the confidentiality of the data being sent. Asymmetric cryptography does protect confidentiality of the data being sent. Asymmetric cryptography does protect confidentiality, but its size and speed make it more efficient at protecting the confidentiality of small units, such as for electronic key exchange. In all the cases, it is strength of the algorithms and the length, and the length of the keys that ensure the secrecy of the data in question.

Integrity is better known as message integrity, and it is a crucial component of message security. When a message is sent, both the sender and recipient need to know that the message was not altered in transmission. This is especially important when it comes to legal contracts—recipients need to know that the contracts have not been altered. The signers also have to have a way to validate that the contract they signed is not altered in the future. This integrity is provided with one-way hash functions and digital signatures. The hash functions compute the message digests, and his guarantees the integrity of the message by allowing easy testing to determine whether any part of the message has been changed. The message now has a computed function (the hash value) to tell the users to respond the message if it was intercepted and interfered with. This hash value is combined with asymmetric cryptography by taking the message's hash value and encrypting it with the user's private key. This lets anyone with the users public key decrypt the hash and compare it to the locally computed hash, ensuring not only the integrity of the message but positively identifying the sender.

An item of some confusion, nonrepudiation is actually fairly simple. It means that the sender cannot later deny that they sent the message. This is important in electronic exchange of data because of the lack of face-to-face meetings. Nonrepudiation is based upon public cryptography and the principle of only you knowing your private key. The presence of a message signed by you, using your private key, which no body else should know, is an example of nonrepudiation. When a third party can click your signature using your public key, that disproves any claim that you were not the one who actually sent the message. Nonrepudiation is tied to asymmetric cryptography and cannot be implemented with symmetric algorithms.

Authentication is simply being able to prove you are who you say you are. Authentication is similar to nonrepudiation, except that it is often used before communication begins, not after. Authentication is also typically used in both directions as part of a protocol. Authentication can be done in a multitude of ways, the most basic being the use of a simple password. Every time you check your e-mail, you authenticate yourself to the server. This process can grow to need two or three identifying factors like a password, a token, and a biometric. Digital certificates are one form of such tokens. When you log in to a secure website, one-way authentication occurs. You want to know that you are logging into the server that you mean to so your browser checks the server's digital certificates. This is a token that is digitally signed by a trusted third party, assuming you that the sender is genuine. This authentication is one way because the server does not need to know that you are who you are—it will authenticate your credit card letter on. However, two-way authentication can work the same way, where you send your digital certificate signed by a third party, and the other entity you are communicating with sends their. While symmetric encryption can be used as a simple manner of authentication (only the authorized should know the secret, after all) asymmetric encryption is better suited to show, via digital signatures and certificates that you are who you say you are.

4.9 SPEECH CRYPTOGRAPHY

Speech is the most simple and natural form of communication. Modern secure speech communication systems convert the analog speech to digital form, carry out a variety of compression, coding operations and then encrypt the resulting bit stream using a stream or block cipher. We give below a panoramic view of this area.

4.9.1 Speech as a Signal

Speech is a very complex signal representing different kinds of sound as—voiced, unvoiced and silence. A typical speech signal can be expressed as a sum of certain waveforms:

$$A \sin (wt + j)$$

or

$$A \cos (wt + j),$$

where A, w, j are constants and t represents time. Such wave form is called a Sinusoid. Each sinusoid has different frequency. Thus speech is a signal in which a large number of frequencies is present.

For processing speech, one can work with the function $x(t)$ which represents the time waveform containing the information on time and amplitude. Other information hidden in the waveform can be pronounced by transferring the signal into the different domain such as frequency domain using transformations such as FFT(Fast Fourier Transform). Various speech parameters can be expected in this transform domain. The vocal tract parameters are obtained by an algorithm performing a linear predicting coding (LPC), which tries to predict a sample of speech signal given some (say 10) previous samples. The speech signal can be visualized better through spectrogram, which is a three-dimensional representation that has time, frequency and energy density as dimensions.

In some application, one may require to process speech in its analog form but in many cases the processing is done in digital form after A/D conversion. The digitization is also required for utilizing the channel efficiently by reducing the redundancy of the signal in such a way that reconstruction of the analog speech from the digital form is possible with minimum loss of quality and intelligibility.

For secure speech communication, there are various techniques available for both analog as well as digital domain. For digital secure speech communication one has to convert the speech signal coding by using some coding techniques. We briefly describe here some of the common coding techniques.

4.9.2 Speech Coding Schemes

There are many coding techniques available for digitization of the speech signal. Their selection for an application depends on many factors. For securing speech communication in its binary form through some encryption methods there are three coding schemes:

1. PCM (Pulse code modulation)
2. CVSD (Continuously variable slope data modulation)
3. LPC – 10e (Linear predicting coding).

In the case of PCM, each speech sample is quantized using some n bits (n levels of quantization) and hence represented by n-bits. If m is the sampling-rate then $m\ n$ gives the bit-rate. Speech secrecy system based on this coding normally use—16-bit PCM with 8 KHz sampling-rate, thus operating at 128 Kbits/sec.

In the case of CVSD, the difference between adjacent speech samples in encoded using just one bit 1 or 0 depending upon if the current sample value is greater than the previous one or not. The sampling in this case is not uniform but the step size varies, which is adaptive. This reduces the bit-rate and redundancy of the signal, and thus providing more security. However, the quality of the reconstructed speech is affected.

In this case instead of coding speech sample by sample, a group of samples, called a frame is considered and is encoded in terms of 'n' number of parameters each of which can be approximated to 4 to 7 bits. For LPC-10e algorithm, a frame is encoded in terms of 10 parameters, which altogether constitute just 56 bits. Such a high level of compression achieved by developing short-term steady state models of the vocal tract and transmitting only the quantized and encoded parameters of these models. Though the quality of reconstructed speech here would be worse as compared to the other two, security systems based on LPC are supposed to provide better security due to considerable reduction in the redundancy.

4.9.3 Speech Secrecy Systems

There are three main categories for speech secrecy systems:

1. Scrambler (Transposition)
2. Digital speech ciphers (XOR)
3. Speech steganography (Hiding).

Speech scramblers were used in the early days where the communication was mainly in analog form and occasionally in digital form. The basic objective of a scrambler is to do some kind of arrangement of the units of the signal in a specified way. In case of analog scramblers, scrambling is done either in its analog form (e.g. Cutting the time waveform at different time intervals and permuting these pasts) or after A/D conversion but the transmission takes place in analog form. In case digital scramblers, the scrambling is done after digitalization and the transmission is also digital. Scrambling could be done in the time domain or frequency domain or in both. Many techniques have been employed but the main function used for scrambling is permutation of fine parts in which speech is cut (segmentation and choice of frame).

Modern speech secrecy system is mainly based on enciphering techniques. Here, speech is first encoded in binary form using one of the speech coding techniques as described in previous section, and then enciphered using a stream cipher as in case of text ciphers (editing speech bits with binary key sequence bit-by-bit mod 2).

Mathematically, the secrecy of digital speech ciphers as described above lies mainly with the speech coding and the strength of the algorithm that generates the key. In the area of speech ciphers, mainly symmetric key algorithms are used. The strength of a speech cipher system depends on (i) destroying all speech characteristics in all domain of study of speech signals, (ii) complexity of the crypto algorithm, and (iii) the key length or key variability.

For ensuring (i), one has to choose sampling rate, quantization, segments, frames, speech coding etc. suitably. As far as complexity of algorithm (ii) and the variability of key space (iii) are concerned, these are same as in the case of text ciphers as described earlier. The issues related to error correction, synchronization, modulation and communication protocols are all common with text communication.

Secrecy is an issue of utmost importance in military as well as civilian sectors. In case of steganographic communication, the message (text/fax/speech) is encoded in bits by using techniques, which ensure maximum level of compression. These message bits are hidden in another innocuous image or voice recording (called as cover) exploiting the redundancy in the cover. Speech can be used as a cover very conveniently. In case of PCM coded speech, the MSBs (Most Significant Bits) are sufficient to get back or synthesize the original speech to an acceptable level of quality. If we replace the LSBs (Least Significant Bits) of each sample value by the bits of the message to be hidden, then the cover-speech would sound like the original one and the interceptor would not suspect it, but the receiver would be able to locate the hidden bits and reconstruct the secret message easily.

The steganographic process may have to handle low bit-rate (reduced redundancy) voice coding, environment noise, channel distortions and resampling (as expected in a battle field). Such a process of steganography can also be done with other speech coders. Finding the bits in coded speech where another message could be hidden without being detected is a current area of research. Transform domain steganography is another area of research where information bits are hidden in parameters of some transformations in such a way that there is no perceptible difference in the cover and the stego image/voice. Similarly, various techniques and their analysis are being evolved for hiding message in music and multimedia files.

REVIEW QUESTIONS

4.1 Define plaintext, ciphertext, decryption and encryption.

4.2 What is the difference between plaintext and ciphertext?

4.3 What is the difference between encryption and decryption?

4.4 Define cryptosystem, what is difference between symmetric cryptosystem and asymmetric cryptosystem.

4.5 Define cryptanalysis. Explain the purpose of cryptanalysis.

4.6 What is the difference between encryption algorithm and decryption?

4.7 Describe the encryption algorithm.

4.8 What are the categories of encryption methods. Explain substitution ciphers with the help of example.

4.9 Explain transposition ciphers with the help of example.

4.10 Describe the cryptographic algorithm. What is difference between secret key encryption and public key encryption?

4.11 Describe secret key cryptography.

4.12 How many keys are required for two people to communicate via a cipher?

4.13 What are the two basic functions used in encryption algorithms?

4.14 What is the difference between a block cipher and stream cipher?

4.15 Describe code-book ciphers.

4.16 Explain DES algorithm and compare with international data encryption algorithm.

4.17 What is triple DES? How many keys are used in triple DES?

4.18 What is the difference between DES and AES?

4.19 Describe public key cryptography.

4.20 Explain Diffie-Hellman algorithm.

4.21 Explain RSA algorithm.

4.22 Explain message digest and describe secure Hash algorithm.

4.23 Describe the security mechanisms and explain confidentiality, integrity and reliability.

4.24 What is speech cryptography?

4.25 Describe speech-coding schemes.

4.26 Explain speech secracy systems. What are the categories for speech systems?

4.27 Write shortnote on:

- Digital signature
- IDEA

4.28 What is difference between digital speech ciphers and speech steganography?

CHAPTER 5

Network Fundamentals

Chapter Outline

Computers are changing the way we do business and the way we live. Business decisions have to be made ever more quickly, and the decision makers require immediately access to accurate information. But before we ask how quickly we can get hooked up. We need to know how networks operate, what types of technology are available, and which design best fills, which set of needs. When a company adds a new division, the technology has to be flexible enough to reflect changing configurations.

When we communicate, we are sharing information. In the context of computer information systems, data are represented by binary information units (or bits) produced and consumed in the form of 0's and 1's. Data communication is the exchange of data between two devices via some form of transmission medium (such as wire cable). Communicating devices must be part of a communication system made up of a combination of hardware and software. The effectiveness of data communication system depends on three characteristics, i.e. delivery, accuracy and timeliness. There are five components in data communication systems as shown in Figure 5.1.

Message	:	Message is the information (data message)
Sender	:	Device by which sends the data message
Receiver	:	Receiver by which receives the data message
Medium	:	Physical path by which a message travels from sender to receiver
Protocol	:	Set of rules that govern the data communication.

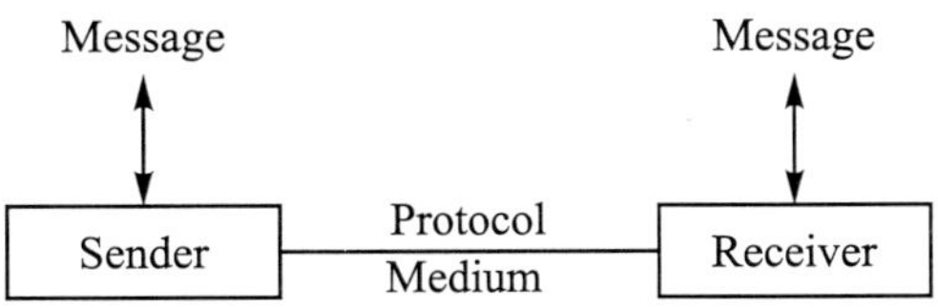

Figure 5.1 Data communication system.

5.1 A BRIEF HISTORY

The field of communications is certainly not new: people have been communicating since early humans grunted and scratched pictures on cave walls, which was based on the auditory and visual senses, you either heard someone speaking or saw the letters and symbols that define a message.

Communications changed drastically in 1837, after invention of Telegraph by Samuel Morse. Telegraph invention made it possible to send the information using electrical impulses over a copper wire. Messages were sent by translating each character into a sequence of long or short electrical impulses and transmitting them. Morse code is the association of characters with electrical impulses.

In 1937, Howard A. Aliken of Harvard University began work on the design of fully automatic calculating machine using the concepts of Babbage and punch cards in collaboration with the IBM (International Business Machine). Seven-year later in January 1944 the design became a reality and was named MARK I. This was considered to be the *first digital computer*. MARK I could accept data from PUNCH Cards, store them in memory, make calculations by means of automatically-controlled electromagnetic relays and arithmetic counters which were mechanical. It could be programmed, i.e. given a set of commands to carry out certain operations. It performs arithmetic and logical operations and solved scientific problems.

Another event important to communications occurred in 1945 with the invention of the *first electronic computer*, ENIAC (Electronic Numerical Integrator and Calculator). It contains vacuum tubes, registers, capacitors and switches, and it was faster than the MARK I. Although ENIAC played no direct role in data or computer communications, it did show that calculations and decision making could be done electronically, an important ability in today's communications systems.

The relation between computers and communications began to emerge after the invention of transistor in 1947 allowed smaller and cheaper computers to be built. The new generation of computers that emerged during the 1960s made new applications such as processing and routing telephone calls economically feasible.

Another milestone in computer-networking occurred with the development of ARPANET. It was developed by US Department of Defense. It was the pioneering network of Advanced Research Project Agency of the US Department of Defense. Operation of ARPANET was started in 1969 and connects over 100 computers spanning half the globe from Hawaii to Norway.

The 1970s and 1980s saw the merger of the fields of computer sciences and data communications that profoundly changed the technology, products and companies of the now combined computer-communication industry.

The computer-communications revolution has produced several remarkable facts:

- There is no fundamental difference between data-processing (computers) and data communications (transmission and switching equipment).
- There are no fundamentals differences among data, voice, and video communications.
- The distinction among single-processor computer, multi-processor computer, local network, metropolitan network and long-haul network has blurred.

The 1990s saw the emergence of the World Wide Web, an application that makes information from around the world easily accessible from one's desk. With the click of mouse button, computer users can access files, programs, video clips, and sound bits.

Computer and communications have progressed to the point where most businesses or schools can no longer function without them. Our almost total dependence on them demand that we understand them and their abilities and limitations.

5.2 COMPUTER NETWORKS

A network is a set of devices (often referred to as nodes) connected by media links. A node can be a computer printer, or any other device capable of sending and for receiving data generated by other notes on the network, the links connecting the devices are often called communication channels.

Computer network can be defined as interconnected collection of autonomous computers. Two computers are said to be interconnected, if they are able to exchange the information. For example, company has set-up the network as shown in Figure 5.2.

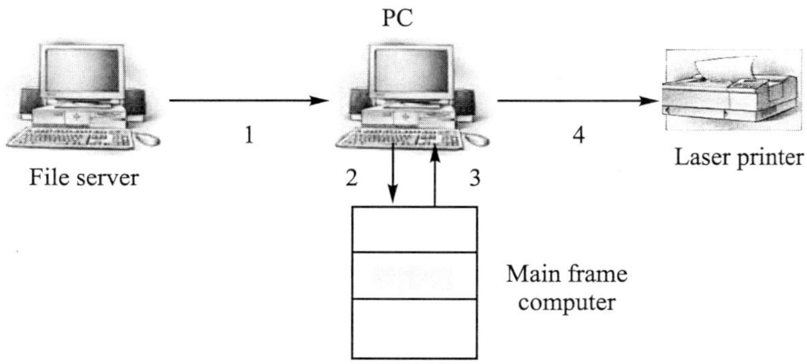

Figure 5.2 Computer network.

Sales executive is planning a presentation to the Board of Directors that includes an analysis of last month's sales. Data is available in a file server and statistical software is available in a PC, which has to analyze the data. Program forecasting future, sales runs on the mainframe.

Sales executive has to follow the following steps to prepare the presentation.

Step 1: Transfer data from files server to PC and run statistical software to get the result.

Step 2: Transfer data from step 1 to mainframe and run forecasting program.

Step 3: Transfer results from step 2 back to PC for printing formatting.

Step 4: Sends results to the laser printer.

We have shown the illustration of network with the help of example. Many network, however, involve many people using many PC's, each of which can access any of many printers or servers. Devices must be connected in a way that allows data to travel among many users with little or no delay. Topology is the layout of the connections formed between computers. To some extent, the reliability and efficiency of a network is determined by its structure. There are five basic topologies possible: bus, star, ring, tree, and mesh.

5.2.1 Bus Topology

A network that uses a bus topology usually consists of a single, long cable to which computers attach. Any computer attached to a bus can send a signal down the cable, and all computers receive the signal. Figure 5.3 illustrates the topology.

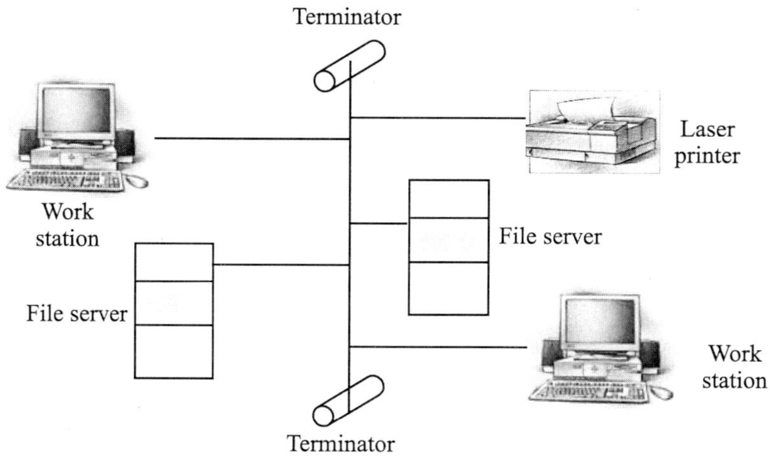

Figure 5.3 Bus topology.

Because all computers attached to the cable can sense an electrical signal, any computer can send data to any other computers. Of course, the computers attached to a bus network must coordinate to ensure that only one computer sends a signal at any time or choas results. In bus topology the failure or removal of device does not cause the network to fail.

5.2.2 Star Topology

The star topology is the oldest communications design method, with roots in telephone switching systems. Although it is the oldest design method, advances in network technology have made the star technology a good option for modern networks. A network uses a star topology if all computers attach to a central point. Figure 5.4 illustrates the star topology.

A hub is a central device that joins single cable segments or individual LANs into one network.

A typical hub consists of an electronic device that accepts data from a sending computer and delivers it to the appropriate destination. In practice, star networks seldom have a symmetric shape in which the hub is located at equal distance from all computers. In a star topology, the failure of hub (Central Computer) brings down the entire network.

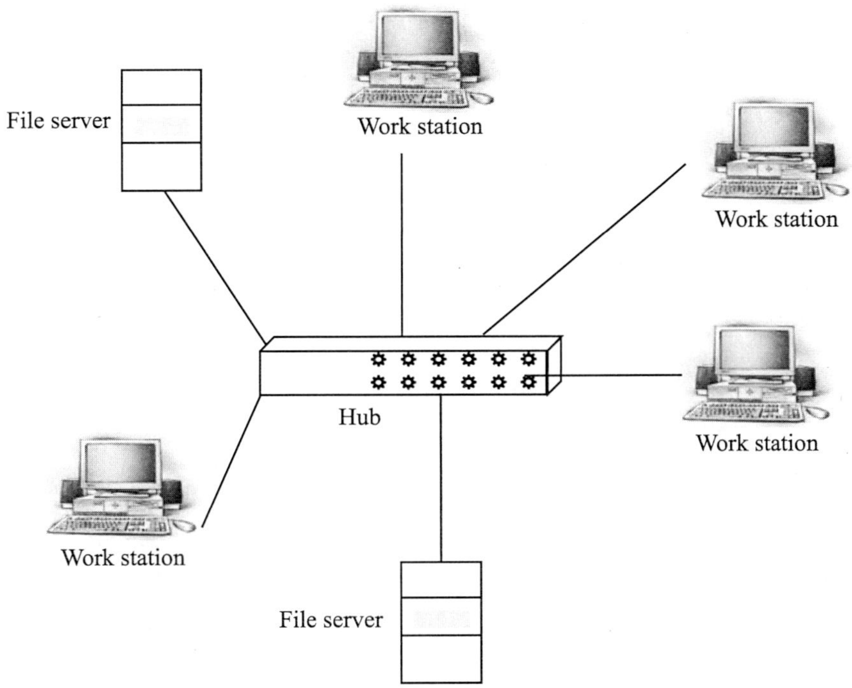

Figure 5.4 Star topology.

5.2.3 Ring Topology

The ring topology is a continuous path for data with no logical beginning or ending points, and thus, no terminators. Workstations and file servers are attached to the cable at points around the rings. Figure 5.5 illustrates the ring topology.

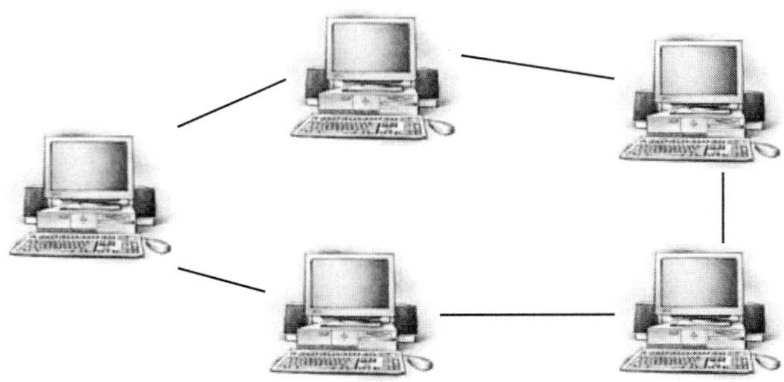

Figure 5.5 Ring topology.

When data is transmitted onto the ring, it goes around the ring from node to node, finds its destination, and then continues until it ends at the source node. A ring network may be either unidirectional or bidirectional. Unidirectional means that all transmissions travel in the same direction. Thus, each device can communicate with only one neighbor. Bidirectional means that data transmissions travel in either direction, and device can communicate with both neighbors.

The ring topology is easier to manage than the bus because the equipment used to build the ring makes it easier to locate a defective node or cable problem. Overall, the ring topology enables more reliable communications than the bus.

5.2.4 Tree Topology

A tree topology is a variation of a star. As in star, nodes in a tree are linked to a central hub that controls the traffic to the network. However, not every device plugs directly into the central hub. The majority of devices connect to a secondary hub that in turn is connected to the central hub as shown in Figure 5.6.

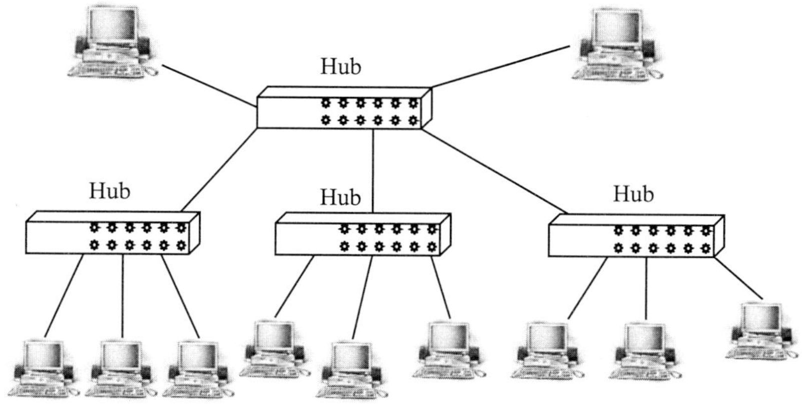

Figure 5.6 Tree topology.

A good example of tree topology can be seen in cable TV technology, where the main cable from the main office is divided into main branches and each branch is divided into smaller branches and so on. The hubs are used when a cable is divided.

5.2.5 Mesh Topology (Fully Connected Topology)

The mesh topology has a direct connection between every pain of devices in the network. This is an extreme design. Communication becomes very simple because there is no competition for common lines. If two devices want to communicate, they do so directly without involving other devices. Figure 5.7 illustrates the mesh topology.

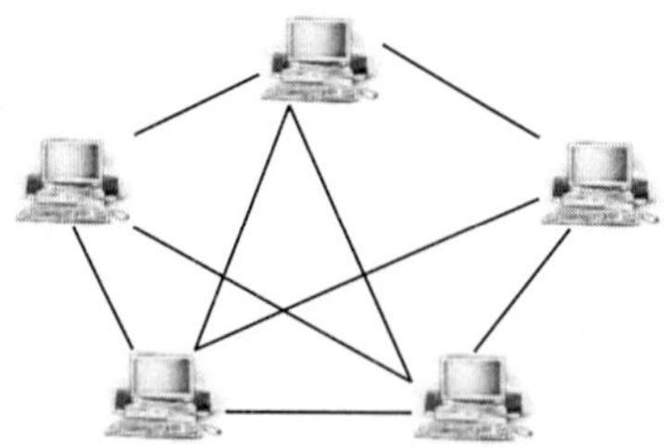

Figure 5.7 Mesh topology.

5.2.6 Combined Topologies

Many computer networks use combinations of the various topologies. Figure 5.8 shows a possible combination. It has a common bus, sometimes called the backbone, which allows users to access mainframes and high-volume or frequency accessed storage (Figure 5.8).

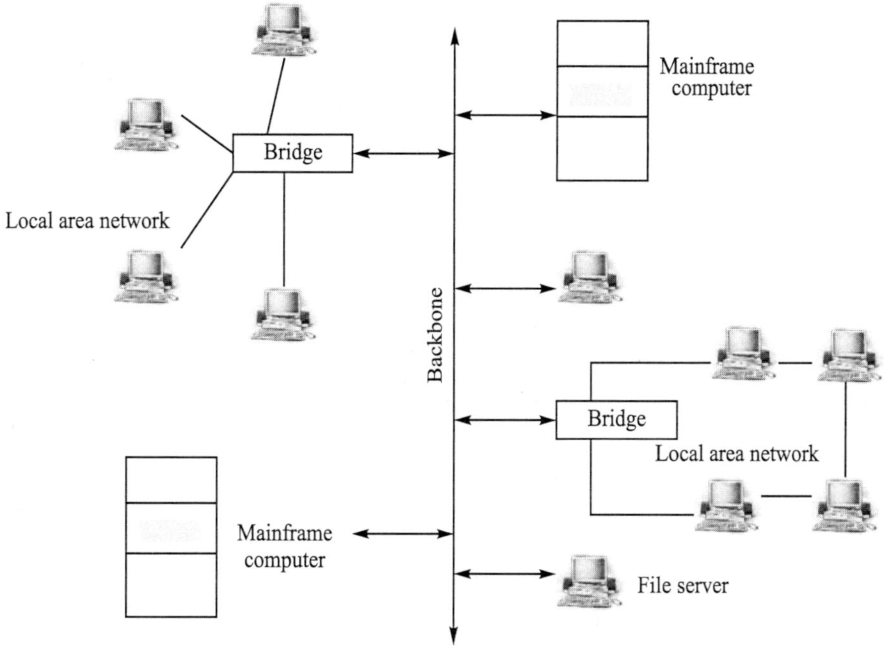

Figure 5.8 Combined topology.

5.3 CATEGORIES OF NETWORKS

Broadly speaking, there are two types of networks based on transmission technology:

1. Broadcast networks
2. Point-to-point networks.

Broadcast networks have a single communication channel that is shared by all the machines on the network. Short messages are called packets in certain context, sent by any machine are received by all the others. Upon receiving a packet is intended for itself, it processes the packet, if the packet is intended for some other machine, it is just ignored.

Broadcast systems generally also allow the possibility of addressing a packet to all destinations by using a special code in the address field. When a packet with this code is transmitted, it is received and processed by every machine on the network. This mode of operation is called Broadcasting.

Point-to-point networks consist of many connections between individual pairs of machines. To go from the source to the destination, a packet on this type of network may have to first visit one or more intermediate machines. Often multiple routes, of different lengths are possible, so routing algorithms play an important role in point-to-point networks.

Today when we speak of networks, we are generally referring to three primary categories: local area networks (LAN), metropolitan area network (MAN) and wide area network (WAN). Network categories can be specified based on its size, its ownership, the distance it covers and its physical architecture.

5.3.1 Local Area Network (LAN)

LAN normally refers to local area networks or LANs, are used to interconnect distributed communities of computer-based data terminal equipments located within a single building or localized group of buildings.

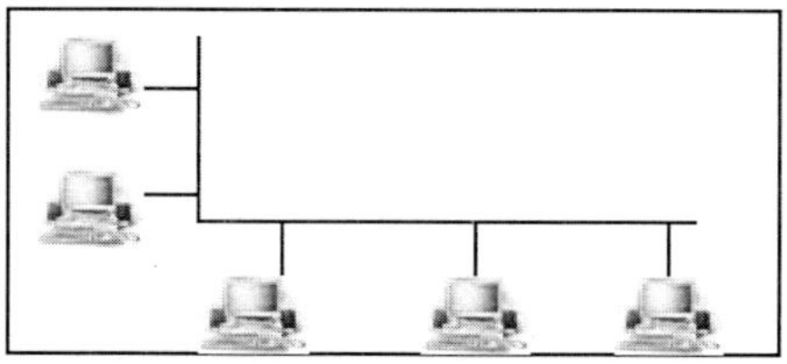

Figure 5.9(a) Single building LAN.

For example, we may use a LAN to interconnect workstations distributed around offices within a single building or group of buildings such as a university campus, to interconnect computer-based equipment distributed around a factory or hospital campus, shown in Figure 5.9.

However, since all the equipment is located within a single establishment, LANs are normally installed and maintained by the organization. Hence they are also reformed to as private data networks.

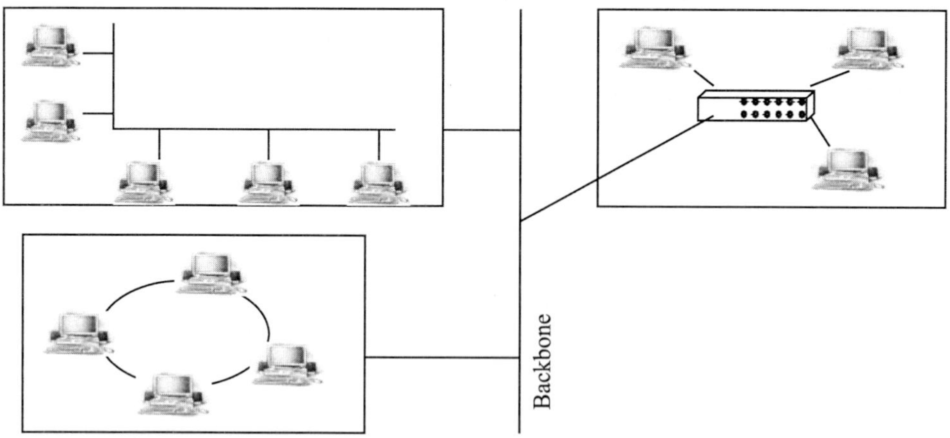

Figure 5.9(b) Multiple building LAN.

In addition to size, LANs are distinguished from other types of networks by their transmission media and topology. In general, a given LAN will use only one type of transmission medium. The most common LAN topologies are bus, ring and star. Traditionally, LANs have data rates in the 4 to 16 Mbps range.

5.3.2 Metropolitan Area Network (MAN)

MAN is basically a bigger version of a LAN and normally uses similar technology. MAN is designed to extend over an entire city. It may be single network such as a cable television network or it may be a means of connecting a number of LANs into a large network so that resources may be shared LAN-to-LAN as well as device-to-device. The high speed links between LANs within a MAN are made possible by fiber-optic connections.

5.3.3 Wide Area Network (WAN)

A wide area network is at far end of the spectrum because it is far-reaching system of networks that forms a complex whole. One WAN is composed of two or more LANs that are connected across a distance of more than 30 miles. Large WANs may have many constituent LANs and MANs on different continents. The most well-known WAN is the Internet, which consists of thousands of LANs and MANs throughout the world.

5.4 OPEN SYSTEMS AND OSI MODEL

A set of protocols that would allow any two different systems to communicate regardless of their underlying architecture is called an open system. International Organization for Standardization (ISO) has addressed the problem of allowing many systems to communicate ISO has developed a Open Systems Interconnections (OSI) model for a computer protocol architecture and as a framework for developing protocol standards. OSI guidelines specify:

- How network devices contact each other, and how devices using different protocols communicate
- How a network device knows when to transmit or not transmit data
- How the physical network devices are arranged and connect
- Methods to ensure that network transmissions are received correctly
- How network devices maintain a consistent rate of data-flow
- How electronic data is represented on the network media.

OSI model consists of seven layers:

1. Application layer
2. Presentation layer
3. Session layer

4. Transport layer
5. Network layer
6. Data link layer
7. Physical layer.

OSI model divides the basic communication functions into seven layers shown in Figure 5.10. Here, it is assumed that application A in one computer is communicating with application B in another computer. Applications A and B communicate using an application layer (Layer 7) protocol.

The purpose of the application layer is to provide user services such as electronic mail, file transfers, remote job entry, and resource allocation. Application layer protocols have been developed for file transfer, e-mail, network management and other applications.

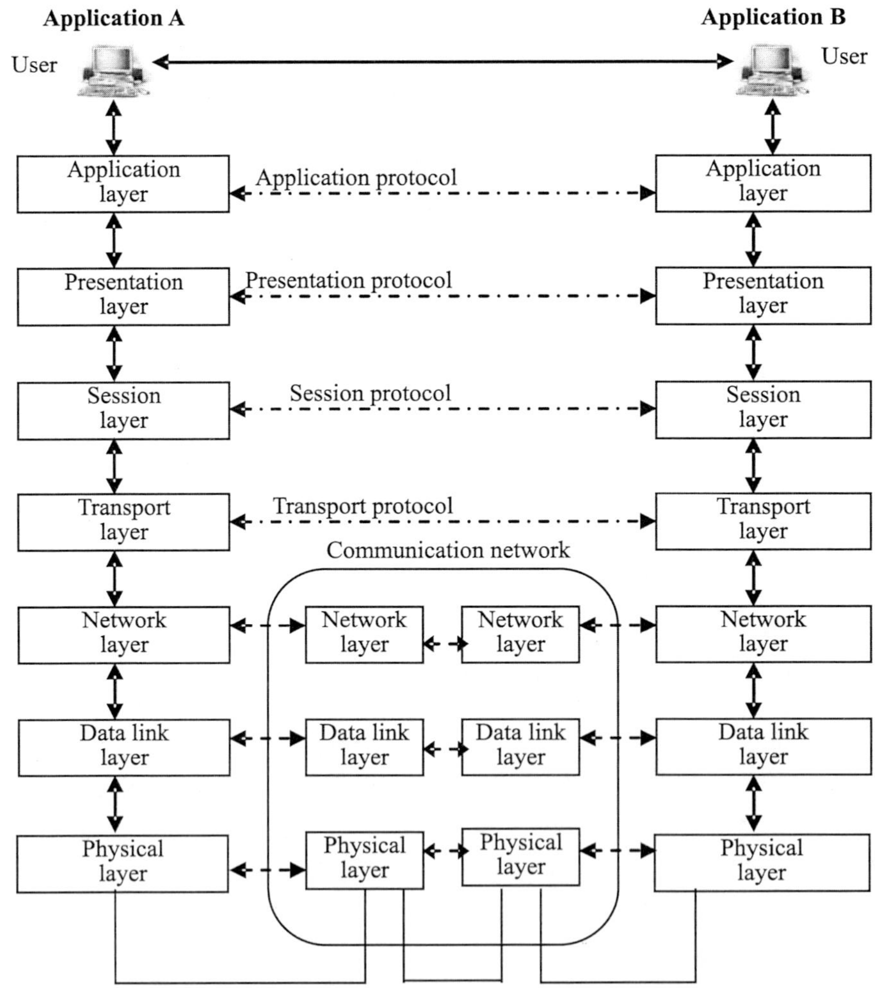

Figure 5.10 The OSI model.

The presentation layer is responsible for presenting data in the format, its user can understand for example, suppose two different computers use different numeric and character formats. The presentation layer translates data from one representation to another and insulates the user from such differences. So user can exchange information, not raw bit steams. The presentation layer can also provide security measures. It may encrypt data before handing it to the lower layers for transfer. The presentation layer at the other end would decrypt the data after receiving it.

The session layer allows applications on two different computers to establish a session, or logical connection. For example, a user may logon to a remote system and may communicate by alternately sending and receiving messages. The session layer concerns file management and overall networking functions. Access availability and system time allocations are included at this layer. Session layer protocols provide a method by which presentation sessions can organize, synchronize, and manage the transfers of information between themselves.

Transport layer is responsible to ensure that data is sent reliably from the sending node to the destination node (Computer). Transport layer provides end-to-end error recovery and flow control.

The network layer deals with routing strategies, which is responsible for delivery of a pocket from source to destination. For example, if two systems are connected in a bidirectional ring network, there are two paths between any two points. Should an entire message follow the same route or should part of it be transferred independently?

If two systems are connected to the same link there is usually no need for network layer. However, if the two systems are attached to different networks (links) with connecting devices between the networks (links), there is often a need for the network layer to accomplish source-to-destination delivery. The network layer controls the communication subset, the collection of transmission media and switching elements required for routing and data transmission.

The data link layer provides for the transfer of frames (blocks of information) across a transmission link that directly connects two nodes. The data link layer also recognizes a format. Data are often transmitted in the frames, which consist of a group of bytes organized according to a specified format. Data link layer uses error detection and correction techniques to ensure that a transmission contains no errors. It also uses flow control techniques, which controls how much information is sent at a time.

The physical layer deals with the transfer of bits over a communication channel, for example, copper wire pairs, coaxial cable, radio or optical fiber. It defines the mechanical, electrical, functional and procedural specifications will define items like the connectors and cable types used as the medium of communications link. Electrical specifications cover aspects that affect the impedance operating power, attenuation, frequency and bandwidth limitations etc. that affect the transfer of data. Functional aspects define the use of any interconnecting lines such as data and control functions. Procedural concerns define the lowest type of protocol rules that are required to assure a good communication link. Functions of the seven OSI layers are given in Table 5.1.

Table 5.1 Functions of the seven OSI layers

Layer	*Functions*
Physical Layer	• Provides the transfer medium (such as cable) • Translate data into a transmission signal appropriate to the transfer medium • Determine the voltage levels used for data signal transmissions and to synchronize transmissions. • Determines the signal type digital or analog. • Includes the physical layout of the network.
Data Link Layer	• Constructs data frames using the appropriate format for the network. • Creates CRC information and checks error using CRC information. • Retransmits data if there is an error. • Examines device address and acknowledges receipt of frame.
Network Layer	• Determine the network path on which to route packets. • Helps reduce network congestion. • Establishes virtual circuits. • Routes frames to other networks, resequencing packet transmission when needed.
Transport Layer	• Ensures reliability of packet transmissions from node to node. • Ensures data is sent and received in the same order. • Provides acknowledgement when a packet is received. • Monitors for packet transmission errors, and resends damaged packets.
Session Layer	• Initiates the communications link • Makes sure the communications link is maintained • Determines which node transmits at any point in time, for example which one transmit first.
Presentation Layer	• Translate data to a format the receiving node understands, for example from EBCDIC to ASCII. • Performs data encryption. • Performs data compression.
Application Layer	• Enables sharing of remote derives and printers • Handles e-mail messages. • Provides file transfer services and file management services.

5.5 TRANSMISSION CONTROL PROTOCOL/INTERNET PROTOCOL (TCP/IP)

When computers talk over the Internet, the language they speak is the TCP/IP. TCP/IP is also the protocol of choice for most medium and large–sized networks. Novell Netware, UNIX, and Window NT networks can all implement TCP/IP, particularly on growing networks and on ones that use client/server or web-based applications. TCP/IP is one of the oldest protocols and is proven technology that is used by millions of computer users around the globe. Its broad acceptance, reliable history, and extensive capabilities make it a good choice for most LAN-to-WAN installations.

The TCP/IP protocol suite, used in the Internet, was developed prior to the OSI model. Therefore, the layers in the TCP/IP protocol suite do not match exactly with those in the OSI model. The TCP/IP protocol suite is made of five layers.

- Application layer
- Transport layer
- Internet layer
- Network access layer
- Physical layer.

The first four layers provide physical standards, network interface, Internet working, and transport functions that correspond to the first four layers of the OSI model. The three top most layers in OSI model, however, are represented in TCP/IP by a single layer called the application layer (Figure 5.11).

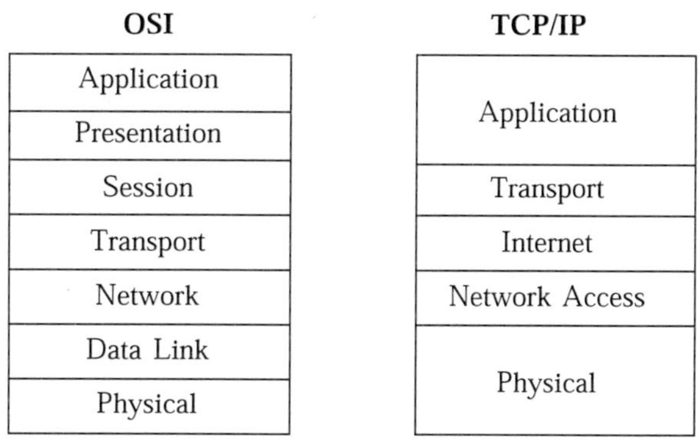

Figure 5.11 Comparison of OSI and TCP/IP.

A number of applications have been standardized to operate on top of TCP. We mention three of the most common here.

5.5.1 Simple Mail Transfer Protocol (SMTP)

SMTP provides a basic electronic mail facility. It provides a mechanism for transferring messages among separate hosts. Features of SMTP include mailing lists, return receipts and forwarding. Once a message is created, SMTP accepts the message and makes use of TCP to send it to an SMTP module on another host. The target SMTP module will make use of local electronic mail package to store the incoming message in user's mailbox.

5.5.2 File Transfer Protocol (FTP)

FTP is used to send files from one system to another under user command. Both text and binary files are accommodated, and the protocol provides features for controlling user access. When a user wishes to engage in file transfer, FTP sets up a TCP connection to the target system for the exchange of control messages. This connection allows user ID and password to be transmitted, and allows the user a file transfer is approved a second TCP connection is set-up for the data transfer. The file is transferred over the data connection, without the overhead of any headers of control information at the application level. When the transfer is complete, the control connection is used to single the completion and to accept new file transfer commands.

5.5.3 TELNET (Terminal Network)

The main task of the Internet and its TCP/IP protocol suite is to provide services for users. For example, users want to be able to run different application programs at a remote site and create results that can be transferred to their local site. One way to satisfy these demands is to create different client-server application programs for each desired service. Program such as file transfer programs (FTP), e-mail (SMTP), and so on are already available. But it would be impossible to write a specific client-server program for each demand.

The better solution is a general purpose client-server program that lets user access any application program on a remote computer; in other words, allow the user to log on to a remote computer. After logging on, a user can use the services available on the remote computer and transfer the results back to the local computer. TELNET is an abbreviation of TErminaL NETwork. Client-server application program is called TELNET.

REVIEW QUESTIONS

5.1 Identify the five components of data communication systems.

5.2 List five communication applications and how they might be used.

5.3 Discuss computer network and its topology.

5.4 What are some of the factors that determine whether a communication system is a LAN, MAN or WAN?

5.5 Discuss bus topology, ring topology and star topology.

5.6 Define the type of topology in Figures (a & b).

(a)

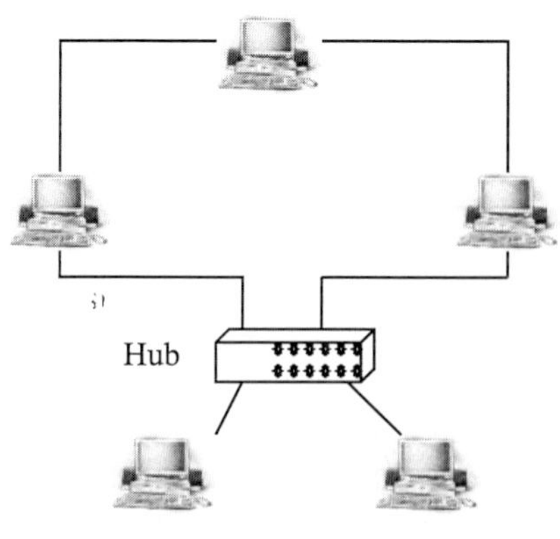

(b)

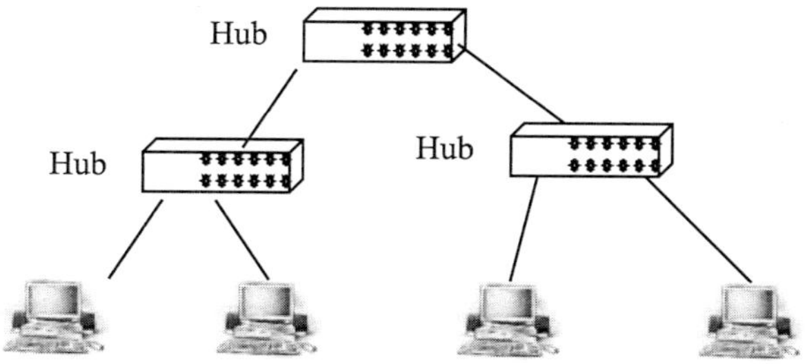

5.7 What is de facto standard?

5.8 Why are standards needed? And what is the purpose of ITU-T?

5.9 Which agency defines the standards and protocol for OSI model?

5.10 Find at least three standards defined by ITU-T.

5.11 Find at least three standards defined by IEEE.

5.12 Discuss OSI model. Which of the OSI model layers deals primarily with network operations?

5.13 What is the concession of the physical layers?

5.14 Discuss TCP/IP.

5.15 How do the layers of TCP/IP protocol suite correlate to the layers of the OSI model?

5.16 Discuss simple mail transfer protocol (SMTP) and file transfer protocol.

CHAPTER 6

Hardware and Software Security

Chapter Outline

Software security depends on hardware security. If the hardware can be stolen or surreptitiously replaced, secure software will not help. Before the invention of the personal computer, computer mainframes were so huge that they took up an entire room. To secure these machines IT managers locked the rooms. Now small and portable laptop and palmtop computers are easily stolen. Companies use computers for storing sensitive information, doing online transactions and accessing private and public networks. IT managers looking to protect their investments must consider securing the perimeter and allowing only authorized user access to their computers.

Both in its hardware and its software, the computer has the ability to protect itself. That's true even of PC's and networks, despite what large-system partisans sometimes claim. Nevertheless, there are two important points to remember:

- No form of security is automatic. Whatever is the size of your system, you must work to make it secure. Networks require more work than centralized systems.
- No form of security can do it all. Even the most advanced and comprehensive forms of large-system security can do only part of the job.

The increased use of networks and personal computers has directed new attention of technical types of protection. The nature of a network makes it necessary. Physical protection is obviously much more difficult than it was withhold centralized systems. There is also the vastly increased number of users. Once, only a few people knew how to use computers. Now, those who don't know are usually seen as targets for retraining. These numbers make it infinitely more difficulty to manage a system of procedural controls. Meanwhile, computer systems and the networks, that link them are constantly getting better. Thus, technical protection is becoming both easier and more important. It is now possible to design technical measures that will protect you against most types of crime and abuse. Technical security can also be cost-effective. Often, the protection requires more ingenuity than it does money.

Built-in security is a combination of controls within your hardware, software and communication systems. The three types of security interact and support each other as given below:

1. Hardware controls are used to make sure the operating system functions properly and to control access to the programs and data.
2. Software controls are used primarily to identify users and controls their access. They also let you monitor use of the system.
3. Communication controls are applied to networks, modems, and other communication system components to control access and the flow if data over the system.

Most technical security methods are aimed at one or more of these objectives:

- Maintaining the integrity of your computer system and its contents. The computer should do its job correctly and consistently your data must be reliable, and your programs must process it without error. These qualities can be important in such functions as payroll, inventory and finances. Poor integrity can leave you open to fraud, theft and embezzlement.
- Keeping sensitive information in confidence. This is largely a matter of access control. The information in your database files often is essential to the operation of your business. It may include critical financial details or trade secretes which if revealed or corrupted, can have a catastrophic effect on your business. You also must be careful to protect the privacy of personal data on your employers and customers.
- Making the computer's services available whenever they are needed. You certainly know the perils and frustration of a computer that goes down. Good technical controls can help you minimize that problem, protecting the system from sabotage, accidents, misuse and even poor design.

A secure system should meet these requirements:

- It must implement an explicitly defined security policy. This policy should fully describe how you wish to grant access to information.
- All information should be classified according to its security level.
- Every individual who is authorized to use the system should be positively identified and granted access only to designated processes.
- Any action that might affect security must be recorded.
- The hardware and software components of the system should be designed so each can be evaluated independently.
- The system must provide as much protection to your security mechanisms as it does to the information it is supposed to guard.

6.1 HARDWARE SECURITY

Hardware security is more than locking the door to the computer room. Companies are using the Internet, Intranets and Extranets to exchange information. Their employees use laptops wherever they go, carrying with them proprietary information. Hardware devices such as computer locks and smart cards help companies to protect this information. Securing the organization's perimeter with alarms, surveillance cameras, and security guards make it transparent to intruders that security is enforced. Consider all possible security breaches and implement a security solution that encompasses them all.

Some hardware problems are common:

- Equipment and removable media can be stolen or substituted.
- Changing hardware setup parameter scan circumvent security.
- Systems can be booted by unauthorized users or unauthorized software.
- Boot media can be rewritten by unauthorized software.
- Unauthorized software can be executed from removable media.

Some of the safeguards that can be taken are:

- Locking doors and security equipment.
- Having lockable cases and keyboards and removable media drives.
- Having a key or password-protected configuration and set-up.
- Requiring a password to boot.
- Requiring a password to mount removable media.
- Using read-only media.
- Staring removable media in secured areas.

Organizations that stores and transit sensitive and valuable information over both public and private networks should be concerned with information security. For example, security breach can occur in hardware, software, network connection, or authentication procedures.

Developing a Security System

When planning a security system, form a strategy rather than randomly deploying gizmos. Three possible strategies are perimeter security, interior security, and physical protection of individual assets. While you want to keep intruders out, you also want to limit the amount of damage they can do once they are inside.

Perimeter security means preventing entry by criminals, who choose the easiest points, usually doors and windows can be protected with small, easily mounted devices that sound an alarm when the glass is broken. Authorization can take many forms, including entering a code into a keypad, sliding a card through a scanner, or pressing a button on a wireless remote control.

Interior security is as much about deferring intruders as about catching them. Motion detector can be used to set off alarms. Surveillance cameras can detect theft when they are located so as to catch the intruder's eye.

Many computing devices are small enough to be put in a briefcase and carried away. Cable kits can be an inexpensive solution to this problem. Some hardware devices can be connected to computers and set to trigger an alarm. Software can be installed in a laptop to let police track down stolen laptops.

6.2 SMART CARD

A smart card is a credit-card size device that has an embedded microprocessor, a small amount of memory, and an interface that allows it to communicate with a workstation or network. With smart cards, passwords and IDs are securely encrypted on the card; when combined with biometrics finger. Scanning technologies, users can ever skip the PIN code.

A smart card can be personalized to the user. For example, a company using smart cards to provide access to network services would store network privileges and preferred system settings on each employee's card, which could then be used from any terminal with a card reader, customizing the desktop to the employee's preference.

Two characteristics make smart cards especially well-suited for security, sensitive or personal data applications:

1. The onboard processor can service requests from the network and return the results without divulging the sensitive data. For example, a smart card could digitally sign data without divulging the user's private key.
2. The user can carry data on the smart card rather than entrusting it to network storage. For example, a smart card could be used to carry personal information about the user, such as medical records or digital certificates.

Microsoft windows NT4, windows 95 and windows 98 all support smart cards and smart card readers based on specifications established by the personal computer smart card (PC/SC) workgroup of leading companies. Windows-compatible smart card solutions can be used with Internet Explorer to authenticate a secure connection and with Outlook Express for sending and receiving secure e-mail.

Through the use of public key cryptography and X.509 certificates, smart cards securely store private as well as public key certificates. Embedded private key is the digital certification representation of a user's identity. Smart card allows you to digitally sign and encrypt messages, provides access to protected Intranet sites, and can enable a single network sign on.

6.3 BIOMETRICS

Access controls that utilize something you know (e.g., combinations) or something you have (e.g., keys) are not the only methods to limit facility access to authorized individuals. A third approach is to utilize something unique about the individual, their finger prints, for example, to identify them. Unlike the other two methods, something you are known as biometrics, does not rely on the individual to either remember something or to have something in their possession. Biometrics is a more sophisticated access control approach and is also more expensive. Other methods to accomplish biometrics include handwriting analysis, retinal scans, voiceprints, hard geometry and facial geometry.

Biometrics can be used to control access to computer systems and networks as well as to serve as physical access control device.

Biometrics identifies people based on unique physical characteristics or behavioral traits using body features such as fingerprints, eyes, or faces, and ways of doing things such as speaking or writing signatures. The catalyst for biometrics is the growing realization that passwords can get lost, misplaced, forgotten, or written on notes and stick on computer monitors for anyone to use. Valuable corporate data is often compromised as a result.

The term "biometrics product" has multiple definitions:

- A component that captures a human characteristics
- Associated hardware
- Application software
- Image-matching software
- A stand-alone product
- A complete solution
- A platform or environment that supports biometric authentication.

This technology is still expensive without being as effective as other security products. Moreover, people see having their eyeballs scanned as an invasion of privacy. They fear a Big Brother-like agency keeping tabs on fingerprints and voiceprints. Once they understand how limited the data needed in, they are likely to become more comfortable with the technology.

Some of the commercially-available biometric identification methods are:

Voiceprint: Sound waves generated by an individual speaking a given word or password are compared to stored patterns.

Fingerprints: Ridges on fingers are converted to a digital template that can be compared with database records.

Palmprints: The ridges of the palm are measured for comparison with a database.

Hand geometry: Measures the size and shape of the hand.

Hand veins: The vein pattern on the back of the hand is scanned, creating a digital template that can be matched against stored patterns.

Handwriting acoustic emissions: Analyze sounds generated when a person signs his or her name.

Iris map: A video image of the colored portion of the eye is mapped by computer, creating a digital code based on the individual pattern of the iris.

Facial thermographs: Use an infrared camera to capture heat emission patterns; there is a unique signature when heat passes through facial tissue.

Facial identification: Converts a video image of the face to a digital template to be compared with a recorded image. Generally, biometric authentication is a two-phase process. The first is scanning personal characteristics of user's such as fingerprints irises, faces, signatures, or voiceprints, into the computer. Key features are then converted to unique templates, which are stored in the computer as encrypted numerical data. In the second phase, the user presents that personal characteristic and the computer compares it with the template in the database. But in the real world, matches will rarely be perfect due to extraneous factors and background interference.

6.4 VIRTUAL PRIVATE NETWORKS (VPNs)

It is widely accepted fact that Internet technologies have changed the way that companies do business in today's marketplace. The growing necessity for secure access to business—critical information and enterprise resources from various remote locations has brought virtual private network (VPN) technology to the forefront of IT initiatives. VPNs offer secure communications between network application using a public or unsecured medium such as the Internet through the use of various technologies offering user authentication, data integrity and access control. A VPN is not a single technology, but a complex interaction of different technologies. VPNs also represent cost-savings over a true private networks such as leased line and frame relay because they reduce connectivity costs.

VPNs have three different uses in todays' business environment:

(i) Remote access for the mobile workforce
(ii) Internet connectivity or site-to-site
(iii) Extranet connectivity or business-to-business (B2B)

A successful VPN deployment is much more than simple data encryption. A complete VPN solution includes:

Security: User authentication, standards-based data encryption to guarantee the security of network connections, authenticity of users, and privacy and integrity of data communications.

Traffic control: Bandwidth management, quality of service, and acceleration of data encryption/decryption to guarantee VPN reliability and performance.

Enterprise management: A comprehensive security policy that integrates enterprise-wide VPNs and centralized policy-based management.

6.4.1 Types of VPNs

VPNs are generally separated into two types: User VPNs and Site VPNs. The difference between them is the way the two types are used, not because of the way traffic is segregated by each type.

User VPNs

User VPNs are virtual private networks between an individual user machine and an organization site or network. Often user VPN's are used for employees who travel or work from home. The VPN server may be the organization's firewall or it may be a separate VPN server. The user connects to the Internet via a local ISP dial-up, DSL line, or cable modem and initiates a VPN to the organization site via the Intranet.

The organization's site requests the user to authenticate and, if successful, allows the user to access to the organization's internal network as if the user were within the site, and physically on the network. Obviously, the network speed will be slower since the limiting factor will be the user's Internet connection.

User VPN may allow the organization to limit the systems or files that the remote user can access. This limitation should be based on organization policy and depends on the capabilities of the VPN product.

While the user has a VPN back to the organization's internal network, he or she also has a connection to the Internet and can perform other activities like a normal Internet user. The VPN is handled by a separate application on the user's computer as shown in Figure 6.1.

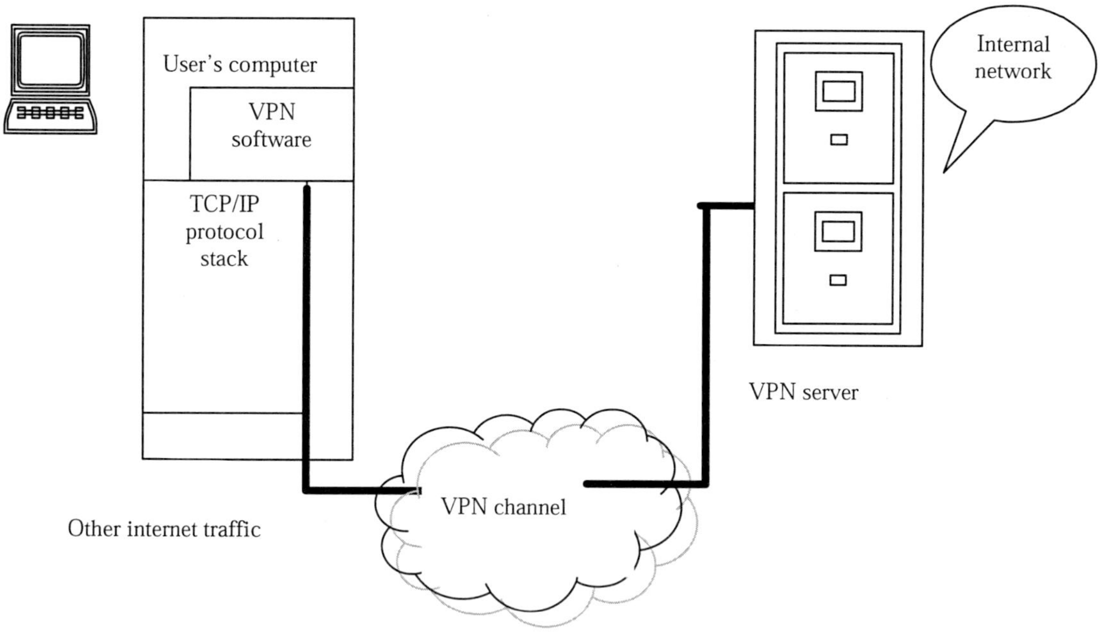

Figure 6.1 User VPN configuration.

In some cases a user's computer can act as a router between the Internet and the VPN (and thus the organization internal network). This type of attack should be investigated before was VPN's are deployed. Some VPN clients provide a policy component that can limit this type of exposure.

There are two primary benefits of user VPNs:

- Employees who travel can have access to e-mail files, and internal systems wherever they are without the need for expensive long distance calls to dial-in servers.
- Employees who work from home can have the same access to network services as employees who work from the organization facilities without the requirement for expensive leased lines.

Site VPNs

Site VPNs are used by organizations to connect remote sites without the need for expensive leased lines or to connect two different organizations that wish to communicate for some business purpose. Generally, the VPN connects one firewall or border router with another firewall or border router as shown in Figure 6.2.

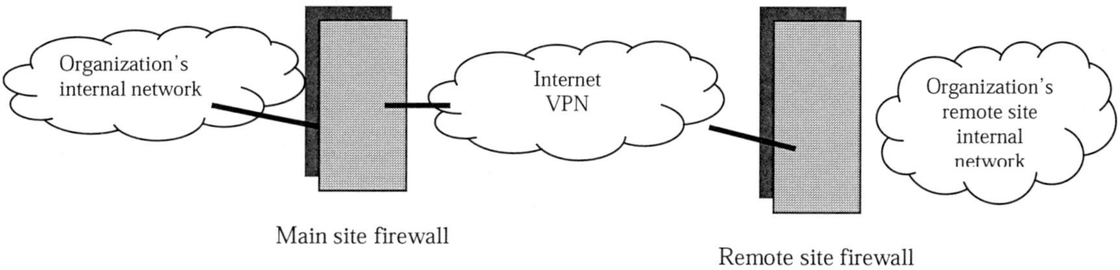

Figure 6.2 Site-to-site VPN across the Internet.

To initiate the connection, one site attempts to send traffic to the other. This causes the two VPN end points to initiate the VPN. The two end points will negotiate the parameters of the connection depending on the policies of the two sites. The two sites will also authenticate each other by using some shared secret that has been preconfigured or public key certificate. Some organizations use site VPNs as backup links for leased lines.

Care must be taken with this type of configuration to make sure that the routing is configured properly and that the physical line used for the VPN is different than the line used for the leased connection. You may find that the two lines travel over the same physical cable and thus may not provide as much redundancy as you expect.

As with the user VPN, the primary benefit of the site VPN is cost-savings. An organization with small remote offices can create a virtual network that connects all remote offices to the central site (or even with each other) at a significantly reduced cost. The network infrastructure may also be implemented much faster as local ISP (Internet Service Providers), can be used for ISDN or DSL lines at the remote offices. Rules can be established based on organization policy for how the remote sites can connect to the central site or each other. If the site VPN is to connect two organizations, strict limitations can be placed on access to internal networks and computer systems.

6.4.2 Virtual Private Network Software

To provide virtual private networking capabilities using the Internet as a network backbone, specialized tunneling protocols were developed to establish private, secure channels between connected systems. Four VPN protocols that have been developed include the following:

(i) Microsoft's Point-to-Point Tunneling Protocol (PPTP)
(ii) The Internet Engineering Task Force (IETF) Internet Protocol Security (IPSec.)
(iii) Cisco's Layer 2 Forwarding (L2F) Protocol
(iv) A Combination of the two called Layer 2 Tunneling Protocol (L2TP)

Figure 6.3 depicts the use of tunneling protocols to build a virtual private network across the Internet. Various tunneling protocols including L2F, L2TP and PPTP are used to pass traffic across the VPN, a process that is transparent to the end users. A key component of VPN is tunneling, which is a vehicle for encapsulating packets inside a protocol that is understood at the entry and exit points of a given network. These entry and exit points are defined as tunnel interfaces. The tunnel itself is similar to hardware interface, but is configured in software.

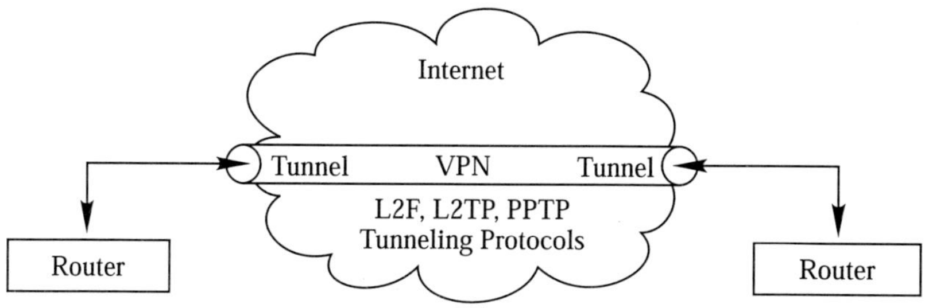

Figure 6.3 Utilizing tunneling protocols.

Point-to-Point Tunneling Protocol

The Point-to-Point Tunneling Protocol (PPTP) was first created by a group of companies calling themselves the PPTP Forum. The group consisted of 3 Com, Ascend Communication, Microsoft, ECI Telematics, and U.S. Robotics. The basic idea behind PPTP was to split up the functions of remote access in such a way where individuals and corporations could take advantage of the Internet's infrastructure to provide secure connectivity between remote clients and private networks. Remote users would dial into the local number of the ISP and then securely tunnel into their corporate network.

The most commonly used protocol for dial-up access to the Internet is the Point-to-Point Protocol (PPP). The first connection is to the remote access host using PPP. A second connection is then made over the PPP connection to a PPTP server on a private LAN. A typical example of a PPTP installation is a client computer running PPP and PPTP to access an ISP. Figure 6.4 illustrates this connectivity.

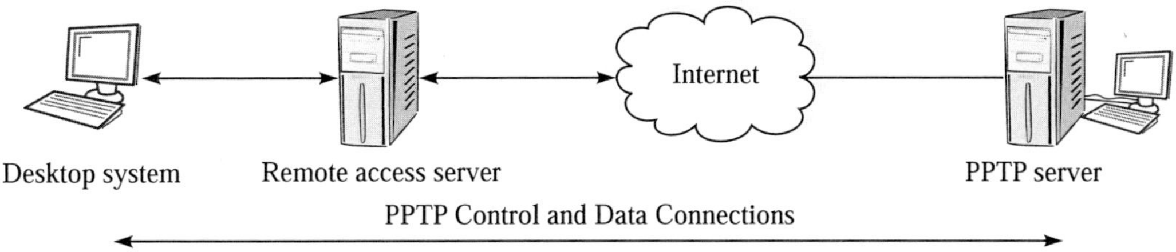

Figure 6.4 PPTP environment

PPTP permits a user running Window 95 to dial into a Windows NT Server running the Remote Access Service (RAS), and it supports the equivalent of a private, encrypted dial up session across the Internet. Similarly, a VPN could be established permanently across the Internet by leasing dedicated lines to an ISP at each end of a two-way link, and maintaining ongoing PPTP-based communications across that dedicated link.

Since it is based on PPT, PPTP is well suited to handling multiprotocol network traffic, particularly IP, IPX and NetBEUI protocols, PPTP's design also makes it easier to outsource some of the support tasks to an ISP.

Layer 2 Tunneling Protocol

The Layer 2 Tunneling Protocol (L2TP) was created as a successor to two tunneling protocols, PPTP and L2F (Layer 2 Forwarding Protocol). Like PPTP, L2F was designed as a tunneling protocol, using its own definition of an encapsulation header for transmitting packets at Layer 2. One major difference between PPTP and Packets at Layer 2. One major difference between PPTP and L2F is that L2F tunneling is not dependent on IP, enabling it to work with other physical media.

There are two levels of authentication of the user. Level 1 is by the ISP prior to setting up the tunnel and Level 2 is when the connection is set up at the corporate gateway.

Layer 2 Tunneling Protocol defines its own tunneling protocol, based on the work of L2F. Work has continued on defining L2TP transport over a variety of packetized media such as X.25, Frame Relay, and ATM. Although many initial implementation of L2TP focus on using UDP on IP networks, it is possible to set up an L2TP system without using IP as a tunnel protocol entirely. A network using ATM or Frame Relay can also be deployed for L2TP tunnels. Figure 6.5 depicts the protocols involved in an L2TP connection between an access concentrator and a network server.

Because L2TP is a Layer 2 protocol, it offers users the same flexibility as PPTP for handling protocols other than IP, such as IPX and NetBEUI. Also because it uses PPP for dial-up links, L2TP includes authentication mechanisms within PPP. The components of an L2TP system are essentially the same as those for PPTP: point-to-point protocols, tunnels, and authentication systems.

L2TP should be considered the next-generation VPN protocol, particularly for dial-in VPNs. Many vendors already have plans to supplant PPTP-based products with L2TP products. L2TP offers a number of advantages of PPTP, particularly for handling multiple sessions over a single tunnel as well as assigning QoS parameters of different tunnels to the same site. In addition, L2TP's capabilities to run over such technologies as X.25, Frame Relay, and ATM

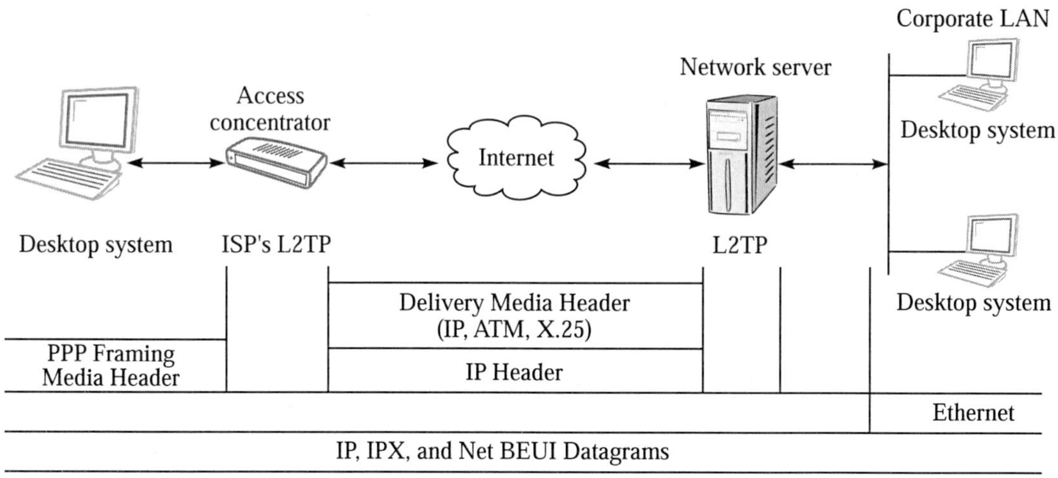

Figure 6.5 L2TP connection protocol.

while handling multiple network layer protocols, in addition to IP, affords users and ISP's a considerable amount of flexibility in designing VPNs. L2TP also provides stronger security for the corporate data, because it uses IPSec's Encapsulating Security Payload (ESP) for encryption packets, even over a PPP link between the end-user and the ISP.

Layer 2 Forwarding Protocol

Layer 2 Forwarding (L2F) Protocol is tunneling protocol developed by Cisco Systems Inc. The key management requirements of service that are provided by Cisco's L2F implemented are as follows:

- Neither the remote end system nor its corporate hosts should require any special software to use this service in a secure manner.
- Authentication is provided by dial-up PPP and the various authentication protocols, as well as support for smart cards and one-time passwords; the user can manage the authentication independent of the ISP.
- Addressing will be as manageable as dedicated dial-up solutions; the address will be assigned by the remote user's respective corporation, and not by the ISP.
- Authorization will be managed by the corporation's remote user's, as it would in a direct dial-up solution.
- Accounting will be performed by both the ISP and the user.

These requirements are primarily achieved based on the functionality provided by tunneling the remote user directly to the corporate location using the L2F protocol. In the case of PPP, all link control protocol and network control protocol negotiations take place at the remote user's corporate location. PPP is allowed to flow from the remote user and terminate at the corporate gateway.

Internet Protocol Security (IPSec)

Internet Protocol Security (IPSec) is a standard created to add security to TCP/IP networking. It is a collection of security measures that addresses data privacy, integrity, authentication, and key management, in addition to tunneling. The IPSec system includes a considerable amount of flexibility in authentication and encryption algorithms, allowing it to meet the demands of both current and future networking situations.

The original TCP/IPs did not include any inherent security features. To address the issue of providing packet level security in IP, the IETF has been working on the IPSec protocols within their IP Security Working Group. The first protocols comprising IPSec, for authenticating and encrypting IP datagrams, were published by the IETF as RFCs 1825 to 1829 in 1995. Current specifications are included in RFCs 2401, 2402, 2406, 2408, and 2411.

These protocols set out the basics of the IPSec architecture, which include two different headers designed for IP packets. The IP Authentication Header (AH) is for authentication and the other, the Encapsulating Security Payload (ESP) is for encryption purposes. In addition, Security Association (SA), which is a security agreement on key management, is an important concept in IPSec. An SA is a one-way relationship between a sender and a receiver that affords security services to the traffic carried on it.

The AH and ESP protocols can be applied either to authenticate or decrypt just the packets payload or entire IP header, including the IP addresses of the source and destination. Applying authentication and encryption in tunnel mode provides the greatest degree of security.

To enable secure communications between two parties, a system for exchanging keys is required. An IPSec Security Association is created between VPN sites to exchange keys and any pertinent details on the cryptographic algorithms that will be used for session. Although manual exchanges of security associations and keys are possible for a small number of VPN sites, IP Sec includes an involved, but workable framework for automatic key management called Internet Key Exchange (IKE).

- IPSec has multiple modes and services, including the following:
- Connectionless integrity
- Confidentiality
- Data origin authentication
- Key management
- Replay protection

IPSec software can reside in stationary hosts, mobile clients, or security gateways. Only security gateways are needed if LAN-to-LAN tunnels are to be created. Mobile workers would require IPSec client software if they wanted to connect to a VPN site.

6.5 OPERATING SYSTEMS

The OS, being the system's resources regulator, must provide for security mechanisms. It must not only secure the information to protect the privacy but also prevent misuse of system resources.

Operating systems are the prime providers of security in computing systems. They support many programming capabilities, permit multiprogramming and sharing of resources, and enforce restrictions on programs and user behavior. Because they have such power, operating systems are also targets for attack, because breaking through the defenses of an operating system gives access to the secrets of computing systems.

6.5.1 A Bit of History

Once upon a time, there were no operating systems: users entered their programs directly into the machine in binary by means of switches. In many cases, program entry was done by physical manipulation of a toggle switch; in other cases, the entry was performed with a more complex electronic method, by means of an input device such as a keyboard. Because each user had exclusive use of the computing system, users were required to schedule blocks of time for running the machine. These users were responsible for loading their own libraries of support routines—assemblers, compliers, shared subprograms—and "cleaning up" after use by removing any sensitive code or data.

The first operating systems were simple utilities, called executives, designed to assist individual programmers and to smooth the transition from one user to another. The early executives provided linkers and loaders for relocation, easy access to compilers and assemblers, and automatic loading of subprograms from libraries. The executives handled the tedious aspects of programme support, focusing on a single programmer during execution.

Operating systems took on a much broader role (and a different name) as the notion of multiprogramming was implemented. Realizing that two users could interleave access to the resources of a single computing system, researchers developed concepts such as scheduling, sharing, and parallel use. Multiprogrammed operating systems, also known as *monitors*, oversaw each program's execution. Monitors took an active role, whereas executives were passive. That is, an executive stayed in the background, waiting to be called into service by a requesting user. But a monitor actively asserted control of the computing system and gave resources to the user only when the request was consistent with general good use of the system. Similarly, the executive waited for a request and provided service on demand; the monitor maintained control overall resources, permitting or denying all computing and loaning resources to users as they needed them.

Multiprogramming brought another important change to computing. When a single person was using a system, the only force to be protected against was the user himself or herself. A user making an error may have felt foolish; but one user could not adversely affect the computation of any other user. However, multiple users introduced more complexity and risk. User A might rightly be angry if user B's programs or data had a negative effect on A's program's execution. Thus, protecting one user's programs and data from other user's programs became an important issue in multiprogrammed operating systems.

6.5.2 Trusted Operating Systems

We say that an operating system is trusted if we have confidence that it provides the following services in a consistent and effective way.

- Memory protection
- File protection
- General object access control
- User authentication.

Every system can be described by its requirements: statements of what the system should do and how it should do it. An operating system's security requirements are a set of well-defined, consistent and implementable rules that have been clearly and unambiguously expressed. If the operating system is implemented to meet these requirements, it meets the user's expectations. To ensure that the requirements are clear, consistent, and effective the operating system usually follows a stated security policy: a set of rules that layout what is to be secured and why.

To create a trusted operating system, the designers must be confident that the proposed system will meet its requirements while protecting system will meet its requirements, while protecting appropriate objects and relationships. They usually begin by constructing a model of the environment to be secured. The model is actually a representation of the policy the operating system will enforce. Designers compare the model with the system requirements to make sure that the overall system functions are not compromised or degraded by the security needs. Then they study different ways of enforcing that security.

After having selected a security model, designers choose a means to implement it. Thus, the design involves both what the trusted operating system is (that is, its intended functionality) and how it is to be constructed (its implementation). Our trust in the system is rooted in two aspects: *features* (the operating system has all the necessary functionality needed to enforce the expected security policy) and *assurance* (the operating system has been implemented in such a way that we have confidence it will enforce the security policy correctly and effectively).

Trusted systems incorporate technology to address both features and assurance. The design of a trusted system is delicated, involving selection of an appropriate and consistent set of features with an appropriate degree of assurance that the features have been assembled and implemented correctly. Key features of a trusted operating system are:

- User identification and authentication
- Mandatory access control
- Discretionary access control
- Object reuse protection
- Complete mediation
- Trusted path
- Audit
- Audit log reduction
- Intrusion detection.

We must be able to tell who is requesting access to an object, and we must be able to verify the subjects identity. Trusted operating systems require secure identification of individuals and each individual must be uniquely identified.

Mandatory access control means that access control policy decisions are made beyond the control of the individual owner of an object. A central authority determines what information is to be accessible by whom, and the user cannot change access rights. By contrast, discretionary access control, as its name implies, leaves a certain amount of access control to the discretion of the object's owner or to anyone else who is authorized to control the objective access.

Reusable objects must be carefully controlled, least they create a serious vulnerability. Malicious user may claim a large amount of disk space and then scavenge for sensitive data. This kind of attack is called object reuse.

For mandatory or discretionary access control to be effective, all accesses only to files if the attack will acquire access through memory or an outside port or a network or a covert channel. Trusted operating systems perform complete mediation, meaning that all accesses are checked.

For critical operations such as setting a password or changing access permissions, users want an unmistakable communication, called a trusted path, to ensure that they are supplying important, protected information only to a legitimate receiver.

A security-relevant action may be as simple as an individual access to an object, such as a file, or it may be as major as a change to the central access control database affecting all subsequent accesses. Accountability usually entails maintaining a log of security relevant events that have occurred, listing each event and the person responsible for addition, deletion or change. This audit log must obviously be protected from outsiders, and every security-relevant event must be recorded. Some trusted systems perform audit reduction using separate tools to reduce the volume of the audit data. In this way, if there is an event, all the data have been recorded and can be consulted directly. However, for most analysis, the reduced audit log is enough to review.

Intrusion-detection software builds patterns of normal system usage, triggering an alarm any time the usage seems abnormal. After a decade of promising research results in intrusion detection, products are now commercially available.

6.5.3 Security Breaches

We first need to comprehend the types of security breaches that may happen. Breaches may happen with malicious intent or may be initiated by users inadvertently, or accidentally. They may end up committing a security breach through a mis-typed command or ill-understood interpretation of some command. In both these instances, the OS must protect the interest of legitimate users of the system. Unix also does not rule out a malicious access with the intent to abuse the system. It is well known that former disgruntled employees often attempt access to systems to inflict damages or simply corrupt some critical information. A malicious user's action may result in one of the following three kinds of security breaches:

- Disclosure of information
- Compromising integrity of data
- Denial of service to legitimate users of the system.

To launch an attack, an attacker may correctly guess a weak password of a legitimate user. He can then access the machine and all hardware and software resources made available to that user. Note that a password is an intended control (a means to authenticate a users) to permit legitimate access to system resources. Clearly, a malicious user may employ password cracking methods with the explicit intent to bypass the intended controls. He may access classified information and may also misuse the system resources. An unauthorized access may be launched to steal precious processor cycles, resulting in denial of service. Or, he may be able to require privileged access to modify critical files corrupting sensitive data. This would be an act of active misuse. Some activities like watching the traffic on a system or browsing without modifying files may be regarded as an act of passive misuse. Even this is a breach of security as it does lead to disclosure. It may result in some deterioration, albeit not noticeable, in the overall services as well.

Here, we shall discuss a few well-known attacks that have happened and have been recorded. A study of these examples helps us to understand how security holes get created.

(i) *External masquerading:* This is the case of unauthorized access. The access may be via a communication media, recording and playback. For instance, login session may be played back to measurable another user. The measures require a network-based security solution.

(ii) *Pest programs:* A malicious user may use a best program to cause a subsequent harm. Its effect may manifest at some specified time or event. The Trojan horse and virus attacks fall in this category. The main difference between a Trojan horse and a virus is that a virus is a self-reproducing program. Some virus writers have used the Terminate and Stay Resident (TSR) program facility in Microsoft environments to launch such attacks. The best programs require internal controls to counter. Generally, the tim lag helps the attacker to cover the tracks.

Typically, a virus propagation involves the following steps:

(a) *Remote cope:* In this step, a program is copied to a remote machine.

(b) *Remote execute:* The copied program is instructed to execute. The step required to repeat the previous step o the other connected machine, thereby propagating the virus.

(iii) *Use a given facility for a different purpose:* This form of attack involves use of a given facility for a purpose other than it was intended for. For example, in unix we can list files in any directory. This can be used to communicate secret information without being detected. Suppose 'User B' is not permitted to communicate or access files of 'User A'. When 'User B' accesses the files of 'User A,' he will always get a message permission denied. However, 'User A' may name his files as at nine, tonight, we meet. When 'User B' lists the files in the directory of 'User A', he gets the message at nine tonight we meet', thereby defeating the access controls.

(iv) *Active authority misuse:* This happens when an administrator (or an individual) abuses his user privileges. A user may misuse the resources advanced to him in good faith and trust. An administrator may falsiyfy bookkeeping data, or a user may manipulate accounts data, or some unauthorized person may be granted an access to sensitive information.

6.6 KERBEROS

Kerberos is an authentication service developed at Massachusetts Institute of Technology. The problem that Kerberos addresses is this: Assume an open distributed environment in which users at workstations wish to access services on the server distributed throughout the network. We would like for servers to be able to restrict access to authorized users and to be able to authenticate requests for service. In this environment, a workstation cannot be trusted to identify its users correctly to network services. In particular, the following three threats exist:

(i) A user may gain access to a particular workstation and pretend to be another user operating from that workstation.

(ii) A user may alter the network address of a workstation so that the requests sent from the altered workstation appear to come from impersonated workstation.

(iii) A user may eavesdrop on exchanges and use a reply attract to gain entrance to a server or to disrupt operations.

In any of these cases, an unauthorized user may be able to gain access to services and data that he or she is not authorized to access. Rather than building in elaborate authentication protocols at each server, kerberos provides a centralized authentication server whose function is to authenticate users to servers and servers to users. Kerberos relies exclusively on symmetric encryption, making no use of public-key encryption.

Kerberos is a system that supports authentication in distributed systems. Kerberos is used for authentication between intelligent processes, such as client-to-server tasks, or a user's workstation to other hosts. Kerberos is based on the idea that a central server provides authenticated tokens, called *Tickets*, to requesting applications. A ticket is an unforgeable, nonreplayable, authenticated object. That is, it is an encrypted data structure naming a user and a service that the user is allowed to obtain. It also contains a time value and some control information.

The first step in using Kerberos is to establish a session with the Kerberos server, as shown in Figure 6.6.

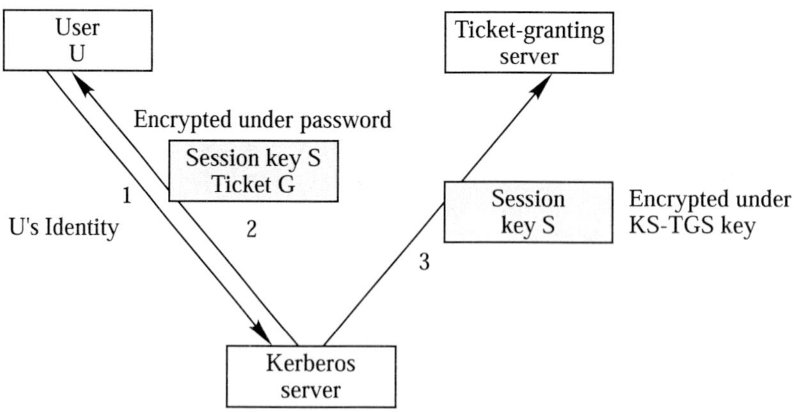

Figure 6.6 Initiating a Kerberos session.

A user's workstation sends the users's identity to the Kerberos server when a user logs in. The Kerberos server verifies that the user is authorized. The Kerberos server sends two messages.

(a) to the user's workstation, a session key S_G for use in communication with the ticket-granting server (G) and a ticket T_G for the ticket-granting server; S_G is encrypted under the user's password: $E(S_G + T_G, pw)^4$

(b) to the ticket-granting server, a copy of the session key S_G and the identity of the user (encrypted under a key shared between the Kerberos server and the ticket-granting server).

If the workstation can decrypt $E(S_G + T_G, pw)$ using pw, the password typed by the user, then the user has succeeded in an authentication with the workstation.

Notice that passwords are stored at the Kerberos server, not at the workstation, and that the user's password did not have to be passed across the network, even in encrypted form. Holding passwords certainly but not passing them across the network is a security advantage.

Next, the user will want to exercise some other services of the distributed system, such as accessing a file. Using the key S_G provided by the Kerberos server, the user U request a ticket to access file F from the ticket-granting server.

As shown in Figure 6.7 after the ticket granting server verifies U's access permission, it returns a ticket and a session key. The ticket contains U's authenticated identity (in the ticket U obtained from the kerberos server), an identification of F (the file to be accessed), the access rights (for example, to read), a session key S, for the file server to use while communicating this file to U, and an expiration date for ticket. The ticket is encrypted under a key shared exclusively between the ticket-granting server and the file server. This ticket cannot be read, modified, or forged by the user U (or anyone else). The ticket-granting server must, therefore, also provide U with a copy of S_F, the session key for the file server. Requests for access to other services and servers are handled similarly. (In Kerberos version 5, only S_G is encrypted: in Kerberos version 4, both the session key and the ticket were encrypted when returned to the user.)

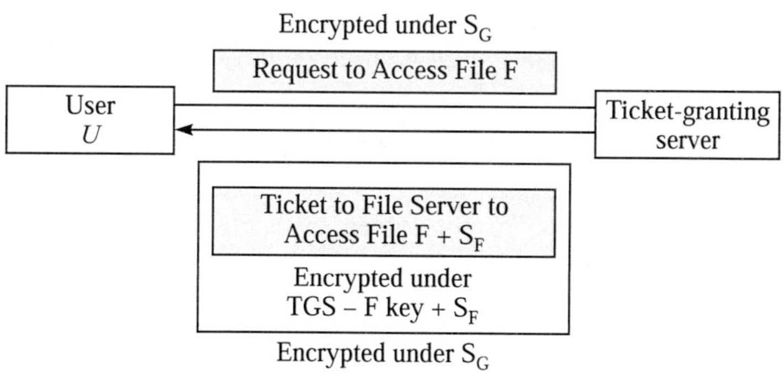

Figure 6.7 Obtaining a ticket to access a file.

Kerberos was carefully designed to withstand attacks in distributed environment.

- *No passwords communicated on network.* As already described, a user's password is stored only at the Kerberos server. The user's password is not sent from the user's workstation when the user initiates a session. (Obviously, a user's initial password must be sent outside the network, such as in a letter).

- *Cryptographic protection against spoofing.* Each access request is mediated by the ticket-granting server, which knows the identity of the requester, based on the authentication performed initially by the Kerbero's server and on the fact that the user was able to present a request encrypted under a key that had been encrypted under the user's password.
- *Limited period of validity.* Each ticket is issued for a limited time period; the ticket contains a time stamp with which a receiving server will determine the tickets validity. In this way, certain long-term attacks, such as brute force cryptanalysis, will usually be neutralized because the attacker will not have time to complete the attack.
- *Time stamps to prevent replay attacks.* Kerberos requires reliable access to a universal clock. Each user's request to a server is stamped with the time of the request. A server receiving a request will compare this time to the current time and fulfil the request only if the time is reasonably close to the current time. This time-checking prevents most replay attacks, since the attacker's presentation of the ticket will be delayed too long.
- *Mutual authentication.* The user of the service can be assured of any server's authenticity by requesting an authenticating response from the server. The user sends a ticket to a server and then sends the server a request encrypted under the session key for the server's service; the ticket and the session key were provided by the ticket-granting server. The server can decrypt the ticket only if it has the unique key it shares with the ticket-granting server. Inside the ticket is the session key, which is the only means the server has of decrypting the user's request. If the server can return to the user a message encrypted under this same session key but containing 1+ the user's timestamp, the server must be authentic. Because of the mutual authentication, a server can provide a unique channel to a user and the user may not need to encrypt communications on that channel to ensure continuous authenticity. Avoiding encryption saves time in the communication.

Kerberos imposes five assumptions on the environment in which it can properly function. These include the following:

(i) A Denial of Service (DoS) attack is not solved with Kerberos.
(ii) Principle must keep these secret keys secret.
(iii) Password guessing attacks are not solved by Kerberos.
(iv) Each host on the network must have a clock that is 'loosely synchronized' to the time of the other hosts.
(v) Principle identifies are not recycled on a short-term basis.

6.7 PUBLIC KEY INFRASTRUCTURE (PKI)

Many security protocols rely on public-key cryptography to provide service such as confidentiality, data integrity, data origin authentication, and no repudiation. The public-key infrastructure (PKI) can provide a structure for verifying and authenticating the parties involved in transactions on the Internet, Intranets, or Extranents.

The purpose of a PKI is to provide a secure infrastructure for managing public keys that allows any one to exchange private documents with anyone else without knowing these people in advance. A PKI is defined by the Internet X.509 Public Key Infrastructure PXIX Roadmap as the set of hardware, software, people, policies, and procedures needed to create, manage, stose, distribute, and revoke certificates based on public key cryptography. The reason for developing a PKI is essentially to build an infrastructure of trust. If a user wants to send a private message to someone, he can obtain the recipient's public key, encrypt the message, and send it. The recipient can then decrypt the message with their private key.

A PKI consists of five types of components. A brief description of each component and its function follows:

(i) *Certificate authorities (CA):* issue and revoke certificates.

(ii) *Certificate holders:* are issued certificates and can sign digital documents.

(iii) *Clients:* Validate digital signatures and their certification paths from a known public key of a trusted certificate authority.

(iv) *Repositories:* store and make available certificates and certificate revocation lists.

(v) *Organizational registration authorities:* vouch for the binding between public keys, certificate holders identities, and other attributes.

Note that X.509 is an International Telecommunication Union Telecommunication Sector (ITU-T) standard. Also, the National Institute of Standards and Technology (NIST) is working on Certificate authorities and digital certificate based on X.509 standards. The X.509 standard constitutes widely accepted basis for a PKI infrastructure, defining data formats and procedures related to the distribution of public keys using certificates digitally signed by certificate authorities.

X.509 defines authentication protocols based on the use of public key certificates. X.509 is an important standard because the certificate structure and authentication protocols defined in X.509 certificate format is used in S/MIME, IP security and SSL/TLS and SET. X.509 is based on the use of public key cryptography and digital signatures. The standard does not dictate the use of a specific algorithm but recommends RSA. The digital signature scheme is assumed to require the use of a hash function. Again, the standard does not dictate a specific hash algorithm. The 1988 recommendation included the description of a recommended hash algorithm; this algorithm has since been shown to be insecure and was dropped from the 1993 recommendation.

6.8 PRETTY GOOD PRIVACY (PGP)

PGP provides a confidentiality and authentication service that can be used for electronic mail and file storage applications. It was invented by Phil Zimmerman in 1991. Originally a free package, it become a commercial product after being bought by Network Associates in 1996.

A freeware versions is still available. PGP is widely available, both in commercial versions and freeware, and it is heavily used by individuals exchanging private e-mail.

PGP addresses the key distribution problem with what is called a "ring of trust" or a user's "keyring". One user directly gives a public key to another, or the second user fetches the first's public key from a server. Some people include this PGP public keys at the bottom of e-mail messages. And one person can give a second person's key to a third (and a fourth, and so on). Thus, the key association problem becomes one of cavent emptor: "let the buyer beware". If I am reasonably confident that an e-mail message really comes from you and has not been tampered with, I will use your attached public key. If I trust you, I may also trust the keys you give me for other people. The model breaks down intellectually when you give me all the keys you received from people, who in turn gave you all the keys that got from still other people, who gave them all their keys and so faith.

You sign each key you give me. The keys you give me may also have been signed by other people. I decide to trust the veracity of a key-and-identity combination, based on who signed the key.

PGP does not mandate a policy for establishing trust. Rather each user is free to decide how much to trust each key received. The PGP processing performs some or all the following actions, depending on whether confidentiality, integrity, authenticity or some combination of these is selected.

- Create a random session key for a symmetric algorithm.
- Encrypt the message, using the session key (for message confidentiality).
- Encrypt the session key under the recipient's public key.
- Generate a message digest or hash of the message: sign the hash by encrypting it with the sender's private key (for message integrity and authenticity).
- Attach the encrypted session key to the encrypted message and digest.
- Transmit the message to the recipient.

The recipient reverses these steps to retrieve and validate the message content.

PGP has grown explosively and is now widely used. A number of reasons can be cited for this growth.

(i) It is available free worldwide inversions that run on a variety of platforms, including windows, UNIX and many more.

(ii) It is based on algorithms that survived extensive public review and are considered extremely secure. Specifically, the package includes RSA, DSS and Diffie-Hellman for public key encryption.

(iii) It has a wide range of applicability, from corporations that wish to select and enforce a standardize scheme for encrypting files and messages to individuals who wish to communicate securely with others worldwide over the Internet and other networks

(iv) It was not developed by, nor it is controlled by, any governmental or standard organization.

The services of PGP have been summarized in Table 6.1

Table 6.1 Summary of PGP services

Function	*Algorithms used & Description*
Digital signature	*Algorithm:* DSS/SHA or RSA/SHA *Description:* A hash code of a message is created using SHA-1. This message digest is encrypted using DSS or RSA with the sender's private key, and included with the message.
Message encryption	*Algorithm:* IDEA or three-key Triple DES with Diffie-Hellman or RSA *Description:* A message is encrypted using IDEA or 3 DES with a one-time session key generated by the sender. The session key is encrypted using Diffie-Hellman or RSA with the recipient's public key, and included with the message.
Compression	*Algorithm:* ZIP *Description:* A message may be compressed, for storage or transmission, using ZIP.
E-mail compatibility	*Algorithm:* Radix 64 conversion *Description:* To provide transparency for e-mail applications, an encrypted message may be converted to an ASCII starting using radix 64 conversion.
Segmentation	*Algorithm:* — *Description:* To accommodate maximum message size limitations, PGP performs segmentation and reassembly.

6.9 SECURITY PROTOCOLS

Security is becoming more and more crucial as the volume of data being exchanged on the Internet increases. Various protocols have been developed to measure security, which can be applied to the application layer, transport layer, and IP layer.

6.9.1 Secure Socket Layer

Secure Sockets Layer (SSL) is the Internet security protocol for point-to-point connections. With the growth of the Internet, many applications need to securely transmit data to remote applications and computers. SSL was designed to solve this problem. Many popular web browsers like Netscape Communication and Internet Explorer use SSL to protect again eavesdropping, tampering, and forgery. In SSL, when clients and servers make connections, they authenticate each other. Once authenticated a "secure pipe" is established and data can be securely exchanged as shown in Figure 6.8. SSL uses the strong encryption technologies from RSA Data Security.

Some practical applications of SSL are:

- **Client/Server systems:** Securing database access
- **Financial:** Remote banking programs

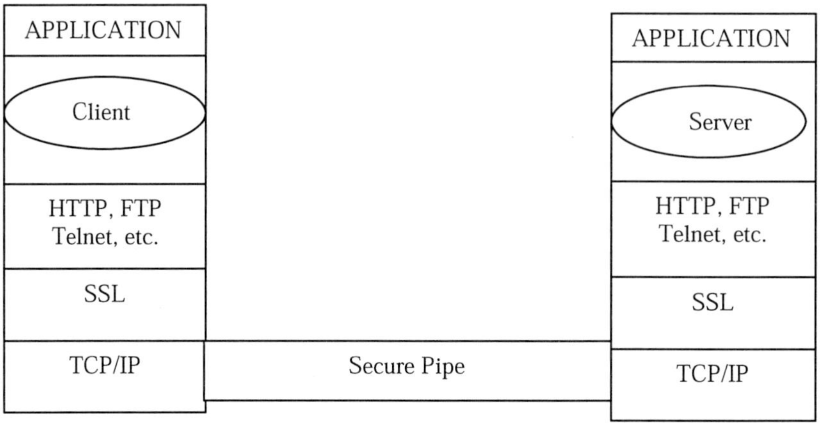

Figure 6.8 Secure socket layer.

- **Information systems:** Remote access and administration application
- **Travel industry:** Create online reservation systems and secure information transfer

6.9.2 Transport Layer Security

The IETF established the TLS working group in 1996 to develop a standard transport security protocol. The working group began with SSL version 3, as its basis and released RFC 2246, TLS protocol version 1.0 in 1999 as a proposed standard. The working group also published RFC 2712, "Addition of Kerberos Cipher Suites to Transprt Layer Security (TLS)", as a proposed standard, and two RFCs on the use of TLS with HTTP. Like its predecessor, TLS is a protocol that ensures privacy between communicating applications and their uses on Internet. When a server and client communicate, TLS ensures that no third party may eavesdrop or tamper with any message.

Transport Layer Security (TLS) is composed of two parts. The TLS Record Protocol and the TLS Handshake Protocol. The TLS Record Protocol provides connection security by using supported encryption methods, such as the Data Encryption Standard (DES). The TLS Record Protocol can also be used without encryption. The TLS Handshake Protocol allows the server and the client to authenticate each other and to negotiate a sension encryption algorithm and cryptographic keys before data is exchanged.

Though TLS is based on SSL and is sometimes referred to as SSL, they are not interoperable. However, the TLS protocol does contain a mechanism that allows a TLS implementation to back down to SSL 3.0. The difference between the two is in the way they perform key expansion and message authentication computations. TLS uses the MD5 and SHA (Secure Hash Algorithm) algorithms together to determine the session key. Though SSL also uses both hashing algorithms, SSL is considered less secure because the way it uses them forces a reliance on MD5 rather than SHA. The TLS Record Protocol is a layered protocol. At each layer, message may include fields for length, description and content. The record protocol takes messages to be transmitted, fragments the data into manageable blocks, optionally compressed the data, applied a message authentication code (MAC) to the data, encrypt it, and transmits the result. Received data is decrypted, verified, decompressed and reassembled, and then delivered to higher level clients. The TLS Handshake Protocol involves the following steps, which are summarized in Figure 6.9.

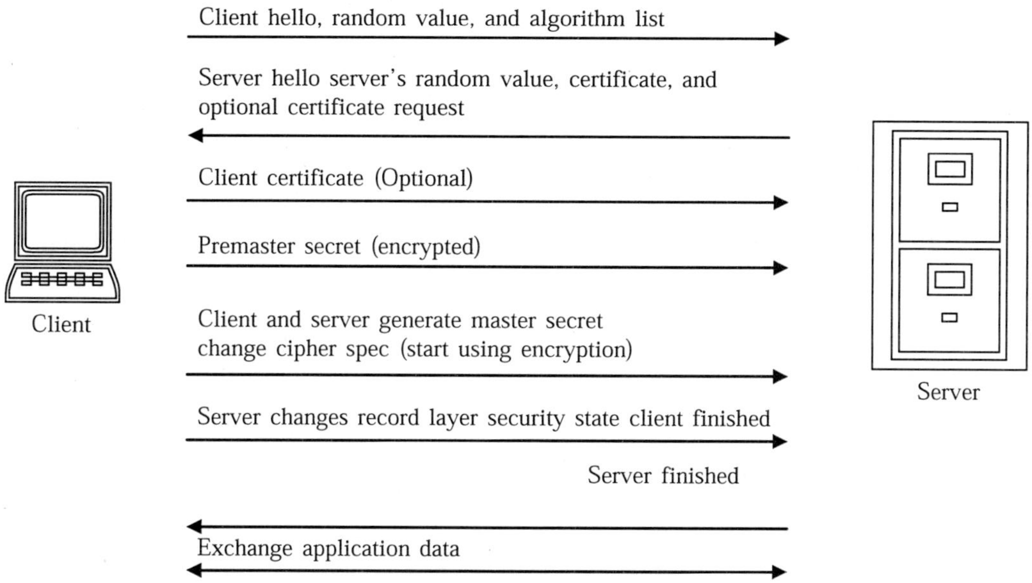

Figure 6.9 TLS handshake protocol.

Step 1: Exchange hello messages to agree on algorithms, exchange random values, and check for session resumption.

Step 2: Exchange the necessary cryptographic parameters to allow the client and server to agree on a pre-master secret.

Step 3: Exchange certificates and cryptographic information to allow the client and server to authenticate themselves.

Step 4: Generate a master secret from the premaster secret and exchanged random values.

Step 5: Provide security parameters to the record layer.

Step 6: Allow the client and server to verify that their peer has calculated the same security parameters and that the handshake occurred without tempering by an attacker.

Though it has been designed to minimize this risk, TLS still has potential vulnerabilities to a man in the middle attack. A highly-spilled and well-placed attacker can force TLS to operate at lower security levels. Regardless, through the use of validated and rusted certificates, a secure cipher suit can be selected for the exchange of data. Once established, a TLS session remains active as long as data is being exchanged. If sufficient inactive time has elapsed for the secure connection to time out, it can be reinitiated.

6.9.3 IPSec

Internet Protocol Security (IPSec), a set of protocols developed by the Internet Engineering Task Force (IETF) for encryption and authentication of TCP/IP traffic, is the leading standard for cryptographically-based authentication, integrity and privacy services.

At the IP layer, computers on a network communicate by routing datagram packets that contain data, destination addresses, source addresses, and other information. In a corporate LAN or the Internet, where packet datagram's are transmitted "as is", unencrypted a malicious attacker could hijack, forge, or modify them. IPSec secures the network packets to create a secure network of computers over insecure channels. It enables users to communicate securely with a remote host over the Internet via VPNs. Where SSL authentication and encrypts communication between clients and servers at the application layers, IPSec secures the underlying network layers. IPSec provides the capability to secure communication across a LAN, across private and public WAN's and across the Internet. Some practical applications of IPSec are:

- A company can build a secure virtual private network over the Internet or over a public WAN. This enables a business to rely heavily on the Internet and reduce its need for private networks, saving costs and network management overhead.
- An end user whose system is equipped with IP security protocols can make a local call to an Internet Service Provider (ISP) and gain secure access to a company network. This reduces the cost of toll charges for traveling employees and telecomputers.
- IPSec can be used to secure communication with other organizations, ensuring authentication and confidentiality and providing a key exchange mechanism.

The principle feature of IPSec that enables it to support these varied applications is that I can encrypt and/or authenticate all traffic at the IP level. Thus all distributed applications, including remote login, client/server, email, file transfer, web access, and so on, can be secured.

List the following benefits of IPSec:

(i) When IPSec is implemented in a firewall or router, it provides strong security that can be applied to all traffic crossing the perimeter. Traffic within a company or workgroup does not incur the overhead of security-related processing

(ii) IPSec in a firewall is a resistant to bypass if all traffic from the outside must use IP, and the firewall is the only means of entrance from the Internet into the organization.

(iii) IPSec is below the transport layer (TCP, UDP) and so is transparent to applications. There is no need to change software on a user or server system when IPSec is implemented in the firewall or router. Even if IPSec is implemented in end systems, upper-layer software, including applications, is not affected.

(iv) IPSec can be transparent to the end users. There is no need to train users on security mechanisms issue keying material on a peruser basis, or revoke keying material when users leave the organization.

(v) IPSec can provide security for individual users if needed. This is useful for offsite workers and for setting up a secure virtual subnetwork within an organization for sensitive applications.

IPSec provides security services at the IP layer by enabling a system to select required security protocols, determine the algorithm(s) to use for the service(s) and put in place any cryptographic keys required to provide the requested services. Two protocols are used to provide security: an authentication protocol designed by the header of the protocol, Authentication Header (AH); and a combined encryption/authentication protocol designated by the format of the packet for that protocol, Encapsulating Security Payload (ESP). The services are provided by the AH and ESP protocols which are shown in Table 6.2.

Table 6.2 IPSec services

Services	*AH*	*ESP (Encryption Only)*	*ESP (Encryption plus Authentication*
Access control	√	√	√
Connectionless integrity	√		√
Data origin authentication	√		√
Rejection of replayed packets	√	√	√
Confidentiality (encryption)		√	√
Limited traffic flow confidentiality		√	√

A key concept that appears in both the authentication and confidentiality mechanisms for IP is the security association (SA). In any IP packet, the security association is uniquely identified by the destination address in the IPv4/IPv6 header.

Authentication Header (AH): The Authentication Header provides connectionless integrity and data origin authentication for IP datagrams. It also optionally provides protection against replays. The AH header is shown in Figure 6.10. It is either follows the IPv4/IPv6 header or is an IPv6 extension header, depending on which version of IP it is used with.

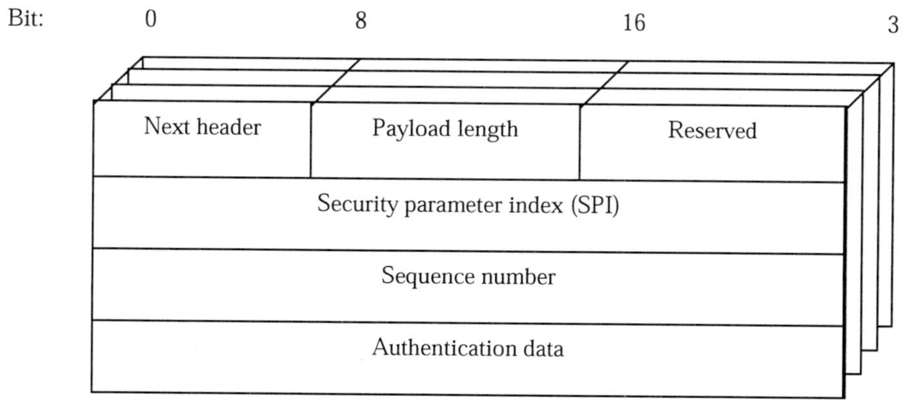

Figure 6.10 IPSec authentication header.

The next header field identifies the type of the next payload after the Authentication Header. The payload length field specifies the length of the AH in 32-bit words (4-byte units), minus 2. The reserved field is reserved for future use; it is set to zero for now. The security parameter index (SPI) field is an arbitrary 32-bit value that, in combination with the destination IP address, uniquely identifies the security association for this datagram.

The sequence number field contains a monotonically increasing counter or sequence number. This field is used to protect against replay, but it is present even if the receiver does not elect to enable the antireplay service for a specific SA (Security Association). The sender counter and the receiver's counter are initialized to 0 when an SA is established. If antireplay is enabled, which is the default, the transmitted sequence number must never be allowed to cycle. Thus the sender's counter and the receiver's counter must be reset by establishing a new SA—and thus a new key prior to transmitting the 2^{32nd} packet on an SA.

Finally, Authentication Data is a variable length field that contains the message integrity code for this packet. The field must be an integral multiple of 32 bits in length. All does not prescribe a specific message digest algorithm. DES and MD5, among others can be used.

Encapsulating Security Payload (ESP): The Encapsulating Security Payload provides confidentiality services, including confidentiality of message contents and limited traffic flow confidentially. As an optional feature, ESP can also provide the same authentication services as AH.

ESP header is designed to provide a mix of security services in IPv4 and IPv6. ESP may be applied alone, or in combination with AH. The ESP header is inserted after the IP header and before the upper-layer protocol header (when used between a pairs of hosts), or before an encapsulated IP header when used to tunnel between a pair of security gateways.

Like AH, the ESP header either follows the IPv4/header or is an IPv6/extension header. Its format is shown in Figure 6.11. The Security Parameter Index (SPI) field has the same function as in the AH. It helps the receiving host identify the security association to which the packet belongs.

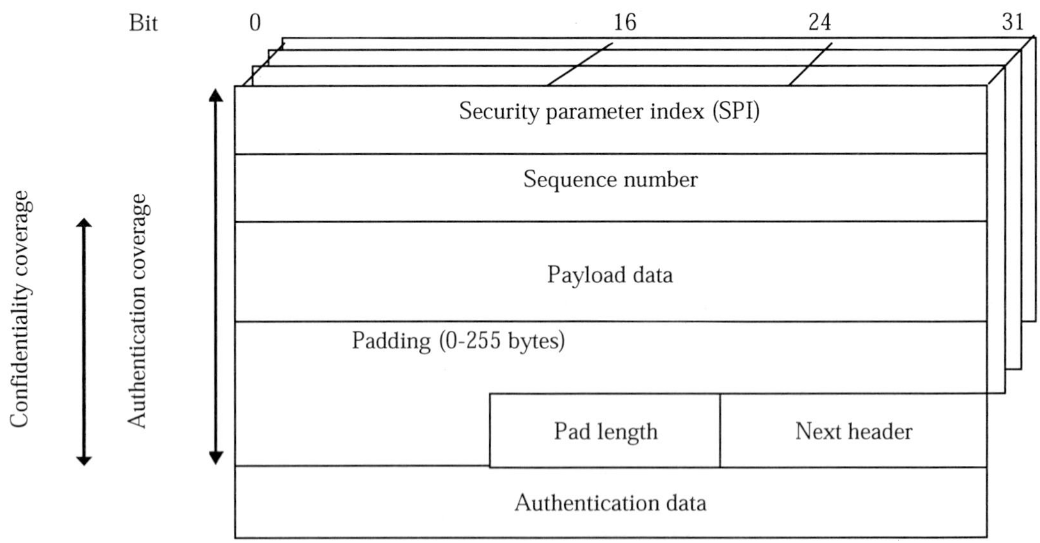

Figure 6.11 IPSec ESP header.

Similarly, the sequence number field protects against replay attacks. The packets Payload Data contains the data described by the next header field. If confidentiality is selected, then the data is encrypted by whatever encryption algorithm was associated with the Security Association. Padding is sometimes necessary, for example, because the encryption algorithm requires the plaintext to be a multiple of some number of bytes, or to ensure that the resulting ciphertext terminates on a 4-bytes boundary. The pad length field records how much padding was added to the data. Finally, the Authentication Data Carrier Variable Field (must be an integral number of 32-bit words) that contains the integrity check value computed over the ESP packet minus the Authentication Data Field.

One of the most popular ways to use the ESP is to build an "IPSec tunnel" between two routers. For example, a corporation wanting to link two sites using the Internet could configure a tunnel from a router at one site to a router at the other site. This tunnel may also be configured to use the ESP with confidentiality and authentication, thus preventing unauthorized access to the data that traverses this virtual link and ensuring that no spurious data is received at the far end of the tunnel.

6.9.4 S/MIME (Secure/Multipurpose Internet Mail Extension)

S/MIME is the electronic standard that protects, messages from unauthorized interception and forgery. S/MIME user public–key encryption technology to secure transmission, storage, authentication and forwarding of secret data, where SSL secures a connection between a client and a server over an insecure network, S/MIME is used to secure users, applications and computers.

S/MIME is a security enhancement to the MIME (Multipurpose Internet Mail Extension) Internet e-mail format standard based on technology from RSA Data Security. To understand MIME, we need first to have a general understanding of the underlying e-mail format that it uses, namely MIME.

MIME is an extension to the RFC 822 framework that is intended to address some of the problems and limitations of the use of SMTP (Simple Mail Transfer Protocol).

- SMTP cannot transmit executable file or other binary objects. A number of schemes are in use for converting binary files into a text form that can be used by SMTP mail systems.
- SMTP cannot transmit text data that includes national language characters because these are represented by 8-bit codes with values of 128 decimal or higher, and SMTP is limited to 7-bit ASCII.
- SMTP servers may reject message over a certain size.
- SMTP gateway that translate between ASCII and the character code EBCDIC do not use a consistent set of mappings, resulting in translation problem.

MIME is intended to resolve these problems in a manner that is compatible with existing RFC822 implementations. The MIME specification includes the following elements:

1. Five new message header fields are defined, which may be included in an RFC 822 header. These fields provide information about the body of the message.

2. A number of content formats are defined, thus standardizing representations that support multimedia electronic mail.
3. Transfer encodings are defined that enable the conversion of any content format into a form that is protected from alternation by the mail system.

In terms of general functionality, S/MIME is very similar to PGP. Both offer the ability to sign and/or encrypt messages. S/MIME provide the following functions:

Enveloped data: This consists of encrypted content of any type and encrypted content encryption keys for one or more recipients.

Signed data: A digital signature is formed by taking the message digest of the content to be signed and then encrypting that with the private key of the signer. The content plus signature are then encoded using base 64 encoding. A signed data message can only be viewed by a recipient with S/MIME capability.

Clear-signed data: As with signed data, a digital signature of the content is formed. However, in this case, only the digital signature is encoded using base 64. As a result, recipients without S/MIME capability can view the message content, although they cannot verify the signature.

Signed and enveloped data: Signed-only and encrypted-only entities may be nested, so that encrypted data may be signed and signed data or clear-signed data may be encrypted.

Some practical applications of S/MIME are:

- Electronic data exchange: Digital signatures on contracts
- Financial messaging: Store and transfer bank statements
- Content delivery: Electronic bill payment
- Health care: Secure patient records and health claims

Like SSL, IPSec and S/MIME is based on RSA algorithm for digital signature and digital envelopes as shown in Table 6.3.

Table 6.3 Security protocols overview

Protocol	*Summary*
SSL(Secure Socket Layer)	Allows a "Secure Pipe" between any two application for transfer of data and mutual authentication
IPSec(IP Security Protocol)	Standard for Cryptographically-based authentication, integrity and confidentiality services at the IP datagram layer
S/MIME(Secure MIME)	Guarantees the secure communication, storage, authentication and forwarding of secret data at the application level

In virtually all distributed environments, electronic mail is the most heavily used network-based application. It is also the only distributed application that is widely used across all architectures and vendor platforms. Users expect to be able to, and do, send mail to others who are connected directly or indirectly to the Internet, regardless of host operating system or communications suite.

With the explosively growing reliance or electronic mail for every conceivable purpose, there grows a demand for authentication and confidentiality services. Two schemes standout as approaches that are likely to enjoy widespread use in the next few years: Pretty God Privacy (PGP) and S/MIME.

6.10 SOFTWARE SECURITY

Software is everywhere. It controls your cell phone. It is how you access your bank's financial services; how you receive electricity, water and natural gas; how you fly from coast to coast. Whether we recognize it or not, we all rely on complex, interconnected, software-intensive information systems that use the Internet as their means for communicating and transporting information.

The security of computer systems and networks has become increasingly limited by the quality and security of their software. Security defects and vulnerabilities in software are commonplace and can pose serious risks when exploited by malicious attacks. Over the past ten years, this problem has grown significantly.

Core security properties of secure software are shown in Figure 6.12 and are described below.

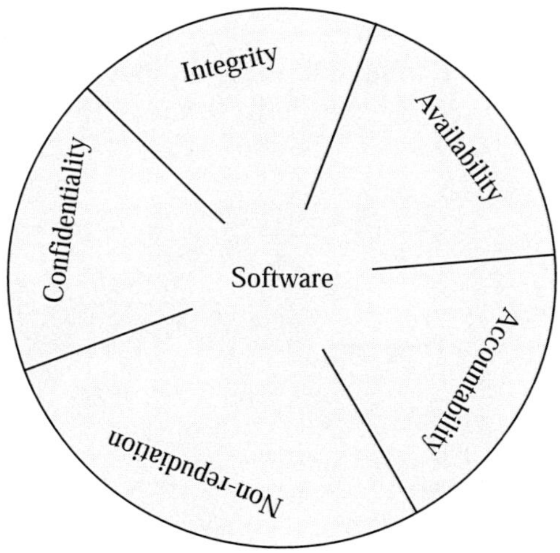

Figure 6.12 Core security properties of secure software.

Confidentiality: The software must ensure that any of its characteristics (including its relationships with its execution environment and its users), its managed assets, and/or its content are obscured or hidden from unauthorized entities. This remains appropriate for cases such as open-source software; its characteristics and content are available to the public (authorized entities in this case), yet it still must maintain confidentiality of its managed assets.

Integrity: The software and its managed assets must be resistant and resilient to subversion. Subversion is achieved through unauthorized modifications to the software code, managed assets, configuration, or behaviour by authorized entities, or any modifications by unauthorized entities. Such modifications may include over-writing, corruption, tempering, destruction, insertion of unintended (including malicious) logic, or deletion. Integrity must be preserved both during the software's development and during its execution.

Availability: The software must be operational and accessible to its intended, authorized users (humans and processes) whenever it is needed. At the same time, its functionality and privileges must be inaccessible to unauthorized users (humans and processes) at all times.

Two additional properties commonly associated with human users are required in software entities that act as users (e.g. proxy agents, web services, peer processes)

Accountability: All security-relevent actions of the software-as-user must be recorded and tracked, with attribution of responsibility. This tracking must be possible both while and after the recorded actions occur. The audit-related language in the security polity for the software system should indicate which actions are considered 'security relevent'!

Non-repudiation: This property pertains to the ability to prevent the software-as-user from disproving or denying responsibility for actions it has performed. It ensures that the accountability property cannot be subverted or circumvented.

These core properties are most typically used to describe network security. However, their definitions have been modified here slightly to map these still valid concepts to the software security domain. The effects of a security breach in software can, therefore, be described in terms of the effects on these core properties.

Some properties of software, although they do not directly make software secure, nevertheless make it possible to characterize how secure software is (shown in Figure 6.13).

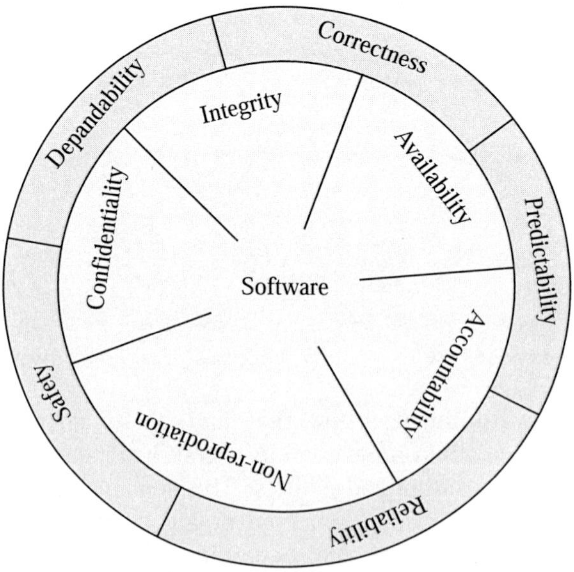

Figure 6.13 Influential properties of secure software.

- Dependability
- Correctness
- Predictability
- Reliability
- Safety

These influential properties are further influenced by the size, complexity, and traceability of the software.

6.10.1 Reliability, Safety, and Security

The focus of reliability for software is on preserving predictable, correct execution despite the presence of unintentional defects and other weaknesses and unpredictable environment stage changes. Software that is highly reliable is often referred to as high-confidence software (implying that a high level of assurance of that reliability exists) or fault-tolerant software (implying that fault tolerance techniques were used to achieve the high-level of reliability).

Software safety depends on reliability and typically has very real and significant implications if the property is not met. These consequences, if reliability is not preserved in a safety critical system, can be catastrophic such as human life may be lost, or the sustainability of the environment may be compromised.

Software security extends the requirements of reliability and safety to the need to preserve predictable, correct execution even in the face of malicious attack on defects or weaknesses and environmental state changes. It is this maliciousness that makes the requirements of software security somewhat different from the requirements of safety and reliability. Failures in a reliability or safety context are expected to be random and unpredictable. Failures in a security context, by contrast, result from human efforts (direct through malicious code). Attackers tend to be persistent, and once they successfully exploit a vulnerability, they tend to continue exploiting that vulnerability on other systems as long as the vulnerability is present and the outcome of the attack remains satisfactory.

Until recently, many software reliability and safety practitioners have not concerned themselves with software security issues. Indeed, the two domains have traditionally been viewed as separate and distinct. The truth is that safety, as a property of software, is directly dependent on security properties such as dependability. A failure in the security of software, especially one that is intentional and malicious, can directly change the operational and environmental presumptions on which safety is based, thereby compromising and possible assurance in its safety properties. Any work toward assuring the safety of software that does not take security properties into consideration is incomplete and unreliable.

Without security architecture and features, adequate levels of confidentiality, integrity, accountability, and non-repudiation may be unattainable. However, fully addressing these properties (as well as availability) requires the development team not only to provide functionality to manage the security behaviour of the software, but also to ensure that the functionality and architecture of the software do not contains weaknesses that could render the software vulnerable to attack in potentially unexpected ways. Many activities and practices are available across the life cycle of software systems that can help reduce and mitigate weakness present in the software. While application defense takes a somewhat after-the-fact approach, practice associated with 'software security' and its role in secure software engineering processes focus on preventing weaknesses from entering the software in the first place or, if that is unavoidable, at least removing them as early in the life cycle as possible and before the software is deployed as shown in Figure 6.14.

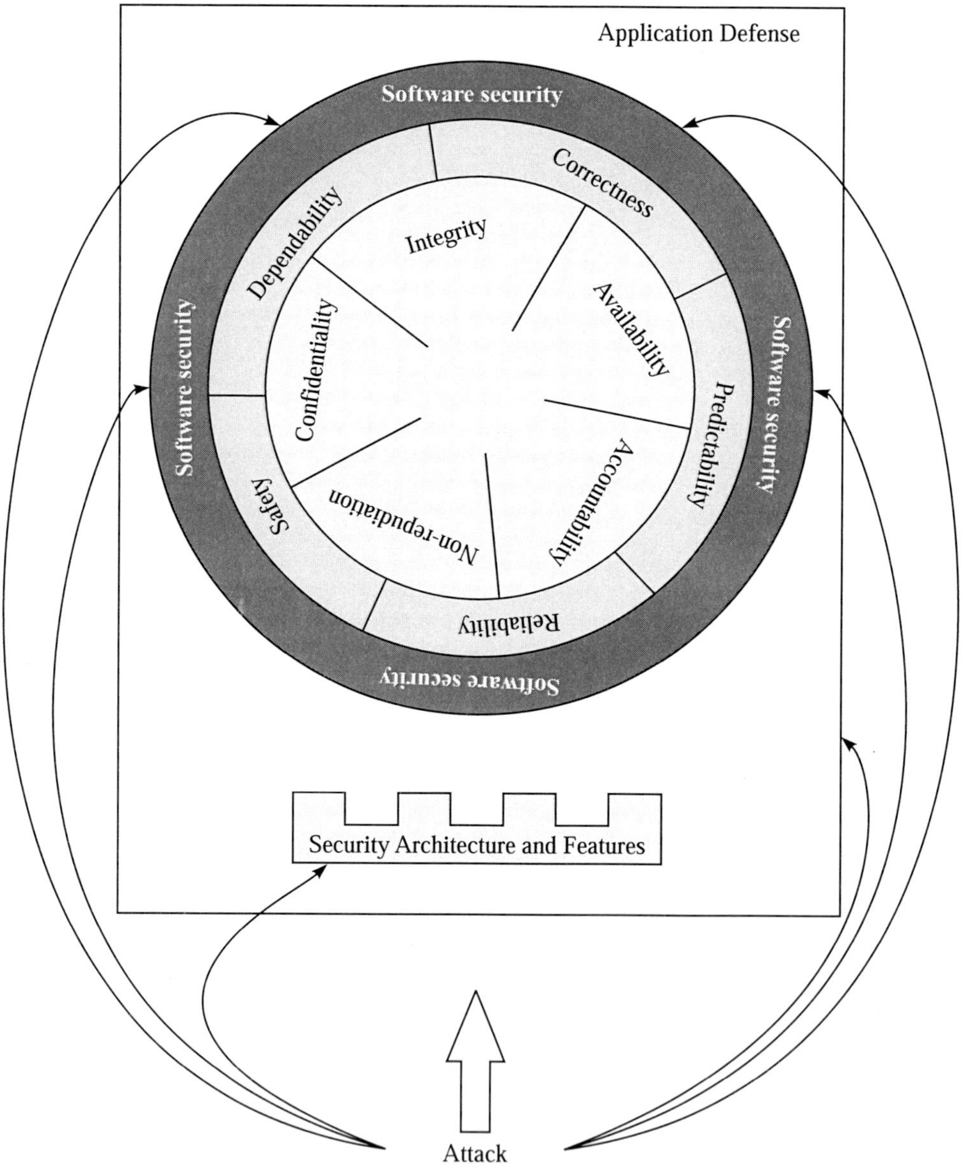

Figure 6.14 Addressing the unexpected through software security.

These weaknesses, whether unintentional or maliciously inserted, can enter the software at any point in the development process through inadequate or incorrect requirements; ambiguous, incomplete, unstable, or improper architecture and design; implementation errors; incomplete or inappropriate testing; or insecure configuration and deployment decisions.

Contrary to a common misconception, software security cannot be the sole responsibility of the developers who are writing code, but rather requires the involvement of the entire development team and the organization supporting it. Luckily, a wide variety of security—focused practices are available to software project managers and their development teams that can be seamlessly integrated throughout any typical software engineering SDLC (Software Development Life Cycle). Among other things, these practices include security requirements engineering with misuse/abuse cases, architectural risk analysis, secure code review, risk-based security testing, and software penetration testing. Software security practices and knowledge associated with various phases of the SDLC that are of value to development teams looking to minimize weakness and thereby build more secure software that is resistant, tolerant, and resilient to attack.

Attack resistance is the ability of the software to prevent the capability of an attacker to execute an attack against it. Attack tolerance is the ability of the software to 'tolerate' the errors and failures that result from successful attacks and in effect, to continue to operate as if the attacks had not occurred. Attack resilience is the ability of the software to isolate, contain, and limit the damage resulting from any failures caused by attack-triggered faults that the software was unable to resist or tolerate and to recover as quickly as possible from these failures.

REVIEW QUESTIONS

6.1 Explain hardware security. Give an example of common hardware problem.

6.2 Explain the objective of technical security methods.

6.3 Explain the requirements for secure system.

6.4 What are the safeguards for hardware security? Explain how security breach can occur in hardware.

6.5 What is the relation between hardware and software security?

6.6 What is the difference between perimeter security and interior security?

6.7 How smart card helps to security? How company uses smart cards?

6.8 How biometrics can be used to control access to computer networks?

6.9 What are biometric identification methods?

6.10 What is the difference between fingerprints and palmprints?

6.11 What is the difference between hand geometry and hand veins?

6.12 Explain handwriting acoustic emissions.

6.13 Explain iris map.

6.14 What is the difference between facial thermographs and facial identification?

6.15 Explain virtual private network and its importance. What are the VPN protocols.

6.16 What is difference between point-to-point tunneling protocol and layer 2 tunneling protocol.

6.17 What is difference between point-to-point tunneling protocol and layer 2 forwarding protocol.

6.18 What is KERBEROS. How KERBEROS supports authentication in distribution system.

6.19 Explain Public-Key Infrastructure (PKI) and describe the various components of PKI.

6.20 What is the difference between site VPNs and user VPNs?

6.21 Describe trusted operated system and write the key features of a trusted operating system.

6.22 What are the services provided by trusted operating system?

6.23 Explain pretty good privacy and write the summary of PGP.

6.24 What is the importance of secure socket layer?

6.25 Explain transport layer security and write the importance of TLS record protocol and TLS handshake protocol.

6.26 Explain internet protocol security and list the benefits of IP Sec.

6.27 Explain encapsulating security payload.

6.28 What is the importance of Secure/Multipurpose Internet Mail Extension?

6.29 Explain core secure properties of secure software and influential properties of secure softwares.

6.30 Discuss reliability, safety and security of software.

CHAPTER 7

Database Security

Chapter Outline

Database and database systems have become an essential components of everyday life in modern society. In the course of the day, most of us encounter several activities that involve some interaction with a database. For example, if we go to the bank to deposit or withdraw funds, if we make a hotel or airline reservation, if we access a computerized library catalog or search for a bibliographic item, or if we buy some item—such as a book, toy, or computer—from an Internet vendor through its web page, chances are that our activities will involve someone or some compute program accessing a database. Even purchasing items from a supermarket nowadays in many cases involve an automatic update of the database that keeps the inventory of supermarket items.

Protecting data is at the heart of many secure systems, and many user (People, Programs, or Systems) relay on Database Management System (DBMS) to manage protection. For this reason, we devote this chapter to the security of database management systems, as an example of how application security can be designed and implemented for a specific task. Databases are essential to many business and government organizations, holding data that reflect the organization's core competencies.

7.1 INTRODUCTION TO DATABASES

A database is a collection of related data. By data, we mean known facts that can be recorded and that have implicit meaning. For example, consider the names, telephone numbers and addresses of the people you know. You may have recorded this data in an index address book, or you may have stored it on a hard drive, using a personal computer and software such as Microsoft Access or Excel. This is collection of related data with an implicit meaning and hence is a database.

The preceding definition of database is quite general, for example we may consider the collection of worlds that make up the page of text to the related data and hence to constitute a database. However, the common use of the term database is usually more restricted. A database has the following implicit properties:

(i) A database represents some aspect of the real world, sometimes called the miniworld or the universe of discourse (UoD), changes to the miniworld are reflected in the database.

(ii) A database is a logically-coherent collection of data with some inherent meaning. A random assortment of data cannot correctly be referred to as a database.

(iii) A database is designed, built and populated with date for a specific purpose. It has an intended group of users and some preconceived applications in which these users are interested.

In other words, a database has some source from which data is derived some degree of interaction with events in the real world, and an audience that is actively interested in the contents of the database. A database may be generated and maintained manually or it may be computerized. For example, a library card catalog is a database that may be created and maintained manually either by a group of application programs written specifically for that task or by a database management system.

A database is a collection of data and a set of rules that organize the data by specifying certain relationship among the data. Through these rules, the user describes a logical format for the data. The data items are stored in a file, but the precise physical format of the file is of no concern to the user.

A *database administrator* is a person who defines the rules that organize the data and also controls who should have access to what parts of the data. The user interacts with the database through a program called a *database manager* or a database management system (DBMS).

The DBMS is a general purpose software system that facilitates the processes of defining, constructing, manipulating and sharing databases among various users and applications.

Other important functions provided by the DBMS include protecting the database and maintaining it over a long period of time. Protection includes both system protection against hardware and software malfunctions (or crashes) and security protection against unauthorized or malicious access. A typical large database may have a life cycle of many years, so the DBMS must be able to maintain the database system by allowing the system to evolve as requirements change over time.

7.2 CHARACTERISTICS OF DATABASE APPROACH

The number of characteristics distinguished the database approach from the traditional approach of programming with files. In traditional file processing, each user defines and implements the files needed for specific software application as a part of programming the application. For example, one user, the grade reporting office, may keep a file on students and their grades. Programs to print a students transcript and to enter new grades into the file are implemented as part of the application. A second user, the accounting office, may keep track of students fees and their payments. Although both users are interested in data about students, each user maintains separate files and program to manipulate these files, because each requires some data not available from the other user's files. This redundancy is defining and storing data results in wasted storage space and in redundant efforts to maintain common data up to date.

In the database approach, a single repository of data is maintained that is defined once and then is accessed by various users. The main characteristics of the database approach verses the file-processing approach are the following:

- Self-describing nature of a database system
- Insulation between programs and data, and data abstraction
- Support of multiple views of the data
- Sharing of data and multiuser transaction processing.

A fundamental characteristic of the database approach is that the database system contains not only the database itself but also a complete definition or description of the database structure and constraints. This definition is stored in the DBMS catalogue, which contains information such as the structure of each file, the type and storage format of each data item, and various constraints of the data. The information stored in the catalogue is called metadata and it describes the structure of primary database as shown in Figure 7.1.

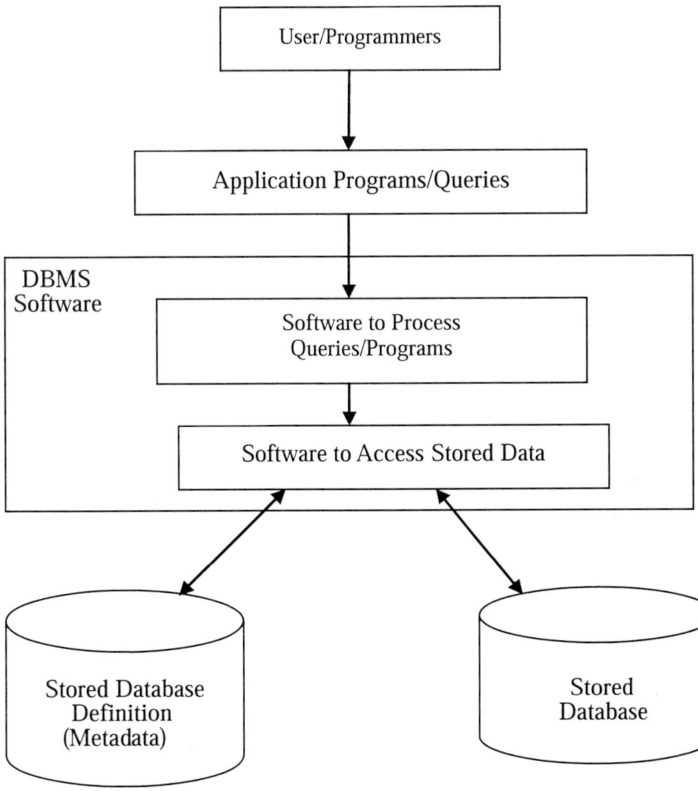

Figure 7.1 Database system.

To compare our initial definitions, we will call the database and DBMS software together as a database system.

The catalogue is used by the DBMS software and also by the database users who need information about the database structure. A general purpose DBMS software package is not written for a specific database application, and hence it must refer to the catalogue to know the structure of the files in a specific database, such as the type and format of the data. It will access the DBMS software must work equally well with any number of database applications, for example a university database, a banking database, or a company database—as long as the database definition is stored in the catalogue.

7.3 DATABASE SECURITY ISSUES

Database security is a very broad area that addresses many issues, including the following:

- Legal and ethical issues regarding the right to access certain information. Some information may be deemed to be private and cannot be accessed legally by unauthorized persons.
- Policy issues at the governmental, institutional, or corporate level as to what kinds of information should not be made publicly available, for example credit ratings and personal medical records.
- System-related issues such as the system levels at which various security functions should be enforced, for example whether a security function should be handled at the physical hardware level, the operating system level or the DBMS level.
- The need in some organizations to identify multiple security levels and to categorize the data and users based on these classifications, for example top secret, secret, confidential and unclassified. The security policy of the organization with respect to permitting access to various classifications of data must be enforced.
- Threats to databases result in the loss or degradation of some or all of the following security goals: integrity, availability, and confidentiality.

Loss of integrity: Database integrity refers to the requirement that information be protected from improper modification. Modification of data includes creation, insertion, modification, changing the status of data and deletion. Integrity is lost if unauthorized changes are made to the data by either internal or accidental acts. If the loss of system or data integrity is not corrected, continued use of the contaminated system or corrupted data could result in inaccuracy, fraud or erroneous decisions.

Loss of availability: Database availability refers to making objects available to a human user or a program to which they have a legitimate right.

Loss of confidentiality: Database confidentiality refers to the protection of data from unauthorized disclosure. The impact of unauthorized disclosure of confidential information can range from violation of the Data Privacy Act to the National Security Act. Unauthorized, unanticipated or unintentional disclosure could result in loss of public confidence, embarrassment, or legal action against the organization.

To protect database against these types of threats four kinds of countermeasures can be implemented:

- Access control
- Inference control
- Flow control
- Encryption.

A security problem common to all computer systems is that of preventing unauthorized persons from accessing the system itself, either to obtain information or to make malicious changes in a portion of the database. The security mechanisms of DBMS must include provisions for restricting access to the database system as a whole. This function is called *Access Control* and is handled by creating user accounts and passwords to control the login process by the DBMS.

A security problem associated with databases is that of controlling the access to a statistical database, which is used to provide statistical information or summaries of values based on various criteria. For example, a database for population statistics may provide statistics based on age groups, income levels, size of household, education levels, and other criteria. Statistical database users such as government statisticians or market research firms are allowed to access the database to retrieve statistical information about the population but not to access the detailed confidential information or specific individuals. Security for statistical databases must ensure that information on individuals cannot be accessed. It is sometimes possible to deduce or infer certain facts concerning individuals from queries that involve only summary statistics on groups. This must not be permitted either. This problem called Statistical Database Security. The corresponding counter measures are called *Inference Control Measures*.

Another security issue is that of *Flow Control*, which prevents information from flowing in such a way that it reaches unauthorized users. Channels that are pathways for information to flow implicitly in a ways that violate the security policy of an organization are called *Covert Channels*.

A final security issues is data encryption, which is used to protect sensitive data (such as credit card numbers) that is being transmitted via some type of communication network. Encryption can be used to provide additional protection for sensitive portions of a database as well. The data is encoded using some coding algorithm. An unauthorized user who accesses encoded data will have difficulty, deciphering it, but authorized users are given decoding or decrypting algorithms (or keys) to decipher data. Encrypting techniques that are very difficult to decode without a key have been developed for military applications.

In a multiuser database system, the DBMS must provide techniques to enable certain users or user groups to access selected portions of a database without gaining access to the rest of the database. This is particularly important when a large integrated database is to be used by many different users within the same organization. For example, sensitive information such as employee's salaries or performance reviews should be kept confidential from most of the database system's users. A DBMS typically includes a database security and authorization subsystem that is responsible for ensuring the security of portions of a database against unauthorized access. It is now customary to refer to two types of database security mechanisms.

- **Discretionary security mechanism:** These are used to grant privileges to users, including the capability to access specific data files, records, or fields in a specified mode (such as read, insert, delete or update).
- **Mandatory security mechanism:** These are used to enforce multilevel security by classifying the data and users into various security classes (or levels) and then implementing the appropriate security policy of the organization. For example, a typical security policy is to permit users at a certain classification level to see only the data items classified at the user's own (or lower) classification level. An extension of this is role-based security, which enforces policies and privileges based on the concept of roles.

7.3.1 Security Requirements

List of requirements for database security is given below:

(i) **Physical database integrity:** The data of a database are immune to physical problems, such as power failures and someone can reconstruct the database if it is destroyed through a catastrophe.

If a database is to serve as a central repository of data, users must be able to trust the accuracy of the data values. This condition implies that the database administrator must be assured that updates are performed only by authorized individuals. It also implies that the data must be protected from corruption, either by an outside illegal program action or by an outside force such as fire or a power failure. Two situations can affect the integrity of a database: When the whole database is damaged (as happens, for example, if its storage medium is damaged), or when individual data items are unreadable.

Integrity of the database as a whole is the responsibility of the DBMS, the operating system, and the computing system manager. From the perspective of the operating system and the computing system manager, databases and DBMS are files and programs, respectively. Therefore, one way of protecting the database as a whole into regularly back up all files on the system. These periodic backups can be adequate controls against catastrophic failure.

(ii) **Logical database integrity:** The structure of the database is preserved with logical integrity of a database, a modification to the value of one field does not affect other fields.

Sometimes it is important to be able to reconstruct the database at the point of a failure. For instance, when the power fails suddenly, a bank's clients may be in the middle of making transactions or students may be in the midst of registering online for their classes. In these cases, we want to be able to restore the system to a stable point without forcing users to redo their recent transactions. To handle those situations, the DBMS must maintain a log of transactions. For example, suppose the banking system is designed so that a message is generated in a log (electronic or paper or both) each time a transaction is processed. In the event of a system failure, the system can obtain accurate account balances by reverting to a backup copy of the database and reprocessing all later transactions from the log.

(iii) **Element integrity:** The data contained in each element are accurate.

The integrity of database elements is their correctness or accuracy. Ultimately, authorized users are responsible for entering correct data in databases. However, users and programs make mistakes collecting data, computing results, and entering values. Therefore, DBMS sometimes takes special action to help catch errors as they are made and to correct errors after they are inserted.

(iv) **Auditability:** It is possible to track who or what has accessed (or modified) the elements in the database.

For some applications it may be desirable to generate an audit record can help to maintain the database's integrity, or at least discover after the fact who had affected what values and when. A second advantage is that users can access protected data incrementally; that is, no single access reveals protected data, but a set of sequential accesses viewed together reveals the data, much like discovering the clues in a detective novel. In this case, audit trial can identify which clues a user has already been given as a guide to whether to tell the user more.

Audit events in operating systems are actions like open file or call procedure; they are seldom as specific as write record 3 or execute instruction I. To be useful for maintaining integrity, database audit trails should include accesses at the record, field, and even element levels. This detail is prohibitive for most database applications.

Furthermore, it is possible for a record to be accessed but not reported to a user, as when the user performs a selected operations. (Accessing a record or an element without transferring to the user the data received is called the pass-through problem.) Also, you can determine the values of some elements without accessing them directly. (For example, you can ask for the average salary in a group of employees when you know the number of employees in the group is only one.) Thus, a log of all records accessed directly may both overstate and understate what a user actually knows.

(v) **Access control:** A user is allowed to access only authorized data, and different users can be restricted to different modes of access (such as read or write).

Databases are often separated logically by user access privileges. For example, all users can be granted access to general data, but only the personnel department can obtain salary data and only the marketing department can obtain sales data. Databases are very useful because they centralize the storage and maintenance of data. Limited access is both a responsibility and a benefit of this centralization.

The databases administration specifies who should be allowed access to which data, at the view, relation field, record, or even element level. The DBMS must enforce this policy, granting access to all specified data or no access where prohibited. Furthermore, the number of modes of access can be many. A user or program may have the right to read, change, delete, or append to a value, add or delete entire fields or records, or organize the entire database.

Superficially, access control for a database seems like access control for operating systems or any other component of a computing system. However, the database problem is more complicated. Operating system objects such as files, are unrelated items, whereas records, fields, and elements are related. Although a user cannot determine the contents of one file by reading others, a user might be able to determine one data element just by reading others. The problem of obtaining data values from others is called *Inference*.

It is important to notice that you can access data by inference without needing direct access to the secure object itself. Restricting inference may mean prohibiting certain path to prevent possible inferences. However, restricting access to control inference also limits queries from users who do not intend unauthorized access to values. Moreover, attempts to check requested accesses for possible unacceptable inference may actually degrade the DBMS's performance.

Finally, size or granularity is different between operating system objects and database objects. An access control list of several hundred files is much easier to implement than an access control list for a database with several hundred files of perhaps a hundred fields each. Size affects the efficiency of processing.

(vi) User authentication: Every user is positively identified both for the audit trial and for permission to access certain data.

The DBMS can require rigorous user authentication. For example, a DBMS might insist that a user pass both specific password and time-of-day checks. This authentication supplements the authentication performed by the operating system. Typically, the DBMS runs as an application program on top of the operating system. This system design means that there is no trusted path from the DBMS to the operating system, so the DBMS must be suspicious of any data it receives, including user authentication. Thus, the DBMS is forced to do its own authentication.

(vii) Availability: Users can access the database in general and all the data for which they are authorized.

The three aspects of computer security—integrity, confidentiality and availability—clearly relate to database management systems. As we have described, integrity applies to the individual elements of a database as well as to the database as a whole. Thus, integrity is a major concern in the design of database management systems. Confidentiality is a key issue with database because of the inference problem, whereby a user can access sensitive data indirectly.

Availability is important because of the shared access motivation underlying database development. However, availability conflicts with confidentiality.

A DBMS has aspects of both a program and a system. It is a program that uses other hardware and software resources, yet to many users it is the only application run. Users often take the DBMS for granted, employing it as an essential tool with which to perform particular tasks. But when the system is not available—busy serving other users or down to be repaired or upgraded—the users are very aware of a DBMS's unavailability. For example, two users may request the same record, and the DBMS must arbitrate; one user is bound to be denied access for a while or the DBMS may withhold unprotected data to avoid revealing protected data, leaving the requesting user unhappy. Problems like these result in high availability requirements for a DBMS.

7.4 DATABASE SECURITY

As the use of the web grows on both Intranets and the public Internet, information security is becoming crucial to organizations. The web provides a convenient, cheap and instantaneous way of publishing data. Now, that it is extremely easy to disseminate information, it is equally important to ensure that the information is only accessible to those who have the rights to use it. With many systems implementing dynamic creation of web pages from a database, corporate information security is even more vital. Previously, strict database access or specialized client software was required to view the data. Now anyone with a web browser can view data in a database that is not properly protected. Never before has information security had so many vulnerable points. As the computing industry moves from the mainframe era to the client/server era to the Internet era, a substantially increasing number of points of penetration have opened up.

For much of Internet security, database specialists have had to rely on network administrators implementing precautions such as firewalls to protect local data. Because of the nature of Intranet/Internet information access, however, many security functions fall into a gray area of responsibility. We describe the primary areas where security fall within the domain of the DBA (Database Administrator), who must create the information solutions. For web security, you must address three primary areas.

(a) **Server security:** Ensuring security relating to the actual data or private HTML files stores on the server.

(b) **User-authentication security:** Ensuring login security that prevents unauthorized access to information.

(c) **Session security:** Ensuring the data is not intercepted as it is broadcast over the Internet or Intranet

You can view these layers as layers of protection. For each layer of security added, the system becomes more protected. Like a chain, however, the entire shield may be broken if there is a weak link.

7.4.1 Server Security

Server security involves limiting access to data stored on the server. Although this field is primarily the responsibility of the network administrator, the process of publishing data to the web often requires information systems specialists to take an active hand in installing and implementing the security policy. The two primary methods in which information from databases is published to the web are the use static web pages and active dynamic web page creation. These two methods require almost completely different security mechanisms.

Static Web Pages

Static web pages are simply HTML files stored on the server. Many database specialists consider static page creation the simplest and most flexible method of publishing data to the web. In a nutshell, a client program is written to query data from a database and generate HTML pages that display this information. When published as static web pages, web files can be uploaded to any server; for dynamic creation, however, the web server usually must be modified (or new scripts or application software installed). Static pages have the secondary advantage of being generated by traditional client/server tools such as visual basic or power builder. Because almost any development system can output text files, only the necessary HTML codes must be added to make them web pages. The creation of the pages, therefore, user standard methods of database access control such as database security and login controls.

Once created, the files must be uploaded to the web server. Protecting the documents stored there occurs in the same manner that any other web documents would be secured. One of the most straight forward ways to protect sensitive HTML documents is to limit directory browsing. Most FTP and web servers allow directories to be configured so that files stored within them may be read but the files may not be listed in the directory. This technique prevents any user who does not know the exact filename from accessing it. Access may be permitted by simply distributing the exact filenames to authorized personnel. Directories may also be protected using the integrated operating systems security. Some web servers allow security limitations to be placed on particular folders or directories using standard operating system techniques (such as file attributes) and then use this security to restrict access. This implementation will vary among web servers. These security implementations to gain access to particular files or folders fall under the user—authentication category of security.

Dynamic Page Generation

Favored by large organizations, this method is gaining popularity as the technology to generate the web pages instantly from a database query becomes more robust. A dynamic web page is stored on the web server with no actual data but instead a template for the HTML code and a query. When a client accesses the pages, the query is executed and an HTML page containing the data is generated on the fly. The necessary data is filled into the slots defined in the template file in much the same way that a mail merge occurs in a word-processing program. A program may be active on the web server to generate the necessary web page, or a CGI (Common Gateway Interface) script might dynamically create it (CGI: with web servers, CGI is a predefined system for transferring data across the Internet. Current scripting languages hide the details, so you can simply retrieve data as it is needed).

One of the first security issues that a DBA must confront is setting up access to the database from the web server. Whether using a CGI script, server-based middleware or a query tool, the server itself must have access to the database.

7.4.2 User-Authentication Security

Authentication security governs the barrier that must be passed before the user can access particular information. The user must have some valid form of identification before access is granted. Logins are accomplished in two standard ways: Using an HTML form or using an HTTP security request.

If a pass-through is provided to normal database access traditional security controls can be brought into play. For example, a standard security login through the Netscape communications corp.'s Netscape Navigator browser. The HTML login is simply an HTML page that contains the username and password form fields. The actual IDs and passwords are stored in a table on the server. This information is brought to the server through a Common Gateway Interface (CGI) script or some piece of database middleware for lookup in a user identification database. This method has the advantage of letting the DBA define a particular user's privilege. By using a table created by the DBA, numerous security privileges specific to a particular project can be defined.

Once a login has occurred, a piece of data called a "cookie" can be written onto the client machine to track the user session. A cookie is data (similar to a key and a value in an.ini file) sent from the web server and stored by a client's browser. The web server can then send a message to the browser, and the data is returned to the server. Because an HTTP connection is not persistent, a user ID could be written as a cookie so that the user might be identified during the duration of the session.

HTML form login security, however, must be implemented by hand. Often this means reinventing the wheel. Not only is database table/other file a must to track users and passwords, but authentication routines must be performed whether through CGI script or via another method. Additionally, unless using a secured connection (see the secure sockets layer) both the user name and password are broadcast across the network, where they might be intercepted.

HTML form login is excellent when security of the data is not paramount yet specialized access controls are required. Browser login is most useful when it is integrated with existing database security through some type of middleware. Even with users properly authenticated, additional security concerns arise.

7.4.3 Session Security

After the user has supplied proper identification and access is granted to data, session security ensures that private data is not intercepted or interfered with during the session. The basic protocols of the network do not set up a point-to-point connection, as a telephone system does. Instead, information is broadcast across a network for reception by a particular machines.

TCP/IP is the basic protocol for transmission on the Internet. The protocol was never designed for security, and as such it is very insecure. Because data sent from one machine to another is actually broadcast across the entire network, a program called "packet sniffer" can be used to intercept information packets bound for a particular user. Therefore, even though a user has properly logged into a system, any information that is accessed can be intercepted and captured by another user on the network. There is no easy way to prevent this interception except by encrypting all of the information that flows both ways.

7.5 VENDOR-SPECIFIC SECURITY

Individual vendors largely determines the security scheme that will be implemented to provide the link between the database and the published HTML page. Following are some of the security components provided by major vendors like, client/server systems solutions must be pieced together using multiple vendor products.

7.5.1 Oracle

Oracle Corp (Redwood shores, California) while providing SSL and S–HTTP security, is planning on using JAVA as a basic component of its security model. The company created its Oracle Web Server to work most effectively with oracle clients such as Oracle Power Browser and solutions created with the Developer/2000 development tools.

Oracle also modified the HTTP protocol to allow a state connection to be established between the client and the server. This connection actually defines a session in which the user is identified by a generated ID to identify the user. These enhancements are present in the Secure-network Server (SNS) include in the Oracle Universal Database. The SNA incorporates support for the Kerberos security standard. Through a Kerberos system, single login permits access to any oracle database in an enterprise system. The JAVA security classes are used by the Oracle development tools to provide complete security integration with the client.

7.5.2 Sybase

Sybase Inc. (Emeryville, Calif) provides a rather elegant way of protecting data access through the web. Rather than construct its own custom web framework, the login security present in the web server simply passes through to the database server for authentication taking advantage of the native security present in the database.

Sybase provides a piece of middleware called web. sql that is used to interface with the Netscape Web Servers. Communication between the Netscape suite spot servers and the database passes through the API for web sql.

7.5.3 Microsoft

Microsoft Corp (Redmond, Wash) is one of the most active players in the Internet Security Field because of its pursuit of the twin markets of Internet deployment and Internet commerce, both of which require extensive security. By taking an active role in the security standards debate, Microsoft hopes to shape policy to its advantage.

With Internet Information Server (IIS), Microsoft has included most of the key security technologies. For user authentication, Microsoft provides its tried-and true challenge/response mechanism. Traditional login on the web-features the same security present at basic window NT login. Unfortunately only the Microsoft Internet Explorer browser supports this login approach, and Netscape has made no announcements to integrate it into Navigator.

For database access, Microsoft has integrated IIS security with Microsoft SQL server through the Internet Database Connector. User begins must occur through an HTML login form, but the information may be verified using a SQL server stored procedure. Look for better integrated security with the release of SQL server 7.0.

Microsoft is also integrating the Kerberos security architecture into windows NT server 5.0. By releasing the server, Microsoft hopes to integrate the keyboard native to NT server with public security. Microsoft already released a certificate server API in an attempt to create a certificate server standard.

7.5.4 Netscape

Netscape Communication Corp. (Mountain view, Calif.) intends to market its suite of servers as a complete system for security on the Internet, Login occurs originally through the browser and then, as in Novell Directory Services, all certification is unified in this model. Therefore, once login to the browser occurs, any resources that are permitted to the user are now accessible. Currently, user-authentication occur by passing information to the data source via middleware. Most companies, including Sybase, Oracle provide the necessary connectors for this process to occur.

Netscape's certificate server will be the cornerstone of this secure system. It can generate a key pair (Public and private keys) for users and store the public certificates for automated retrieval. Netscape positions its certificates server along with SSL/S-HTTP as the primary means of providing security for web access. The certificate server complies with the public standard X.509, SSL and PKCS.

Making your data secure for broadcast over the Internet or Internet is no easy task. The best way to evaluate your security needs is to weigh the disadvantages of unauthorized users seeing your data. The more privacy your data requires, the more security you should have in place. Security is often far easier to implement than to maintain. Make sure that the necessary processor in your organization. Keep your system current. Security is often neglected or bypass by day-to-day users for convenience. By the time loss of data or security breaks have been discovered, much damage may have already been done. Database and web server vendors are constantly upgrading their systems, so staying current on the particular architectures is a must.

7.6 DATABASE BACKUP AND RECOVERY

An integral part of any overall database security strategy should be providing for database backup and recovery. Backups serve many different purposes. Most often, it seems that systems administrator perform backups to protect information in the case of server hardware failures. Although this is very real danger in most environments. It is often not the most likely. Data can be lost due to accidental human errors, flawed application logic, defects in the database server or operating system platform and, of course, malicious users who are able to circumvent security measures. In the event that data is incorrectly modified or destroyed altogether, the only real method to recover information is from backups.

Since all relational database systems provide some method for performing database backups while a server is still running, there is not much of an excuse for not implementing backups. The real challenge is in determining what backup strategies apply to your own environment. You will need to find out what your working limitations are. This was not an easy task, even in the best-managed organizations. It involves finding information from many different individuals and departments within your organization. You will have to work hard to find existing data, and make best guesses and estimates for areas in which data is not available.

To further complicate issues, there are many constraints in the real world that can affect the implementation of backup processes. First, resources such as storage space, network bandwidth, processing time, and local disk I/O bandwidth are almost always limited. Additionally, human resources—especially knowledgeable and experienced database administrators—may be difficult to find. And, performance requirements, user load, and other factors can prevent you from taking all the time you need to implement an ideal backup solution.

So, how do you decide what to protect? One method is to classify the importance of the relative types of information you need to protect. For example, your sales databases might be of "mission critical" importance, whereas a small decision support system might rank" Low priority" on the scale (since the data can relatively easily be re-created, if necessary). It is also importance to keep in mind that business managers may have a very different ideas of the importance of data when compared to other users who actually deals with this information frequently. Keep in mind that determining how to protect information must be a team effort if it is to be accurate and successful. An example of high-level data protection requirements is shown in Table 7.1.

Table 7.1 A sample categorization of data based on importance

Resource	*Importance*	*Notes*
OLTP server	Critical	Information can't be easily re-created, and data loss will lead to inaccurate or misleading reports.
E-mail server	High	Recovering lost messages and user mail boxes is very difficult.
Decision-support server (Data warehouse)	Medium	Information can be regenereated from other sources.
Internet Web Server	Medium	Content is important, but is replicated among multiple machines as part of development process.

It is important to keep in mind that the purpose of data protection is not to create backups. The real purpose is to provide the ability to recover information, in case it is lost! To that end, a good practice is to begin designing a backup solution based on your recovery requirements you should take into account the cost of downtime, the value of the data, and the amount of acceptable data loss in a worst-case scenario. Also, keep in mind the likelihood of certain types of disasters.

7.7 DATA WAREHOUSE CONTROL AND SECURITY

Data Warehouse (DW) is a collection of integrated databases designed to support managerial decision-making and problem-solving functions. It contains both highly detailed and summarized historical data relating to various categories, subjects or areas. All units of data are relevant to appropriate time horizons. DW is an integral part of enterprise—wide decision support system, does not ordinarily involve data updating. It empowers and end users perform data access and analysis. This eliminates the need for the IS function to perform informational processing from the legacy system for the end-users. It also gives an organization certain competitive advantages, such as: fostering a culture of information sharing; enabling employees to effectively and efficiently solve dynamic organizational problems; minimizing operating costs and maximizing the employee's turnovers.

The security requirements of the DW environments are not unlike those of other distributed computing systems. Thus, having an internal control mechanism to assure the confidentiality, integrity and availability of data in a distributed environment is of paramount importance. Unfortunately, most data warehouses are built with little or no consideration given to security during the development phase. Achieving proactive security requirements of DW there are seven phase processes:

- Identifying the data
- Classifying the data
- Quantifying the value of data
- Identifying data security vulnerabilities
- Identifying data protection measures and their costs
- Selecting cost-effective security measures
- Evaluating the effectiveness of security measures.

These phases are parts of an enterprise—wide vulnerability assessment and management program.

7.7.1 Identifying the Data

The first security task is to identify all digitally-stored corporate data placed in the Data Warehouse. This is an often ignored, but critical phase of meeting the security requirements of the DW environment since it forms the foundation for subsequent phases. It entails taking a complete inventory of all the data that is available to the DW end-users. The installed data monitoring software—an important component of the DW can provide an accurate information about all databases, tables, columns, rows of data and profiles of data residing in the DW environment as well as who is using the data and how often they use the data.

A manual procedure would require preparing a checklist of the same information described above. Whether the required information is gathered through an automated or a manual method, the collected information needs to be organized, documented and retained for the next phase.

7.7.2 Classifying the Data

Classifying all the data in the DW environment is needed to satisfy security requirements for the data confidentiality, integrity and availability in a prudent manner. In some cases, data classification is a legally mandated requirement. Performing this task requires the environment of the data owners, custodians and the end-users. Data is generally classified on the basis of criticality or sensitivity to disclosure, modification and destruction. The sensitivity of corporate data can be classified as least sensitive data, moderately-sensitive data, most sensitive data. Classifying data into different categories is not as easy as it seems.

7.7.3 Quantifying the Data

In most organizations, senior management demands to see the smoking gun (e.g. Cost vs benefit figures, or hard evidence of committed frauds) before committing corporate funds to support security initiatives. Cynic managers will be quick to point out that they deal with hard reality —not soft variables connected hypothetically. Quantifying the value of sensitive data warranting protective measures is as close to the smoking gun as one can get the trigger senior manager's support and commitment to security initiative in the DW environment.

The quantifying process is primarily concerned about assigning "Street Value" to data grouped under different sensitivity categories. By itself, data has no intrinsic value. However, the definite value of data is often measurable by the cost to

(a) reconstruct lost data
(b) restore the integrity of corrupted, fabricated, or intercepted data
(c) not make timely decision due to denial of service
(d) pay financial liability for public disclosure of confidential data.

The data value may also include lost revenue from leakage of trade secrets to competitors, and advance use of secret financial data by rogue employees in the stock market prior to public release.

7.7.4 Identifying Data Vulnerabilities

This phase requires the identification and documentation of vulnerabilities associated with DW environment. Some common vulnerabilities of DW include the following:

- In-built DBMS security
- DBMS limitations
- Inference attacks
- Availability factor
- Human factor
- Inside threats

- Outsider threats
- Natural factors
- Utility factors.

A comprehensive inventory of vulnerabilities inherent in the DW environment need to be documented and organized (e.g. as major or minor) for the next phase.

7.7.5 Identifying Protective Measures and Their Cost

Vulnerabilities identified in the previous phase should be considered in order to determine cost-effective protection for the DW data at different sensitivity levels. Some protective measures for the DW data include:

- Human wall
- Access user classification
- Access controls
- Data encryption
- Partitioning
- Development controls.

The estimated costs of each security measure should be determined and documented for the next phase. Measuring the costs usually involves determining the development, implementation and maintenance costs of each security measure.

7.7.6 Selective Cost-Effective Security Measures

All security measures involve expenses, and security expenses require justification. This phase relies on the results of previous phases to access the fiscal impact of corporate data at risk and select cost-effective security measures to safeguard the data against known vulnerabilities.

However, the cost factor should not be the only criterion for selecting appropriate security measures in DW environment. Compatibility, adaptability and potential impact on the DW performance should also be taken into consideration.

7.7.7 Evaluating the Effectiveness of Security Measures

A winning basketball formula from the John Wooden School of Thought teaches that good team should be prepared to rebound every shot that goes up, even if it is made by the greatest player on the court. Similarly, a winning security strategy is to assume that all security measures are breakable, or not permanently effective. Every time we identify and select cost-effective security measures to secure our strategic information assets against certain attacks, the attackers tend to double their efforts in identifying methods to defeat our implemented security measures.

The best we can do is to prevent this from happening, make the attacks difficult to carryout, or be prepared to rebound quickly if our assets are attacked. We will not be well-positioned to do any of these if we do not evaluate the effectiveness of security measures on an ongoing basis.

Evaluating the effectiveness of security measures should be conducted continuously to determine whether the measures are:

(i) Small, simple and straightforward
(ii) Carefully analyzed, tested and verified
(iii) Used properly and selectively so that they do not exclude legitimate accesses.
(iv) Elastic so that they can respond effectively to changing security requirements, and
(v) Reasonably efficient in terms of time, memory space, and user-centric activities so that they do not adversely affect the protected computing resources. It is equally important to ensure that the DW end-user understand and embrace the propriety of security measures through an effective security awareness program. The data warehouse administrator (DWA) with the delegated authority from senior management is responsible for ensuring the effectiveness of security measures.

The size of historical data in the DW environment grows significantly every year, while the user of the data tends to decrease dramatically. This increase storage, processing and operating costs of the DW annually. It necessitates the periodic phasing out of least and most accessed data over a long time horizon. A prudent decision has to be made as to how long historical data should be kept in the DW environment before they are phased our on mass. The DWA may not meet effectively these challenges without the necessary tools (activity and data monitors), resources (funds and staffing support) and management philosophy (strategic planning and management). For these reasons, the DWA should be a good strategist, an effective communicator and a competent technician. It is generally recognized that the goal of DW is to provide decision-makers access to consistent, reliable and timely data for analytical, planning and assessment purposes in a format that allows for easy retrieval, exploration and analysis. The need for accurate information in the most efficient and effective manner is congruent with the security requirements for data integrity and availability.

REVIEW QUESTIONS

7.1 Why it is important to protect data? Justify protecting data is at heart of many secure system.

7.2 What are the implicit properties of database?

7.3 Why database administrator is important? Explain with example.

7.4 Explain characteristics of database approach.

7.5 Explain database system and its importance.

7.6 Discuss the various issues of database security.

7.7 What is the difference between loss of integrity and loss of availability?

7.8 Explain the requirements for database security.

7.9 What is the difference between physical database security and logical database security?

7.10 Explain the statistical database security.

7.11 Explain the requirements for database security. What is difference between physical database integrity and logical database integrity.

7.12 How server security helps to database security?

7.13 Explain static web pages and its importance.

7.14 Explain dynamic page generation and its importance.

7.15 How user-authentication security helps to database security?

7.16 Describe vendor-specific security.

7.17 Explain data warehouse. How it is possible to make secure data warehouse?

7.18 What is the difference between classifying the data and quantifying the data?

7.19 How to identify data vulnerabilities? Explain database backup and recovery.

7.20 How to evaluate the effectiveness of security measures.

CHAPTER 8

Information Systems Security

Chapter Outline

An information system can be defined technically as a set of interrelated components that collect (or retrieve), process, store, and distribute information to support decision making, coordination, and control in an organization. In addition to supporting decision, making, coordination and control, information systems may also help managers and workers analyze problems, visualize complex subjects, and create new products.

Information systems contain information about significant people, places, and things within the organization or in it the environment surrounding it. By information we mean data that have been shaped into a form that is meaningful and useful to human beings. Data, in contrast, are streams of raw facts representing events occurring in organizations or the physical environment before they have been organized and arranged into a form that people can understand and use.

Three activities in an information system produce the information that organizations need to make decisions, control operations, analyze problems and create new products or services. These activities are input, processing, and output. Input captures or collects raw data from within the organization or from its external environment. Processing converts this raw input into a meaningful form output transfers the processed information to the people who will use it or to the activates for which it will be used.

Information systems play such a critical role in business, government, and daily life that firms need to make security and control a top priority. Security refers to the policies, procedures and technical measures used to prevent unauthorized access, alteration, theft, or physical damage to information systems. Controls consist of all the methods, policies and organizational procedures that ensure the safety of the organization's assets, the accuracy and reliability of its accounting records, and operational adherence to management standards. Let us see how information systems can be controlled and made secure so that they serve the purposes for which they are intended.

8.1 DISTRIBUTED SYSTEMS SECURITY

The Internet is basically worldwide infrastructure which uses a standardized communications protocol, known as TCP/IP. Many people often confuse the Internet with World Wide Web (www), but the www is just one of the applications of the Internet. Some of its other uses are outlined in Figure 8.1.

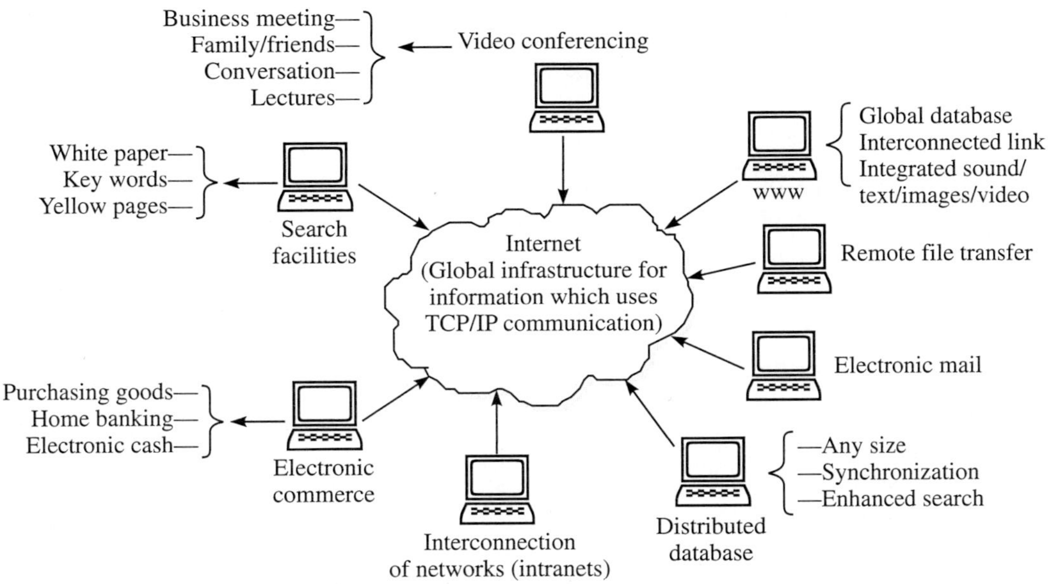

Figure 8.1 Some applications of the internet.

The Internet, networks and increased computing power will have great effects on all areas of life, whether they are in commerce, in industry, or in home life.

The Internet is likely to have a great effect on how companies do business.

For any business, information must be protected. Major issues include protection of data and information storage and the methods used to ensure confidentiality and integrity. The Enterprise organization must apply security principles and methods, which include authentication and authorization techniques. Integrity of the database and the software that processes the transactions must be assured.

Electronic commerce involves customers using electronic-communication to purchase goods, typically using the Internet. This will change the way that many busineses do business, and the way that consumers purchase their goods. An important key to the acceptance of Internet-based purchases is that they must be secure, and cannot be used by criminals to make false purchase, or criminals setting up companies which take payments for incorrect services.

8.2 DISTRIBUTED COMPUTING ENVIRONMENT

How does one describe the distributed computer and networking environment? There are many entities and components that makeup this complex environment. There are a number of terms and definitions that must be understood before proceeding further. They include the following:

- *Distributed network:* A communication network comprises two or more processing centres. The processing may be distributed between each centre and each processor must be in communications with all others.
- *Distributed processing:* A network of computers where the processing of information is initiated in local computers, and the resultant data is sent to a central computer for further processing with the data of other local systems?
- *Distributed data processing:* A data processing arrangement where the computers are decentralized, or located apart from each other.
- *Distributed environment:* A network environment, or topology, where decision making, file storage, and other network functions are not centralized but, instead, are found throughout the network.
- *Distributed computing environment:* A comprehensive integrated set of services that supports the development, use, and maintenance of distributed applications.
- *Distributed architecture:* A bus or ring LAN that uses shared communication media and shared access methods.

A distributed enterprise computer network can include a number of different platforms located across a wide geographic area, accessible over a corporate network or the Internet. These include, but are not limited to, laptop computers, servers, and computer systems as shown in Figure 8.2.

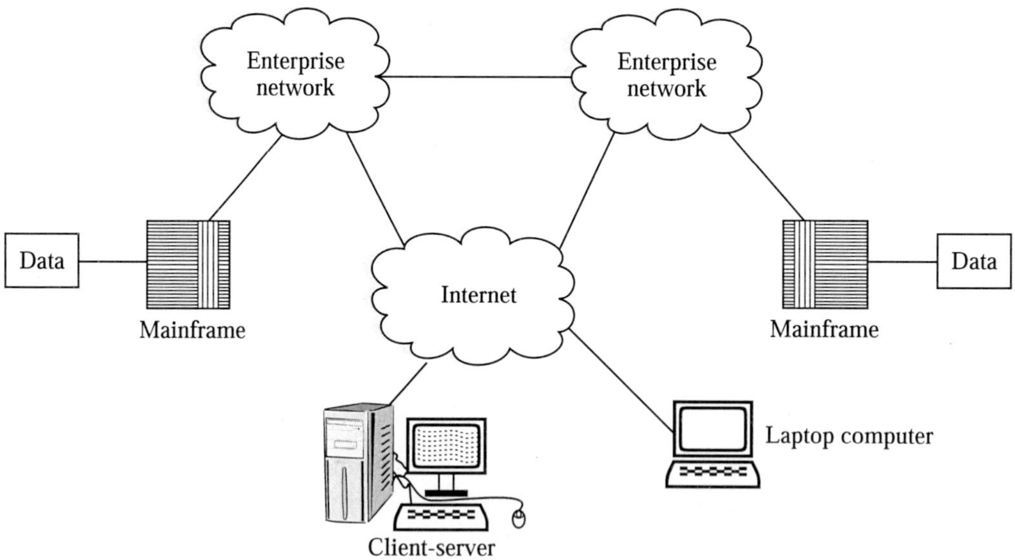

Figure 8.2 Distributed enterprise computer network.

The distributed environment contains a variety of complex components and, therefore, has numerous security issues. A concept that fits in all these environments is electronic commerce (e-commerce).

8.3 SYSTEM VULNERABILITY AND ABUSE

Before computing automation, data about individuals or organizations were maintained and secured as paper records dispersed in separate business or organizational units. Information systems concentrate data in computer files that can potentially be accessed by a large number of people and by group outside the organization.

When large amounts of data are stored in electronic form, they are vulnerable to many more kinds of threats than when they exist in manual form. Through communications, networks, information systems in different locations can be interconnected. The potential for unauthorized accesss, abuse, or fraud is not limited to a single location but can occur at any access point in the network.

Figure 8.3 illustrates the most common threats against contemporary information systems. They can stem from technical, organizational, and environmental factors compounded by poor management decisions.

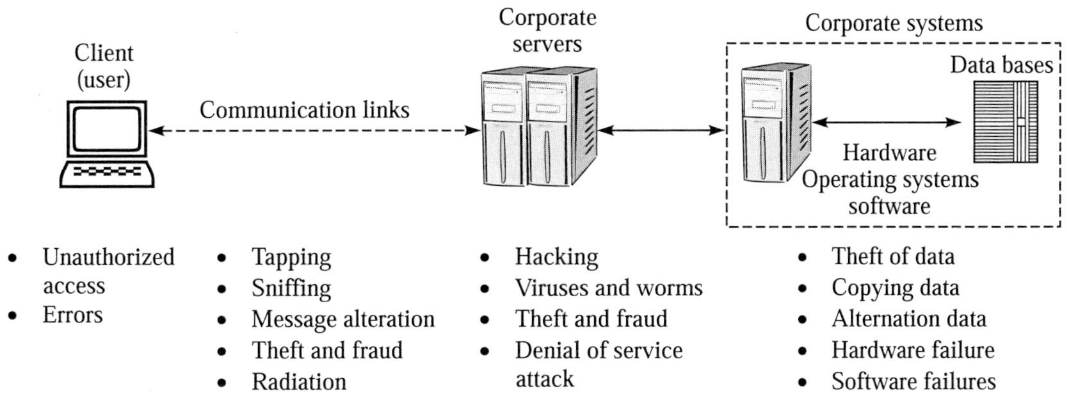

Figure 8.3 Contemporary security challenges and vulnerabilities.

In the multilayer client/server computing environment illustrated here, vulnerabilities exist at each layer and in the communication between the layers. Users at the client layer can cause harm by introducing errors or by accessing systems without authorization. It is possible to access data flowing over networks, steal valuable data during transmission, or alter messages without authorization. Radiation can disrupt a network at various points as well. Intruders can launch denial of service attacks or malicious software to disrupt the operation of web sites. Those capable of penetrating corporate systems can destroy or alter corporate data stored in databases or files. Domestic or offshore outsourcing to another company adds to system vulnerability because valuable information will reside on networks and computers outside the organization's control. Without strong safeguards, valuable data could be lost, destroyed, or could fall into the wrong hands, revealing important trade secrets or information that violates personal privacy. Some worry that outsourcing application development to offshore companies might provide opportunities for programmers to insert hidden code that would later enable someone to gain control over an application or its data.

8.3.1 Internet Vulnerabilities

Large public networks such as the Internet are more vulnerable than internal networks because they are virtually open to anyone. The internet is so huge that when abuses do occur, they can have an enormously widespread impact. When the Internet becomes part of the corporate network, the organization information systems are even more vulnerable to actions from outsiders.

Computers that are constantly connected to the Internet by cable modems or Digital Subscriber Line (DSL) are more open to penetration by outsiders because they use fixed Internet addresses where they can be easily identified. (With dial-up service, a temporary Internet address is assigned for each session.) A fixed Internet address creates a fixed target for hackers.

Telephone service based on Internet technology can be more vulnerable than the switched voice if it does not run over a secure private network. Most Voice over IP (VoIP) traffic over the public Internet is not encrypted, so anyone linked to a network can listen in on conversations. Hackers can intercept conversations to obtain credit card and other confidential personal information or shut down voice service by flooding servers supporting VoIP with bogus traffic.

Vulnerability has also increased from widespread use of e-mail and instant messaging (IM). E-mail can contain attachments that serve as springboards for malicious software or unauthorized access to internal corporate systems. Employees may use e-mail messages to transmit valuable trade secrets financial data, or confidential customer information to unauthorized recipients. Popular instant messaging applications for consumers do not use a secure layer for text messages, so they can be intercepted and ready by outsiders during transmission over the public Internet. Instant messaging over the Internet can in some cases be used as a backdoor to an otherwise secure network. (IM systems designed for corporations, such as IBM's sometime, include security features.)

8.3.2 Malicious Software: Viruses, Worms, Trojan Horses, and Spyware

Malicious software programs referred to as malware include a variety of threats such as computer viruses, worms and Trojan horses. A *computer virus* is a vogue software program that attaches itself to other software programs or data files in order to be executed, usually without user knowledge or permission. Most computer viruses deliver a "payload". The payload may be relatively benign, such as the instructions to display a message or image or it may be highly destructive—destroying programs or data, clogging computer memory, reformatting a computer's hard drive, or causing programs to run improperly. Viruses typically spread from computer to computer when humans take an action such as sending an e-mail attachment or copying an infected file. Many recent attacks have come from *worms*, which are independent computer programs that copy themselves from one computer to other over a network. (unlike viruses, they can operate on their own without attaching to other computer program files and rely less on human behaviour in order to spread from computer to computer. This explains why computer worms spread much more rapidly than computer viruses). Worms can destroy data and programs, as well as disrupt or even halt the operation of computer networks.

Worms and viruses are often spread over the Internet from files of downloaded software, from files attached to e-mail transmissions or from computerized e-mail messages. Viruses have also invaded computerized information systems from "infected" disks or infected machines. Today e-mail attachments are the most frequent source of infection, followed by Internet downloads and Web browing.

A *Trojan horse* is a software program that appears to be benign, but then does something other than expected. The Trojan horse is not itself a virus because it does not replicate, but is often a way for viruses or other malicious code to be introduced into a computer system. The term 'Trojan horse' is based on the huge wooden horse used by the Greeks to trick the Trojans into opening the gates to their fortified city during the Trojan war. Once inside the city walls, Greek soldiers hidden in the horse revealed themselves and captured the city.

Some types of *spyware* can act as malicious software. These small programs instal themselves on computers to monitor user web surfing activity and serve up advertising. Some web advertisers use spyware to obtain information about users buying habits and serve tailored advertisements. Many users find such spyware annoying and some critics worry about its infringement on computer user's privacy.

Other forms of spyware, however, are much nefarious. Key loggers record every key-stroke made on a computer to steal serial numbers for software, to launch Internet attacks, to gain access to e-mail accounts, to obtain passwords to protected computer systems, or to pick up personal information such as credit card numbers. Other spyware programs reset web browser home pages, redirect search requests, or slow down computer performance by taking up too much memory. Nearly, 1000 forms of spyware have been documented.

8.3.3 Hackers, Spoofing, and Sniffing

A hacker is an individual who intends to gain unauthorized access to a computer system. Within the hacking community, the term 'cracker' is typically used to denote a hacker with criminal intent, although in the public press, the terms 'hacker' and 'cracker' are used interchangeably. Hackers and crackers gain unauthorized access by finding weaknesses in the security protections employed by Web sites and computer systems, often taking advantage of various features of the Internet that make it an open system that is easy to use.

Hackers attempting to hide their true identity often spoof, or misrepresent themselves by using fake e-mail addresses or masquerading as someone else. Spoofing also can involve redirecting a web link to an address different from the intended one, with the site masquerading as the intended destination. Links that are designed to lead to one site can be reset to send users to a totally unrelated site, one that benefits the hacker. For example, if hackers redirect customers to a fake web site that looks almost exactly like the true site, they can then collect and process orders, effectively stealing business as well as sensitive customer information from the true site. Other forms of spoofing is in computer crime. Most hacker activities are criminal offences, and the vulnerabilities of systems we have just described make them targets for other types of computer crime as well. The U.S. Department of Justice defines computer crime as "any violation of criminal that involve a knowledge a computer technology for their perpetration, investigation, or prosecution." The computer can be a target of a crime or an instrument of a crime.

A *sniffer* is a type of eavesdropping program that monitors information traveling over a network. When used legitimately, sniffers can help identify potential network trouble-spots or criminal activity on networks, but when used for criminal purposes, they can be damaging and very difficult to detect. Sniffers enable hackers to steal proprietary information from anywhere on a network, including e-mail messages, company files, and confidential reports.

8.3.4 Denial of Service Attacks

In a denial of service (DoS) attack, hackers flood a network server or web server with many thousands of false communications or requests for services to crash the network. The network receives so many queries that it cannot keep up with them and is thus unavailable to service legitimate requests. A distributed denial of service (DDoS) attack uses numerous computers to inundate and overwhelm the network from numerous launch points. Although DoS attacks do not destroy information or access restricted areas of a company's information systems, they can cause a web site to shut down, making it impossible for legitimate users to access the site.

8.3.5 Internal Threats: Employees

We tend to think the security threats to a business originate outside the organization. In fact, the largest financial threats outside the organization. In fact, the largest financial threats to business institutions come from insiders. Some of the largest disruptions of service, destruction of e-commerce sites, and diversion of customer credit data and personal information have come from insiders—once trusted employees. Employees have access to privileged information, and in the presence of sloppy internal security procedures, they are often able to roam throughout an organization's systems without leaving a trace.

Studies have found that the user's lack of knowledge is the single greatest cause of network security breaches. Many employees forget their passwords to access computer systems or allow other coworkers to use them, which compromises the system. Malicious intruders seeking system access sometimes trick employees into revealing their passwords by pretending to be legitimate members of the company in the need of information. This practice is called *social engineering.*

Employees—both end users and information systems specialists—are also a major source of errors introduced into an information system. Employees can introduce errors by entering faulty data or by not following the proper instructions for processing data and using computer equipment. Information systems specialists can also create software errors as they design and develop new software or maintain existing programs.

8.3.6 Software Vulnerability

Software errors also pose a constant threat to information systems, causing untold losses in productivity. A major problem with software is the presence of hidden bugs, or program code defects. Studies have shown that it is virtually impossible to eliminate all bugs from large programs. The main source of bugs is the complexity of decision-making code. Important programs within most corporations may contain tens of thousands or even millions of lines of code, each with many alternative decision paths. Such complexity is difficult to document and design—designers may document some reactions incorrectly or may fail to consider some possibilities. Even after rigorous testing, developers do not know for sure that a piece of software is dependable until the product proves itself after much operational use.

Commercial software often contains flaws that create not only performance issues but also security vulnerabilities that open networks to intruders. These vulnerabilities and bugs can enable malware to slip past antivirus defenses. A great deal of malware has been trying to exploit vulnerabilities in the Microsoft Windows operating system and other Microsoft products, but malware targetting the Linux operating system is on the rise as well.

To correct software flaws once they are identified, the software vendor creates lines of code called *patches* to repair the flaw without distributing proper operation of the software. An example is Microsoft XP Service Pack 2 (SP2) introduced in 2004, which features added firewall protection against viruses and intruders, capabilities for automatic security updates, and an easy-to-use interface for managing the security applications on the user's computer. It is up to users of the software to track these vulnerabilities, test, and apply all patches. This process is called *patch management.*

8.4 MANAGEMENT FRAMEWORK OF SECURITY AND CONTROL

Technology is not the key issue in information systems security and control. It provides a foundation, but in the absence of intelligent management policies, even the best technology can be easily defected. For instance, experts believe that over 90 per cent of successful cyber attacks could have been prevented by technology available at the time. Inadequate human attention made these attacks so prevalent.

The protection of information resources requires a sound security policy and set of controls. ISO 17799, an international set of standards for security and control, provides helpful guidelines. It specifies best practices in information systems security and control, including security policy, business continuity planning, physical security, access control, compliance, and creating a security function within the organization.

The protection of information resources requires a well-designed set of controls. Computer systems are controlled by a combination of general controls and application controls.

General controls govern the design, security, and use of computer programs and the security of data files in general throughout the organization information technology infrastructure. On the whole, general controls apply to all computerized applications and consist of combination of hardware, software, and manual procedures that create an overall control environment.

Application controls are specific controls unique to each computerized application such as payroll or order processing. They consist of controls applied from the business functional area of a particular system and from programmed procedures.

Before an organization commits resources to controls, it must know which assets require protection and the extent to which these assets are vulnerable. A risk assessment helps answer these questions and also helps the firm determine the most cost-effective set of controls for protecting assets.

A firm must develop a coherent corporate policy, that takes into account the nature of the risks, the information assets that need protecting and the procedures and technologies required to address the risks, as well as implementation and auditing mechanisms.

Disaster recovery planning devises plans for the restoration of computing and communications services after they have been disrupted by an event such as an earthquake, flood, or terrorist attack. Disaster recovery plans focus primarily on the technical issues involved in keeping systems up and running, such as which files to back up and the maintenance of back-up computer systems or disaster recovery services.

Business continuity planning focuses on how the company can restore business operations after a disaster strikes. The business continuity plan identifies critical business processes and determines action plans for handling mission-critical functions if systems go down.

Business managers and information technology specialists need to work together on both types of plans to determine which systems and business processes are most critical to the company. They must conduct a business impact analysis to identify the firm's most critical systems and the impact a system's outage would have on the business. Management must determine the maximum amount of time the business can survive with its systems down and which parts of the business must be restored first.

8.4.1 Role of Auditing in the Control Process

How does management know that information systems security and controls are effective? To answer this question, organizations must conduct comprehensive and systematic audits. An information system audit identifies all of the controls that govern individual information systems and assesses their effectiveness. To accomplish this, the auditor must acquire a thorough understanding of operations, physical facilities, telecommunications, security systems, security objectives, organizational structure, personnel, manual procedures, and individual applications.

The auditor usually interviews key individuals who use and operate a specific information system concerning their activities and procedures. Security, application controls, overall integrity controls, and control disciplines are examined. The auditor should trace the flow of sample transactions through the system and perform tests, using appropriate, automated audit software.

Security audits should review technologies, procedures documentation, training and personnel. A very thorough audit will even simulate an attack or disaster to test the response of the technology, information systems staff, and business employees.

The audit lists and ranks all control weaknesses and estimate the probability of their occurrence. It then assesses the financial and organizational impact of each threat.

8.4.2 Technology and Tools for Safeguarding Information Resources

Companies require special measures to support electronic commerce and digital business processes. They can use fault-tolerant computer systems or create high-availability computing environments to make sure that their information systems are always available and performing without interruptions. Firewalls are placed between an organization's private network and external networks such as the Internet to prevent unauthorized users from accessing the private network. Intrusion detection systems monitor private networks. Intrusion detection systems monitor private networks for suspicious network traffic and attempts to access corporate systems. Passwords, Tokens, and biometric authentication can be used for authenticating system users. Antivirus software can check computer systems for infection by viruses and worms and often eliminate the malicious software. Encryption, the coding and scrambling of messages, is a widely used technology for securing electronic transmission over the Internet and over Wi-Fi networks. Digital certificates combined with Public Key encryption provide further protection of electronic transactions by authenticating a user's identity.

The quality and reliability of software can be improved by thorough testing procedures and by allocating resources to put more emphasis on secure software design. Reliability of information system has been defined as "the probability of system, performing its purposes adequately for the period of time intended under the stated operating conditions."

8.5 E-COMMERCE SECURITY

There is considerable apprehension concerning the lack of security on the Internet. There are a number of initiatives to set security standards for electronic commerce. To transact business, organizations must have a means to conduct secure, confidential, and reliable transactions. To achieve this goal, four cornerstones of secure electronic transactions must be present. These include the following attributes:

- Possess the ability to prevent unauthorized monitoring of traffic.
- Prevent the content of messages from being altered after transmission and provide a method to prove they have or have not been altered.
- Determine whether a transmission is from an authentic source or a masquerade.
- Prevent a sender from denying the receipt or transmission of a message (nonrepudiation).

Cryptographic systems provide a method to transmit information across an untrusted communication system without disclosing the content of the information to a snoop. Cryptographic systems provide confidentiality and can also provide proof that the transmission's integrity has not been compromised.

Securing Electronic Transactions

Individuals, organizations, industries, and commerce use the Internet to transmit e-mail, purchase goods and services, transact banking, and perform other unique services that depend on secure transmissions. There are methods that can provide secure transmission for each.

An e-mail often contains confidential information such as credit card numbers or social security numbers. It is essential that the contents and the sender of a message be authenticated. An e-mail might be considered a legal document when conducting a transaction such as responding to an official competitive bid. Therefore, it is essential that both the sender and the recipient be assured of the integrity of the transmission.

Many network users purchase goods and services over the Internet. Buyers select the items and authorize payment using the web. These items are then delivered through the normal shipment channel. Typical items include books, CDs, and auction items. Software and recording can be delivered immediately by downloading through the Internet. All of these transactions must be validated and tracked.

It is now possible to conduct banking transactions through an electronic bank. These banks offer users virtually all the services and functions provided by conventional banks. Functions include checking of account balances and statements, transferring funds between accounts, and electronic payments. Authentication and authorization are two security functions that must occur with these transactions. The user must be identifiable and have authority to access a particular account with a particular transaction.

There are a number of Internet transactions that fall in the general category. The Internet lends itself to the supply of small quantities of information and other services to many users. The development of the web as a high-quality publishing medium depends on the extent to which information suppliers of books and documents can obtain payment from users for that information. The use of the Internet for voice and video-conferencing is another service that is likely to be supplied when it is paid for by end-users.

Transactions such as these can be safely executed only when protected by approximate security policies and mechanisms. A client must be protected against the disclosure of credit and debit card numbers during transmission and against a fraudulent vendor who obtains payment without delivering the goods or services. Conversely, vendors must obtain payment before releasing the items selected for the purchase, whether they are supplied online or through a normal delivery method. In addition, the cost to achieve the required protection must be reasonable in comparison to the value of the transaction.

8.5.1 Security Services and Protocols

Security services provide a range of services and protocols for e-commerce, including private communications, access controls, security in business transactions, and electronic cash management. Users who engage in business transactions over the Internet need secure connections.

This level of security is provided by secure channel service called *Secure Sockets Layer* (SSL) protocol. With SSL, the client and the server use a handshaking technique to agree on the level of security required during session. Authentication takes place over a secure channel and all information transmitted during the session is encrypted. The protocol authenticates the client, then exchanges a master key, which is used to encrypt subsequent data exchanges.

With the growth of e-commerce, security over the Internet has become increasingly important. *Secure Electronic Transaction* (SET) was designed to replace the SSL standard and provide electronic customers and merchants with the assurance that e-commerce's can be conducted in a sequence manner. Note that SET is an encryption standard for secure credit card authorization over the Internet. SET offers the prospect of lower business costs because non-secured credit card transactions on the Internet carry high fees and are generally considered high risk by credit card companies.

The SET standard addressed the following major business requirements:

(i) Guarantee confidentiality of payment information.
(ii) Guarantee integrity of all transmitted data.
(iii) Provide cardholder authentication.
(iv) Provide vendor authentication,.
(v) Provide security practices to protect e-commerce transactions.
(vi) Develop an open protocol.
(vii) Provide for interoperability between software and network components.

Many problems have occurred with SSL. Therefore, a new standard such as SET is needed. With SSL, online merchants encrypt confidential information during transmission, so there is not a method of preventing fraudulent use of this information. SET provides increased security to prevent such occurrences, since it authenticates both merchants and cardholders. The specification guarantees that transaction content is not altered during the transmission between the originator and the recipients. Also, unlike SSL, SET allows impromptu (done without advance preparation) shopping expeditions by consumers equipped with digital certificates.

To meet the business requirements of e-commerce, SET incorporates the following features:

- Cardholder account authentication
- Confidentiality of information
- Integrity of data
- Merchant authentication

The Secure Electronic Transaction (SET) protocol was developed so merchants could automatically and safely collect and process payments from Internet clients.

Security protocols that can be deployed to provide security services in the e-commerce environment include SSL, IPSec, and AES. SSL provides for privacy, authentication, and message integrity and is standard for securing web traffic. IPSec secures each packet of data by encrypting it inside another packet that is then sent over the Internet. At the receiving end, the message is unpacked and decrypted. AES is in development and will provide a more robust encryption method using 128-bit keys instead of the 56-bit DES key.

IPSec provides the capability to secure communications across a LAN, private and public WANs, and the Internet. Functions that allow e-commerce systems to operate with a high degree of integrity and security include the following:

- Enhanced e-commerce security provisions
- Secure remote access over the Internet
- Secure branch office connectivity over the Internet

- Extranet connectivity with partners over the Internet
- Intranet and Extranet connectivity to the Internet.

The principal features of IPSec that enables it to support these varied applications is that it can encrypt and/or decrypt all traffic at the IP level. This means that all distributed applications that are used to make e-commerce work can be secured. These applications include remote login, e-mail file transfer, web access, and client/server access.

8.5.2 E-security Versus E-thieves

E-merchants must evaluate the steps being taken to prevent online fraud, security and privacy violations, and intruders attacks. Although the cost of implementing these e-security measures can be significant, the alternative is even more costly. There are actions that can be taken to prevent theft, protect sensitive information, and foil destructive attacks.

Online fraud can occur in a number of ways. However, identification fraud and electronic price tag alteration are the most predominant forms. Identification fraud occur when e-thieves use a consumer's credit card to make online purchases or when consumers make an online purchase and then later deny that they made the transaction. E-merchants often have little or no recourse and are held liable when transactions conducted at their sites are later determined to be fraudulent. This means that the merchants must pay higher discount rates and fees and higher penalties based on their charge-back percentages. Electronic price tag alteration occurs when hackers manipulate the shopping cart software code and alter prices. It is estimated that one-third of all shopping cart applications have software holes.

Traditional password protection, which is used to control system and database access, is not sufficient for e-commerce security. Secure e-commerce requires both parties to a transaction be positively mutually identified. This mutual authentication process prevents intruders from acquiring valuable information or goods under false pretences. E-commerce transaction information must be secured against theft. Encrypting the information before it is sent, then decrypting it when received, can protect transaction communications. This security technique is designed to foil intruders who may intercept the transaction somewhere in the transmission path.

E-commerce transaction information, which is stored on computer systems and servers, must be carefully protected. This is usually accomplished by defensive hardware and software, which can include firewall and intrusion detection mechanisms. The goal is to keep systems safe from external and internal theft attempts. Confidential data, such as credit card numbers and account information, should be encrypted. Encryption can make the information usable in the event that e-thieves gain access to the system.

Attacks that use destructive techniques such as denial of service and viruses also pose a threat to e-commerce. Interruption of service caused by such attacks can be very costly to an e-commerce organization. Since access to the site may be blocked, both immediate customers and potential customers may be lost. A number of security measures can be effective in mitigating these types of attacks. Antivirus software and the same measures used to foil theft are useful against these threats.

REVIEW QUESTIONS

8.1 What is information system and explain its role in business and government.

8.2 What is distributed system? Explain with example.

8.3 What is the difference between data and information?

8.4 Explain information system. Distinguish between a computer, a computer program, and an information system.

8.5 What are the Internet and World Wide Web? How have they, changed the role played by information systems in organizations?

8.6 Describe the distributed computing environments and its components.

8.7 Explain system vulnerability and abuse and illustrate the most common threats against contompory information system.

8.8 Explain e-commerce and its importance.

8.9 Distinguish between a virsus, a worm and a Trojan horse.

8.10 What security problems are created by employees?

8.11 Distinguish between general controls and application controls.

8.12 How can management framework or security and control be established?

8.13 Describe the secure socket layer.

8.14 Describe the SET standard.

8.15 Explain IPSec and e-commerce.

8.16 Comment on the issue of e-merchantes versus e-thieves.

CHAPTER 9

Intrusion Detection Systems

Chapter Outline

Intrusion Detection System (IDS) has existed for a long time. Some of the earliest forms included night watchman and guard dogs. In this case, the watchman and guard dogs served two purposes: they provided a means of identifying that something bad was happening and they provided a deterrent to the perpetrator. Most thieves were not interested in facing a dog so they were unlikely to attempt to rob a building with dogs. The same is true for a night watchman. Thieves did not want to be spotted by a watchman who might have a gun or who would call the police.

Burglar and car alarms are also forms of IDS. If the alarm system detects an event that it is programmed to notice (such as the breaking of a window or the opening of a door), lights go on, an alarm sounds, or the police are called. The deterrent function is provided by a window sticker or a sign in the front yard of the house. Cars often have a red light visible on the dash bond to give an indication that an alarm is active.

All of these examples share a single, principle aim: detect any attempt to penetrate the security perimeter of the item (business, building, car and so on) being protected. In the case of building or car the security perimeter is easy to identify. The walls of the building, a fence around the property or the doors and windows of the car clearly defined the security perimeter. Another characteristic that all of these examples have in common is well-defined criteria for what constitutes a penetration attempt and what constitutes the security perimeter.

If we translate the concept of the alarm system into the computer world, we have the base concept of an IDS.

Intrusion detection (ID) is the process of monitoring the events occurring in a computer system or network and analyzing them for signs of intrusions. An intrusion can be defined as any set of actions that attempts to compromise the integrity, confidentiality or availability of resources. IDS are software or hardware products that automate this monitoring and analysis process.

A firewall is a system designed to present unauthorized access to or form a different part of a network architecture. Firewall can be implemented in hardware and software, or a combination of both. Several types of firewall techniques are available. Packet files, application gateway, circuit-level gateway and proxy server. In practice, many firewalls use two or more of these techniques is concert. A firewall is generally considered a first line of defense in protecting private systems or information.

An Intrusion Detection System (IDS) is a next line of defense system. IDS is a device, typically another separate computer, that monitors activity to identify malicious or suspicious events. A model of IDS is shown in Figure 9.1. The components in the figure are the basic elements of an IDS, based on the common Intrusion Detection Framework. An IDS receives raw inputs from sensors. It saves those inputs, analyze them, and take some controlling action.

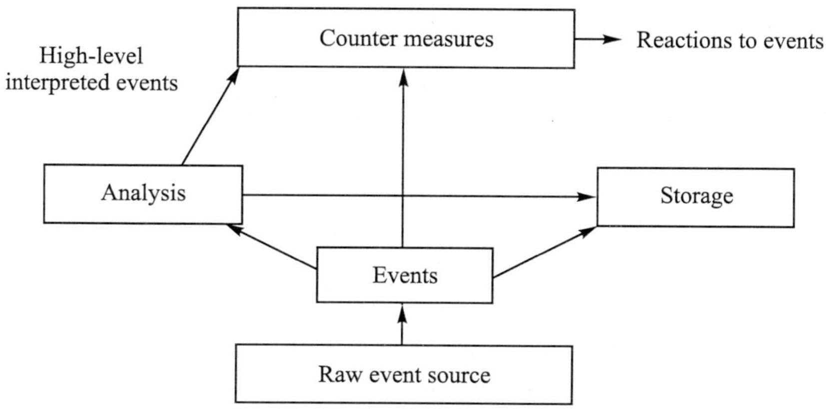

Figure 9.1 Common components of an IDS framework.

Intrusion detection system perform a variety of functions:

(i) Monitoring users and system activity.
(ii) Auditing system configuration for vulnerabilities and misconfigurations.
(iii) Assessing the integrity of critical system and data files.
(iv) Recognizing known attack patterns in system activity.
(v) Identifying abnormal activity through statistical analysis.
(vi) Managing audit trails and highlighting user violation of policy or normal activity.
(vii) Installing and operating traps to record information about intruders.

IDS tools are capable of distinguishing between inside attacks originating from inside the organization (coming from own employees or customers) and external ones (attacks and the thread posed by hackers).

9.1 WHAT IS NOT AN IDS?

Contrary to popular market belief and terminology employed in the literature on intrusion detection systems, not everything falls into this category. In particular, the following security devices are not IDSs.

- Network logging system used, for example to detect complete vulnerability to any denial-of-service (DoS) attack across a congested network. These are network traffic monitoring systems.
- Vulnerability assessment tools that check for bugs and flaws in operating systems and network services (security scanners), for example Cyber Cop Scanner.
- Anti-virus products designed to detect malicious software such as virus, Trojan horses, worms, bacteria, and logic bombs. Although feature-by-feature these are very similar to intrusion detection systems and often provide an effective security breach detection tool.
- Firewalls
- Security/cryptographic systems for example VPN, SSL, S/MIME etc.

Since intrusion detection system deals with hacking breaches, let us take a closer look at these dangerous activity. To assist in the discussion of their taxonomy, some definitions will be helpful although they may vary.

- **Intrusion**—A series of concatenated activities that pose threat to the safety of IT resources from unauthorized access to a specific computer or address domain.
- **Incident**—Violation of system security policy rules that may be identified as a successful intrusion.
- **Attack**—Failed attempt to enter the system (no violation committed).
- **Modeling of intrusion**—A time-based modeling of activities that compose an intrusion. The intruder starts his attack with an introductory action followed by auxillary ones (or evasions) to proceed to successful access; in practice, any attempt undertaken during the attack by any person, for example by the IT resource manager can be identified as a threat.

Generally, attack can be categorized in two areas:

- Passive attack (aimed at gaining access to penetrate the system without compromising IT resources.
- Active attack (results in an unauthorized state change of IT resources).

In terms of the relation intruder—victim, attacks are categorized as:

- Internal, coming from own enterprise's employees or their business partners or customers.
- External, coming from outside, frequently via the Internet.

Attacks are also identified by the source category, namely those performed from internal systems (local network), the Internet or from remote dial—in sources. Now, let us see what types of attacks and abuses are detectable (sometimes hardly detectable) by IDS tools to put them in the ad hoc categorization. The following types of attacks can be identified.

(a) Those related to unauthorized access to the resources (often an introductory steps toward more sophisticated actions):

— Password cracking and access violation.

— Trojan horses.

— Interceptions; most frequently associated with TCP/IP stealing and interceptions that often employee's additional mechanisms to compromise operation of attacked system (for example by flooding); man in the middle attacks.

— Spoofing (deliberately misleading by impersonating or masquerading the host identity by placing forget data in the cache of the named server, i.e. DNS spoofing).

— Scanning ports and services, including ICMP scanning (ping), UDP, TCP stealth scanning TCP that takes advantage of a partial TCP connection establishment protocol etc.

— Remote OS Fingerprinting, for example by testing typical responses on specific packets, addresses of open ports, standard application responses (banner checks), IP stack parameters etc.

— Network packet listening (a passive attack that is difficult to detect but sometimes possible).

— Stealing information, for example disclosure of propriety information.

— Authority abuse; a kind of internal attack, for example, suspicious access of authorized users having odd attributes (at unexpected times, coming from unexpected addresses).

— Unauthorized network connections.

— Usage of IT resources for private purposes, for example to access pornography sites.

— Taking advantage of system weakness to gain access to resources or privileges.

(b) Unauthorized alternation of resources (after gaining unauthorized access):

— Falsification of identity, for example to get system administrator rights.

— Information altering and deletion.

— Unauthorized transmission and creation of data (sets), for example, arranging a database of stolen credit card numbers on a government computer (e.g. the spectacular theft of several thousand numbers of credit cards in 1999).

— Unauthorized configuration changes to systems and network services (servers)

(c) Denial of Service (DoS): Flooding–compromising a system by sending huge amounts of useless information to lock out legitimate traffic and deny services:
- Ping flood—a large number of ICMP packets sent to a broad cast address
- Send mail flood—flooding with hundreds of thousands of messages in a short period of time; also POP and SMTP relaying.
- Distributed a denial of service—coming from a multiple source

Compromising the systems by taking advantage of their vulnerabilities:
- Buffer overflow, for example Ping of Death—sending a very large ICMP (exceeding 64 KB)
- Remote System shutdown

9.2 INFRASTRUCTURE OF IDS

The main task of intrusion detection system is defense of a computer system by detecting an attack and possibly repelling it. Detecting hostile attacks depends on the number and type of appropriate actions, as shown in Figure 9.2. Intrusion prevention requires a well-selected combination of "baiting and trapping" aimed at both investigations of threats. Diverting the intruder's attention from protected resources is another task. Both the real system and a possible trap system are constantly monitored. Data generated by intrusion detection system is carefully examined (this is the main task of IDS) for detection of possible attacks (intrusions)

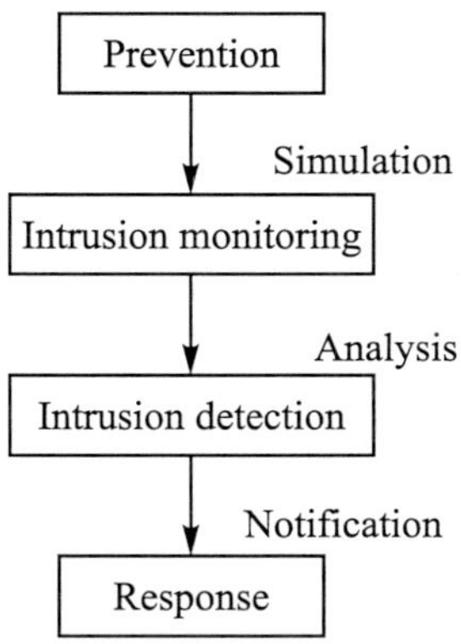

Figure 9.2 Intrusion detection system activities.

Once the intrusion has been detected, IDS issues alert notifying administrators of this fact. The next step is undertaken either by the administrators or the IDS itself by taking advantage of additional countermeasures (specific block functions to terminate sessions, backup system, routing connections to a system trap, legal infrastructure etc.)—following the organization security policy as shown in Figure 9.3. An IDS is an element of the security policy.

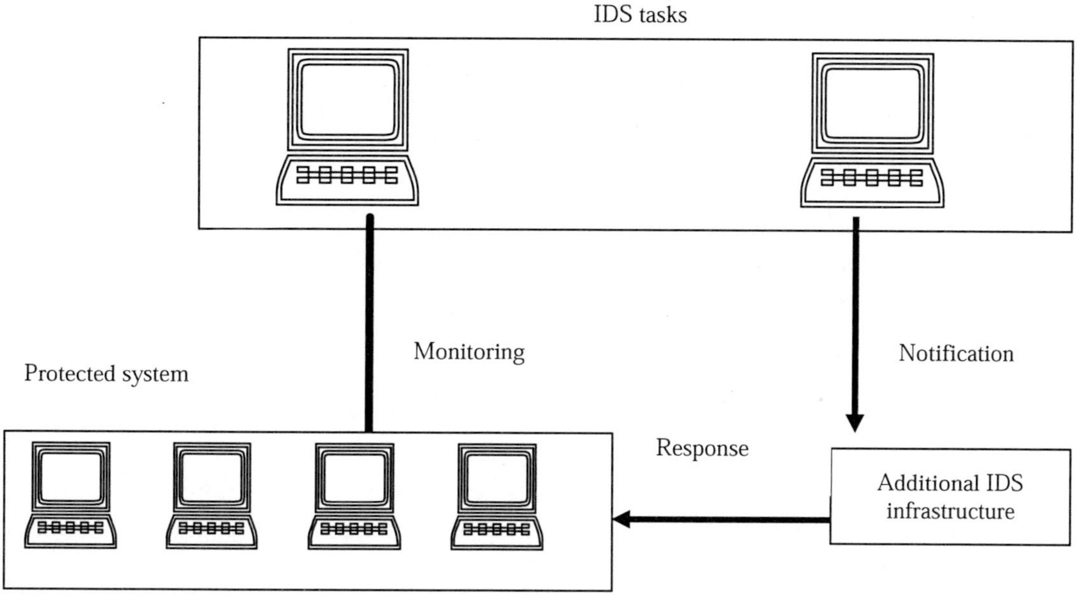

Figure 9.3 Infrastructure of IDS.

Among various IDS tasks, intruder identification is one of the fundamental ones. It can be useful in the forensic research of incidents and installing appropriate patches to enable the detection of future attempts targeted on specified persons or resources.

Intrusion detection may some time produce false alarms, for example as a result of malfunctioning network interface or sending attack description or signature via e-mail.

9.3 CLASSIFICATION OF IDS

Primarily, an IDS is concerned with the detection of hostile actions. This network security tool uses either of two main techniques. The first one, anomaly detection, explores issues in intrusion detection associated with deviations from normal system or user behavior. The second employees signature detection is to discriminate between anomaly or attack patterns (signatures) and known intrusion detection signatures. Both methods have their distinct advantages and disadvantages as well as suitable application areas of intrusion detection.

As we mentioned earlier that IDS is somewhat like a burglar alarm. An IDS watches the activity going on around it and tries to identify undesirable activity. Intrusion detection systems are typically divided into two main categories, depending on how they monitor activity: Host-based and network-based.

- A host-based IDS examines activity on an individual system, such as a mail server, web server or individual PC. It is concerned only with an individual system and usually has no visibility into the activity on the network or systems around it.

- A network-based IDS examines activity on the network itself. It has visibility only into the traffic crossing the network link it is monitoring and typically has no idea of what is happening on individual systems.

Whether or not it is network-or host-based, an intrusion detection system will typically consists of several specialized components working together. These components are often logical and software-based rather than physical and will vary slightly from vendor-to-vendor and product-to-product. Typically, an IDS will have the following logical components:

Traffic collector: This component collects activity/events for the IDS to examine. On a host-based IDS, this could be log files, audit logs or traffic coming to or having a specific system. On a network-based IDS, this is typically a mechanism for copying traffic off the network link basically functioning as a sniffer.

Analysis engine: This component examines the collected network traffic and compares it to known patterns of suspicious or malicious activity stored in the signature database. The analysis engine is the "brains" of the IDS.

Signature database: This signature database is a collection of patterns and definitions of known suspicious or malicious activity.

User interface and reporting: This is the component that interfaces with the human elements providing alerts, when appropriate and giving the user a means to interact with and operate the IDS.

The definition of an intrusion detection system does not include preventing the intrusion from occurring, only detecting it and reporting it to an administrator/operator.

9.4 HOST-BASED IDS

Host-based IDS is designed to only examine activity on a specific host. A host-based IDS is a system that examines log files audit trails and network traffic coming into or leaving a specific host. Host-based IDS can operate in real time looking for activity as it occurs, or batch mode, looking for activity on an activity on a periodic basis.

Host-based IDS can be installed on many different types of machines namely servers, workstations and notebook computers. Host-based IDS is a system of sensors that are loaded on various machines and controlled by central manager. There are five basic types of host-based IDS sensors:

(i) Log analyzers
(ii) Signature-based sensors
(iii) System call analyzers
(iv) Application behavior analyzers
(v) File integrity checkers.

Log analyzers do exactly what its name implies. A process runs on the server and watches the appropriate log files on the system. If a log entry appears that matches some criteria in the host-based IDS sensor process, an action will be taken. The log analyzers are particularly well-adapted to track the activity of authorized users on internal systems. Thus, if an organization is concerned about the system administrators or other authorized users of its systems, a log analyzer could be used to track activity and move the record of this activity to a system beyond the reach of the administrator or user.

Signature-based sensor has a set of built-in security event signatures that are matched against either incoming network traffic or log entries. The difference between the signature-based and log analyzer sensors in the addition of the ability is to analyze incoming traffic. Signature-based systems have the ability to see attacks as they come into the system, so they can give some additional notification of attacks, However, it is likely that the attack will either succeed or fail before the host-based IDS sensor can take action, making these reactive sensors as well. A signature-based sensor is also useful in tracking authorized users on internal systems.

System call analyzers analyze calls between applications and the operating system to identify security events. This type of host-based IDS sensor places a software shim between the operating system and the applications. When an application want to perform an action, the call to the operating system to perform the action is analyzed and compared to a database of signatures.

System call analyzers differ from log analyzers and sensor-based sensors. Log analyzers and sensor-based sensors are able to prevent an action from occurring. In case of system call analyzers, if an application makes a call that matches the signature of a buffer overflow (for example), the sensor can prevent this call from taking place and save the system from being compromised.

Application behavior analyzer's are similar to system call analyzers in that they are implemented as a software shim between the applications and the operating systems. In the case of behavior analyzers, the sensor examines the call to see if the application is allowed to perform the action rather than examine the call to see if it looks like an attack. In configuring such sensors, a list of actions allowed for each application must be created.

File integrity checkers check for changes in files. This is accomplished through the use of a cryptographic check sum or digital signature of the file. The resulting signature will change if any bit in the original file changes (this can include attributes such as creation time and size). The algorithms used for this process were developed to make it extremely difficult for changes to be made that would leave the same signature. Upon the initial configuration of the sensor, each file to be monitored for changes in run through the algorithm to create an initial signature. This number is stored in a secure location. Periodically, each monitored file has its signature recomputed and compared to the original. If they match, the file has not changed. If they do not match, the file has changed. A file integrity checker does not give any indication of an attack, but rather, details the results of the attack.

9.5 NETWORK-BASED IDS

Network-based IDS came along a few years after host-based systems. After running host-based IDS system for a while, many organizations grew tired of the times, energy and expense involved with managing the first generation of these systems. The desire for a "better way" grew along with the amount of malicious activity seen coming across the networks themselves.

A network-based IDS, as the name suggests, focuses on network, traffic—the bits and bytes traveling along the cables and wires that interconnect the systems. Network-based IDSs are typically deployed so that they can monitor traffic in and out of an organization's major links; connections to the Internet, remote offices, partners etc.

Network-based IDS exists as a software process on a dedicated hardware system. The network-based IDS places the network interface card on the system into promiscuous mode, meaning that the card passes all traffic on the network (rather than just traffic destined for the system) to the network-based IDS software. The traffic is then analyzed according to a set of rules and attack signatures to determine if it is traffic of interest. If it is, an event is generated.

At this time, network-based IDS systems are primarily signature-based. This means that a set of attack signatures has been built into the systems and these are compared against the traffic on the wire. If an attack is used that is not in the signature file, the network-based IDS will not pick it up. Network-based IDS systems also have the capability to specify traffic of interest based on the source address, destination address, source port, or destination port. This allows organizations to define traffic to watch for that is outside of the attack signatures.

The most common configuration for a network-based IDS is to use two network interface cards as shown in Figure 9.4. One card is used to monitor a network. This card is placed in a "stealthy" mode so that it does not have an IP address, and therefore, does not respond to incoming connections.

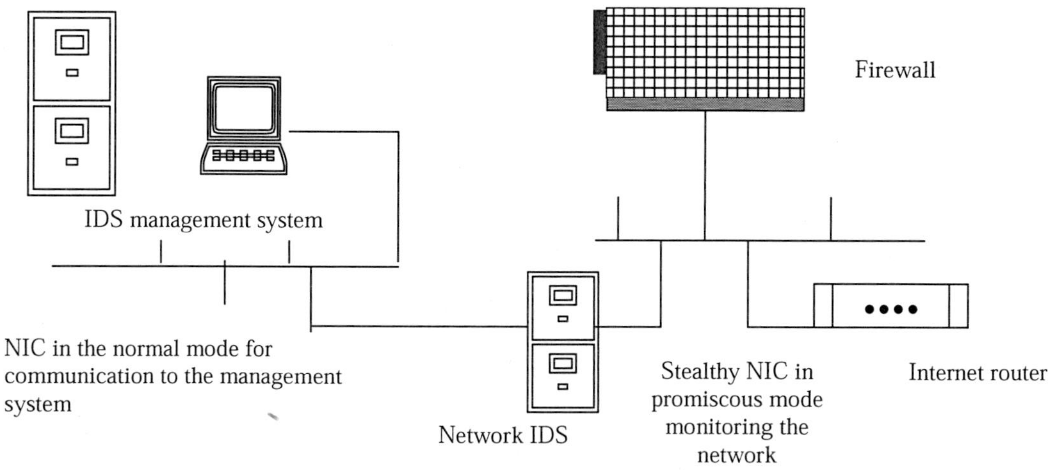

Figure 9.4 Network-based IDS configuration with two network interface cards.

The stealthy card does not have a protocol stack bound to it, so it cannot respond to probes such as a ping. The second card is used to communicate with the IDS management system and to send alarms. This card is attached to an internal network that is not visible to the network being monitored.

9.6 ANOMALY VS SIGNATURE DETECTION

Intrusion detection system must be capable of distinguishing between normal (not security–critical) and abnormal user activities, to discover malicious attempt in time. However, translating user behaviors (or a complete user session) in a consistent security-related decision is often not that simple—many behavior patterns are unpredictable and unclear as shown in Figure 9.5.

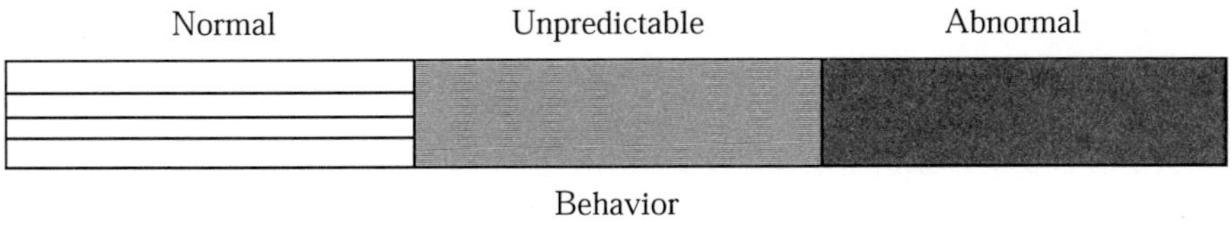

Figure 9.5 Behavior of the user in the system.

In order to classify actions, intrusion detection systems take advantage of the anomaly detection approach, sometimes referred to as behavior-based or attack signatures, i.e. a descriptive material on known abnormal behavior (signature detection), also called knowledge-based.

9.6.1 Normal Behavior Patterns—Anomaly Detection

Normal behavior patterns are useful in predicting bot user and system behavior. Here, anomaly detectors construct profiles that represent normal usage and then use current behavior data to detect a possible mismatch between profiles and recognize possible attack attempts.

In order to match event profiles, the system is required to produce initial user profiles to train the system with regard to legitimate user behaviors. There is a problem associated with profiling: When the system is allowed to "learn" on its own, experienced intruders (or users) can train the system to point where previously intrusive behavior becomes normal behavior. An inappropriate profile will be able to detect all possible intrusive activities. Furthermore, there is an obvious need for profile updating and system training which is a difficult and time consuming task.

Given a set of normal behavior profiles, everything that does not match the stored profile is considered to be a suspicious action, hence these systems are characterized by very high detection efficiency (they are able to recognize many attacks that are new to the system), but their tendency to generate false alarms is generally a problem.

Advantages of this anomaly detection methods are: possibility of detection of novel attacks on intrusions; anomalies are recognized without getting inside their causes and characteristics; less dependence of IDSs on operating environment (as compared with attack signature-based systems); ability to detect abuse of user privileges.

The biggest disadvantages of this method are:

- A substantial false alarm rate. System usage is not monitored during the profile construction and training phases. Hence, all users activities skipped during these phases will be legitimate.
- User behaviors can vary with time, thereby requiring a constant update of the normal behavior profile database (this may imply the need to close the system from time-to-time and may also be associated with greater false alarm rates.
- The necessity of training the system for changing behavior makes a system immune to anomalies detecting during the training phase (false-negative)

9.6.2 Misbehavior Signatures—Signature Detection

Systems processing information on abnormal, unsafe behavior (attack signature-based systems) are often used in real-time intrusion detection system (because of their low-computational complexity).

The misbehavior signatures fall into two categories:

(i) *Attack signatures:* They describe action patterns that may pose a security threat. Typically, they are presented as a time-dependent relationship between series of activities that may be interlaced with neutral ones.

(ii) *Selected text strings:* Signatures to match that text strings which look for suspicious action (for example—calling/etc/password)

Any action that is not clearly considered prohibited is allowed. Hence, their accuracy is very high (low number of false alarms). Typically, they do not achieve completeness and are not immune to novel attacks.

There are two main approaches associated with the signature detection:

(i) *Verification of the pathology of lower layer packets:* Many types of attacks (ping of death or TCP stealth scanning) exploit flaws in IP, TCP, UDP or ICMP packets. With a very simple verification of flags set on specific packets, it is possible to determine whether a packet is legitimate or not. Difficulties may encountered with possible packet fragmentation and the need for reassembly. Similarly, some problems may be associated with the TCP/IP layer of the system being protected. It is well known that hackers use packet fragmentation to bypass many IDS tools.

(ii) *Verification of application layer protocols:* Many types of attacks exploit programming flaws, for example, out of band data sent to as established network connection. In order to effectively detect such attacks, the IDS must have implemented many application layer protocols.

The signature detection methods have the following advantages: very low-false alarm rate, simple algorithms, easy creation of attack signature databases, easy implementation and typically minimal system resource usage.

Disadvantage of this method are:

- Difficulties in updating information on new types of attacks (when maintaining the attack signature database updated as appropriate).
- They are inherently unable to detect unknown, novel attacks. A continuous update of the attack signature database for correction is a must.
- Maintenance of an IDS is necessarily connected with analyzing and patching of security holes, which is a time-consuming process.
- The attack knowledge is operating environment-dependent, so misbehavior signature-based intrusion detection systems must be configured in strict compliance with the operating system (version, platform, application used etc).
- They seemed to have difficulty in handling internal attacks. Typically, abuse of legitimate user privileges is not sensed by the system as a malicious activity (because of the lack of information on user privileges and attack signature structure.

Commercially offered IDS products often use the signature detection method for two reasons. Firstly, it is easier for a given signature to be associated with a known attack abstraction and to assign a name to an attack, e.g. Ping of Death, which is used worldwide (a suitable signature can be attached to the installation version), than the normal behavior of a certain John Brown in an organization. Secondly, the attack signature database must be updated regularly (by adding signatures of newly discovered attacks and exploits), which may create a fairly good source of income for vendors of IDS tools. A database update is at the same time a less cumbersome task than that associated with the change of typical user behavior profiles. In the later case, a temporary closing down of the system may be required, what cannot be tolerated on certain applications.

9.6.3 Parameter Pattern Matching

The third method of intrusion detection is subtler than the two mentioned earlier. It reasons on the fact that system administrators monitor various systems and network attributes (not necessarily targeting security issues). As a rule, information obtained in this way has a constant specific environment. This method involves the use of day-to-day operational experience of the administrators as the basis for detecting anomalies. It can be considered as a special case of Normal Profile Methods. The difference lies in the fact that a profile here is part of the human knowledge.

This is very powerful technique, since it allows intrusions based on unknown type attacks. The system operator can detect subtle change that are not obvious to the operator himself. Its inherent disadvantage is connected with the fact that humans can process and hence understand only a limited portion of information at a time, what means that certain attacks may pass undetected.

9.7 MANAGE AN IDS

Before the decision is made for an organization to implement (commercial or not), the organization should understand what the goals of this program are to be. The level of efforts necessary to properly configure and manage an IDS is a significant and this effort may be better spent performing intrusion prevention (by creating a good security program).

This being said, if an IDS is to be implemented, proper resources are necessary for a successful program. If the goals of the IDS program include the ability to monitor to attacks on a 27/7 basis, staff members will be needed to respond at all hours of the day and night. At the same time, system administrator will be required to work with the security staff to determine if the attack was successful and if so, how the incident should be handled ideally, an incident-handling procedure will be created and tested prior to the implementation of the IDS.

An intrusion detection system can only report what it has been configured to report. There are two components to an IDS configuration. First are the attack signatures that have been programmed in the system. Second are many additional events that the administrator has identified as being of interest. This may include certain types of traffic or certain types of log messages. Assuming that the IDS has been properly configured, there are four types of events that the IDS will show you:

(i) Reconnaissance events
(ii) Attacks
(iii) Policy violations
(iv) Suspicious or unexplained events.

9.8 INTRUSION DETECTION TOOLS

9.8.1 System Intrusion Detection

Assuming you got your system into a reasonable state, you would like to keep it there. Or, at least you would like to know if it is changed.

- **Tripwire**
  - Commercial version, with support, for various flavors of **UNIX** and **Windows.** They also have **Tripwire for Routers** and **Tripwire for Apache Webservers**— http://www.tripwiresecurity.com/
  - A **Linux-only open-source version of the commercial one.** Midway between the commercial and the ASR in terms of features: http://www.tripwire.org/
  - Academic Source Release (ASR), free and unsupported, for **UNIX:**
    - ftp://coast.cs.purdue.edu/pub/tools/unix/Tripwire/
    - ftp://info.cert.org/pub/tools/tripwire/
- **AIDE** (Advanced Intrusion Detection Environment) is a free replacement for Tripwire — http://www.cs.tut.fi/~rammer/aide.html

- **Osiris** is a free replacement for Tripwire—http://www.hostintegrity.com/osiris/
- **Samhain** is a free replacement for Tripwire—http://samhain.sourceforge.net/
- **SNARE (System Ntrusion Analysis and Reporting Environment)** provides host-based intrusion detection for Linux, including graphical configuration, monitoring, and reporting tools: http://www.intersectalliance.com/projects/Snare/index.html
- **BackLog for Solaris** replaces the normal Solaris C2 Audit log collection and reporting sybsystem: http://www.intersectalliance.com/projects/BackLogSolaris/index.html
- **BackLog** is a Windows NT service to collect and process Event Log information: http:/ /www.intersectalliance.com/projects/BackLogNT/index.html
- Also see **Purdue's CERIAS group,** http://www.cerias.purdue.edu/ for current research in this challenging area.

9.8.2 Network Intrusion Detection (NID)

Note carefully that most "network intrusion detection" system really detect an *attack* and not an *intrusion.* Still possibly useful, just make sure you understand what a tool really does.

Also be somewhat skeptical of the real need for NID. If you are running BSD, do you *really* care that someone on the other side of the planet is trying to exploit a risk only found on Microsoft SQL Server? Is it appropriate to waste your time being "warned" about this complete non-risk? Aggressive NID *can* be a denial-of-service attack against yourself.

- **Snort** is a great tool that detects and diagnoses scans, probes, and attempted attacks. http://www.snort.org/
  - **RazorBack** is another graphical tool for analyzing **Snort** logs: http://www.intersectalliance.com/projects/RazorBack/index.html
  - **ACID-XML** analyzes Snort logs and generates XML tables: http://www.maximumunix.org/
- Tools to automatically analyze audit trails for suspicious events.
  - **CMDF,** SAIC, San Diego CA.
  - **NetRanger,** WheelGroup Corp, San Antonia TX.
  - **NetStalker,** Haystack Labs Inc., Austin TX.
  - **ID-Trak,** Internet Tools, Inc., http://www.internettools.com/
  - **GrIDS,** Computer Security Laboratory, University of California, Davis. The most ambitious, still under development.
- Also see **Purdue's CERIAS group,** http://www.cerias.purdue.edu/ for current research in this challenging area.

9.8.3 Freeware Intrusion Detection Tools

Ido Dubrawsky

Firewalls and access control lists were once thought to be the ultimate solutions in preventing network intrusion. Unfortunately, neither tool provides the capability to respond to or provide real-time detection of an intrusion attempt. This is the gap that an Intrusion Detection System (IDS) fills. An IDS provides continual real-time or near-real-time monitoring of a host or a network.

Intrusion detection systems can be divided into two primary categories: network-based and host-based. Network-based IDS tools monitor network traffic on the local LAN, analyzing traffic that "fits" a known signature for a given exploit, and then notifies the proper contacts of its findings. Host-based IDS tools provide detection of an intrusion on a system within the network. Although the ideal case would be to prevent a system intrusion from happening, the fact is that even with a network IDS in place, it is still possible for an attacker to find ways around it. If that happens, a host-based IDS may be able to determine whether the attacker has succeeded in penetrating a given system.

Network-based IDS tools come in two forms: real-time and near-real-time. Real-time network-based IDS report suspicious traffic as soon as it is detected on the wire. Near-real-time IDS work by gathering network traffic and then at a predetermined time interval (such as once an hour) provide an analysis of the previous interval's data. One of the benefits of real-time IDS is the capability to respond to an attack as it is happening. Near-real-time IDS also provide sufficient notification of an attack in progress.

Host-based IDS monitor system files (such as **wtmp/utmp** on UNIX systems) and log files as well as check the integrity of system binaries to determine whether an intrusion has occurred. These types of IDS utilize an agent that resides on the host being monitored.

Some of the more popular network IDS tools include commercial products, such as the Cisco Secure Intrusion Detection System (CSIDS, formerly NetRanger), ISS's RealSecure, and NFR's Network Flight Recorder. Some popular host-based IDS tools include Tripwire (in its commercial form), Symantec's Intruder Alert, and Entercept by Entercept Security Technologies. However, you don't have to spend thousands of dollars to get the benefits of an IDS. Several freeware network and host-based intrusion detection systems are available on the Internet, and they can provide a comparable level of protection as their commercial brethren.

Snort

Snort is defined as a "Lightweight Intrusion Detection System". By definition, lightweight IDS should have a small system footprint, provide for cross-platform support, and easy installation. Snort fits all three requirements. It utilizes the libpcap library (originally developed at Lawrence Berkeley Laboratory) for sniffing traffic and then analyzing the packet payloads.

Snort is configured by command-line options as well as Berkeley Packet Filter Commands. The heart of the Snort detection engine is a set of rules written in a simple language that allows for per packet tests and actions. Snort's detection rules can also be modified and extended by the end user. There are three primary subsystems to Snort:

1. Packet decoder
2. Detection engine
3. Logging and alerting system.

The packet decoder engine's subroutines impose order on the packet data in each of the TCP/IP layers by overlaying data structures on top of the raw network traffic. The detection engine utilizes a two-dimensional linked list of rules to identify network attacks. Finally, the logging and alerting system provides various mechanisms to notify the proper individuals of suspicious activity. The alert mechanisms include sending messages to **syslog**, logging to an alert text file, and using the WinPopup messages through **sambaclient**.

Imposing order on network traffic involves inspecting packets from the data link layer to the application layer, copying each layers data into internal data structures and then setting pointers to these data structures. In essence, Snort copies the essential traffic data into memory and then passes those data structures to the detection engine for analysis.

Snort monitors network traffic looking for predefined suspicious activity. The activity which snorts considers suspicious is contained within a database made up of rules that characterize various attack signatures. Attacks are not just identified based upon traffic to a port, but also by inspecting the packet payloads. For example, in order to recognize a IIS Unicode directory traversal attack, Snort must look at the data being sent to the Web server, which may be the target. However, other attacks may be identified based on destination port. Traffic on a network destined for port 12345 on a host may indicate the presence of the NetBus trojan on that host.

Installation

Snort is currently supported under many operating systems. The main requirement for installing Snort is the presence of the **libpcap** library. Although the **libpcap** library was originally developed at the Lawrence Berkeley Laboratory, development of the library is now done by the "TCPdump Group" (http://www.tcpdump.org). Libpcap-0.6.2 is the most recent version of the **libpcap** library as of this writing. Most BSD-based systems (i.e., FreeBSD, NetBSD, OpenBSD) as well as some Linux systems already come with **libpcap** installed. Be sure to check whether your system already has the **libpcap** software installed.

Snort can be downloaded from the main Snort web site: http://www.snort.org

The software is available as a source-code tarball, RPM package, a Solaris package, a Win32 prebuilt executable in a WinZip file, or as a Win32 source code in a WinZip file. The current version of Snort as of this writing is version 1.7. The installation described here will assume that the source-code tarball is being used to install the Snort software.

The software can be unpacked after it is downloaded:

```
$ gzip -dc snort-1.7.tar.gz | tar -xvf -
snort-1.7/contrib/ACID-0.9.5b9.tar.gz
snort-1.7/contrib/SnortSnarf-111500.1.tar.gz
snort-1.7/contrib/Spade-0922001.tar.gz
...
snort-1.7/README.Spade.Usage
snort-1.7/LICENSE
snort-1.7/cdefs.h
```

To build the software, **cd** to the Snort directory and run the configure script. To determine all of the possible flags that the configure script takes, use the **./configure —help** command. Snort allows for various options including the use of a database back-end for log writes. The databases currently supported include mySQL, postgreSQL, and Oracle. To build the basic version of Snort:

```
$./configure
...(output from the configure script)
$ make
...(output from make), and
$ make install
```

Snort uses a configuration file called **snort.conf**. This sample file provides detailed instructions on how to configure Snort. One of the first things to do when configuring Snort is to set the **HOME_NET** variable to reflect the local network. The network can be specified explicitly using network/mask style notation or it can be specified using a global environment variable **$<intname>_ADDRESS**. For example, if the local network was 192.168.1.1 with a netmask of 255.255.255.252, the configuration would be:

```
var HOME_NET 192.168.1.1/30
```

If the IP address assigned to the system running Snort is provided dynamically by an ISP, you can use the **$<intname>_ADDRESS** to have Snort determine the IP address upon startup. In this case, the **HOME_NET** variable would be similar to:

```
var HOME_NET $ppp0_ADDRESS
```

With the **HOME_NET** variable defined, the next section to configure for Snort are the preprocessors.

Plug-ins

Plug-ins have been available in Snort as of version 1.5. Snort Plug-ins come in two forms: detection plug-ins, and preprocessors. Preprocessors provide for complex functions, such as TCP stream reassembly, IP defragmentation, or HTTP request normalization. Preprocessors are only called once per packet, can directly manipulate packet data, and even call the detection engine directly with their modified data. The IP defragmentation, HTTP request normalization, and portscan preprocessors are active by default in the **snort.conf** file. To activate additional preprocessors, simply uncomment the preprocessor directive in the configuration file.

Detection plug-ins check a single aspect of a packet for a value defined within a rule and determine whether the packet data meets the acceptance criteria. Detection plug-ins can be called multiple times per packet.

The configuration file allows for the definition of the Snort output. This is accomplished using the output plugins. These plug-ins allow for logging to **syslog**, a dedicated file, or a SQL database. The directive for output plug-ins has the form:

```
output <name of plugin>: <configuration options>
```

A typical output would be:

```
output alert_syslog: LOG_AUTH LOG_ALERT
```

This output says to log all Snort output to the **syslog** daemon using the **LOG_AUTH** facility and **LOG_ALERT** level. To log to a dedicated logfile:

```
output log_tcpdump: snort.log
```

It is possible to define new rule types and associate one or more output plug-ins with that type. To have logs go to both the **syslog** facility as well as a dedicated logfile:

```
{
type filelog
output log_tcpdump: snort.log
output alert_syslog: LOG_AUTH LOG_ALERT
}
```

Rule Set Configuration

The final item to configure in the **snort.conf** log is the rule set. The latest Snort rules are available at http://www.snort.org or http://www.whitehats.com. Using all of the rule sets defined in the **snort.conf** at the same time can result in performance degradation. If you're not running a Web server, the Web plug-ins can be disabled in the **snort.conf** file. It is best to tailor the plug-ins to the services you provide. The current default list of rule sets in the **snort.conf** are:

web-lib — For generic web traffic
webcgi-lib — CGI specific exploits
webcf-lib — Coldfusion exploits
webiis-lib — Microsoft IIS specific exploits
webfp-lib — Microsoft FrontPage exploits
webmisc-lib — Miscellaneous web exploits
overflow-lib — Buffer Overflow ruleset
finger-lib — Finger exploit ruleset
ftp-lib — FTP exploit ruleset
smtp-lib — SMTP exploit ruleset
telnet-lib — Telnet exploit ruleset
misc-lib — Miscellaneous exploit (i.e. SNMP, DNS, etc.) ruleset
netbios-lib — NetBIOS exploit ruleset
scan-lib — Monitors for scans (such as Nmap Fingerprinting, etc.)
ddos-lib — Monitors for traffic between DDoS clients and handlers
backdoor-lib — Monitors for traffic to and from backdoor software such as BackOrifice, Netbus, and others
ping-lib — Monitors ICMP traffic
rpc-lib — RPC exploit ruleset

Once the **snort.conf** file is tailored to the specific environment, the Snort program can be started. To start Snort in network intrusion detection mode:

```
# /usr/local/bin/snort -de -l /var/log/snort/packets -c /etc/snort.conf
```

The **-de** flag tells Snort to dump the application layer data as well as log the layer 2 packet header data. The **-l** specifies the directory where suspicious packets should be logged. The **-c** flag specifies the Snort configuration file. (For more information on Snort, refer to Kristy Westphal's articles in the September 2000 and June 2001 issues of *Sys Admin*.)

Shadow

Another network IDS package is the Shadow system. Shadow grew out of another project called the Cooperative Intrusion Detection Evaluation and Response (CIDER) project. While Snort provides for a real-time network intrusion detection capability, Shadow provides a near-real-time intrusion detection. This difference grows out of the fact that Shadow updates its information at a predefined interval (the Shadow documentation speaks in terms of one hour time intervals). On the other hand, Shadow provides for data analysis. This analysis helps reduce false alarms.

One of the advantages of Shadow is that it provides for the ability to look at events over user-defined periods. If, for instance, an admin wishes to see all of the events of the previous 24 hours, Shadow can do that. Shadow comes with various scripts that allow an administrator to look for patterns in network traffic over a given period. One big advantage of the Shadow system over Snort is the ability to have a more distributed IDS model. Shadow allows an administrator to deploy sensors all over the network and have a single analysis system to collect all the logs from the sensors. This provides a single location where all data from the sensors can be viewed.

The Shadow system usually comprises two systems: a sensor and an analyzer. The sensor usually sits between an organization's firewall and its Internet connection. The analyzer is located behind the firewall. The Shadow sensor collects traffic going to and from the organization.

Shadow relies on the **tcpdump** software package (available at: http://www.tcpdump.org) as well as the **libpcap** library (also available at: http://www.tcpdump.org). The Shadow software can be obtained from the Naval Surface Warfare Center's Dahlgren Lab Web site at http://www.nswc.navy.mil/ISSEC/CID. The analyzer then collects the traffic logs from the sensor, examines the data and filters it, and finally, displays the network traffic on a Web page. The Shadow software package comes with a wide variety of filters that can be used to sift through the data collected from the sensor, and identify suspicious events. This helps the administrator remove any traffic that does not match the patterns defined in the filters before it is displayed. This also helps focus the administrator on the key events that may be traversing the network. Also, Perl, **tcpdump**, **libpcap**, **nmap**, **tcpshow**, **sudo**, and **gzip** are required for the Shadow system to work. Secure shell is also necessary. In essence, a Linux- or BSD-based host works very well as either a sensor, an analyzer, or both under Shadow.

Installation

The sensor is a UNIX-based system. Because of the way the Shadow software collects data, the authors recommend a system with at least 32 MB of memory and at least 9 GB of disk space. It is probably more reasonable to have 64 MB of memory and 20 GB of disk space, especially if the sensor will be capturing application layer data as well as the IP headers.

The Shadow software requires a large partition mounted onto the **/LOG** directory of the sensor. After the sensor system is installed, compile and install the **libpcap** library and the **tcpdump** software package:

```
# gzip -dc libpcap-0.6.2.tar.gz | tar -xvf -
... output from tar
# cd libpcap-0.6.2
# ./configure
# make
# make install
```

When **libpcap** is built and installed, **tcpdump** can be built.

```
# gzip -dc tcpdump-3.6.2.tar.gz | tar -xvf -
...output from tar
# cd tcpdump-3.6.2
# ./configure
# make
# make install
```

By default, the configure script looks for the **libpcap.a** library in **../libpcap-0.6.2**, so be sure to build the **libpcap** library in the same parent directory as you build the **tcpdump** software. Also by default, cryptographic support is built into **tcpdump** to help analyze IPSec traffic. With the **libpcap** and **tcpdump** built and installed on the sensor, Shadow can now be installed. Unpack the Shadow tarfile (downloaded from the Naval Warfare Center's Web site mentioned previously):

```
# gzip -dc step.tar.gz
# cd SHADOW-1.6
# ls
accessories/ fetchem.pl* one_day_pat.pl* sites/
analyzer_crontab filters/ one_day_script.pl* sort_and_resolve.pl*
cleanup.pl find_scan.pl* pat_match.pl* strip.pl*
docs/ httpd/ sensor/
```

The files for the sensor can be found in the sensor directory.

```
# ls sensor
README.scripts sensor_crontab start_logger.pl* stop_logger.pl*
gmt.filter sensor_driver.pl std.filter
gmt.ph sensor_init.sh std.ph
```

These files are written in Perl and include a start script, **sensor_init.sh**, which should be installed in **/etc/rc.d/init.d** if the sensor is a Linux system. This file is Linux specific and must be modified to work under a non-Linux system. Copy over the Perl files, the Perl header files, and the filter files to the **/usr/local/logger/sensor** directory on the sensor.

Once the files are installed on the sensor, you will need to install the cronjobs listed in the **sensor_crontab** file into **cron**. The **sensor_crontab** file contains three commands:

/usr/bin/rdate -s time-a.nist.gov,
/sbin/hwclock —systohc (meaningful only on Linux systems), and
/usr/local/logger/sensor/sensor_driver.pl std > /dev/null 2>&1

The last command is the one that starts and stops the **tcpdump** process on the sensor and also manages the **tcpdump** output files in **/LOG**. Because **tcpdump** requires access to the network interface, it will require root privileges. To avoid running **tcpdump**, **suid** root the Shadow **crontab** entries should be put into root's **crontab**.

With the sensor installed, the analysis station can be set up. The **fetchem.pl** script should be installed in **/usr/local/logger** and an hourly cronjob should be added:

7 * * * * /usr/local/logger/fetchem.pl > /dev/null 2>&1

The **fetchem.pl** script will copy over the **tcpdump** output file and place it on the analysis system. It then calls **tcpdump** to read the file and output the information to the Web page. Some of the other scripts in the shadow system include one to clean up the sensor's **/LOG** directory to prevent data loss due to the partition filling up, a script to search through a **tcpdump** log file for signs of port scans, scripts to look for patterns across a whole day's worth of **tcpdump**, output, and scripts to sort the data by source IP, date, and time.

To customize all of these scripts, create a Perl header file, **GENERIC.ph**, in the sites directory. This file should be renamed to the name of your site, because the Perl scripts all require the site name on the command line. This Perl header file contains default values for variables used in all of the other Perl scripts.

Shadow also comes with CGI scripts written in Perl and other files for use on the analyzer. These should be installed in the appropriate places of the web server root directory. After all of this is complete, the Shadow will be ready for production use.

9.8.4 Host-Based Intrusion Detection

Host-based IDS utilize logfile information as well as file signatures to determine whether a system has been compromised. In this category are software packages such as Tripwire, AIDE, SWATCH, FCheck, LIDS, and Psionic Software's LogCheck, PortSentry, and HostSentry packages.

Tripwire

Possibly the original host IDS, Tripwire was originally developed in 1992 by Dr. Eugene Spafford and one of his graduate students, Gene Kim, while at Purdue University's COAST lab. In 1997, Gene Kim led the founding of Tripwire Inc. and licensed the Tripwire source code from Purdue. The original source of Tripwire is still available through Tripwire, Inc. as Tripwire 1.3.1-ASR (ASR stands for Academic Source Release). An open source version of Tripwire (based on the Tripwire 2.0 release) is available from: http://www.tripwire.org in pre-built binary form. The source code to the open source Tripwire can be found at:

http://sourceforge.net/projects/tripwire. The rest of my discussion about Tripwire will focus on the open source version (currently 2.3.1).

Tripwire works by compiling a database of signatures (usually message digests) of specified system files. It then periodically compares the signatures of those specified files against the database. If the calculated signature of a file does not match the signature for that file in the database, a system compromise is assumed and the proper party (usually the systems administrator) is notified.

Installing Tripwire is fairly straightforward. To build the latest version of Tripwire, you will need **gcc** 2.95.2 or better on your system. When you have the software, unpack the gzipped tarfile and **cd** to the **tripwire-2.3.1-2/src** directory to edit the master makefile. This makefile controls the creation of the programs: **Tripwire, twadmin**, **twprint**, and **siggen**. Specify the platform type (Linux or FreeBSD) in the makefile by changing the value of the SYSPRE variable to the appropriate type. Then type "**make release**" to build the above binaries.

By default, Tripwire looks in **/etc/tripwire** for its configuration file, **tw.cfg**, its policy file, **tw.pol**, and its key files, **site.key** and **$(HOSTNAME)-local.key**. The tripwire database is stored in **/var/lib**, and the default report directory is **/var/lib/tripwire/report**.

The first step in setting up Tripwire once it has been built and installed is running it in Database Initialization Mode. This creates a baseline database of the system. It is recommended that database initialization be done in single-user mode, right after the system has been installed so that there is no doubt that the database was created on a fresh, non-compromised system. Once database initialization is done, Tripwire should be periodically run from **cron** in the Integrity Checking Mode. Here, Tripwire scans through the system looking at the files and directories it scanned in Database Initialization Mode. Tripwire calculates the signatures of these files and directories and compares them against the signatures stored in its database. If a difference is found between two signatures for the same file or directory, Tripwire notifies the systems administrator of the problem either through e-mail or in a system logfile.

Another mode found in Tripwire is the Database Update Mode. This mode is used to update the tripwire database in case a patch or a new software package has been added to the system. In this way, the installation of the patch or software will not produce a false alarm because of the change in the signature of the files or directories affected.

AIDE

AIDE stands for Advanced Intrusion Detection Environment, and the software is meant as a free replacement to Tripwire. AIDE originally appeared when Tripwire was a strictly commercial product. AIDE is written in C and provides a variety of features including using a Postgres SQL database as a back-end for storing the hash signatures of the files AIDE is configured to monitor. The AIDE tarfile can be obtained from the Web site: http://www.cs.tut.fi/~rammer/aide.html. To install AIDE and compile:

```
# gzip -dc aide-0.7.tar.gz | tar -xvf -
# cd aide-0.7
# ./configure
# make
# make install
```

To configure the software, edit the **aide.conf** file. There are basically three types of lines in the configuration file: configuration lines, selection lines, and macro lines. Configuration lines have the format of **parameter=value**; selection lines determine which files and directories AIDE will monitor; and macro lines define variables in a similar fashion to Tripwire. AIDE supports md5, sha1, rmd160, and tiger checksums but also permits custom rules to define multiple checksums. AIDE can monitor file or directory permissions, inode changes, size, and other parameters to determine whether a system compromise has occurred.

FCheck

FCheck, written by Michael Gumienny, is another freely available file integrity checker similar to Tripwire and AIDE. FCheck has the capability to monitor files, directories, or even complete filesystems for any additions, deletions, or modifications. It is a Perl program and requires only one other file, the **fcheck.cfg** configuration file. To install FCheck, simply download it from Michael Gumienny's page at: http://www.geocities.com/fcheck2000. The software can run on UNIX or Windows systems. To install, simply untar the gzipped FCheck tarfile, copy the FCheck program and the **fcheck.cfg** configuration file to wherever you want them kept and edit the configuration file to set a few variables. For example:

```
# gzip -dc FCheck_2.07.59.tar.gz | tar -xvf -
fcheck/
fcheck/license
fcheck/fcheck
fcheck/fcheck.cfg
fcheck/README
fcheck/install
# cd fcheck
# cp fcheck fcheck.cfg /usr/local/fcheck
# cd /usr/local/fcheck
# vi fcheck.cfg
```

The **fcheck.cfg** contains information such as which directories, files, and filesystems to monitor, as well as what signature type to use, where to keep the FCheck database, and even how to notify the systems administrator when a discrepancy has been discovered, thus making FCheck a very versatile and flexible tool.

SWatch

SWatch (short for the Simple Watcher) monitors the system logfiles for any suspicious activity. SWatch is written in Perl and relies heavily on regular expression matching. To operate, SWatch requires several Perl modules including Time::HiRes (which will require the Bit::Vector module), Date::Calc, Date::Format, and File::Tail. If these modules are not installed on the system, the SWatch **Makefile.PL** will ask if you want to download the module from CPAN. SWatch can be downloaded from: http://www.stanford.edu/~atkins/swatch and the latest version as of this writing is 3.01. Installing SWatch is straightforward. Once the downloaded tarfile is untarred:

```
# Perl Makefile.PL
# make
# make test
# make install
# make realclean
```

Configuration and customization of SWatch is done through the **swatchrc** file. The SWatch configuration file utilizes two keywords: **watchfor** and **ignore**. The **watchfor** keyword notifies SWatch of a regular expression value to look for in the logfiles it is monitoring; the ignore keyword provides SWatch with the ability to bypass messages containing the expression values defined on that line. The configuration file also contains action values like **echo**, **bell**, **exec**, **pipe**, **mail**, and **write**. These actions can be used to define how Swatch notifies the systems administrators of possible problems.

Logcheck/HostSentry/PortSentry

Logcheck, PortSentry, and HostSentry are products from Psionic Software. They are available from Psionic's Web site: http://www.psionic.com. Each package is designed to perform a unique function. HostSentry reacts to login/logout activity by monitoring the **utmp/wtmp** files on UNIX systems, LogCheck spots problems and security violations by processing information in various system log files on UNIX systems, and PortSentry can detect and respond in real-time to port scans against a target host. Of the three packages, HostSentry is still in the very early alpha stage. Logcheck and PortSentry are mature packages that can be utilized across an organization's network.

HostSentry

HostSentry is written entirely in the Python programming language. If you have Python already installed on the system, you will need to recompile it to activate the **syslog** and **dbm/gdbm** functions. Once Python is installed properly, simply type "**make install**" in the HostSentry directory. This will install the HostSentry software in the **/usr/local/abacus directory**.

To configure HostSentry, edit the **hostsentry.conf** file in **/usr/local/abacus**. There are several variables defining files that HostSentry needs. These must be defined in the **hostsentry.conf**. The file **hostsentry.modules** defines which modules HostSentry will use to generate alerts. The **hostsentry.ignore** file contains a list of users for which HostSentry should never generate an alert. Once all the configuration files have been edited, HostSentry can be started with the simple command:

```
# python hostsentry.py
```

PortSentry

PortSentry uses one of four "stealth" detection modes to identify whether a port scan is occurring. If it detects a portscan, PortSentry can do one of four possible actions:

1. Log the incident via **syslog()**,
2. Drop the "attacking" host by adding its IP address into **/etc/hosts.deny**,

3. Reconfigure the local host to that all traffic from the attacker to the target is then sent to a dead host, or
4. Reconfigure the local host to drop all packets from the attacker using a local packet filter (**ipfw** for BSD, or **ipchains** for Linux).

Installation of PortSentry requires editing the **portsentry_config.h** file. This file contains definitions for the location of the **portsentry.conf** file as well as the TCP_wrappers **hosts.deny** file. It also contains the definition of what **syslog** level and facility PortSentry will use when sending incident information to **syslog**. Once that is done, simply type:

```
# make <OS type>
```

where **<OS type>** is either **linux**, **bsd**, **solaris**, **hpux**, **hpux-gcc**, **freebsd**, **openbsd**, **netbsd**, **bsdi**, **aix**, **osf**, or **generic**. If the PortSentry build succeeds, then type:

```
# make install
```

The default installation directory for PortSentry is **/usr/local/psionic**, but this can be changed. With PortSentry installed, edit the **portsentry.conf** file and define which ports PortSentry will monitor and how it will respond to a suspected port scan. One variable to be especially careful with is the value of **SCAN_TRIGGER**. This variable determines the number of port connects permitted before an alarm is raised. The default is 0, which means react immediately. A value of 1 or 2 will reduce false alarms. It is possible to configure PortSentry in such a way that it will have a "hair trigger" and literally block out every other host on the network, especially if the LAN is a large broadcast domain. PortSentry if very useful when you wish to have the ability to respond to port scan in real-time.

Logcheck

The third software package available from Psionic Software is Logcheck. Logcheck runs automatically and checks system log files for security violations and unusual activity. Logcheck is comprised of a shell script and a C program called logtail. Logtail remembers the last position it read from in a log file and then uses this position on subsequent runs to process any new information. The **logcheck.sh** shell script is the heart of the Logcheck package. The **logcheck.sh** script is run from cron at a predetermined interval. This script calls logtail on the various logfiles it monitors, extracts the events that occurred since the last time it was called, and then mails the report to the systems administrator.

To build Logcheck, simply type:

```
# make <OS type>
```

where **<OS type>** is one of **linux**, **bsdos**, **freebsd**, **sun**, **generic**, **hpux**, or **digital**. This will both build the logtail program as well as install it in **/usr/local/bin**. The **logcheck.sh**, and the configuration files will be installed in **/usr/local/etc**. Once the package is built and installed, add a line to the root crontab launching **logcheck.sh** at a desired interval. For example, to run Logcheck once per hour at five minutes past the hour:

```
5 * * * * /usr/local/etc/logcheck.sh
```

9.8.5 Linux Intrusion Detection System (LIDS)

LIDS is a kernel patch for the Linux kernel as well as an admin tool for enhancing security. LIDS implements a reference monitor and mandatory access control in the Linux kernel. When LIDS is in effect, file access, system and network administration operations, raw device file access, and memory and I/O access can be made impossible, even for root! LIDS not only provides protection but detection as well. Like PortSentry, LIDS can detect port scans against the host and notify the systems administrator. LIDS can also detect other access rule violations as well.

LIDS can also respond to any access rule violation. This response can either be through logging to **syslog** or even terminating a user session. LIDS' flexibility make it ideal as a host intrusion detection and response tool.

The kernel patch and LIDS administrative software can be downloaded from the LIDS web site: http://www.lids.org. Incorporating LIDS into a Linux system requires that the proper kernel patch be applied to the kernel source tree—that is for kernel 2.2.19, the LIDS patch lids-0.9.15-2.2.19 should be used. Once the patch is applied, the kernel should be rebuilt and installed. Also, the **lidsadm program** should be built and the LIDS system configured. After all of that is done, the system should be rebooted with the new kernel and then sealed. A detailed discussion of the LIDS system is beyond the scope of this article, however, the LIDS Web site contains excellent documentation of the LIDS software as well as how to integrate it into a Linux system.

Network IDS and host-based IDS can be used together to help protect a network. The network IDS can monitor all traffic on the network and identify an attack while the host-based IDS can provide administrators with the ability to detect if an attack against succeeded in compromising a host. As stated earlier, a network IDS only knows about attacks that match the patterns in its filters. All network IDS have this "blind spot". This is where a host-based IDS is handy in conjunction with a network IDS. A host-based IDS can remove the blind spot by providing continuous monitoring of hosts so that if an attack succeeds in evading the network IDS, a host compromise can still be detected.

Intrusion Detection Systems come in two predominant forms: host-based and network. These two categories can then be broken down further into real-time and near-real-time response systems. In the real-time category for freeware network IDS is Snort, whereas the near-real-time freeware IDS is Shadow. Under host-based IDS, the real-time packages include the Linux Intrusion Detection System (LIDS), PortSentry, and HostSentry. Near-real-time host IDS include Tripwire, FCheck, AIDE, and Logcheck. Utilizing any of these to protect a network or host provides systems and network administrators with greater capabilities in securing their systems.

Ido Dubrawsky has been working in UNIX and network administration field for nine years. When not working on security, he spends his free time with his wife, Diana, their two children, and their dog, Reidy. He is currently employed by Cisco Systems in the Cisco Secure Consulting Service as a Network Security Engineer.

9.9 IDS PRODUCTS AND VENDORS

These are quite a few intrusion detection products available in the market today, with prices ranging from free to very expensive. Table 9.1 provides a list of some of the IDS products and vendors currently available.

Table 9.1 List of IDS vendors and products

Name	*Product*	*Where to find more information*
Cisco Systems, Inc	Cisco IDS	www.cisco.com
Computer Associates	ETrust	www.ca.com
Enterasys Network	Dragon	www.enterasys.com
Internet Society Systems Inc	RealSecure	www.ISS.net
Intrusion, Inc	SecureNet, Secure Host	www.intrusion.com
Interuvert Networks	Intrushielf	www.interuvert.com
Ipolicy Networks	IpEnforcer	www.ipolicynetworks.com
Netscreen	Netscreen IDP	www.netscreen.com
NFR Security, Inc	NFR	www.nfr.com
Snort	Snort(Free, Open Source)	www.snort.org
Symantec Corporation	Intruder Alert	www.symantec.com
Tipping Point Technologies	Unity One	www.tippingpoint.com
Tripwire, Inc	Tripwire	www.tripwiresecurity.com

REVIEW QUESTIONS

9.1 What is intrusion detection?

9.2 What is firewall?

9.3 What is the difference between intrusion detection and firewall?

9.4 What are the functions performed by intrusion detection system?

9.5 What is not an IDS?

9.6 What is the difference between passive attack and active attack?

9.7 Describe intrusion detection activity.

9.8 Explain intrusion detection infrastructure.

9.9 Describe classification of intrusion detection systems.

9.10 Explain host-based IDS.

9.11 Explain network-based IDS.

9.12 What are the host-based IDS sensors?

9.13 Explain signature-based sensor.

9.14 Explain system call analyzers.

9.15 How system call analyzer differs from log analyzer and signature-based sensor?

9.16 Describe anomaly vs signature detection.

9.17 Describe normal behavior patterns—anomaly detection.

9.18 Describe misbehavior signature—signature detection.

9.19 Write the disadvantages of normal behavior pattern—anomaly detection.

9.20 Write the disadvantages of misbehavior signature—signature detection.

9.21 Explain parameter pattern matching.

9.22 How to manage an IDS?

Chapter 10

Network Security

Chapter Outline

In the past few years government and military organizations have widely adopted LAN, WAN and Internet to take advantage of advancement in technology. Connecting private and internal network to an outside un-trusted network has advantages and disadvantages. There are advantages because the exchange of information is greatly facilitated. There are disadvantages because valuable network resources are exposed to the outside world. The vast connectivity and growing interest in the Internet has also posed several risks.

The common motives for computer crimes could be lure for money, revenge, terrorism, fun, recognition or curiosity. Information systems can be attacked by outsiders who may penetrate a computer system or by insiders who are authorized to use the resources but misuse their authorization. An attacker may disrupt the information system of an organization (active attack) or gain access to its sensitive information (passive attack). Although no direct damage is done in a passive attack, any leak in information could have drastic repercussions for the organization.

In simple words, security has been defined as:

"Protecting information system from unintended access".

Security of information system refers to protecting all components of information system, specifically data, software, hardware and networks. A comprehensive security plan incorporates both security policy and security mechanism.

The factors that influence security policy are:

- Mission of the organization
- Management support
- Risk assessment

- Level of security needed
- Cost effectiveness
- Personal security responsibilities and accountability
- Social factors.

The factors that influence security mechanisms are:

- Network architecture
- Security issues
- Security components
- Factors that make network vulnerable to attack
- Network security administration
- Security awareness and training.

10.1 FUNDAMENTAL CONCEPTS

Here, we discuss objectives, assets, threats, vulnerable, safeguards and potential attacks on information in network environment.

10.1.1 Objectives

Information security has four major objectives as given below:

(i) *Confidentiality:* Ensuring that information is not disclosed or revealed to unauthorized persons.

(ii) *Integrity:* Preventing unauthorized creation or modification of data and maintaining consistency of data.

(iii) *Availability:* Ensuring that authorized users are not denied access to information and resources.

(iv) *Legitimate use:* Ensuring that authorized persons don't use the information in an unauthorized way.

10.1.2 Assets

Assets are valuable resources of the organization that need to be protected. The loss of an asset represents the significant loss to the organization. In some cases, a lost asset can't be replaced, particularly in the case of good will, trust, or confidential research.

Examples of asset categories are: users, application, services, servers, networks, documentation, goodwill, reputations and manpower skills.

10.1.3 Threats

Threat is an impending action by a person or event that poses some danger to an asset. A loss of an asset is caused by the realization of threat. The threat is realized via the medium of vulnerability. Threats come from organization environment, and therefore, can't be totally controlled by the organization. The four major threats are as follows:

(i) *Information leakage:* Information is revealed to unauthorized users which is threat to secrecy.

(ii) *Integrity violation:* Destroying, altering or creating bogus data that results in inconsistency of data.

(iii) *Denial of service:* Using legitimate access rights to disrupt traffic partially or completely.

(iv) *Illegitimate use:* Exploitation of privileges by legitimate users.

The above threats can be realized in different ways as given below:

(a) *Authorization violation:* A person authorized to use resource uses it in an unauthorized manner.

(b) *Bypassing control:* Exploiting system flaws or security weakness in order to acquire higher or unauthorized privileges.

(c) *Eavesdropping:* Leakage of information by monitoring communication channel.

(d) *Interception:* Extracting information from radio frequency or electromagnetic equipment.

(e) *Malicious programs:* Programs that are specially written to damage other programs.

(f) *Masquerade:* Person or entity pretends to be different.

(g) *Traffic analysis:* Leakage of information by analyzing traffic pattern.

(h) *Repudiation:* A person participating in an exchange of information denies having participated.

(i) *Resource exhaustion:* Using resources so as making them unavailable for others. This results in denial or service.

(j) *Social engineering:* Fooling a user to disclosing his password. Learning over someone's shoulder to observe the password and learning about a system by eavesdropping on conversation are also accomplished by social engineering.

10.1.4 Vulnerability

Vulnerability is weakness or absence of safeguards. Unlike threats, vulnerabilities usually exist within the organization. A possible categorization of vulnerability is security policy, procedures, administration, implementation and apathy. Some examples of vulnerability are given in Table 10.1.

Table 10.1 Examples of vulnerability

Category	*Vulnerability*
Security policy	• Granting higher rates to users than required.
Administration	• Circumventing security procedures due to degradation in performance
	• Initializing insecure system
	• Empty root/administrator passwords, particularly during installation.
Implementation	• Failure of protection mechanism
Apathy	• By passing or disabling security procedures for convenience
Procedure	• Duplication of confidential reports
	• Unsafe handling of backups containing confidential reports

A network has many different vulnerabilities, but all derive from an underlying model of computer, communication and information systems security. Threats are raised against the key aspects of security: Confidentiality, integrity, availability, as shown in Table 10.2.

Table 10.2 Network Vulnerabilities

Target	*Vulnerability*
Precursors to attack	—Port scan
	—Social engineering
	—Reconnaissance
	—OS and application fingerprinting
Authentication failures	—Impersonation
	—Guessing
	—Eavesdropping
	—Spoofing
	—Session hijacking
	—Man-in-the middle attack
Programming flaws	—Buffer overflow
	—Addressing errors
	—Parameter modification, time-of-check to time-of-use errors.
	—Malicious active code: Jave Script, Activex
	—Malicious code: virus, worm, Trojan horse
	—Malicious typed code
Confidentiality	—Protocol flaw
	—Eavesdropping
	—Passive wiretap
	—Misdelivery
	—Exposure within the network

(*Contd.*)

Table 10.2 Network Vulnerabilities (*Contd.*)

Target	*Vulnerability*
	—Traffic flow analysis —Cookie
Integrity	—Protocol flaw —Impersonation —Falsification of message —Noise —Web site defacement —DNS attack —Active wiretap
Availability	—Protocol flaw —Transmission or component failure —Connection flooding, e.g. echo-chargen, ping of death —DNS attack —Traffic redirection —Distributed denial of service

10.1.5 Safeguards

Safeguards are physical controls, security policies, security mechanism and procedures that protect assets from threats.

Physical controls: The common physical controls are:

- Physical security
- Personnel security
- Administrative security
- Emanations security.

Security policy: The security policy is a set of rules established by the organization to apply to all security relevant activities. Several levels of security policies have been suggested such as management policy, operational policy and procedural policy.

Authorization is a fundamental part of a security policy. It establishes who is assigned to perform what role. It is carried out using access control mechanism.

Security services: The security mechanisms and procedures, which are main security safeguards are known as security services. The security services are as:

- Identification and authentication service
- Access control service
- Confidentiality service

- Data integrity service
- Non-repudiation service.

10.1.6 Attack

An attack is the realization of threat. Broadly the attackers are hackers, spies, vandals and professional criminals.

Tool: The tools generally used by attacker broadly fall into categories such as physical attack, information exchange, user commands, program and data up.

Actions: Depending on the vulnerability, the attacker can perform different actions such as probe, scan, flood, bypass control, spoof, steal and read/copy/modify.

Target: The targets of attack are generally account, process, data, system components and network.

10.2 IDENTIFICATION AND AUTHENTICATION

Identification and authentication are measures to prevent unauthorized people from entering the system. Identification is the means by which a user provides a claimed identity to the system. The most common form of identification is the user ID. Authentication is the means of establishing vulnerability the validity of a user's claimed identity. The two tasks are generally combined into login process. There are three ways of authenticating a user's identity.

1. Proof by knowledge, e.g. (password)
2. Proof by possession, e.g. (pin card)
3. Proof by property (biometrics), e.g. (fingerprint)
4. Strong Authentication

10.2.1 Proof by Knowledge

A password is associated with each user or entity. Passwords are shared secrets between user and system. To gain access to the system, the user enters a user ID and password. The system authenticates the user if the password matches with that stored in the system corresponding to user ID. There are different ways to store passwords in the system.

Clear passwords: The system stores passwords in clear text in password file, which is 'read' and 'write' protected form users. It provides no protection from system administrator or super-user. Storage of password files on backup media also poses security risk.

Encrypted password: A one-way functions of passwords are stored instead of clear passwords. When a user enters the password, the system computers one-way function of the password and compares with that stored in the system.

Threats on Passwords

Replay: An adversary records the password when it is transmitted in clear text over the communication line. The recorded password is subsequently used to impersonate.

Brute-force attack: An adversary tries all possible passwords, one at a time in the hope to uncover the correct password. The feasibility of the attack depends on number of trials required (password space) and the time taken for each trial.

Password guessing: The adversary guesses the passwords by trying names of user's family members or proper names.

Dictionary attacks: The adversary tries to match the password with dictionary words. Apart from standard dictionary, one line dictionaries of words from foreign languages, specialized words from music and films are also available. Dictionary attack is generally not successful on a single user's password, but it may uncover a weak password to gain access to system.

Safeguards

(a) Password rules are imposed to prevent use of weak passwords such as:
   — Minimum length of passwords and allowable set of characters, uppercase, numeric, non-alphanumeric are specified.
   — The password ageing time frames are specified to enforce change in passwords.
   — Generations of expired passwords being disallowed for use are specified.

(b) A site may use reactive password checking strategy in which password cracker programmer is run periodically to find weak passwords.

(c) A site may use proactive password checking scheme in which the system checks for all allowable password at the time of registration. If the password is weak, it is rejected.

10.2.2 Proof by Possession

A user presents physical token that the system can recognize as belonging to him such as a banking card, smart card or ATM card. Personal Identification Numbers (PINs) are often used along with physical token to identify the user. To prevent brute force attack on PIN, the machine-confiscate the card by locking it and deactivates it if three unsuccessful attempts are made to enter the PIN.

PINs are second level of security in case the card is lost or stolen. However, since users often do not keep the two things separate, theft is a regular occurrence in this case.

10.2.3 Proof by Property

Biometric techniques relay on measuring readily accessible and reliable unique characteristics of users such as fingerprints, written signatures, voice patterns, retinal scans, face geometry and hand geometry. When the system needs to authenticate the user, the system obtains a biometric measure of the user and then compares it against that stored in the database.

10.2.4 Strong Authentication

Passkeys: User password is mapped to a one-way has-function to generate a cryptographic key. Such password-derived keys are known as passkeys. The passkey is used to secure communication link between user and the system.

One time passwords: A special equipment generates a pseudorandom number which is used as password. The password is changed every minute and is time synchronized to the database stored in the computer. This method is expensive because of the additional hardware.

Challenge response protocol: In proof of knowledge method using passwords, the user discloses the passwords to prove the knowledge of the shared secrete. Whereas, in the challenge-response method, a user provides his/her identity by responding correctly to the challenge (question) asked by the verifier. For example, the user and the system agree on function $f = x^2 + 5$. When the user logs in, the system randomly selects a number say 10 and sends it to user, the user has to reply with number 105 for valid authentication.

10.3 ACCESS CONTROL

Once a user or process has been authenticated, the next step in security is to prohibit the user from accessing resources not authorized to it. Access control is a means of enforcing authorization. Access controls are defined by protection rules, which define the possible ways in which subjects and objects are allowed to interact. The subjects, objects and protection rules are described below:

Subject: A subject is an entity, wishing to access and perform operations on objects and to which access authorization are to be granted. The subjects may be processes or users.

Object: An object is an entity to which access must be controlled. An object may be a file, a database, a semaphore, a tree data structure, CPU, memory segment, printer or a site of a network.

Operation: Each object is associated with a set of operations that may be performed on it. For example, for data files, operations could be open, close, create, delete, read and write. Similarly, for program files, the operations could be read, write and execute.

Protection rules: Protection rules govern rules for subject's access to the object. Associated with each (subject, object) pair, is an access right that defines the set of possible operations.

10.3.1 Identity-Based Policies

These are further categorized into individual-based policy, group-based policy and role-based policy. An individual-based policy is expressed in terms of list for each subject stating which subjects may perform which actions on the objects. In group-based policy, several subjects are granted the same permission for one object. In role-based policy, rights are granted to groups of people based on this role in the organization. For example, teller, customer and auditor are granted appropriate rights depending on their roles.

10.3.2 Rule-Based Policy

Rule-based policies are categorized into two categories: Multilevel policy and compartment-based policy.

Multilevel policy operates by assigning to each object a security level from the hierarchy of levels as given below. In compartment-based policy, a set of objects is associated with a named security compartment or category, which isolates them from other sets of objects. Users need to be given a distinct clearance for a compartment to be able to access targets in the compartment.

10.3.3 Security Requirements

The military security evaluation has specified functional requirements for the flow of information as given below:

Security levels: The hierarchical levels are defined such as top secret, confidential and unclassified. Each subject and objects are assigned security level from the same hierarchy. For example, a person having a "Top Secret" clearance is allowed to read documents labeled "Top Secret". A person with "Top Secret" classification can read unclassified documents.

10.3.4 Mandatory Access Control

The security level is assigned to each subject reflecting the degree to which it is trusted not to disclose sensitive information to other objects in accordance with the sensitivity of the information that it contains. Dominance relations have been defined for granting read-only access and write-only access as discussed below:

- Read-only access stipulates that a subject S has read access to object X if security level of S is greater than or equal to security level of X.
- Write-only access stipulates that a subject S has write access to object X if security level of X is greater than that of S.

10.3.5 Discretionary Access Control

In discretionary access control, once a subject has obtained information from the object, it can pass on that information to anyone else without the knowledge of the object's owner.

10.3.6 Labeling

A labeling requirements ensure that all human readable outputs produced by the system is labeled with the security levels of the information attached to the visible output.

10.3.7 Auditing

The auditing requirements ensure that all activities that change the state of the security of the system and actions that might indicate a threat to the integrity of the system are recorded. The records can be analyzed in case the security of the system in compromised.

10.3.8 Convert Channel Analysis

A convert channel is a path not intended for information transfer but subverts security policy of the system. Convert channels are usually based on the ability of one process to indirectly leak information to another process that is carefully monitoring it. Convert channel analysis requirements enforces that the amount of information that can flow through convert channel is limited to an acceptable bandwidth.

10.4 A MODEL FOR NETWORK SECURITY

A model for much of what we will be discussing is captured, in very general terms, in Figure 10.1. A message is to be transferred from one party to another across some sort of Internet. The two parties, who are the principals in this transaction, must cooperate for the exchange to take place. A logical information channel is established by defining a route through the Internet from source to destination and by the cooperative use of communication protocols (e.g. TCP/IP) by the two principals.

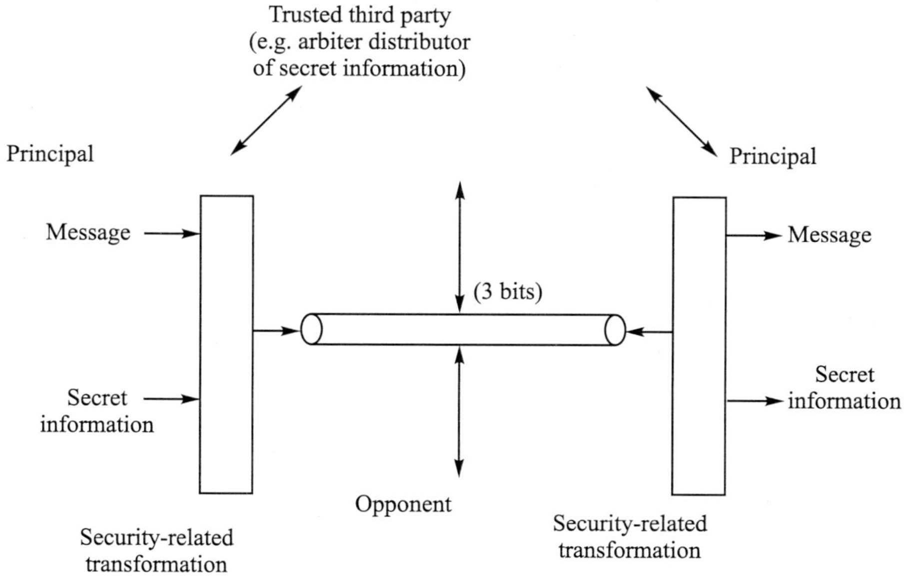

Figure 10.1 Model for network security.

Security aspects come into play when it is necessary or desirable to protect the information transmission from an opponent who may present a threat to confidentiality, authenticity, and so on. All the techniques for providing security have two components:

(a) A security-related transformation on the information to be sent. Examples include the encryption of the message, which scrambles the message so that it is unreadable by the opponent, and the addition of the code based on the contents of the message, which can be used to verify the identity of the sender.

(b) Some secret information should be shared by the two principals and it is hoped, unknown to the opponent. An example is an encryption key used in conjunction with the transformation to scramble the message before transmission and unscramble it on reception.

A trusted third party may be needed to achieve secure transmission. For example, a third party may be responsible for distributing the secret information to the two principals while keeping it from any opponent. Or a third party may be needed to arbitrate disputes between the two principals concerning the authenticity of a message transmission.

This general model shows that there are four basic tasks in designing a particular security service:

1. Design an algorithm for performing the security-related transformation. The algorithm should be such that an opponent cannot defeat its purpose.
2. Generate the secret information to be used with the algorithm.
3. Develop methods for the distribution and sharing of the secrete information.
4. Specify a protocol to be used by the two principals that makes use of the security algorithm and the secret information to achieve a particular security service.

However, there are other security-related situations of interest that do not neatly fit this model. A general model of these other situations is illustrated by Figure 10.2, which reflects a concern for protecting an information system from unwanted access. Most readers are familiar

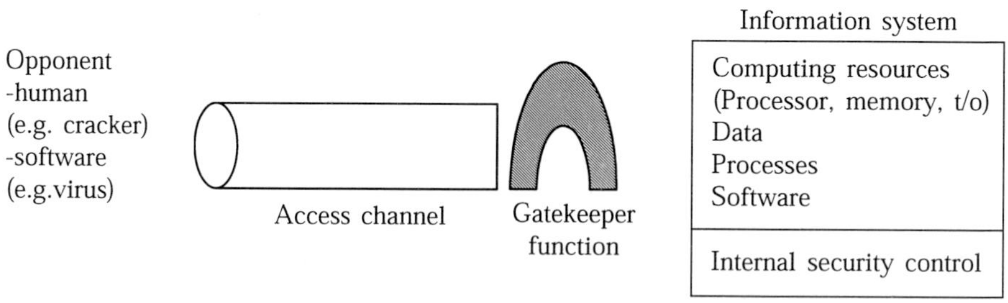

Figure 10.2 Network access security model.

with the concerns caused by the existence of hackers, who attempt to penetrate systems that can be someone who, with no malign Internet, simply gets satisfaction from breaking and entering a computer system. Or, the intruder can be disgruntled employee who wishes to do damage or a criminal who seeks to exploit computer assets for financial gain (e.g. obtaining credit card numbers or performing illegal money transfers).

Another type of unwanted access is the placement in a computer system of logic that exploits vulnerabilities in the system and that can affect application programs as well as utility programs, such as editors and compilers. Two kinds of threats can be presented by programs:

- Information access threats intercept or modify data on behalf of users who should not have access to that data.
- Services threats exploit service flaws in computers to inhibit use by legitimate users.

Viruses and worms are two examples of software attacks. Such attacks can be introduced into a system by means of a diskette that contains the unwanted logic concealed in otherwise useful software. They can also be inserted into a system across a network; this letter mechanism is of more concern in network security.

The security mechanisms needed to cope with unwanted access fall into two broad categories, shown in Figure 10.2. The first category might be termed as a gatekeeper's function. It includes password-based login procedures that are designed to deny access to all but authorized users and screening logic that is designed to detect and reject worms, viruses and other similar attacks. Once access is gained, by either an unwanted user or unwanted software, the second line of defense consists of a variety of internal controls that monitor activity and analyze stored information in an attempt to detect the presence of unwanted intruders.

10.4.1 General Vulnerabilities

Password sniffing: An intruder eavesdrops on a communication line to capture password that are transmitted unencrypted. Having captured a password, the intruder can use it to masquerade as a legitimate user.

The r-commands: The r-tools, where 'r' stands for 'remote' are UNIX system commands to provide services such as remote login—'rlogin', remote shell for executing commands on another computer—'rsh', remote copying—'rcp'. The r-commands, if configured improperly can permit unauthorized access to accounts and commands. The r-tools use the philosophy of trusted host and trusted user. If one host trusts another host, then any user that has the same user name on both hosts can login from one trusted host to another computer without entering a password.

Software flaws: Buffer overflows—a buffer overflow occurs when data is written past the end of memory buffer. The most common reason is that a check is not made on the length of the data before writing into the buffer. In some cases overflow corrupts the execution stack making it convenient for the attacker to execute his code. Shell escapes—string containing shell meta-characters are passed as input arguments to the shell to execute a command. This results in execution of two commands, a desired command and the one requested by attacker. Malicious scripts, scripts containing commands that aid the attacker to exploit a known vulnerability, generally in the operating system.

X window system: The X window system is a network transparent graphical user interface technology for bit-mapped displays. The server program listens and responds to requests from clients. The input activities are relayed to a client as messages called events such as keystrokes, pointer movements or colour changes. A client can request to be notified about all events for any window. As a result, a client can eavesdrop on the activities of any other client. In particular, a client can intercept keystrokes associated with login made from another window on a given display including login passwords.

Denial of service attacks: The attacker renders the system unusable for legitimate users by "hogging" a resource so that it cannot be used by others. The most common form of attack is to flood the target with packets (message overloading) or service overloading. The attack is generally combined with source address spoofing to avoid detection.

10.4.2 Attacks on Internet Protocol

Packet replay: Packet replay refers to recording and retransmission of message packets in the network. Packet replay can be prevented by using timestamps.

IP spoofing: The attacker changes the IP address on message packets to that of another user or host machine. This can be used to masquerade as a trusted host when address-based authentication is used. This lets the attacker execute operating system commands that may compromise the target system's security.

Source routing: Source routing is a routing mechanism whereby the path to a target machine is determined by the source, rather than by intermediate routers. If an attacker has knowledge of some trust relationship between your hosts, source routing can be used to make it appear that the malicious packets are coming from a trusted host.

10.4.3 Attacks on Internet Services

Telnet: The telnet protocol allows a user to log into a remote system and use the system as though the user was sitting at the terminal that was directly connected. Logging into a system using telnet possess a security risk because username and password are transmitted in plain text. It is possible for eavesdropper to capture the password.

File transfer protocol (FTP): FTP allows users to connect to remote system and transfer files back and forth. As with telnet, username and password are transmitted in clear text. Anonymous FTP allows users who do not have an account on the machine to transfer file to and from a specific directory. There is a threat of denial of service attack if too many files transfers are initiated simultaneously.

Trivial file transfer protocol (TFTP): TFTP is a UDP-based file transfer program that is frequently used to allow diskless hosts to boot over the network. TFTP has no user authentication, and therefore, it may be used steal password files.

Attacks through e-mail: E-mail bombing is characterized by repeatedly sending an identical e-mail message to a particular address. E-mail spamming refers to sending e-mail to thousands of users. E-mail spoofing: e-mail bombing/spamming may be combined with e-mail spoofing which alters the identity of the sender making it difficult to detect the originator.

Denial of service: E-mail bombing and spamming to a particular site results in denial of service through loss of network connectivity, system crash and failure of service.

10.5 MALICIOUS SOFTWARE

Malicious software are programs that corrupts other programs or pose severe security threats to system. These fall into two categories. (Those that need a host program and those that are independent. The former are essentially fragments of programs that cannot exist independently of some actual application program, utility, or system program. The latter are self-contained programs that can be scheduled and run by the operating system.)

(a) Host-dependent Programs

Trapdoor: It is secret entry point into a computer program that allows someone who is aware of the trapdoor to gain access without going through normal methods of authentication.

Trapdoors have been used legitimately for many years by programmers to debug and test programs. This usually is done when the programmer is developing an application that has an authentication procedures, or a long setup, requiring the user to enter many different values to run the application. To debug the program, the developer may wish to gain special privileges or to avoid all the necessary setup and authentication. The programmer may also want to ensure that there is a method of activating the program should something be wrong with the authentication procedure that is being built into the application. The trapdoor is code that recognizes some special sequence of input or is triggered by being run from a certain user ID or by an unlikely sequence of events. Trapdoors become threats when they are used by unscrupulous programmers to gain unauthorized access.

Logic bomb: The logic bomb is code embedded in some legitimate program that checks for certain conditions to be met. When the conditions are met, it performs certain unauthorized actions "explodes".

A logic bomb is basically a Trojan horse with a timing device. It initiates some destructive mechanism based on a clock. As an example, a disgruntled employee may create a bomb to execute after leaving the company.

Trojan horse: A program that appears to be useful but contains a hidden code which when executed performs some unwanted functions.

A trojan horse is a program that some unscrupulous person installs on a computer to capture passwords when entered by an unsuspecting user. These programs may perform an ostensibly useful function, but they contain a hidden function that compromises the host system's security. These programs can be installed on a computer when the user leaves the computer logged in when unattended. Individuals may also attempt to capture passwords that are transmitted across communication channels. Some programs and network operating systems send uncrypted passwords that are easy to capture and reuse. Several methods that can thwart this situation are token-based authentication or challenge/response schemes.

The Trojan horse program is the most widely used class of computer attack methods. An attacker must trick the user into running a Trojan horse program by making it appear attractive and disguising its true nature. Some Trojan horse programs are merely designed to destroy data or crash systems, while others allow attackers to steal data or even remotely controls computer systems. Another attacker method closely allied with the Trojan horse is called the backdoor.

After installing a Trojan horse backdoor, attackers often attempt to cover their tracks by manipulating the computer system files. This can be accomplished by deleting or modifying the computer system logs that show all of the processor activity. System log management is important to defend against log-editing attacks.

Trojan mule: A program that simulates the login session and displays login screen that appears genuine. A user unaware of the program enter ID and password. The program records the login session and terminates.

Virus: A self-replicating program that infects other programs, either by modifying them directly or by modifying the environment in which they operate.

There are a number of virus classifications set forth by the National Computer Security Association (NCSA) and the Computer Security Institute (CSI). A brief description of each virus category is as follows:

Boot sector virus: Infact, the master boot record by overwriting the original boot code with an infected version. A boot virus is spread to the disk drive when the system is booted with an infected floppy disk.

File-infecting virus: Infects executable files with com, exe, and ovl extensions. Operating system files are targeted. The original program is often replaced with an infected program.

Macro virus: Includes executable programs that attach themselves to documents created in Microsoft World and Excel. The virus executes and does its damage when the user receives a Word or Excel document and executes a macro.

Multipart virus: Infects boot sectors as well as executable files. They are a real problem because they use stealth and polymorphism to prevent detection.

Polymorphic virus: Changes its appearance to avoid detection by antivirus software. It encrypts itself with a special algorithm that changes every time an infection occurs.

Stealth virus: Attempts to hide itself from the operating system and antivirus software. They stay in memory to intercept attempt to use the operating system and hide changes made to file sizes.

(b) Host-independent Programs

Bacteria: Programs that consume system resources by replicating itself. The program do not explicitly damage any file.

Their sole purpose is replication. A typical bacteria program may do nothing more than execute multiple copies of itself simultaneously on a multiprogramming system. It may create multiple new files, each of which is a copy of the original source file of the bacteria program. Both of these programs may replicate twice, ad infinitum. Bacteria reproduce exponentially, eventually taking up all the processor capacity, memory and disk space, which denies users to those resources.

Worms: Network worm program replicates itself and sends copies from one computer to another across network connections. Once active within a system, it can behave like virus or bacteria. Worms can also implant Trojan horses. In addition to propagation, it usually performs some disruptive or distractive actions.

The primary difference between a worm and a virus is that a worm operates through networks, and a virus can spread through any medium (but usually uses copies program or data files). Additionally, the worm spreads copies of itself as a stand-alone program, whereas the virus spreads copies of itself as a program that attaches to or embeds in other programs.

10.5.1 Safeguards

Scanners: Every virus is constructed from a number of bytes. A unique sequence of these bytes can be selected which can be used to identify the virus. The sequence is known as virus signature. A scanner searches files looking for signature. Most antivirus software are scanners which scans for known signatures. Some kits contain heuristic scanner that scan based on virus behavior.

Integrity checkers: An integrity checker can be used to identify viruses with unknown signatures. This utility calculates checksum for every file that the user chooses and stores the checksums in a file. Periodically, the integrity checker is run again on files and checksums are re-calculated to detect discrepancies.

Behavior blocker: This utility remains in memory and alerts the user of any suspicious activity.

10.6 FIREWALLS

A firewall is a device that filters all traffic between a protected or "inside" network and a less trustworthy or "outside" network. Usually, a firewall runs on a dedicated device; because it is a single point through which traffic is channeled, performance is important, which means non-firewall functions should not be done on the same machine. Because a firewall is executable code, the attacker could compromise that code and execute from the firewalls device. Thus, the fewer pieces of code on the device, the fewer tools the attacker would have by compromising the firewall. Firewall code usually runs on a proprietary or carefully minimized operating system.

The purpose of a firewall is to keep "bad" things outside a protected environment. To accomplish that, firewall implement a security that is specifically designed to address what bad things might happen. For example, the policy might be to prevent any access from outside (while still allowing traffic to pass from the inside to the outside). Alternatively the policy might permit access only from certain places, from certain users, or for certain activities. Part of the challenge of protecting a network with a firewall is determining which security policy meets the needs of the installation.

A firewall is a network access control device that is designed to deny all traffic except that which is explicitly allowed. This definition contrasts with router, which is a network device that is intended to route can be firewall. I will argue that a router can perform some of the functions of a firewall, but one key difference still remains: a router is intended to route all traffic as fast as possible, not to deny traffic. Perhaps a better way to differentiate a router and a firewall is to say that a firewall to flow, while a router is a network device that can be configured to deny certain traffic. In addition to this, firewalls generally provide a more granular level of configuration. Firewalls can be configured to allow traffic based on the service, the IP address of the source or destination, or the ID of the user requesting service. Firewalls can also be configured to log all traffic.

Firewalls have a wide range of capabilities. Types of firewalls include:

- Packet-filtering firewalls
- Stateful inspection firewalls
- Proxy firewalls
- Guards
- Personal firewalls.

10.6.1 Packet-Filtering Firewalls

Packet-filtering firewalls or packet-filtering gateway applies a set of rules to each incoming IP packet and then forwards or discards the packets. The router is typically configured to filter packets going in both directions (from and to the internal network). Filtering rules are based on information contained in a network packet.

- *Source IP address:* The IP address of the system that originated the IP packet.
- *Destination IP address:* The IP address of the system the IP packet is trying to reach.
- *Source and destination transport-level address:* The transport-level (e.g. TCP or UDP) port number, which defines applications such as SNMP or TELNET.
- *IP protocol field:* Defines the transport protocol.
- *Interface:* For a router with three or more ports, which interface of the router the packet came from or which interface of the router the packet is destined for.

The packet filter is typically set up as a list of rules based on matches to fields in the IP or TCP header. If there is a match to one of the rules, that rule is invoked to determine whether to forward or discard the packet. If there is no match to any rule, then a default action is taken.

For example, suppose a company has three LANs at three locations throughout the nation, as shown in Figure 10.3.

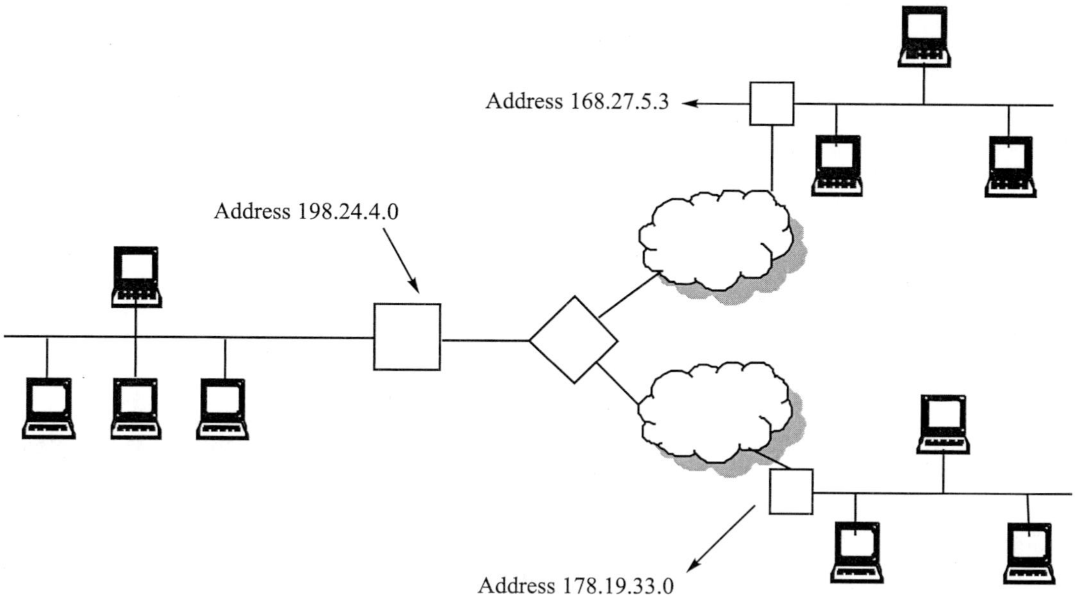

Figure 10.3 Three connected LANs.

In this example, the router has two sides: inside and outside. We say that the local LAN is on the inside of the router, and two connections to distant LANs through the wide area network are on the outside. The company might want communication only among the three LANs of the corporate network. It could use a packet-filtering firewall on the LAN at 198.24.4.0 to allow in only communication destined to the host at 198.24.4.0 and to allow out only communications addressed either to address 168.27.5.3 or 178.19.33.0.

Packet filters do not "see inside" a packet; they block or accept packets solely on the basis of the IP addresses and ports. Thus, any details in the packets data field (for example, allowing certain Telnet commands while blocking other services) is beyond the capability of a packet filter. Packet filter can perform the very important service of ensuring the validity of inside addresses. Inside hosts typically trust other inside hosts for all the reasons described as characteristics of LANs. But the only way an inside host can distinguish another inside host is by the address shown in the source field of a message. Source address in packets can be forged, so an inside application might think it was communicating with another host on the inside instead of an outside forger. A packet filter sits between the inside network and the outside net, so it can know if a packet from the outsider in forging an inside address, as shown in Figure 10.4

A screening packet filter might be configured to block all packets from the outside that claimed their source address was an inside address. In this example, the packet filter blocks all packets claiming to come from any address of the form 198.50.25.x (but course, it permits in any packets with destination 198.50.25.x).

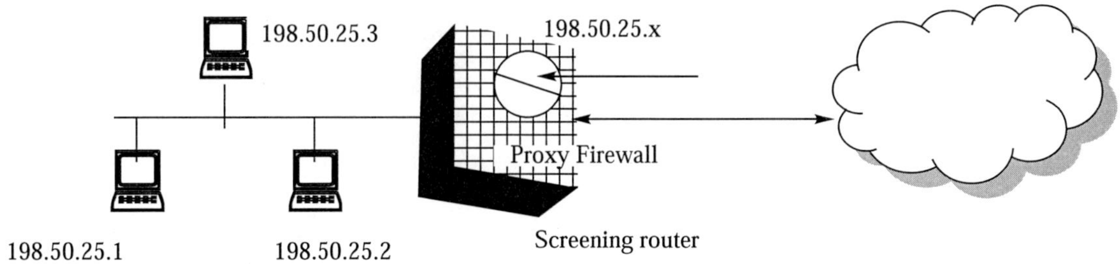

Figure 10.4 Filter screening outside addresses.

10.6.2 Stateful Inspection Firewalls

Filtering firewall work on packets one at a time, accepting or rejecting each packet and moving on to the next. They have no concept of "state" or "context" from one packet to the next. A stateful inspection firewall maintains state information from one packet to another in the input stream.

Policy rules are enforced through the use of packet inspection filters. The filters examine the packets and determine whether the traffic is allowed based on the policy rules and the state of the protocol, this is known as stateful inspection. If the application protocol is running over TCP, state determination is relatively easy as TCP itself maintains state. This means that when the protocol is in a certain state, only certain packets are expected.

One classic approach used by attackers is breaking an attack into multiple packets by forcing some packets to have very shot lengths, so that a firewall will not be able to detect the signature of an attack split across two or more packets (Remember that with the TCP protocols, packets can arrive in any order, and the protocol suite is responsible for reassembling the packet stream in proper order before passing it along to the application). A stateful inspection firewall would track the sequence of packets and conditions from one packet to another to thwart such an attack.

10.6.3 Proxy Firewalls

A proxy firewalls also called an application layer firewalls, is a firewall that simulates the (proper) effects of an application so that the application will receive only requests to act properly. A proxy firewall is a two-headed device: it looks to the inside as if it is the outside (destination) connection, while to the outside it responds just as the insider would.

Policy rules are enforced through the use of proxies. On an application layer firewall, each protocol to be allowed must have its own proxy. The best proxies are those that are built specifically for the protocol to be allowed. For instance, an FTP proxy understand the FP protocol and can determine if the traffic that is flowing is following the protocol and is allowed by the policy rules.

With proxy firewall, all connections terminate on the firewalls as shown in Figure 10.5.

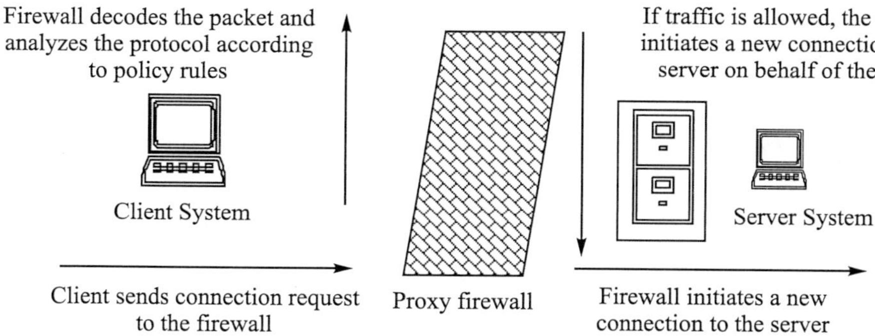

Figure 10.5 Proxy firewalls, proxy connections.

As you can see from the figure a connection starts on the clients system and goes to the internal interface of the firewall. The firewall accepts the connections, analyzes the contents of the packet and the protocol to be used and determines if the policy rules allow the traffic. If so, the firewall initiates a new connection from its external interface to the server system.

Proxy firewall also uses proxies for inbound connections. The proxy on the firewall will receive the inbound connection and process the commands before the traffic is sent to the destination system. In this way, the firewall can protect systems from attacks initiated via applications.

An added benefit of this type of architecture is that it is difficult, if not possible, to "hide" traffic within other services. For example, some system control programs like NetBus or Back office can be configured to use any port that the user wishes. It is possible then to configure them to use port 80 (HTTP). If an application layer firewall with a properly configured HTTP proxy is used, the proxy will not be able to understand the commands coming over the connection, and therefore, the connection will likely fail.

Application layer firewall will have proxies for the most commonly used protocols such as HTTP, SMTP, FTP and telnet. Other proxy may not be available. If a proxy is not available, the protocol cannot be used across the firewall.

The firewall also hides the addresses of the systems behind the application layer firewall. Since all connections originate and terminate on the firewall's interface, internal systems are not directly visible to the outside and thus the internal addressing scheme can be hidden.

10.6.4 Guard

A guard is a sophisticated firewall. Like a proxy firewall, it receives protocol data units, interprets them, and passes through the same or different protocol data units that achieve either the same result or a modified results. The guard decides what services to perform on the user's behalf in accordance with its available knowledge, such as whatever it can reliably know of the (outside) user's identity, previous interactions and so forth. The degree of control a guard can provide is limited only by what is computable. But guards and proxy firewalls are similar enough that the distinction between them is sometimes fuzzy. That is, we can add functionality to a proxy firewall until it starts to look a lot like a guard. Guard activities can be quite sophisticated, as illustrated in the following examples:

(i) A university wants to allow its students to use e-mail up to a limit of so many messages or so many characters of e-mail in the last so many days. Although this result could be achieved by modifying e-mail handlers, it is more easily done by monitoring the common point through which all e-mail flows, the mail transfer protocol.

(ii) A school wants its students to be able to access the worldwide web but, because of slow speed of its connection to the web, it will allow only so many characters per downloaded image (that is, allowing text mode and simple graphics, but disallowing complex graphics, animation, music or the like).

(iii) A library wants to make available certain documents but do support fair use of copyrighted matter, it will allow a user to retrieve only the first so many characters of a document. After that moment, the library will require the user to pay a fee that will be forwarded to author.

(iv) Company wants to allow its employees to fetch files via ftp. However, to prevent introduction of viruses, it will first pass all incoming files through a virus scanner. Even though many of these files will be non-executable text or graphics, the company administrator thinks that the expense of scanning them (which should pass) will be negligible.

Each of these scenarios can be implemented as a modified proxy. Because the proxy decision is based on some quality of the communication data, we call the proxy a guard. Since the security policy implemented by the guard is somewhat more complex, and therefore, more exposed to error. Similar firewalls have fewer possible ways to fail or be subverted.

10.6.5 Personal Firewalls

A personal firewall is an application program that runs on a workstation to block unwanted traffic, usually from the network. A personal firewall can complement work of a conventional firewall by screening the kind of data a single host will accept, or it can compensate for the lack of a regular firewall, as in a private DSL or cable modem connection. Just as a network firewall screens incoming and outgoing traffic for the network, a personal firewall screens traffic on a single workstation. Commercial implementations of personal firewalls include Norton Personal Firewall from Symantec, McAfee Personal Firewall and Zone Alarm from Zone Labs.

The personal firewall is configured to enforce some policy. For example, the user may decide that certain sites, such as computers on the company networks, are highly trustworthy but most other sites are not. The user defines a policy permitting download of code, unrestricted data sharing and management access from the corporate segment but not from other sites. Personal firewalls can also generate logs of accesses, which can be useful to examine in case something harmful does slip through the firewall.

Combining a virus scanner with a personal firewall is both effective and efficient. Typically, users forget to run virus scanners daily, but they do remember to run them occasionally, such as sometimes during the week. With the combination of a virus scanner and a personal firewall, the firewall directs all incoming e-mail to the virus scanner, which examines every attachment the moment it reaches the target host and before it is opened. A personal firewall can provide reasonable protection to clients that are not behind a network firewall.

10.6.6 Limitations of Firewalls

As we have seen, firewalls are not complete solutions to all computer security problems. A firewall protects only the perimeter of its environment against attacks from outsiders who want to execute code or access data on the machines in the protected environment.

Firewall have their limitations, including the following:

- The firewall cannot protect against attacks that bypass the firewall. Internal system may have dial-up capability to connect to an ISP. An internal LAN may support a modem pool that provides dial-in capability for traveling employees and telecommuters.
- The firewall does not protect against internal threats such as a disgruntled employee or an employee who unwittingly cooperates with an external attacker.
- The firewall cannot protect against the transfer of virus-infected programs or files. Because of the variety of operating systems and applications supported inside the perimeter, it would be impractical and perhaps impossible for the firewall to scan all incoming files, e-mail and messages for viruses.
- Firewalls can be "fooled" by source routing or address spoofing. To combat such attacks, firewalls must be configured to support strong identification and authentication techniques.

Commercial firewalls detail are given in Table 10.3.

Table 10.3 Commercial firewalls

Product vendor	*OS/Hardware platforms*	*Contact information*
Actane Controller	SNMPPC	Le California BatD2 2, Rue Jean Andreani 13084 Air-En-Provence CEDEX – 2, France E-mail: L: infor@actane.com
Ascent Secure Access Firewall	PC	One Ascend Plaza 1701 Harbor Bay Parkway Alameda , CA 94502, USA E-mail: info@ascend.com
A Virt Gateway A Virt Gateway Solutions	PC	51 West Centre, Suite 604 Orem, UT 84043, USA E-mail: sales@aVirt.com

(*Contd.*)

Table 10.3 Commercial firewalls (*Contd.*)

Product vendor	*OS/Hardware platforms*	*Contact information*
Cisco IOS Firewall Cisco	Router	170 W. Tasman Dr. San Jose, CA 95134 USA E-mail: info @cisco.com
Cisco PIX Cisco	POS	170 W. Tasman Dr. San Jose, CA 95134 USA E-mail: info@ cisco.com
Citadel Citadel Data Security	UNIX PC	Unit 3, 46 Orange Street Cape Town, 8001 South Africa E-mail:info@cder.com
CONNECT: Firewall Sterling Commence	SUN WS	4600 Lakehurst Court Dublin, OH 43016-2000, USA E-mail: connect@sterling.com
Cyber Guard Cyber Guard Corporation	UNIX WS PC	2000 W. Commercial Blvd. Ft. Lauderdale, FL 33309 USA E-mail: info @cybg.com
Elron Firewall Elron Software	POS	One Cambridge Centre Cambridge, MA 02142 USA E-mail: info@elronsoftware.com
FLUX EF Enhanced Firewall INS Internetworking Systems	Flux OS	INS Gmbh P.O. Box 101312 D-44543 castrop-Rauxel, Germany E-mail: flexo-info@ins.de
IBM Firewall for AIX IBM	AIX WS	IBM Internet Firewall PO Box 12195 Mail Drop B44A/B501 RTP, NC 27709 US E-mail: peter-crotty @vnet.ibm.com
Globe Server Data Quest Information Systems	LINUX PC	7509 Kingstone Pike Suite 313 Knoxville, TN 37919 USA E-mailinfo @ dqisystems.com
Lucent managed Firewall Lucent Technologies	WNT UNIX POS	480 Red Hill Road Middletown, NJ 07748 USA E-mail : firewall @ lucent.com
Nokia IP& VPN Series Nokia Telecommunications	Router	232 Java Drive Sunnyvale, CA 94089 USA E-mail: info @iprg.nokia.com
VCS Firewall The Knowledge Group	UNIX PC	Concorde Road Patchway, Bristol U.K. E-mail: sales@ktgroup.co.uk

POS : Proprietary or embedded operating system
WS : Workstation
PC : Personal computer
WNT : Windows NT

10.7 NETWORK SECURITY TOOLS

Popular open source tools for Network Security are described in Table 10.4.

Table 10.4 Network security tools

Focus area	*Name of the tool and URL*	*Brief description*
Crypta Interfaces	Bouncy cast http://www.bouncycastle.org/	The Bouncy Castle crypto APIs consist of the following: • A light weight cryptography API in Java. • A provider for the JCE and JCA • A clean room implementation of JCE 1.2.1 • A library for reading and writing encoded ASN.1 objects. • Generators for Version 1 and Version 3 X.509 certificates, Version 2 CRLs, and PKCS 12 files. • Generators for Version 2 X.509 attribute certificates. • Generators/Processors for S/MIME and CMS (PKCS 7/RFC 3852), OCS P (RFC 2560), TSP(RFC 3161) and Open PGP(RFG 2440) A signed jar version suitable for JDK 1.4/1.5 and the Sun JCE. The light weight API works with everything from the J2ME to the JDK 1.5.
Secure Sockets Layer	Open SSL http://www.openssl.org/	The open SSL Project is collaborative effort to develop a robust, commercial-grade, full-featured, and open-source tool kit implementing the Secure Sockets Layer (SSL V2/V3) and Transport Layer Security (TSL V1) protocols as well as a full-strength general purpose cryptography library.
Remove Connectivity	Trinux http://www.trinux.sourceforge.net/	Trinux is a ramdisk-based Linux distribution that books from a single floppy or CD-Rom, loads it packages from an HTTP/FTP server, a FAT/NTFS/ISO file system, or additional floppies. Trinux contains the latest versions of popular open source network security tools for port scanning, packet sniffing, vulerability scanning, sniffer detection, packet construction, active/passive OS finger-printing, network monitoring, session-hijacking, backup/recovery, computer forensics, intrusion detection, and more.

(*Contd.*)

Table 10.4 Network security tools (*Contd.*)

Focus area	*Name of the tool and URL*	*Brief description*
		Trinux also provides support for Perl, PHP, and Python scripting languages. Remote Trinux boxes can be managed securely with open SSH.
	Open SSH http://www.openssh.com	Open SSH is a free version of the SSH connectivity tools that technical users of the Internet rely on.Users of telnet, relogin, and ftp may not realize that their password is transmitted across the Internet unencrypted, but it is. Open SSH encrypts all traffic (including passwords)to effectively eliminate eavesdropping connection hijacking, and other attacks. Additionally, Open SSH provides secure tunneling capabilities and several authentication methods and supports all SSH protocol versions. The Open SSH suite replaces relogin and telnet with the ssh program, rcp with scp, and ftp with sftp. Also included is sshd (the server side of the package), and the other utilities like ssh-add, ssh-agent, ssh-keysign, ssh-keyscan, ssh-keygen and sftp-server.
Intrusion Prevention and Detection	Snort http://snort.org	Snort is an open source network intrusion prevention and detection system utilizing a rule-driven language, which combines the benefits of signature, protocol and anomaly based inspection methods. With millions of downloads to date, Snort is the most widely deployed intrusion detection and prevention technology worldwide and has become the defacto standard for the industry.
Network Authentication	Kerberos http://web.mit.edu/kerberos/	Kerberos is a network authentication protocol. It is designed to provide strong, authentication for client/server applications by using secret key cryptography. Kerberos is available in many commercial products as well.
Network Monitoring	nmap http://insecure.org/nmap/	Nmap (Network Mappea) is a free open source utility for network exploration or security auditing. It was designed to rapidly scan large networks, although it works fine against single hosts. Nmap users raw IP packets in novel ways to determine what hosts are available on the network, what services (application name and version) those hosts are offering, what operating

(*Contd.*)

Table 10.4 Network security tools (*Contd.*)

Focus area	*Name of the tool and URL*	*Brief description*
		systems (and OS versions) they are running, what type of packet filters/firewalls are in use, and dozens of other characteristics. Nmap runs on most types of computers and both console and graphical versions are available.
	nagious http://www.nagious.org/	Nagious is an open source host, service and network monitoring program.
Host-Based Firewals	IP Tables http://www.netfilter.org/	Netfilter/IP Tables • Build internet firewalls based on stateless and stateful packet filtering. • Use NAT and masquerading for sharing internet access of you do not have enough public IP addresses. • Use NAT to implement transparent proxies. • Aid the tc and iproute 2 systems used to build sophisticated QOS and policy routers. • Do further packet maintaining (mangling) like altering the TOS/DSCP/ECN bits of the IP header.
	IPFW htttp://www.freebsd.org/doc/en_vs.ISO8859-1/books/handbook/firewalls-ipfw.html	The IPFIRE WALL (IPFW) is a free BSD sponsored firewall software application authored and maintained by Free BSD Volunteer staff members. It uses the legacy stateless rules and a legacy rule coding technique to achieve what is referred to as simple stateful logic.
J2EE Authentication and Authorization	Tomcat http://tomcat.apache.org/	Apache Tomcat is the servlet container that is used in the official Reference Implementation for the Java Servlet and Java Server Pages technologies. The Java Servlet and Java Server Pages specifications are developed by Sun under the Java Community Process.
	JBoss http://labs.jboss.com	An application server within Java that can host business components developed in Java. Essentially, JBoss is an open source implementation of J2EE that relies on the Enterprise JavaBeans specification for functionality.
	Jetty http://jetty.mortbay.org/	Jetty is the HTTP server and servlet container.

(*Contd.*)

Table 10.4 Network security tools (*Contd.*)

Focus area	*Name of the tool and URL*	*Brief description*
Antivirus	Clam AV http://www.clamer.net	Some features of Clam Antivirus Scanner are mentioned below: • Command-line scanner • Fast, multi-threaded daemon • Milter interface for sendmail. • Database updates with support for digital signatures. • Virus Scanner C library. • On-access scanning (Linux® and Free BSD) • Virus database updated multiple times per day (see home page for total number of signatures) • Built in support for RAR (2.0), Zip, Gzip, Bzip2, Tar, MS OLE_2, MS Cabinet files, MS CHM (Compressed HTML), MS SZDD. • Built in support for mbox, maildir, and raw mail files. • built in support for Portable Executable files compressed with UPX, FSG, and Petite.
Antispam	Spam Assasin http://www.spamassasin.apache.org/	Spam Assassin in a mature, widely-deployed open source project that serves as a mail filter to identify spam. Spam Assassin uses uses a variety of mechanisms including header and text analysis, Bayesian filtering, DNS blocklists, and collaborative filtering databases. Spam Assassin runs on a server and filter spam before it reaches your mailbox.

REVIEW QUESTIONS

10.1 Define security. What is difference between active attack and passive attact?

10.2 What are the factors that influence security policy? Explain how mission of organization will influence security policy.

10.3 What are the factors that influence security mechanism?

10.4 What is the importance of assets in an organization?

10.5 What are the major threats to an organization?

10.6 Explain vulnerability. Write major objectives of information security.

10.7 How are assets protected from threats?

10.8 Explain network vulnerabilities with examples.

10.9 What is the difference between identification and authentication? Explain strong-authentication.

10.10 How is user's identity authenticated?

10.11 Describe identity-based policy and rule-based policy.

10.12 Describe a model for network security and explain the role of confidentiality in model.

10.13 How are the functional requirements for military security evaluation specified?

10.14 Discuss attacks on Internet protocol and Internet services.

10.15 Describe malicious software and explain host-dependent programs and host-independent program.

10.16 What is the purpose of firewalls?

10.17 Describe the types of firewalls?

10.18 Explain packet-filtering firewall and its importance.

10.19 Describe stateful inspection firewall.

10.20 What is the difference between proxy firewalls and personal firewalls?

10.21 Explain limitations of firewalls.

10.22 Describe following network security tools:

(i) Kerberos
(ii) nmap
(iii) Snort
(iv) SSL

CHAPTER 11

Wireless Security

Chapter Outline

WIRELESS networks become more and more prevalent throughout the organization. This is because they are inexpensive and easy to set up and work. Some organizations are looking at the costs of upgrading wiring in their buildings and turning to wireless networks as a cost-saving measures. Unfortunately, while wireless technology can provide a cost saving, it opens up some fairly serious security issues for organizations that use them. Various security mechanisms have been proposed to handle the issues of eaves dropping and authentication, but thus, for the standards that have been proposed and many of the implementations of those standards in the products have had serious security vulnerabilities.

Wireless networking is the transmission of packetized data by means of a physical topology not using direct physical links. We will narrow this definition to apply to networks that use radiowaves to carry the signals, over either public or private bands. While there are proprietary applications that use point-to-point technology with narrowband radios and highly-directional antennas, this technology is not common enough to produce any significant research into its vulnerabilities and anything that was developed would have little usefulness. So, we will focus on point-to-multipoint systems, the two most common of which are the Wireless Application Protocol (WAP) and IEEE 802.11. The Wireless Application Protocol is a system developed to send data to small handheld devices such as cellular phones, wireless e-mail handhelds, and PDAs. The 802.11 protocol has been standardized by the IEEE for wireless local area networks.

11.1 WIRELESS APPLICATION PROTOCOL (WAP)

The Wireless Application Protocol (WAP) is a concerted attempt to develop and implement a standard for communicating information between wireless devices and the Internet. WAP has enjoyed fairly broad industry support, with major contributions from manufacturers Ericssion,

Motorola, Nokia, and phone.com (formerly unwired Planet). These principal organizations created the WAP Forum in the summer of 1997. Since its inception, the Forum has grown to well over 350 commercial firms. WAP is promulgated to:

- Improve productivity and service, Real time information is available anytime, anywhere within the organization, greatly enhancing workforce flexibility and mobility.
- Improve infrastructure installation spud, simplicity, and costs. Eliminate pulling cable through conduit walls, and ceilings.

Because wireless technology provides so many advantages (including portability, mobility, timeliness and easy of installation), its disadvantages (including security and limited spectrum availability) are being aggresively attacked by proponents. To judge from actions, the industry agree that the potential rewards of a robust wireless IT capability exceed the risk of information loss and capital investment. A real question remains, however, as to whether WAP was ready for prime time when first deployed in 1999 and 2000. Wireless devices, as desirable as they are, start out with limitations that make them awkward for communications applications:

- Small display capabilities.
- Limited processing capabilities
- Clumsy input devices
- Low bandwidth—only about 9600 bps.

The WAP Forum aimed not at reengineering devices, but at promoting a standard specification for the technology used to develop applications, services, and platforms that operate through wireless communications networks. Such a standard is desirable to eliminate much of the struggle for device interoperability and open up the field to third party developers. It mitigates some device limitations by greatly reducing the bandwidth needed for interoperability. Initial WAP specifications were published on April 30, 1998, for an open, global wireless protocol, based on existing Internet standards such as XML and IP, for all wireless networks. The WAP Forum still projects that WAP will be a best-of-class standard, although not necessarily the only standard, for wireless access to the Internet.

Wireless Application Protocol (WAP) is designed for access to Internet and advanced telephony services from mobile phones. WAP pays proper sensitivity to the constraints of these devices like small display, limited keys on the keypad, no pointer device like mouse etc. Independent of their network, bearer and terminals, a user will be able to access internet and corporate intranet services while mobile. Net-net using WAP, a mobile user will be able to access the same wealth of information from a pocket-sized device as they can from a desktop. Though WAP can be used from a variety of networks. General Packet Radio Service (GPRS) and 3G networks are more suited for these applications.

WAP forum develops standards for application deployment over wireless devices like PDA's (Personal Digital Assistant) and mobile phones. One primary concept that the WAP specifications have adopted is the concept of layering the protocol. Layering is the concept of breaking up the entire communication process into discrete pieces. Each of these pieces handles a specific function. WAP is based on layered architecture. The WAP protocol stack is simulator to the OSI network model. Figure 11.1 illustrates the WAP protocol architecture. These layers consists (from top to bottom) of:

- Wireless application environment (WAE)
- Wireless session protocol (WSP)
- Wireless transaction protocol (WTP)
- Wireless transport layer security (WTLS)
- Wireless datagram protocol (WDP).

Wireless Application Environment (WAE)	Wireless markup language (WML) WML script (included cryptolibrary) Content formats
Wireless Session Protocol (WSP)	Session state management Session suspend/resume
Wireless Transaction Protocol (WTP)	Transaction protocols: Unreliable one way, reliable one way and reliable two ways. Transaction optimization using a transaction window model
Wireless Transport Layer Security (WTLS)	Data integrity, privacy, authentication, denial-of-service protection Security is optional
Wireless Datagram Protocol (WDP)	Common interface to upper layers protocols from many bearers services. Future bearer service support can be added through extensions at this layer
Bearer	CDMA, GSM, bluetooth.

Figure 11.1 WAP protocol architecture.

The primary objective of WAP application environment (WAE) is to provide an interoperable environment to build services in wireless space. WAE provides facilities like:

- User agent: The browser or a client program:
- Wireless markup language (WML): a lightweight markup language, similar to HTML, but optimized for use in wireless devices.
- WML script: A lightweight client side scripting language, similar to Java script in web.
- Wireless telephony application: Telephony services and programming interfaces.
- Content formats: Set of well-defined data formats, including images, phone book records and calendar information.

The Wireless Session Protocol (WSP) provides a consistent interface between two session services (Client and Server). It provides the cooperating client/server application to:

- Establish a reliable session from client to server and close it in orderly manner.
- Agree on a common level of protocol functionality using capability negotiation.
- Exchange content between client and server using compact encoding.
- Suspend and resume the session.

The Wireless Transaction Protocol (WTP) runs on top of a datagram service and provides a lightweight transaction-oriented protocol that is suitable for implementation in "thin" clients. WTP allows for interactive browsing (request/response) applications and supports three transaction classes: unreliable with no result message, reliable with no result message and reliable with one reliable message.

Wireless Transport Layer Security (WTLS) is a security protocol based upon the transport layer security (TLS) protocol. WTLS and TLS are derived from the secure sockets Lauer (SSL) protocol. WTLS is intended for use with the WAP transport protocols and has been optimized for use over narrow-band communication channels. WTLS provides data integrity, privacy, authentication and denial-of-service protection.

The transport layer protocol in the WAP architecture is referred to as the Wireless Datagram Protocol (WDP). The WDP layer operates above the data capable bearer services supported by the various network type general transport service. WDP offers a consistent service to the upper layer protocols of WAP and communicates transparently over one of the available bearer services. While WDP uses IP as the routing protocol, unlike the Web, WAP does not use TCP. Instead, it uses UDP (User Datagram Protocol), which does not require messages to be split into multiple packets, and sent out only to be reassembled on the client. Due to the nature of wireless communications, the mobile application must be talking directly to a WAP gateway, which greatly reduces the overhead required by TCP.

Since the WDP protocols provide a common interface to the upper layer protocols the security, session, application layers are able to function independently of the underlying wireless network. This is accomplished by adapting the transport layer to specific features of the underlying bearer. By keeping the transport layer and the basic features consistent, global interoperability can be achieved using mediating gateways.

WAP gateway acts as a middleware which performs coding and encoding between cellular device and the web server. The WAP gateway can be located either in a telecom network or within a computer data network (an Internet Service Provider). A user from a WAP device requests for a WAP page using a URL, the gateway establishes a connection to the target WAP site. It collects the document from the site. Then the WAP page is "compiled" and converted into binary code. Binary code takes for less space compared to the WML (Wireless Markup Language) source. This realizes quicker delivery. The code is then sent across to the phone or the wireless device over the air. When the phone receives the stream of octets, it "de-compiles" it. The client browser does the reverse operation of compilation by decompiling the binary code. This will allow the client to regenerate the normal WML page and then displays it on the device. The WAP protocols are designed to operate over a variety of different bearer services, including short message, circuit-switched data, and packet data. The bearers offer different levels of quality of service with respect to throughput, error rate and delays.

11.2 WAP SECURITY

Security is optional in the wireless application protocol (WAP). In the WAP specification, security is provided through the Wireless Transport Security (WTLS) layer, which operates directly on top of the transport protocol layer. The goals of the WTLS specification are to provide authentication, integrity confidentiality through the use of certificates and encryption. WTLS specifically addresses limited storage/memory capacity, low bandwidth, low processing capabilities and long/unpredictable latency.

11.2.1 Authentication

Authentication can be performed in several ways, including digital certificates, tokens or simple passwords. A popular way to perform authentication over the Internet is the use of digital certificates, cryptographic messages issued by a trusted third party. The key provided can then be used to encrypt a private shared key to enable ciphered communication. Authentication in WTLS is done with digital certificates; thpe type of certificates supported by WTLS include the native WTS type, X509, and X9.68. Authentication is optional in the WTLS protocol if the client and the server choose to use authentication, then the process begins immediately after the hello exchange. The server will send its certificate and the client will then provide its certificate, if possible, to the server. Once the certificates are processed, authentication is complete.

11.2.2 Integrity

Integrity means reliable information, when you are sending data to and receiving it from a specific place, you want assurances that what you sent in and what was received. This is typically accomplished not by making the information completely invulnerable to replacement or substitution, by giving indications if the information has been tampered with. Typically, this is done by generating checksum of the message with a one-way hash function. When the receiver gets the data, it hashes it as well and compares the two sums, if they match, then the data was unaltered. WTLS implements integrity through the use of message authentication codes (MACs). A MAC algorithm generates a one-way hash of the compressed WTLS data. WTLS supports the MD5 and SHA MAC algorithms. The MAC algorithm is also decided during the WTLS handshake.

11.2.3 Confidentiality

Confidentiality is easy enough in theory: make sure that no one can read the packets that you are sending and receiving but you and the party are intending to talk to. Confidentiality can be assured in several ways, but because wireless affords no control over the physical medium that the packets are traveling over, there is no way to stop another party from listening in. This is especially true with WAP, as central aggregation point for the network is the cellular provider's tower. So given that anyone can listen in, the best way to ensure data confidentiality is through the use of data encryption. Encryption is explained in detail in this book. The simplest explanation is that the data plaintext is encrypted and then sent over the airwaves as ciphertext. The originator and the recipient both have keys to decrypt the data and reproduce the plaintext.

This method of ensuring confidentiality is very common, and if the encryption is well-designed and implemented, then it is very hard for unauthorized users to take captured ciphertext and reproduce the plaintext that created it. WTLS uses a modified version of the TLS protocol, formerly known as SSL (Secure Sockets Layer). The WTLS protocol supports several popular bulk encryption algorithms, including DES, Triple DES (more commonly referred to as 3-DES), RC5 (Rivest Cipher–symmetric–encryption) and IDEA (International Data Encryption Algorithm). They can support 40- and 56-bit keys in case of DES and 3DE, and 40-, 56-, and 128-bit keys in the case of RC5 and IDEA. These algorithms depend on the client and the server having a shared secret.

To establish what this shared secret is, WTLS must carry out a key exchange, exactly as TLS does every time you log into a secure web site. WTLS supports several keys exchange methods: Diffie-Hellman and RSA. Both the algorithm used to encrypt the session and the method of key exchange in WTLS are decided during the WTLS handshake.

11.3 SECURITY ISSUES WITH WTLS

As WTLS implements the three parts of security into the protocol, it also has to allow for the unique requirements of the devices that are using the protocol. The TLS protocol that WTLS is based on is designed around Internet-based computers, machines that have relatively high-processing power, large amounts of memory, and sufficient bandwidth available for Internet applications. The PDAs and other devices that WTLS must accommodate are limited in all these respects. Thus, WTLS has to be able to cope with small amounts of memory and limited processor capacity, as well as long round-trip times that TLS could not handle well. These requirements are the primary reasons that WTLS has security issues. As the protocol is designed around more capable servers than devices, the specification can allow connections with little to no security. Clients with low memory or CPU capabilities cannot support encryption and choosing null or weak encryption greatly reduces confidentiality. Authentication is also optional in the protocol and omitting authentication reduces security by leaving the connection vulnerable to a man-in-the middle-type attack. In addition to the general flaws in the protocol's implementation, there are several known security vulnerabilities, including those to the chosen plaintext attack and alert message truncation attack.

WTLS has number of inherent security problems, such as weak encryption necessitated by the low-computing power of the devices and the network transition that must occur at the cellular provider's network.

11.4 WIRELESS LAN

A Wireless Local Area Network (WLAN) is a grouping of network components connected through electromagnetic waves. Using electromagnetic waves, WLANs transmit and receive data over the air, minimizing the need for wired connections. WLANs are used to augment or replace wired computer networks, adding flexibility, freedom of movement, and easy of installation within the work place.

Today's business relies heavily on the ability to share information and resources. A wide variety of industries have discovered the benefits that WLAN can bring to daily tasks. WLAN provide roaming by allowing users real-time access to information from anywhere in their organization, without having to find a place to connect to the network with a cable or wire, thereby increasing productivity. WLANs also have inherent ease of implementation and affordability as they do not require expensive and time-consuming cable installations, especially in environments that require frequent moves and changes and are difficult to wire. In addition, fewer wires and connectors imply fewer problems for the users and the network managers and, hence, WLANs are highly reliable. WLAN systems can easily be configured and rearranged to accommodate a variety of office settings and a number of users, from small to extensive. WLANs are, therefore, adaptable to the changing environment.

Fixed wireless refers to wireless devices or systems that are situated in fixed locations, such as an office or home as opposed to devices that are mobile, such as cell phones and PDAs. Fixed wireless devices normally derive their electrical power from utility mains, as opposed to portable wireless devices that normally derive their power from batteries. Mobile technology on the other hand allows different wireless systems and bearer technologies (i.e. air interfaces, and modulation schemes) to coexist on the same backhaul and tower infrastructures at the same time, and new ones to be added at any time. However, wireless LANs can be seen as a combination of fixed wireless and mobile wireless services.

For wireless LAN, wireless technology centers around the 802-11x (a, b, g and so on) series of standards (IEEE wireless LAN standard). These standards allow workstations to establish connections up to 54 Mbps with a wireless access point, which is then connected to the wired LAN or directly to another workstation as shown in Figure 11.2. The standards provide for the exchange of authentication information and for the encryption of the information.

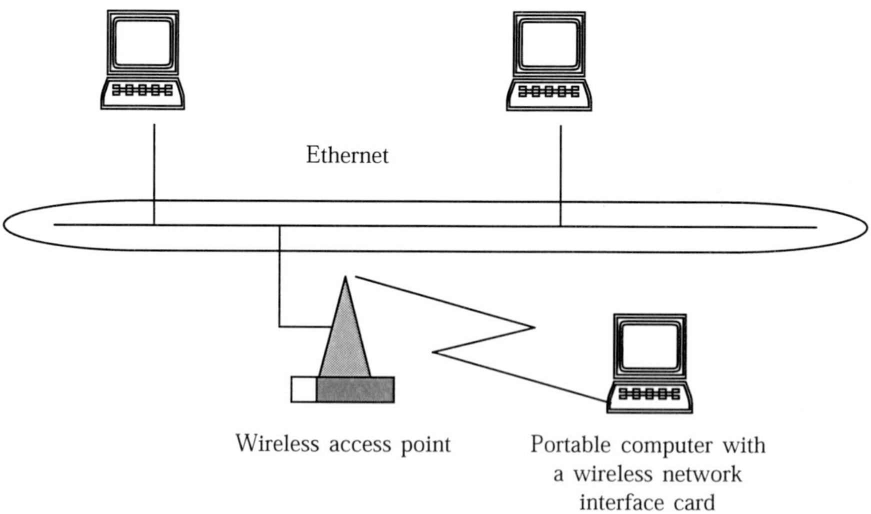

Figure 11.2 Wireless network architecture.

Wireless LANs have two primary components: the wireless network interface card (NIC) in the remote device and the wireless access point (A device connected to the wired local area network that receives signals and transmits signals back to wireless NICs, and that acts as both the base station and bridge for a wireless network). For organizations to effectively use a wireless LAN, there must be sufficient coverage over the areas where the employees or guests will place their computers. Indoors, the range of a typical 802.11x WLAN is approximately 150 feet. Outdoors, the range can be up to 1,500 feet. This means that access point must be placed so that coverage exists in the appropriate areas.

The 802.11 b protocol was an IEEE standard that was ratified in late 1999, launching a range of products that would open the way to a whole new genre of attacks for the attackers and new series of headaches of security administrators everywhere. This was a new standard for sending packetized data traffic over radio waves in the unlicensed 2.4 GHz band. As the products matured and became easy to use and affordable, security experts started to deconstruct the limited security that has been built into the standard. The 802.11 a protocol is another standard for wireless networking, but it works only to improve the speed of the network and does not have security updates. At the time of writing, 802.11 g has just started to appear on the market. This technology has been focused on making traffic in the 2.4 GHz band run at the data rates supported by the 802.11 a's 5 GHz band. While the 802.11 g standard does support a longer WEP key, this does not solve the problems with WEP. What this means is that for security purposes 802.11 b and 802.11 g are virtually identical. The 802.11 b protocol provides the multiple-rate. Ethernet over 2.4 GHz is spread-spectrum wireless. It provides transfer rates of 1 Mbps, 2 Mbps, 5.5 Mbps and 11 Mbps, and typically uses direct-sequence spread spectrum (DSSS). The most common layout is a point-to-multipoint environment with the available bandwidth being shared by all users. Typical range is roughly 100 yards indoors and 300 yards outdoors line of sight.

The 802.11 a protocol is newer, with products only recently becoming available. It operates in the 5 GHz spectrum using Orthogonal Frequency Division Multiplexing (OFDM). Supporting rates of up to 54 Mbps, it is faster brother of 802.11 b. Although it is faster, the higher frequency used by 802.11 a shortens the usable range of devices. The 802.11 g draft uses portions of both of the other standards: it uses the 2.4 GHz band for greater range but uses the OFDM transmission method to achieve the faster 54 Mbps data rates. All these protocols operate in bands that are "Unlicensed" by the "Federal Communications Commission".

All wireless networks can be divided into high-power and long-range wireless WANs; medium-power and medium-range wireless LANs; and low-power and low-range wireless PAN, which has been shown in Figure 11.3.

A WPAN (wireless personal area network) is a personal area network—a network for interconnecting devices centered around an individual persons workplace—in which the connections are wireless. Typically, a wireless PAN uses some technology that permits communication within about 10 meters (33 feet) such as Bluetooth, which was used as the basis for a new standard, IEEE 802.15. Bluetooth is a proprietary open wireless technology standard for exchanging data over short distances (using short wavelength radio transmission) from fixed and mobile devices, creating personal area network with high level of security. A Bluetooth PAN is also called a *piconet.*

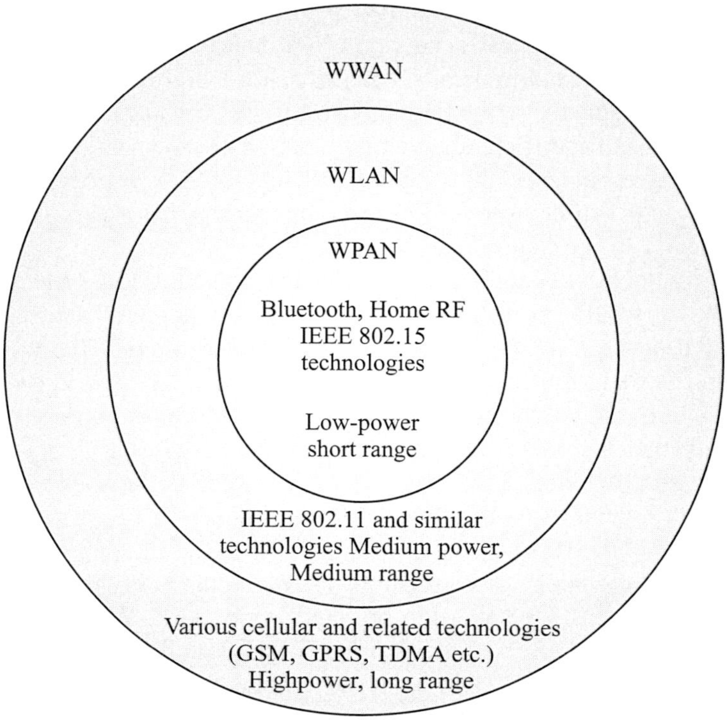

Figure 11.3 Overview of modern wireless network.

11.4.1 WLAN Configuration

There are several ways to configure a WLAN network as explained below:

(i) ***Ad hoc network***

An ad hoc network is a peer to peer network formed by a set of stations within the range of each other that dynamically configure themselves to set up a temporary network. In an ad hoc or independent WLAN as shown in Figure 11.4, two stations communicate directly with each other without an access point. Every mobile station node in a network must be able to act as a router that will pass messages onwards and the nodes must be collectively responsible for network traffic. Also they must be aware which routes are available at a given time. This is a responsibility of the routing protocol used. This type of topology is also referred to as *mesh topology*.

Since ad hoc networks have no formal structures, several nodes try to communicate with one another resulting in the chaos. Several algorithms prevent including a spokesman election algorithm that selects a master from the collective and makes all others slaves. Another possibility is to use broadcast and flooding to all other nodes to establish an addressing scheme.

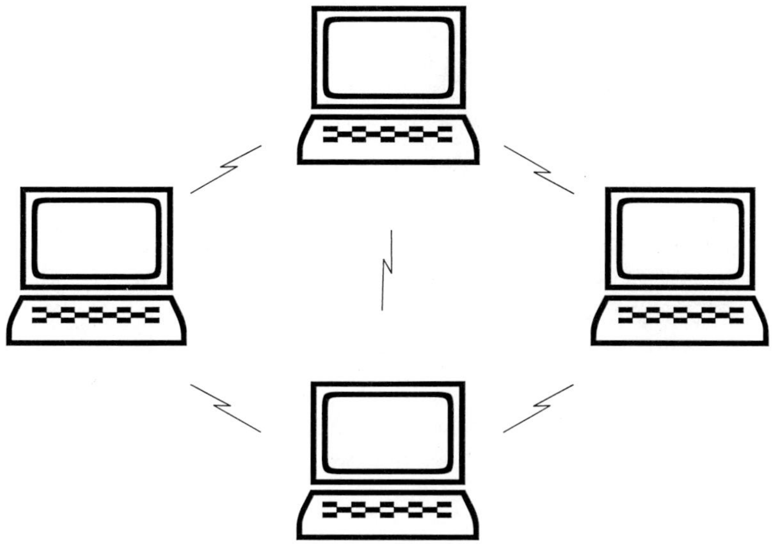

Figure 11.4 Ad hoc WLAN (Mesh configuration).

(ii) ***Infrastructure network***

In an infrastructure network as shown in Figure 11.5, WLAN clients connect to the network through a wireless access point, and then operate as a wired client would. Most corporate wireless LANs operate in infrastructure mode and access the wired network for connections to printers and file servers.

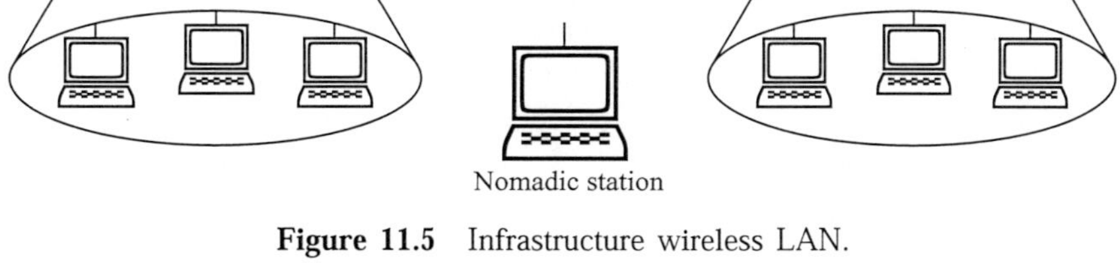

Figure 11.5 Infrastructure wireless LAN.

(iii) ***Hotspots***

A hotspot provides wireless LAN service, free or for a free, from a wide variety of public meeting areas, including coffee shops and airport lounges. To use hotspots, the user's notebook must be configured with the W_i–F_i cutified logo and can send and receive data anywhere within the range of a wireless LAN in the allocated frequency band.

(iv) ***Point-to-point bridge***

A bridge connects two networks. A point-to-point bridge would interconnect two buildings having their own Ethernet networks. For example, a wireless LAN bridge can interface with an Ethernet netwok directly to a particular access point. This may be necessary if there are several devices in different parts of the facility that are interconnected using Ethernet. A wireless bridge, can then, be used to interconnect them wirelessly.

(v) ***Point-to-multipoint bridge***

When connecting three or more LANs that may be located on different floors in a building or across buildings, the point-to-multipoint wireless bridge is utilized. The multipoint wireless bridge configuration is similar to a point-to-point bridge in many ways.

(vi) ***Ethernet to wireless bridge***

An ethernet to wireless bridge as shown in Figure 11.6 connects a single device that has an Ethernet port but not an 802.11 Network Interface Card (NIC), such as a network printer.

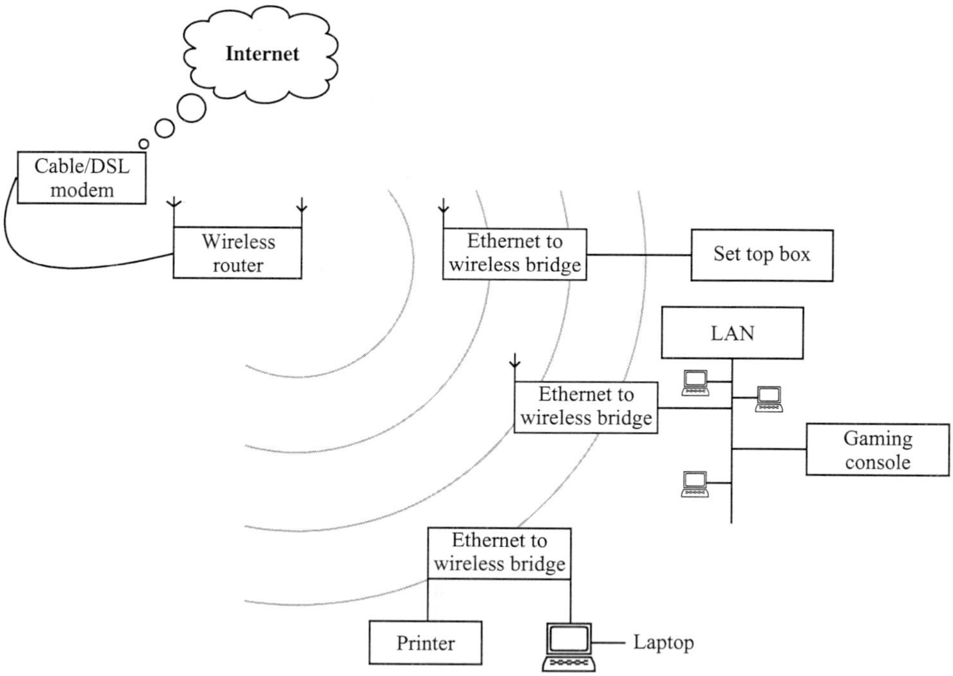

Figure 11.6 Ethernet to wireless bridge.

11.4.2 WLAN Technology Consideration

Manufactures of wireless LANs have a range of technologies to choose from while designing a WLAN solution. Each technology comes with its own set of advantages and limitations.

(i) ***Spread-spectrum***

Most wireless LAN systems use spread-spectrum technology, which is wideband radio frequency technique in which a transmitted signal occupies a bandwidth which is kept much larger than that which is required by a baseband information signal spread-spectrum trades transmission bandwidth for enhanced detectability, interference rejection, and security. In other words, more bandwidth is consumed than that in the case of narrowband transmission, but the tradeoff produces a signal that is, in effect, stronger in strength and thus easier to detect, provided the receiver knows the parameters of the spread-spectrum signal being broadcast. The correlation receiver effectively is integrated over a very wide bandwidth to recover a spread-spectrum signal. The correlator then "spreads" out a narrowband interferer over the receivers total detection bandwidth. Since the total integrated signal density or signal-to-noise ratio (SNR) at the correlators input determines whether there will be interference or not. All spectrum systems have a threshold or tolerance level of interference beyond which useful communication ceases. This tolerance or threshold is essentially the ratio of the RF bandwidth to the information bandwidth.

(a) **Direct-sequence spread-spectrum technology**

Direct-sequence spread-spectrum (DSSS) is a spread spectrum modulation scheme that generates a redundant bit pattern for each transmitted bit. The bit pattern, called a chip or chipping code, enables receivers to filter out signals that do not use the same bit pattern, including noise or interference. The chipping code serves two primary functions:

- It identifies the data so that the receiver can recognize it as belonging to a certain transmitter. The transmitter generates the chipping code and only receivers that know the chipping code can deciper the data.
- The chipping code spreads the data across the available bandwidth as shown in Figure 11.7.

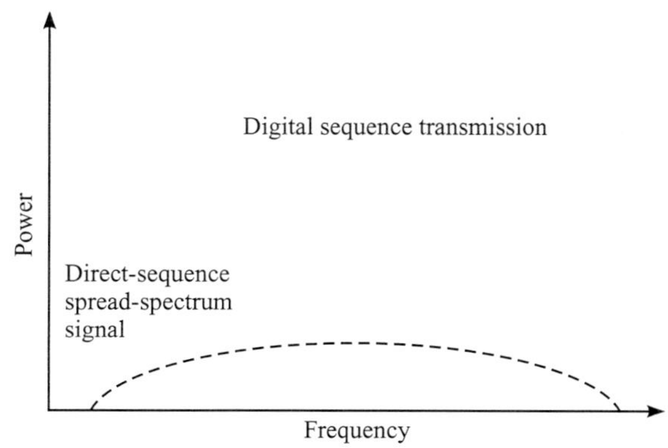

Figure 11.7 Direct-sequence transmission.

Longer chips require more bandwidth but allow a greater probability that the original data can be recovered. Even if one or more bits in the chip are damaged during transmission, technology embedded in the ratio can recover the original data using statistical techniques without the need for retransmission. Figure 11.8 shows the de-spreading of the DSSS signal.

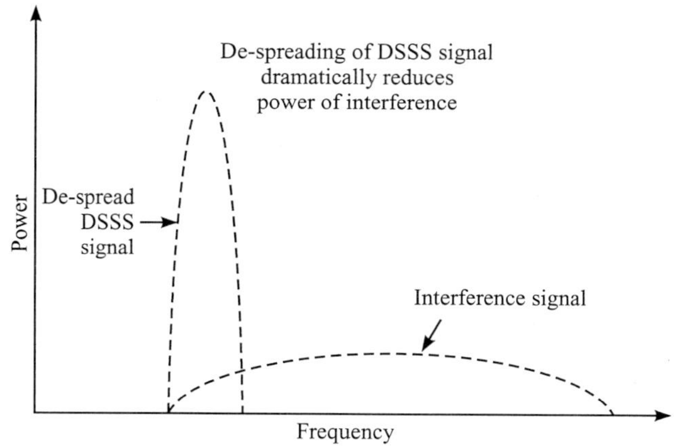

Figure 11.8 De-spreading of DSSS.

The processing gain (bandwidth of the spread-spectrum signal) of 11 (10.4 dB) provides adequate protection against narrowband interference and allows the available frequency band to be segmented into a number of direct sequence centre frequencies. IEEE 802.11 specifies 11 such frequencies. 802.11 b WLANs use DSSS and have higher data throughput than their FHSS counterparts because of the lower overhead of the DSSS protocol.

(b) **Frequency-hopping spread-spectrum technology**

In the frequency-hopping spread-spectrum scheme (FHSS), the frequency of the data transmission is continuously changing (hopping) in time among the 79 frequencies specified in IEEE standard 802.11, as shown in Figure 11.9 the fixed time interval over which data are transmitted on a given frequency is called dwell time. Again, knowing the frequency-hopping spectrum, the frequency synthesizer in the receiver can synchronize with the hopping pattern of the incoming signal and extract the original data. To an unintended receiver, FHSS appears as short-duration impulse noise. FHSS technology uses bandwidth inefficiently in order to assure high security; therefore FHSS systems typically have lower throughput speeds than Direct-sequence spreads-spectrum (DSSS) systems. Slower performing WLAN devices 1 Mbps use FHSS.

Three different sets of frequency-hopping (FH) sequences are defined, each set containing 26 hopping sequences. Use of different FH sequences ensures that adjacent or overlaping BSS (Basic Service Set, Group of stations incl. the AP within an AP transmission range) can operate without interference and maximize throught put of each zone.

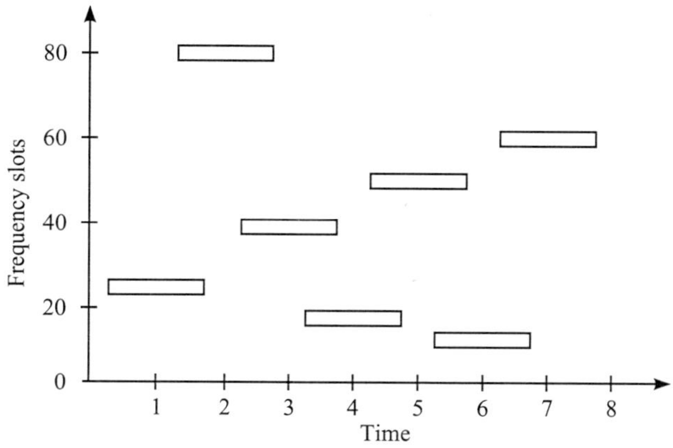

Figure 11.9 Frequency-hopping spread-spectrum.

(c) **Comparison between DSSS and FHSS**

Studies on the system behaviour of DSSS and FHSS have been conducted in recent past with important results as below:

- DSSS provides 11 Mbps capacity links, but it is sensitive technology due to effect of co-location, multipath, near/far, and interference by Bluetooth. The most limiting factor, multipath may be minimized by using the technology for short distance or in a point-to-point application.
- FHSS provides only 3 Mbps capacity links, but it is very robust technology with excellent behaviour in harsh environment characterized by large areas of coverage, multiple co-located cells, noises, multipath, bluetooth presence, etc. The technology allows easy cellular point-to-multipoint deployment, providing excellent reliability.

(ii) ***Orthogonal frequency division multiplexing (OFDM)***

OFDM utilizes multiple carriers (referred to as subcarriers) and is technically not a spread-spectrum technique because the subcarriers remain stationary and are not spread, but it serves the purpose of spreading the signal power over a large band. It does this by breaking the signal into parts and transmitting each of the parts on a different subcarrier at a different centre frequency. Thus, a fast data rate transmission seems to consist of many low data rate transmission, simultaneously, on different frequencies. This effective slowing of the symbol transmission rate, without slowing the actual data transmission rate, makes OFDM resistant to intersymbol interference (ISI) resulting from multipath. In theory, if higher data rates are required, then the signal can be broken up into more parts and transmitted on additional subcarriers, each part still being sent at a slow enough to avoid intersymbol interference.

(iii) ***Narrowband radio technology***

A narrowband radio system transmits and receives information on a specific radio frequency. Narrowband radio keeps the radio signal frequency as narrow as possible just to transmit the information. The listener is required to tune his receiver to that frequency to receive the transmission. Undesirable crosstalk between communication channels is avoided by carefully coordinating different users on different channel frequencies.

A summary of the key characteristics of the most widely used technologies of the wireless LAN is given in Table 11.1.

Table 11.1 Comparison of WLAN technologies

	Infrared		*Spread spectrum*		*Radio*
	Diffused infrared	*Directed-beam infrared*	*Frequency hopping*	*Direct-sequence*	*Narrowband microwave*
Data Rate (Mbps)	1 to 4	1 to 10	1 to 3	2 to 20	10 to 20
Mobility	Stationary/mobile	Stationary with LOS	Mobile	Stationary/mobile	
Range (m)	15 to 60	25	30 to 100	30 to 250	10 to 40
Detectability	Negligible		Little		Some
Wavelength/ frequency	λ: 800 to 900 nm		902 to 928 MHz 2.4 to 2.4835 GHz 5.725 to 5.85 GHz		902 to 928 MHz 5.2 to 5.775 GHz 18.825 to 19.205 GHz
Modulation technique	Ask		FSK	QPSK	FSK/QPSK
Radiated power	—		< 1 W		25 mW
Access method	CSMA	Token Ring, CSMA	CSMA		Reservation ALOHA, CSMA
Licence required	No		No		Yes unless ISM

11.5 WIRELESS LAN SECURITY

Because WLANs use the air as a medium for sending and receiving information (and thus, the signals are open to anyone who happens to be in range), the security of the transmission is very important to the security of the entire system. Without proper protection for the confidentiality and integrity of information as it travels between workstation and access points, there can be little confidence that the information has not been compromised or that the workstations and access points have not been replaced by an intruder.

Security in wireless LANs is addressed primarily through the use of Wired Equivalent Privacy (WEP). WEP uses the RC4 Stream Cipher (Rivest Cipher 4–Symmetric Encryption) to encrypt the data as it is transmitted through the air. This encryption is synchronous and based upon a key shared by the Access point and all the clients using the access point. WEP comes in both 40- and 104-bit key strengths. RC4 is a well-known strong algorithm, and thus, is not easily attacked. The confidential mechanism also relies on RC4.

The authentication service of WEP can be used to authenticate the workstation to the access point. WEP can also use cryptographic authentication mechanism. This mechanism relies on knowledge of a shared secret, which is used with RC4 algorithm, to prove the identity of the workstation to the access point. It does not provide mutual authentication, so the workstation has no proof that the access point is in fact a valid AP on the network. Thus, the use of WEP does not prevent an interception or man-in-the-middle attack as shown in Figure 11.10.

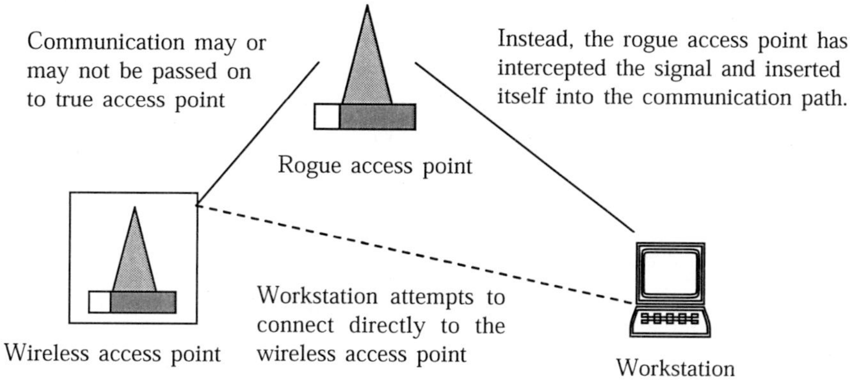

Figure 11.10 Man-in-the-middle attack against WEP.

The WEP protocol specification includes an integrity check on each packet. The integrity check that is used is a cyclic redundancy check (CRC) of 32 bits. The CRC is calculated for each packet before the packet is encrypted and then the data plus the CRC is encrypted and sent to destination, while the CRC is not cryptographically secure, it is protected by the encryption. This might be a sufficiently strong system if the encryption were strong.

11.5.1 Access Point Security

Configuring the AP for security is an important starting point. Ideally, the AP will allow you set a WEP key. Make sure this key cannot be easily guessed. While this will not prevent the cracking of the key, it will make it a little more difficult. If possible, use MAC addresses to limit the workstation that are allowed to connect. This will introduce more management overhead into the entire project, but it can also help to limit some AP detection. Make sure the AP does not broadcast the SSID if possible.

11.5.2 Workstation Security

It is possible to directly attack workstations on a WLAN. If an intruder were to get on the WLAN, sniffers will allow him to identify other workstations. Even if he cannot attack internal systems or eavesdrop on information flowing on the network, he may still be able to attack other workstations.

Protection for workstations on a WLAN is no different than desktops anywhere else. Appropriate antivirus software should be used. If the risk is high, personal firewalls should also be deployed on the workstations.

11.5.3 Safeguarding Wireless LANs

Several levels of security can be implemented to safeguard the wireless LAN. The level of security that is implemented should match the security requirements of the wired LAN and the data that passes over it. Most wireless LAN implementations treat the wireless user as a regular LAN user, and most current wireless LAN devices run the same network applications as wired devices. The same principles that apply to identifying the IC levels of network traffic passing over Bluetooth links or WAP connections apply to wireless LAN connections. The two primary security safeguards that should be considered when implementing wireless LANs are the degree of control that is required in identifying the remote user and the degree to which the network traffic must be safeguard.

REVIEW QUESTIONS

11.1 Explain wireless network and its application.

11.2 What is the purpose of wireless application protocol?

11.3 Explain WAP protocol architecture.

11.4 What is the difference between wireless session protocol and wireless transaction protocol?

11.5 How wireless transport layer security (WTLS) is important for WAP protocol architecture?

11.6 Describe wireless datagram protocol and its importance.

11.7 Describe WAP security.

11.8 What are the security issues with WTLS?

11.9 Explain wireless LAN security.

11.10 What is access point? Explain access point security.

11.11 How to protect workstation on a WLAN?

11.12 How to safeguard wireless LANs?

11.13 Describe WLAN configuration.

11.14 What is the difference between ad hoc network and infrastructure network?

11.15 Differentiate the spread-spectrum technology from frequency-hopping spread-spectrum technology.

CHAPTER 12

Web Security

Chapter Outline

The World Wide Web (the web) is at the heart of the explosion in the business use of the Net. The web is a system with universally accepted standards for storing, retrieving, formatting, and displaying information using a client/server architecture. The web combines text, hypermedia, graphics and sound. It can handle all types of digital communication, making it easy to link resources that are half-a-world apart. The web uses graphical user interfaces for easy viewing. It is based on a standard hypertext language called Hypertext Markup Language (HTML), which formats documents and incorporates dynamic links to other documents stored in the same or remote computers. Using these links, the user need only point at a highlighted keyword or graphic, click on it, and immediately be transported to another document, probably on another computer somewhere else in the world. Users are free to jump from place to place following this own logic and interest.

Web browser software is programmed according to HTML standards. The standard is universally accepted, so anyone using a browser can access any of the millions of web sites. Browsers use hypertext's point-and-click ability to navigate or surf—move from site to site on the web—to another desired site. The browser also includes an arrow or back button to enable the user to retrace his or her steps, navigating back, site by site.

Those who offer information through the web must establish a home page—a text and graphical screen display that usually welcomes the user and explains the organization that has established the page. For most organizations, the home pages lead users to other pages, with all the pages of a company being known as a web site. To access the web site, the user must specify a uniform resource locator (URL) which points to the address of a specific resource on the web. Http stands for hypertext transport protocol, which is the communications standard used to transfer pages on the web. Http defines how messages are formatted and transmitted and what action web servers and browsers should take in response to various commands.

Virtually all businesses, most government agencies, and many individuals now have web sites. The number of individuals and companies with Internet access is expanding rapidly, all of these have graphical web browsers. As a result, businesses are enthusiastic about setting up facilities on the web for electronic commerce. But the reality is that the Internet and the web are extremely vulnerable to compromises of various sorts. As businesses wake up to this reality, the demand for secure web services grows.

12.1 CLIENT/SERVER ARCHITECTURE

The www, or web is basically an infrastructure of information. This information is stored on the www on web servers and it uses the Internet to transmit data around the world. These servers run special programs that allow information to be transmitted to remote computers which are running a web browser, as illustrated in Figure 12.1. The Internet is a common connection in which computers can communicate using a common addressing mechanism (IP) with a TCP/IP connection.

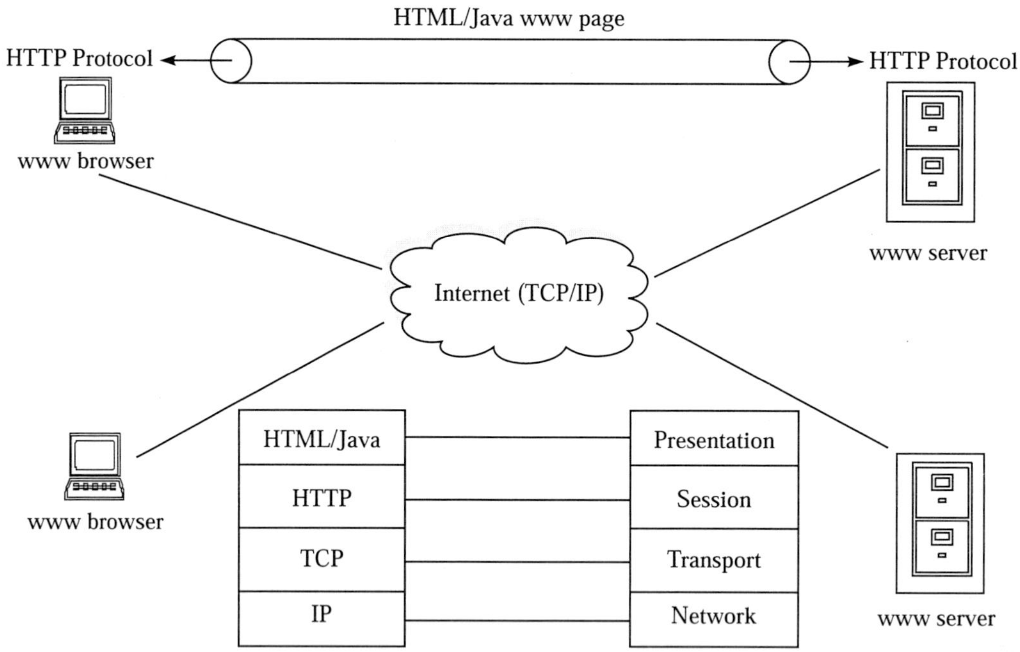

Figure 12.1 Web servers and browsers.

The www is structured with client and servers, where a client accesses services from the server. These servers can either be local or available through a global network connection. A local connection normally requires the connection over a local area network, but a global connection normally requires the connection to an Internet Service Provider. These providers are often known as Internet access providers (ISPs), sometimes as Interconnectivity providers

(ICP). They provide the mechanism to access the Internet and have the required hardware and software to connect from the user to the Internet. This access is typically provided through one of the following:

- Connection to a client computer through a dial-up modem connection (typically at 28.8 kbps or 56 kbps).
- Connection to a client computer through a dial-up ISDN connection (typically at 64 kbps or 128 kbps).
- Connection of a client computer to a server computer which connects to the Internet through a frame relay router (typically 56 kbps or 256 kbps).
- Connection of a client computer to a local area network which connects to the Internet through T1, 1.544 Mbps router.

These connections are illustrated in Figure 12.2

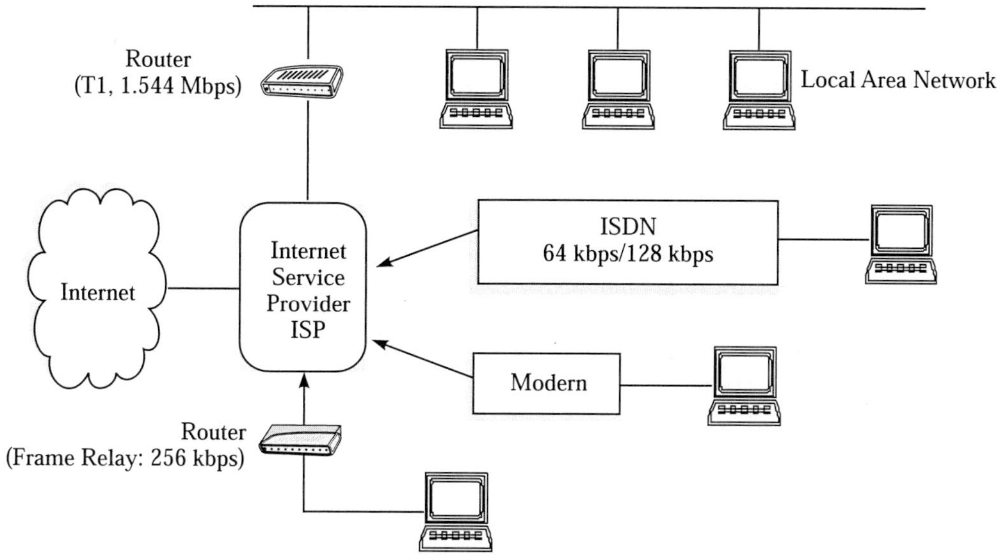

Figure 12.2 Example connections to the internet.

The foundation protocol of the www is the Hypertext Transfer Protocol (HTTP), which can be used in any client–server application involving hypertext. It is used on the www for transmitting information using hypertext jumps and can support the transfer of plaintext, hypertext, audio, images, or any Internet-compatible information. The most recently defined standard is HTTP1.1, which has been defined by the IETF standard.

HTTP is a stateless protocol, where each transaction is independent of any previous transactions. Thus, when the transaction is finished, the TCP/IP connection is disconnected. The advantage of being stateless is that it allows the rapid access of www pages over several widely distributed servers. It uses the TCP protocol to establish a connection between a client and a server for each transaction and then terminates the connection once the transaction completes.

HTTP also supports many different formats of data. Initially, a client issues a request to a server which may include a prioritized list of formats that it can handle. This allows new formats to be easily added and also prevents the transmission of unnecessary information.

A client's www browser (the user agent) initially establishes a direct connection with the destination server which contains the required www page. To make this connection, the client initiates a TCP connection between the client and the server. After this is established, the client then issues an HTTP request, such as the specific command (the method), the URL, and possibly extra information such as request parameters or client information. When the server receives the request, it attempts to perform the requested action. It, then, returns an HTTP response, which includes status information, a success/error code, and extra information. After the client receives this, the TCP connection is closed.

12.2 SECURITY CONSIDERATIONS AND THREATS

The www is fundamentally a client/server application running over the Internet and TCP/IP intranets. Web is increasingly serving as a highly visible outlet for corporate and product information and as a platform for business transactions. Reputation can be damaged and money can be lost if the web servers are subverted.

Web servers are relatively easy to configure and manage, and web content is increasingly easy to develop, the underlying software is extraordinarily complex. This complex software may hide many potential security flaws, which are vulnerable to a variety of security attacks. Common users are clients for web-based services. Clients are not aware of the security risks that exist and do not have the tools or knowledge to take effective countermeasures.

Table 12.1 provides a summary of the types of security threats faced in using the web.

Table 12.1 A comparison of threats on the web

	Threats	*Consequences*	*Countermeasures*
Integrity	Modification of user data Trojan horse browser Modification of memory Modification of message traffic in transit	Loss of information Compromise of machine Vulnerability to all other threats	Cryptographic checksum
Confidentiality	Eavesdropping on the net Theft of information from server Theft of data from client Information about network configuration Information about which client talks to server	Loss of information Loss of privacy	Encryption, web proxies

(*Contd.*)

Table 12.1 A comparison of threats on the web (*Contd.*)

	Threats	*Consequences*	*Countermeasures*
Authentication	Impersonation of legitimate users	Misrepresentation of users	Cryptographic techniques
	Data forgery	Belief that false information is valid.	
Denial of service	Killing of user threats	Disruptive	Difficult to prevent
	Flooding machine with bogus threats	Annoying	
	Filling up disk or memory	Prevent user from getting work done	
	Isolating machine by DNS attacks		

One way to group these threats is in terms of passive and active attacks. Passive attacks include eavesdropping on network traffic between the browser and the server and gaining access to information on a web site that is supported to be restricted. Active attacks include impersonating another user, alternating messages in transit between the client and the server, and altering information on a web site. Another way to classify web security threats is in terms of location of the threats: web server, web browser, and network traffic between the browser and the server.

12.3 WEB TRAFFIC SECURITY APPROACHES

The various approaches have been considered for web security, which are similar in the services they provide, but they differ with respect to their scope of applicability and their relative location within the TCP/IP protocol stack. Relative location of security facilities in the TCP/IP protocol stack is shown in Figure 12.3 and it illustrates the differences.

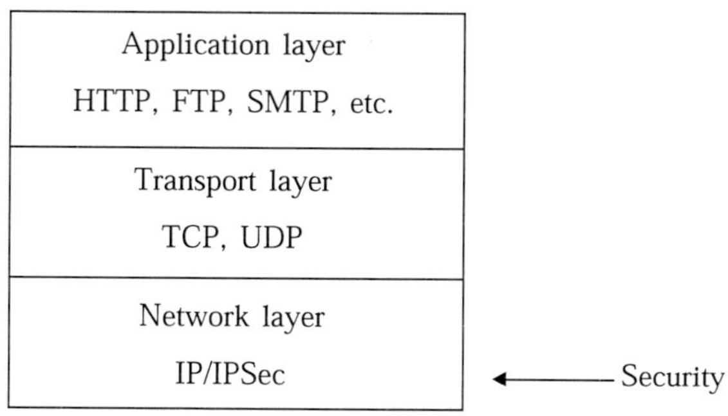

(a) Security provided at the network layer with IPSec

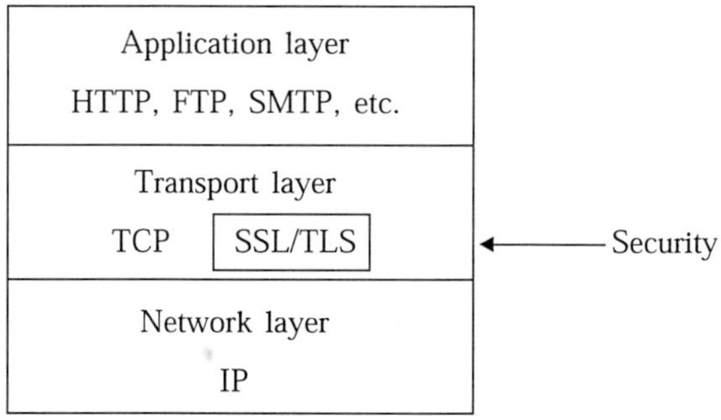

(b) Security provided at the transport layer with SSL/TLS

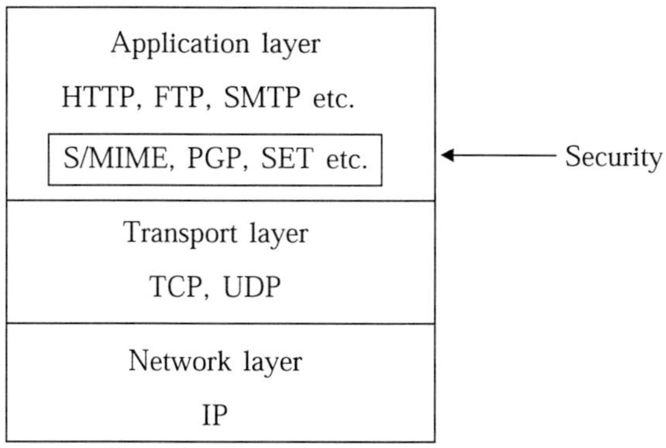

(c) Security provided at the application layer with PGP, SET, etc.

Figure 12.3 Relative location of security facilities in TCP/P protocol stack.

One way to provide web security is to use IP security as shown is Figure 12.3(a). The advantage of using IPSec is that it is transparent to end users and applications and provides a general purpose solution. Further, IPSec includes filtering capability so that only selected traffic need incur the overhead of IPSec processing.

Another way to provide web security is to implement security just above TCP as shown in Figure 12.3(b). The foremost example of this approach is the secure socket layer (SSL) and the follow-on Internet standard known as Transport Layer Security (TLS). SSL can be embedded in specific packages. For example, Netscape and Microsoft Explorer browsers come equipped with SSL, and most web servers have implemented the protocol.

Application-specific security services are embedded within the particular application as shown in Figure 12.3(c). In the context of web security, an important example of this approach is Secure Electronic Transaction (SET).

12.4 SSL/TLS FOR SECURE WEB SERVICES

SSL (Secure Socket Layer) was developed originally by Netscape in 1995 to provide secure and authenticated connections between browsers and servers. SSL provides transport layer security.

Recall from Figure 12.3 that the transport layer is where the TCP and UDP protocols reside in the TCP/IP stack. (Since SSL sits immediately above TCP in the protocol stack, a more precise way of stating this would be that SSL provides session layer security in the OSI model of the internet protocols.)

IETF (Internet Engineering Task Force, the body in charge of the core internet protocols, including the TCP/IP protocol) made SSL version 3 an open standard in 1999 and called TLS (Transport Layer Security) version 1.

SSL/TLS allows for either server-only authentication or server-client authentication.

In server-only authentication, the client receives the server's certificate. The client verifies the server's certificate and generates a secret key that it then encrypts with the server's public key. The client sends the encrypted secret key to the server; the server decrypts it with its own private key and subsequently uses the client-generated secret key to encrypt the messages meant for the client.

In the server-client authentication, in addition to the secret key, the client also sends to the server its certificate that the server uses for authenticating the client. Open SSL is an implementation of the SSL and the TLS protocols.

SSL is actually not a single protocol, or even a single protocol layer. SSL is composed of four protocols in two layers as shown in Figure 12.4.

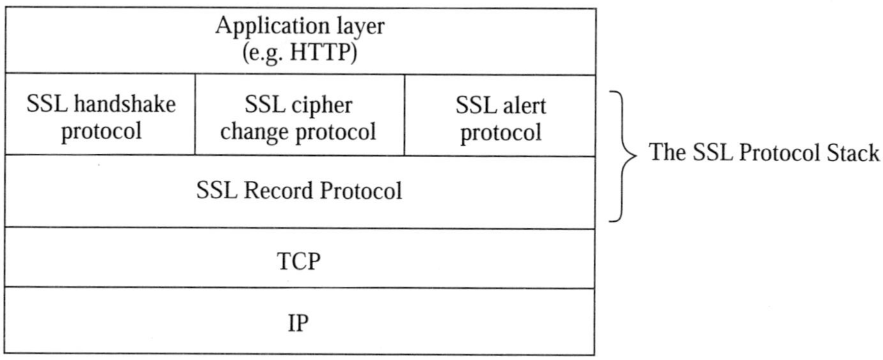

Figure 12.4 SSL protocol stack.

12.4.1 The Twin Concepts of "SSL Connection" and "SSL Session"

In the SSL family of protocols, a connection is a one-time transport of information between two nodes in a communication network.

- A connection constitutes a peer-to-peer relationship between the two nodes.
- Being one-time, connections are transient.
- Every connection is associated with a session.
- A session is an enduring association between a client and a server.
- A session is created by the SSL handshaking protocol.

- A session can consist of multiple connections.
- A session is characterized by a set of security parameters that apply to all the connections in the session.
- The concept of a session eliminates the need for negotiating the security parameters for each separate connection.

12.4.2 SSL Session State

An SSL session state is characterized by the following parameters:

(i) *Session identifier:* An arbitrary byte sequence chosen by the server to identify an active or resumable session state.

(ii) *Peer certificate:* An X509. V3 certificate of the peer. This element of the state may be null.

(iii) *Compression method:* The algorithm used to compress the data prior to encryption.

(iv) *Cipher spec:* Specifics of the bulk data encryption algorithm and the hash algorithm used for MAC (Message Authentication Code) calculations.

(v) *Master secret:* A 48-byte secret shared between the client and the server.

(vi) *Is resumable:* A flag indicating whether the session is allowed to initiate new connections.

12.4.3 SSL Connection State

An SSL connection state is charaterized by the following parameters:

(i) *Server write MAC secret:* The secret key used in calculating the MAC (Message Authentication Code) Value for the data sent by the server.

(ii) *Client write MAC secret:* The secret key used in calculating the MAC value for the data sent by the client.

(iii) *Server write key:* The symmetric-key encryption key for data encrypted by the server and decrypted by the client.

(iv) *Client write key:* The symmetric-key encryption key for data encrypted by the client and decrypted by the server.

(v) *Initialization vectors:* An initialization vector (IV) for each key used by a block cipher operating in the CBC mode (cipher block chaining mode) is maintained. The vectors are initialized by the SSL Handshake Protocol. Subsequently, the final ciphertext block from each record is preserved for use as the IV with the following record.

(vi) *Sequence numbers:* Each party maintains separate sequence numbers for the transmitted and received message through each connection. When a party sends or receives a change cipher spec message, the appropriate sequence number is set to zero. Sequence number may not exceed $2^{64}-1$.

12.4.4 SSL Record Protocol

The SSL record protocol sits directly above the TCP protocol as shown in Figure 12.4. This protocol provides two services:

- Confidentiality
- Message integrity

In a nutshell, this protocol is in charge of taking the actual data that the server wants to send to a client or that the client wants to send to the server, fragmenting the data into blocks, applying authentication and encryption primitives to each block, and handling the block to TCP for transmission over the network. On the receive side, the blocks are decrypted, verified for message integrity, reassembled, and delivered to the higher-level protocol.

The operation of the SSL Record Protocol is shown in Figure 12.5. It consists of the following five steps:

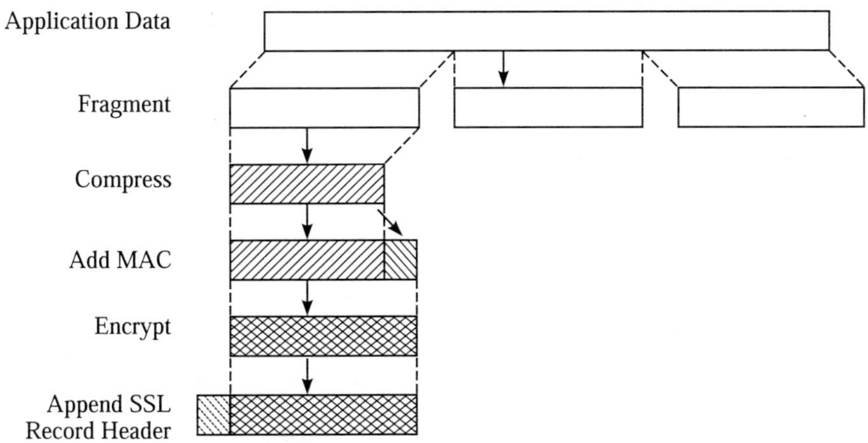

Figure 12.5 SSL record protocol operation.

Fragmentation: The message (either from server to client or from client to server) is fragmented into blocks whose length does not exceed 2^{14} (16384) bytes.

Compression: This optional step requires loss less compression and carries the stipulation that the size of the input block will not increase by more than 1024 bytes. (As you would expect, compression will, in most cases, reduce the length of a block produced by the fragmentation step. But for very short blocks, the length may increase.) SSL V3, the current version of SSL does not specify compression.

Adding MAC: This step computes, the MAC (Message Authentication Code) for the block. The MAC is appended to the compressed message block.

Encryption: The compressed message and the MAC are encrypted using symmetric-key encryption. The encryption may be carried out with a block cipher such as 3DES or with a stream cipher such as RC4-128. A number of choices are available for the encryption steps depending on the level of security needed.

Append SSL Record Header: Finally, an SSL header is pretended to the encrypted block. The header consists of 8 bits for declaring the content type, 8 bits for declaring the major version used for SSL, 8 bits for declaring the minor version used, and 16 bits for declaring the length of the compressed plaintext (or the plaintext if not compression was used). Each output block produced by the SSL Record Protocol is referred to as an SSL record. The length of a record is not to exceed 32,767 bytes.

12.4.5 SSL Handshake Protocol

Before the SSL Record Protocol can do its thing, it must become aware of what algorithms to use for compression, authentication, and encryption. All of that information is generated by the SSL Handshake Protocol. The SSL Handshake Protocol is also responsible for the server and the client to authenticate each other. This protocol must also come up with the cryptographic keys to be used for the encryption and the authentication of each SSL record. The SSL Handshake Protocol works in four phases as shown in Figure 12.6.

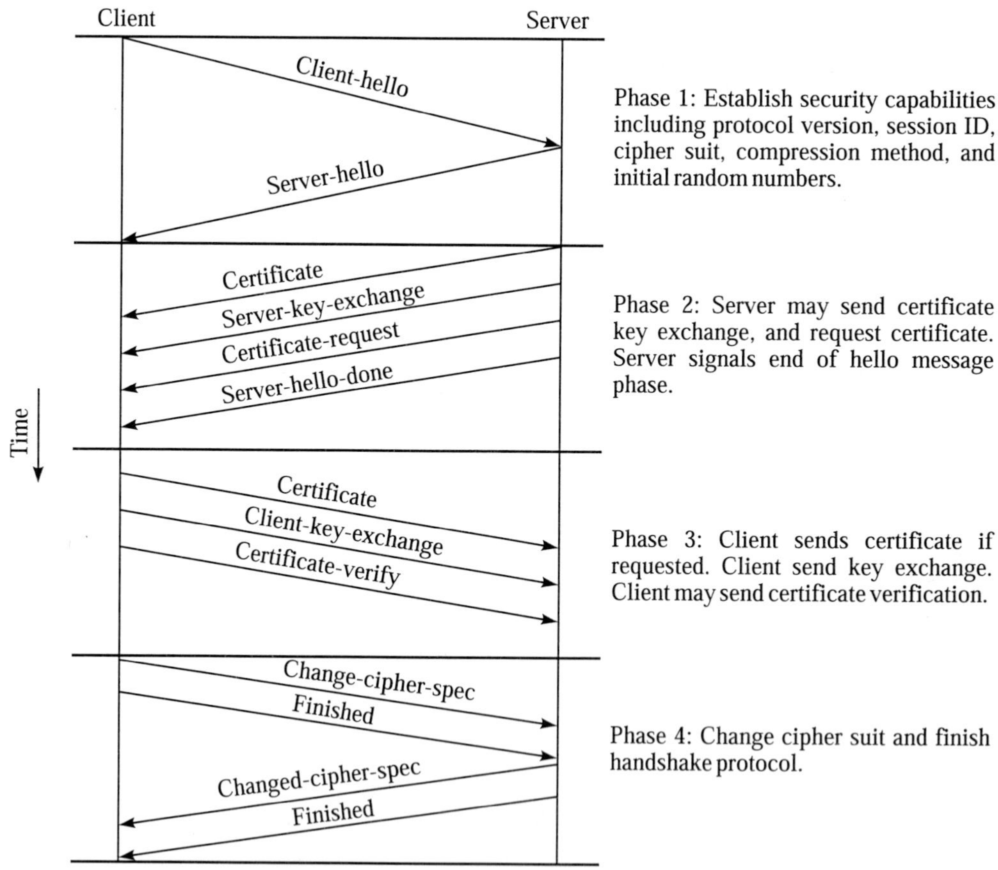

Note: Shared transfers are optional or situation-dependent messages that are not always sent.

Figure 12.6 Handshake protocol action.

PHASE 1 handshaking, initiated by the client, is used to establish the security capabilities present at the two ends of a connection. The client sends to the server a client-hello message with the following parameters:

Version: The highest SSL version understood by the client.

Random: A 32-bit timestamp and 28-byte random field that together serve as nonce's during key exchange to prevent replay attacks.

Passion ID: A variable length session identifier. A nonzero value indicates that the client wishes to update the parameters of an existing connection or create a new connection on this session. A zero value indicates that the client wishes to establish a new connection on a new session.

Cipher suite: A list of cryptographic algorithms supported by the client, in decreasing order of preference.

Compression method: A list of compression methods the client supports.

The server responds with its server hello message that has a similar set of parameters. The server's response, as you would expect, includes the specific algorithms selected by the server from the client's lists for compression, authentication, and encryption.

The cipher suite parameters in the server hello message consists of two elements. The first elements declares the key exchange method selected. (The choice is between RSA, Three different types of Diffie-Hellman, etc.) The second elements of the cipher suite parameter is called cipher spec; it has a number of fields that indicate the authentication algorithm selected, the length of MAC, the encryption algorithm, etc.

PHASE 2 handshaking is initiated by the server if server authentication is needed by the client. The server sends to the client a certificate message containing its one or more certificates validating its public key. This could be followed by a server-key-exchange message and a certificate-request message, both from the server to the client. The server-key exchange message could, for example, consist of the global Diffie-Hellman values (a prime number and a primitive root of that number) and the servers Diffie-Hellman public key. Phase 2 handshaking ends when the server ends the client—a server hello done message.

PHASE 3 handshaking is initiating by the client. If client authentication is required, the client sends to the server the certificate message containing one or more certificates validating its public key. Next, the client sends to the server a mandatory client-key-exchange message that could, for example, consist of a secret session key encrypted with the server's public key. This phase ends when the client sends to the server a certificate verify message to provide a verification of its certificates if they are signed by a certificate authority.

PHASE 4 handshaking completes the setting up of a secure connection between the client and the server. The client sends to the server a change-chipher-spec message indicating that it is copying the pending cipher spec into the current cipher spec. (See phase 1 handshaking for cipher spec.) Next, the client sends to the server the finished message. As shown in Figure 12.6, the server does the same vis-a-vis the client.

The change-cipher-spec message format must correspond to the change cipher spec Protocol. This protocol says that the message must consist of a single byte with a value of 1 indicating the change.

The last of the SSL protocols, Alert Protocol, is used to convey SSL-related alerts to the peer entity.

12.5 SECURE HYPERTEXT TRANSFER PROTOCOL (S-HTTP)

The native protocol that web clients and servers use to communicate is Hypertext Transfer Protocol (HTTP). This protocol is ideal for open communications. However, in its native form, it does not provide authentication or encryption features. Secure HTTP (S-HTTP) works in conjunction with HTTP to enable clients and servers to engage in private and secure transactions. It is essentially useful for encrypting form-based information as it passes between clients and servers. It should be noted that S-HTTP only encrypts HTTP-level messages at the application layer whereas SSL encrypts all data being passed between the client and the server at the IP socket level.

S-HTTP provides considerable flexibility in terms of what cryptographic algorithms and modes of operation can be used. Also, as the need for authenticating among the internet and web grows, users need to be authenticated before sending encrypted files to each other. With S-HTTP, messages may be protected using digital signatures, authentication, and encryption. During the initial contact, the sender and the receiver establish preferences for encrypting and processing secure messages.

12.6 SECURE ELECTRONIC TRANSACTION (SET)

SET is an open encryption and security specification designed to protect credit card transactions on the Internet. It is a set of security protocols and formats that enables users to employ the existing credit card payment infrastructure on an open network, such as the Internet, in a secure fashion. SET provides three services:

1. Provides a secure communications channel among all parties involved in a transaction.
2. Provides trust by the use of X.509 V3 digital certificates.
3. Ensure privacy because the information is only available to parties in a transaction when and where necessary.

Secure transactions are critical for electronic commerce on the Internet. Merchants must automatically and safely collect and process payments from Internet clients: therefore, a secure protocol is required to support the activities of the credit and companies. SET is designed to secure credit card transactions by authenticating cardholders, merchants, and banks by preserving the confidentiality of payment data. SET includes the following features:

- Requires digital signatures to verify that the customer, the merchant, and the bank are all legitimate.
- Uses multiparty messages that allow information to be encrypted directly to bank.

- Prevent credit card numbers from getting in the wrong hands.
- Requires integration into the credit card processing system.

SET includes a layer that negotiates the type of payment method, protocols and transports. This task is the responsibility of the Joint Electronic Payment Initiative (JEPI). Payment methods could include credit cards, debit cards, electronic cash, and cheques. Payment protocols such as SET define the message format and sequence required for completion of the payment transaction. Transports include such protocols as Secure Socket Layer (SSL) and Secure Hypertext Transfer Protocol (S-HTTP). Note that certificate authorities provide digital signatures that are critical for verifying the authenticity of cardholders and others involved in the transactions.

If e-commerce is to succeed, a method must exist for consumers to use credit cards over the Internet. Credit card usage on the internet is still low, but is likely to grow in the future. SET and SSL is used in the credit card transaction to provide security provisions. SSL encrypts a credit card number and other information using a 40-bit key. Because of its size, this key can be hacked; however, it may be adequate for some needs. Even though SSL keeps the credit card number and information private while being transmitted, it does not address the issue of whether the credit card is valid, stolen or being used without permission. SET addresses these limitations by using an "Electronic wallet" that can identify the user and validate the transaction. An electronic wallet is a type of software application used by the consumer for securely storing purchasing information. Furthermore, SET-based systems have an advantage over the mechanisms, in that SET adds digital certificates that associate the cardholder and the merchant with a particular financial institution and the visa or-master card payment system.

12.6.1 Business Requirements

(i) Provide authentication that a cardholder is legitimate user of a credit card account.

(ii) Provide authentication that a merchant can accept credit card transactions through its relationship with a financial institution.

(iii) Provide confidentiality of payment and ordering information.

(iv) Ensure the integrity of all transmitted data.

(v) Ensure the use of the best security practices and system design techniques to protect all legitimate parties in an electronic commerce transaction.

(vi) Create a protocol that neither depends on transport security mechanism nor prevents their use.

(vii) Facilitate and encourage interoperability among software and network providers.

Key Features

- Cardholder account authentication
- Merchant authentication

- Integrity of data
- Confidentiality of information

12.6.2 SET Participants

Figure 12.7 indicates the participants in the SET system, which include the cardholder and the merchant, in addition to the issuer, acquirer, payment gateway, and a certification authority.

Cardholder: In the electronic environment, consumers and corporate purchasers interact with merchants from personal computers over Internet. A cardholder is an authorized holder of a payment card (e-g. Master card, Visa) that has been issued by an issuer.

Merchant: A merchant is a person or organization that has goods or services (offered by web site or by electronic mail) to the cardholder.

Issuer: This is the financial institution, such as a bank that provides the cardholder with the payment card.

Acquirer: This is also financial institution that establishes an account with a merchant and processes payment card authorizations and payments.

Payment gateway: This is the function operated by the acquirer or designed third party that processes merchant payment messages. The payment gateway interfaces between SET and the existing bankcard payment networks for authorization & payment functions.

Certification Authority (CA): This is an entity that is trusted to issue X.509 V3 public-key certificates for cardholders, merchants and payment gateways.

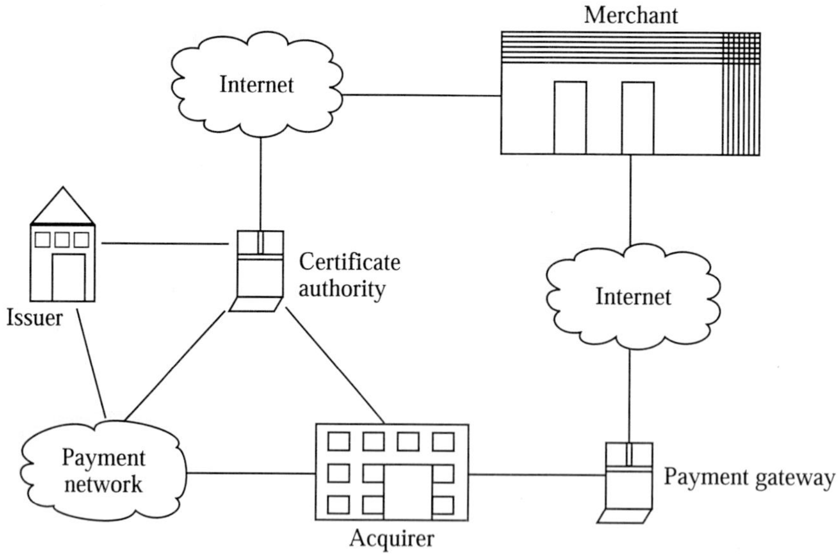

Figure 12.7 SET components and their relationships.

12.6.3 SET Transaction Flow

The sequence of events associated with SET transaction is illustrated through Figure 12.8.

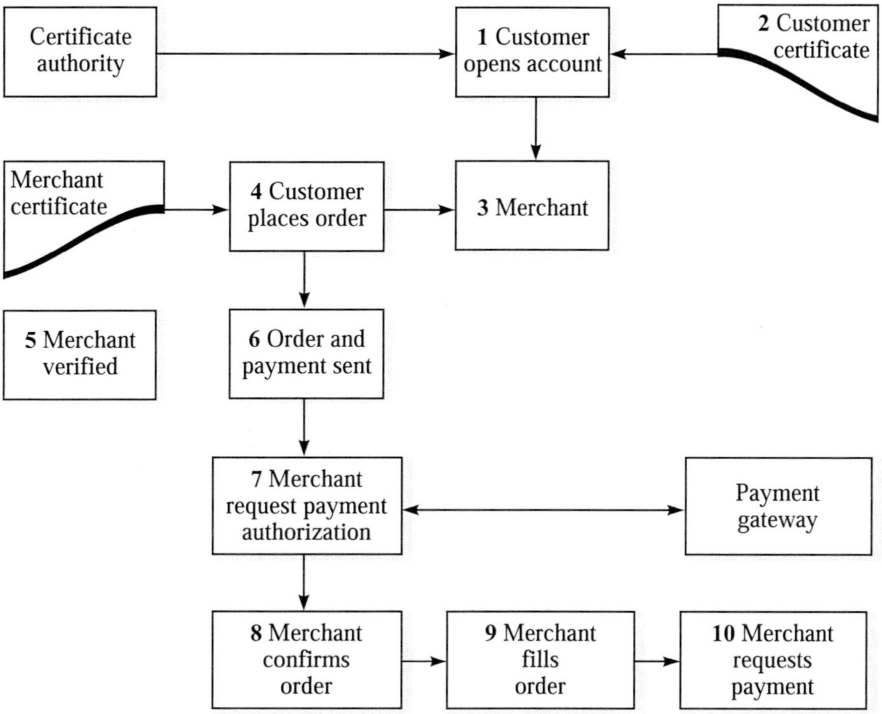

Figure 12.8 SET transaction flow.

1. The customer opens an account and obtains a credit card account with a bank that supports electronic payment and SET.
2. These customers receive a certificate after suitable verification of identity. It establishes a relationship between the customer's key pair and the credit card.
3. Merchants have certificates consisting of one key for signing messages and one for key exchange. They also need a copy of the payment gateway's public key certificate.
4. The customer places an order, which is accepted by the merchant. The order form returned from the merchant includes the items, the cost, and an order number.
5. The customer receives the merchant certificate.
6. The customer sends the order, payment, and this certificate to the merchant.
7. The merchant requests payment authorization through the payment gateway.
8. The merchant provides the customer with order confirmation.
9. The merchant ships the product or service.
10. The merchant request payment gateway, which handles all payment processing.

REVIEW QUESTIONS

12.1 Explain the importance of web security in business.

12.2 Explain the client/server architecture for web.

12.3 Explain the working of web servers and browsers.

12.4 How reputations of business can be damaged if web serves are subverted?

12.5 Write security of threats faced in using the web.

12.6 Write web traffic security approaches.

12.7 Explain the importance of SSL/TLS for secure web services.

12.8 What is the difference between SSL connection and SSL session?

12.9 List and briefly define the parameters that define an SSL session state?

12.10 List and briefly define the parameters that define an SSL session connection.

12.11 What services are provided by the SSL Record Protocol?

12.12 What is the difference between the server-only authentication and server-client authentication in SSL/TLS?

12.13 We say that SSL/TLS is not really a single protocol, but a stack of protocols. Explain. What are the different protocols in the SSL/TLS stack?

12.14 Explain SSL Handshake protocol.

12.15 What is the difference between HTTP and S-HTTP?

12.16 Explain secure Electronic Transaction.

12.17 Explain the set components and their relationships.

12.18 Explain the flow of transaction in SET with diagram.

CHAPTER 13

Network Management

Chapter Outline

Network management can be defined as OAM and P (Operation, Administration, Maintenance and Provisioning) of network and services. The operations group is concerned with daily operations in providing network services. Network administration is concerned with establishing and administering the overall goals, policies, and procedure of network management. The installation and maintenance group handles functions that include both installation and repairs of facilities and equipment. Provisioning involves network planning and circuit provisioning, traditionally handled by the engineering or provisioning department. We will describe each of these functions.

13.1 GOAL OF NETWORK MANAGEMENT

The goal of network management is to ensure that the users of a network receive the information technology services with the quality of service that they expect. Toward meeting this goal, management should establish policy to either formally or informally contract a service level agreement with the users.

From a business administration point of view, network management involves strategic and tactical planning of the engineering, operations and maintenance of a network and network services for current and future needs at minimum overall cost. Well-established, communication and interaction among the various groups are necessary to perform these functions. Figure 13.1 represents the top-down view of network management functions. It comprises three major groups:

1. Network provisioning
2. Network operations
3. Network installation and maintenance.

It is useful to consider the different functions as belonging specific administrative groups, although there are other ways of assigning responsibilities based on organizational structure.

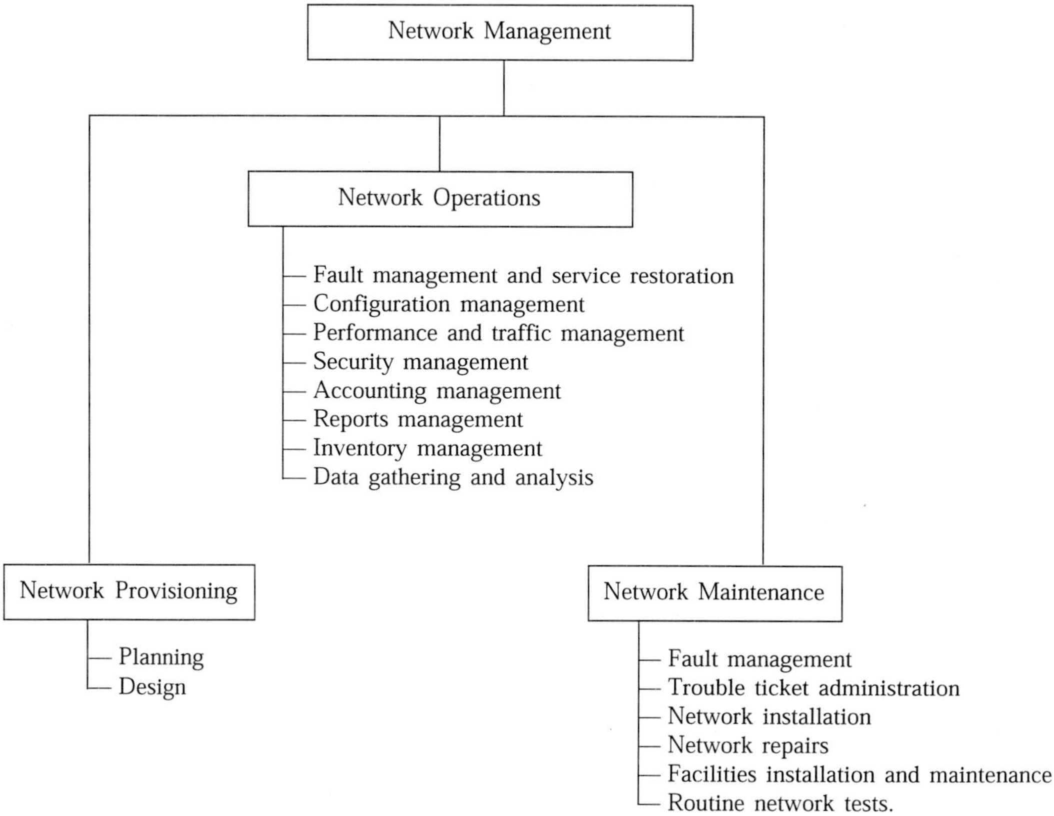

Figure 13.1 Network management functional groupings.

Network provisioning is the primary responsibility of the engineering groups; and network installation and maintenance is the primary responsibility of the plant facilities group. The interactions among the groups are shown in Figure 13.2. The normal daily operations are the function of the network operations group, which controls and administers a network operation center (NOC).

The functions of NOC are concerned primarily with network operations; its secondary responsibilities are network provisioning and network installation and maintenance (I&M).

Network provisioning consists of network planning and design, and is the responsibility of the engineering group. The engineering group keeps track of new technologies and introduces them as needed. Determination of what is needed and when is made through analysis of the traffic and performance data provided by the network operations. Modifications to network provisioning may also be initiated by management decisions. Planning and efficient use of equipment can be achieved with good inventory management of modifications of network configuration by the network provisioning group.

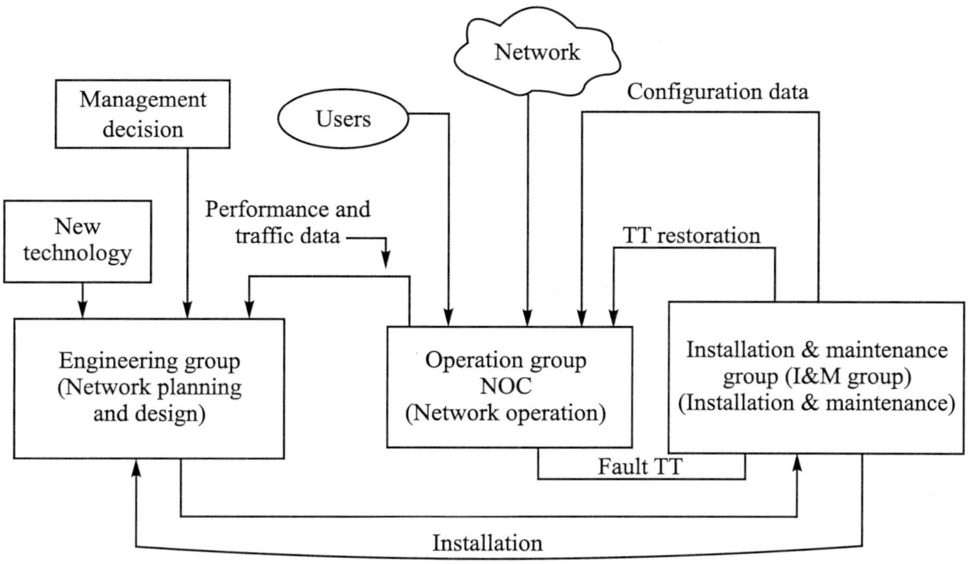

Figure 13.2 Network management functional flow chart.

Network management tools are helpful to the engineering group in gathering statistics and studying the trends of traffic patterns for planning purposes. Automated operations systems help in the design of circuits and measurement of the performance tune-up.

The function of network operations, listed in Figure 13.1 are administered by the network operation center (NOC). They are concerned with daily operation of the network and providing network services. The International Organization for Standardization (ISO) has defined five OSI network management applications:

- Performance management
- Fault management
- Configuration management
- Accounting management
- Security management.

13.1.1 Performance Management

Performance management of a computer network comprises two broad functional categories—monitoring and controlling. Monitoring is the function that tracks activities on the network. The controlling function enables performance management to make adjustments to improve network performance. Some of the performance issues of concern to the network manager are:

- Which is the level of capacity utilization?
- Is there excessive traffic?
- Has throughput been reduced to unacceptable levels?

- Are there bottlenecks?
- Is response time increasing?

To deal with these concerns, the network manager must focus on some initial set of resources to be monitored in order to assess performance levels. This includes associating appropriate metrics and values with relevant network resources as indicators of different levels of performance. For example, what count of retransmissions on a transport connection is considered to be a performance problem requiring attention? Performance management, therefore, must monitor many resources to provide information in determining network operating level. By collecting this information, analyzing it, and then using the resultant analysis as feedback to the prescribed set of values, the network manager can become more and more adept at recognizing situations indicative of present or impending performance degradation.

Before using a network for a particular application, an end user may want to know such things as the average and worst case response time and the reliability of network services. Thus performance must be known in sufficient detail to assess specific end user queries. End users expect network services to be managed in such a way as to consistently afford their applications good response time.

Network managers need performance statistics to help them plan, manage, and maintain large networks. Performance statistics can be used to recognize potential bottlenecks before they cause problems to the end users. Appropriate corrective action can then be taken. This action can take the form of changing routing tables to balance or redistributed traffic load during time of peak use or when a bottleneck is identified by rapidly growing load in one area. Over the long term, capacity planning based on such performance information can indicate the proper decisions to make, for example, with regard to expansion of lines in that area.

The goal of performance management is to quantity, measure, report, analyze and control the performance (for example, utilization, throughput) of different network components. These components include individual devices (for example, links, routers, and hosts) as well as end-to-end abstractions such as path through the network. We will discuss shortly that protocol standards such as the Simple Network Management Protocol (SNMP) play a central role in Internet Performance Management.

13.1.2 Fault Management

To maintain proper operation of a complex network, care must be taken that system as a whole, and each essential component individually, are in proper working order. When a fault occurs, it is important, as rapidly as possible to:

- Determine exactly where the fault is.
- Isolate the rest of the network from the failure so that it can continue to function without interference.
- Reconfigure or modify the network in such a way as to minimize the impact of operation without the failed component or components.
- Repair or replace the failed components to restore the network to its initial state.

Central to the definition of fault management is the fundamental concept of a fault. Faults are to be distinguished from errors. A fault is an abnormal condition that requires management attention (or action) to repair, whereas an error is a single event. A fault is usually indicated by failure to operate correctly or by excessive errors. For example, if a communication line is physically cut, no signals can get through. Or a crimp in the cable may cause wild distortions so that there is persistently high bit error rate. Certain errors (for example, a single bit error on a communication line) may occur occasionally and are not normally considered to be faults. It is usually possible to compensate for errors using the error control mechanisms of the various protocols.

End users expect fast and reliable problem resolution. Most end users will tolerate occasional outages. When these infrequent outages do occur, however the end user generally expects to receive immediate notification and expects that the problem will be corrected almost immediately. To provide this level of fault resolution requires very rapid and reliable fault detection and diagnostic management functions. The impact and duration of faults can also be minimized by the use of redundant components and alternate communication routes to give the network a degree of 'fault tolerance'. The fault management capability itself should be redundant to increase network reliability.

Users expect to be kept informed of the network status, including both scheduled and unscheduled disruptive maintenance. Users expect reassurance of correct network operation through mechanisms that use confidence tests or analyze dumps, logs, alters or statistics. After correcting a fault and restoring a system to its full operational state, the fault management service must ensure that the problem is truly resolved and that no new problems are introduced. This requirement is called *problem tracking and control.* As with other areas of network management, fault management should have minimal effect on network performance.

The goal of the fault management is to log, detect, and respond to fault conditions in the network. The line between fault management as the immediate handling of transient network failures (for example, link, host or router hardware or software outages), while performance management tapes the longer time view of providing acceptable levels of performance in the face of varying traffic demands and occasional network device failures. As with performance management the SNMP protocol plays a central role in fault management.

13.1.3 Configuration Management

Configuration management allows a network manager to track, which devices are on the managed network and the hardware, and software configurations of these devices.

Modern data communication networks are composed of individual components and logical subsystems (for example, the device driver in an operating system) that can be configured to perform many different applications. The same device, for example, can be configured to act either as a router or as an end system node or both. Once it is decided how a device is to be used, the configuration manager can choose the appropriate software and set of attributes and values (for example, a transport layer retransmission timer) for that device.

Configuration management is concerned with initializing a network and gracefully shutting down part or all of the networks. It is also concerned with maintaining, adding, and updating the relationships among components and the status of components themselves during network operation.

Start-up and shut-down operations on a network are the specific responsibilities of configuration management. It is often desirable for these operations on certain components to be performed unattended (for example, starting or shutting down a network interface unit). The network manager needs the capability to identify initially the components that comprise the network and to define the desired connectivity of these components. Those who regularly configure a network with the same or a similar set of resource attributes need ways to define and modify default attributes and to load these predefined sets of attributes into the specified network components. The network manager needs the capability to change the connectivity of network components when end user's needs change. Reconfiguration of a network is often desired in response to performance evaluation or in support of network upgrade, fault recovery, or security checks.

End users often need to, or want to, be informed of the status of network resources and components. Therefore, when changes in configuration occur, end users should be notified of these changes. Configuration reports can be generated either on some routine periodic basis or in response to a request for such a report. Before reconfiguration, end users often want to inquire about the upcoming status of resources and their attributes. Network managers usually want only authorized end users (operators) to manage and control network operation (for example, software distribution and updating).

13.1.4 Accounting Management

Accounting management allows the network manager to specify, log, and control uses and device access to network resources. Usage quotas, usage-based changing, and the allocation of resource—access privileges all fall under accounting.

In many corporate networks, individual divisions or cost centres, or even individual project accounts, are charged for the use of network services. These are internal accounting procedures rather than actual cash transfers, but they are important to the participating end users nevertheless. Furthermore, even if no such internal charging is employed, the network manager needs to be able to track the use of network resources by end user or end user class for a number of reasons, including the following:

- An end user or group of end users may be abusing their access privileges and burdening the network at the expense of other end users.
- End users may be making inefficient use of the network, and the network manager can assist in changing procedures to improve performance.
- The network manager is in a better position to plan for network growth if end user activity is known in sufficient details.

The network manager needs to be able to specify the kinds of accounting information to be recorded at various nodes. The desired interval between sending the recorded information to higher-level management nodes, and the algorithms to be used in calculating the charging. Accounting reports should be generated under the network manager's control.

To limit access to accounting information, the accounting facility must provide the capability to verify end users' authorization to access and manipulate that information.

13.1.5 Security Management

Security management is concerned with managing information protection and access control facilities. These include generating, distributing, and storing encryption keys. Passwords, and other authorization or access control information, must be maintained and distributed. Security management is also concerned with monitoring and controlling access to computer networks and access to all or part of the network management information obtained from the network nodes. Logs are an important security tool, and therefore, security management is very much involved with the collection, storage, and examination of audit records and security logs, as well as with the enabling and disabling of these logging facilities.

Security management provides facilities for protection of network resources and end user information. Network security facilities should be available for authorized users only. End users want to know that the proper security policies are in force and effective and that the management of security facilities is itself secure.

The goal of security management is to control access to network resources according to some well-defined policy. The key distribution centers and certification authorities are components of security management. The use of firewalls to monitor and control external access points to one's network, is another crucial components.

The Network Installation and Maintenance (I&M) Group takes care of installation and maintenance of equipment and cables. This group is the service arm of the engineering group for installation and fixing troubles for network operations. The I&M group works closely with the help desk in responding to the problems reported from the field.

13.2 NETWORK MANAGEMENT STANDARDS

Several network management standards are in use today. Table 13.1 lists four standards and its salient points, and fifth standard based on emerging technology. They are the OSI model, the Internet model, Telecommunications Management Network (TMN), IEEE LAN/WAN, and Web-based management.

Table 13.1 Network management standards

Standard	*Salient points*
OSI/CMIP	— International standard (ISO/OSI) — Management of data communication networks—LAN and WAN — Deals with all server layers — Most complete — Object-oriented — Well-structured and layered — Consumes large resource in implementation

(*Contd.*)

Table 13.1 Network management standards

Standard	*Salient Points*
SNMP/Internet	— Industry standard (IETF) — Originally intended for management of Internet components, currently adopted for WAN and telecommunication systems — Easy to implement — Most widely implemented
TMN	— International standard (ITU-T) — Management of telecommunication network — Based OSI network management framework — Addresses both network and administrative aspects of management
IEEE	— IEEE standards adopted internationally — Address management of LAN and MAN — Adopts OSI standards significantly — Deals with first two layers of the OSI reference model
Web-based management	— Web-based enterprise management (WBEM) Java management extension (JMX)

The Open System Interconnection (OSI) Management Standard is the standard adopted by the International Organization for Standardization (ISO). The OSI management protocol standard is Common Management Information Protocol (CMIP), and has built-in services, Common Management Information Service (CMIS), that specify the basic services needed to perform the various functions. It is the most set of specifications and address all seven layers of the OSI reference model. The specifications are object-oriented and hence managed objects are based on object classes and inheritance rules. Besides specifying the management protocols, CMIP/CMIS also address the network management applications. Both LAN and WAN can be managed using CMIP/CMIS. Two of the major drawbacks of the OSI management standard are that it is complex and that the CMIP stack is layer. Until recently, memory of an ordinary desktop workstation was not sufficient to load a complete CMIP stack.

In contrast to CMIP, Simple Network Management Protocol (SNMP) is truly simple, as its name indicates. It is stated as an industry standard and has become very much like the standard specifications of a standard setting organization. The Internet Engineering Task Force (IETF) is responsible for all Internet specifications including network management. The managed objectives are defined as scalar objectives in SNMP, which was primarily intended to manage Internet components, but is now used to manage WAN and telecommunications systems. Probably because it is easy to implement, SNMP is the most widely implemented network management system today.

The Telecommunications Management Network (TMN) is designed to manage the telecommunications network and is oriented towards the needs for telecommunications service provided. TMN is standard of the International Telecommunication Union (ITU) and is based on OSI CMIP/CMIS specifications. TMN extends the concept of management beyond managing networks and network components; its specifications address service and business considerations.

The IEEE standards for LAN and MAN specifications are concerned only with OSI layer-1 (physical) and layer-2 (data link) and they as structured similarly to OSI specification. Both OSI/CMIP and Internet/SNMP protocols use IEEE standards for the lower layers. The IEEE 802.x series of specifications define the standards for the various physical media and data link protocols. IEEE 802.1 specifications present overview, architecture and management. The IEEE 802.2 standards specify the logical link control (LLC) layer. The LLC layer provides transparency of the various physical media and protocols to the network layer. The other specifications as in the IEEE services as for specific media and protocols, For example, 802.3 specifications as for Ethernet LANs.

The last category in Table 13.1 is web-based management, which is based on using web technology, a web server for the management system, and web browsers for network management stations. Because this is an evolving technology, no standards exist at present. Two technologies are vogue, Web-based Enterprise Management (WBEM) and Java Management Extensions (JMX). A recently formed task force, Desktop Management Task Force (DMTF) is developing specifications for WBEM. The DMTF has chosen the Microsoft object-oriented managed model, common information model. JMX is based on a special subset of Java applets developed by Sun Micro Systems that runs in the network components.

Network management is further complicated when the management system uses the new technology. The SNMP, based on scalar technology and simple definition of managed objects, was widely favored over CMIP. With the need for a total management of network, service, and business for telecommunications service providers, TMN, which uses CMIP is being revived. CMIP, which was hard to implement because it required large memory and a better understanding of object-oriented technology, is now easier to implement. However, because of the numerous existing SNMP-based agents, SNMP is also being explored for implementing TMN. Both SNMP and CMIP using polling methodology, which puts an additional load on the network. Besides, both require dedicated workstations for the network management system. With the new web-based management system, not only can object-oriented technology be implemented, but also the dedicated workstation constraint is removed by the uses of web browser.

13.3 NETWORK MANAGEMENT MODEL

The OSI network model is an ISO standard and is the superior of all the models; it is structure and it addresses all aspects of management. Figure 13.3 shows an OSI network management architecture model that comprise four models, organizational model, information model, communication model, and functional model.

Although the above classification of models is based on OSI architecture, and only some of the models are applicable to other architecture, it helps us understand the picture of different aspects of network management.

The organization model describes the components of a network management system, their functions, and their infrastructure. The organization model is defined in ISO 10040 OSI System Management Overview. If defines the terms *object, agent,* and *manager.* Network objects consist of network elements such as hosts, bridges, routers and so on. They can be classified into managed and unmanaged objects or elements. The managed elements have a management

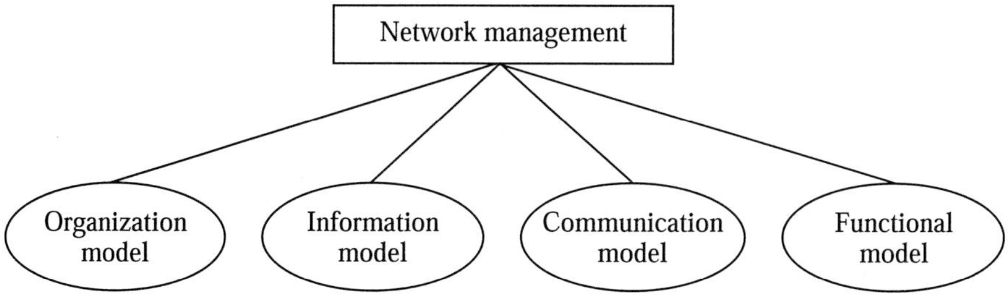

Figure 13.3 OSI network management model.

process running in them, called an *agent*. The unmanaged elements do not have a management process running in them. The *manager* manages the managed element. There is a database in the manager, but not in the agent. The manager queries the agent and receives management data, process it and stores it in its database. The agent can also send minimal set of alarm information to the manager unsolicited.

The OSI information model deals with the structure and organization of management information. ISO 10165 specifies the structure of management information (SMI) and the information database, management information base (MIB). SMI describes how the management information is structured and MIB deals with the relationship and storage of management information.

The third model in OSI management is the communication model, which has three components: management application processes that function in the application layer, layer management between layers and layer operation within the layers.

The functional model is the fourth component of OSI management, and it deals with the user-oriented requirement of network management. OSI defines five functional application areas, namely—configuration, fault performance, security and accounting. These are defined as system management functions in OSI.

13.4 INFRASTRUCTURE FOR NETWORK MANAGEMENT

Network management includes the deployment, integration, and coordination of the hardware, software, and human elements to monitor, test, poll, configure, analyze, evaluate and control the network and element resources to meet the real-time, operational performance, and quality of service requirements at a reasonable cost. So that network management requires the ability to "monitor, test, poll, configure, ... and control" the hardware and software and components in a network. Because the network devices are distributed, this will minimally require that the network administrator be able to gather data (for example, for monitoring purposes) from a remote entity and be able to affect changes (for example, control) at that remote entity. A human analogy will prove useful here for understanding the infrastructure needed for network management.

Imagine that you are the head of a large organization that has branch offices around the world. It is your job to make sure that the pieces of your organization are operation smoothly. How would you do so? At a minimum, you will periodically gather data from your branch offices in the form of reports and various quantitative measures of activity, productivity, and budget. You will occasionally (but not always) be explicitly notified when there is a problem in one of the branch offices; the branch manager who wants to climb the corporate ladder (perhaps to get your job) may send you unsolicited reports indicating how smoothly things are running at his/her branch. You will sift through the reports you receive, hoping to find smooth operations everywhere, but no doubt finding problems in need of your attention. You might initiate a one-on-one dialogue with one of your problem branch offices, gather more data in order to understand the problem, and then pass down an executive order "Make thing change!" to the branch office manager. Implicit in this very common human scenario is an infrastructure for controlling the organization, the boss (you), the remote sites being controlled (the branch offices), your remote agents (the branch office managers), communication protocols (for transmitting standard reports and data, and for one-on-one dialogues), and data (the report contents and the quantitative measures of activity, productivity, and budget). Each of these components in human organizational management has a counterpart in network management.

The architecture of a network management system is conceptually identical to this simple human organizational analogy. The network management field has its own specific terminology for the various components of network management architecture, and so we adopt that terminology here. As shown in Figure 13.4 there are three principle components of network

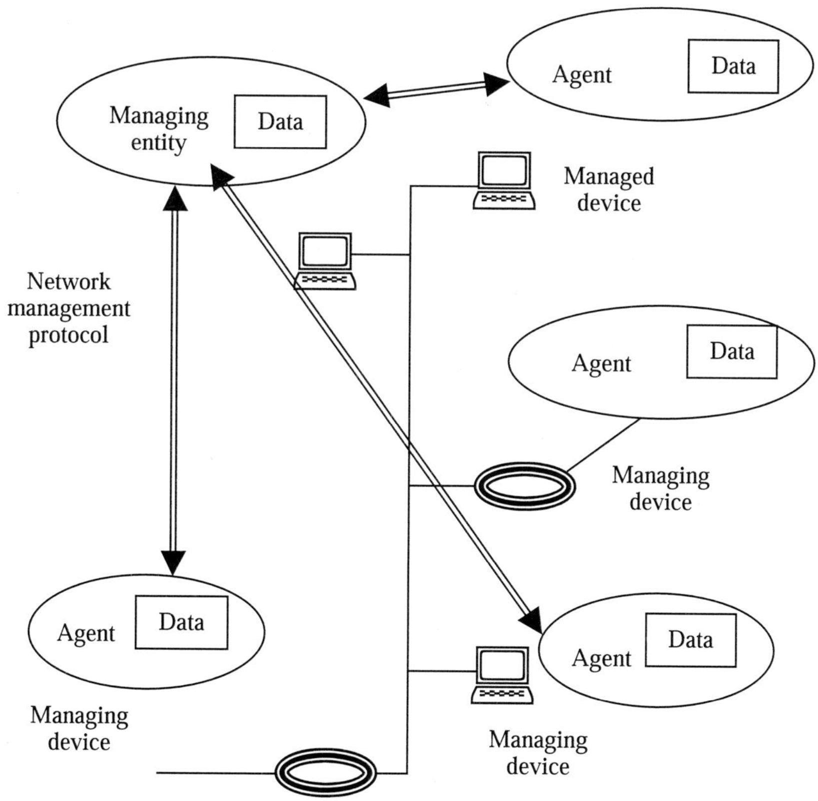

Figure 13.4 Principal components of a network management architecture.

management architecture: a managing entity (the boss in our above analogy-you), the managed devices (the branch office), and the network management protocol.

The managing entity is an application, typically with a human in the loop, running is a centralized network management station in the network operations center (NOC). The managing entity is the locus of activity for network management; it controls the collection, processing, analysis, and/or display of network management information. It is here that actions are initiated to control network behaviour and here that the human network administrator interacts with the network devices.

A managed device is a piece of network equipment (including its software) that resides on a managed network. This is the branch office in our human analogy. A managed device might be host, router, bridge, hub, printer, or modem device. Within a managed device, there may be several so-called managed objects. These managed objects are the actual pieces of hardware within the managed device (for example, a network interface card), and the sets of configuration parameters for the pieces of hardware and software (for example, an intra-domain routing protocol such as RIP: Routing Information Protocol). In our human analogy, the managed objects might be the departments within the branch office. These managed objects have pieces of information are available to the managing entity. In our human analogy, the MIB corresponds to quantitative data (measures of activity, productivity, and budget, with the latter being settable by the managing entity) exchanged between the branch office and the main office. Finally, also resident in each managed device is a network management agent, a process running in the managed device that communicates with the managing entity, taking local actions on the managed device under the command and control of the managing entity. The network management agent is the branch manager in our human analogy.

The third piece of network management architecture is the network management protocol. The protocol runs between the managing entity and the managed devices, allowing the managing entity to query the status of managed devices and indirectly take actions at these devices via its agents. Agents can use the network management protocol to inform the managing entity of exceptional events (for example, component failures or violation of performance thresholds). It is important to note that the network management protocol does not itself manage the network. Instead, it provides a tool with which the network administrator can manage monitor, test, poll, configure, analyze, evaluate and control the network. This is the subtle, but important distinction.

Although the infrastructure for network management is conceptually simple, one can often get bogged down with the network-management-speak vocabulary of "managing entity", "managed device", "managing agent", and "managing information base". For example, in network-management-speak, our simple host monitoring scenario, "managing agents" located at "managed devices" as periodically queried by the "managing entity"—a simple idea, but a linguistic mouthful! Hopefully, keeping the human organizational analogy and its obvious parallels with network management in mind will be of help to understand the concept.

Our discussion of network management architecture above has been generic, and broadly applies to a member of the network-management standards and efforts that have been proposed over the year. Network Management Standards began maturing in the late 1980's with OSI CMISE/CMIP (the Common Management Service Element/Common Management Information Protocol) and the Internet SNMP (Simple Network-Management Protocol) emerging as the two most important standards. Both are designed to be independent of vendor-specific products or networks. Because SNMP was quickly designed and deployed at a time when the need for network management was becoming painfully clear, SNMP found widespread use and acceptance. Today, SNMP has emerged as the most widely used and deployed network management framework.

13.5 SIMPLE NETWORK MANAGEMENT PROTOCOL (SNMP)

13.5.1 Review

SNMP management began in the 1970's. Internet Control Message Protocol (ICMP) was developed to manage ARPANET. ICMP is a mechanism to transfer control message between nodes. A popular example of this is Packet Internet Groups (PING), which is part of the TCP/IP suite now. PING is very simple tool that is used to investigate the health of a node and the robustness of communication with it from the source node. It started as an early form of a network-monitoring tool.

The ARPANET, which started in 1969, developed into the Internet in the 1980's with the advent of UNIX and the popularization of client/server architecture. Data was transmitted in packet form using routers and gateways. TCP/IP-based networks grew rapidly, mostly in the defense and academic communities and in small enter-premarital companies that took advantage of the electronic media for information exchange. The National Science Foundation officially dropped the name ARPANET in 1984, and adopted the name Internet. Note that Internet is spelled with capital I and is limited to TCP/IP-based network. An Internet Advisory Board (IAB) was formed to administer Internet-activities.

With the growth of the Internet, it became essential to have the capability to monitor and configure gateways remotely. The Simple Gateway Monitoring Protocol (SGMP) was developed for this purpose—an interim solution. The Internet Advisory Board recommended the development of SNMP, which is enhancement of SGMP. Even SNMP was intended to be another interim solution, with the long-term solution being migration to the OSI standard CMIP/CMIS. However, due to the enormous simplicity of SNMP and its extensive implementation, it has become de facto standard. SNMPv2 was developed to make it independent of the OSI standard, as well as to add features SNMPv2 has only partially overcome some of the limitations of SNMP. The final version of SNMPv2 was released without one of the major enhancement on its security features there are strong differences of opinion among working group members on the specifications. SNMPv3 addresses the security feature.

13.5.2 Simple Network Management Protocol

The SNMP is a management protocol designed to make sure network protocols and devices not only work but work well. It allows managers to locate problems and make adjustments by exchanging a sequence of commands between a client and a server. Figure 13.5 shows the SNMP architecture. A network manager runs a management client program at a site that

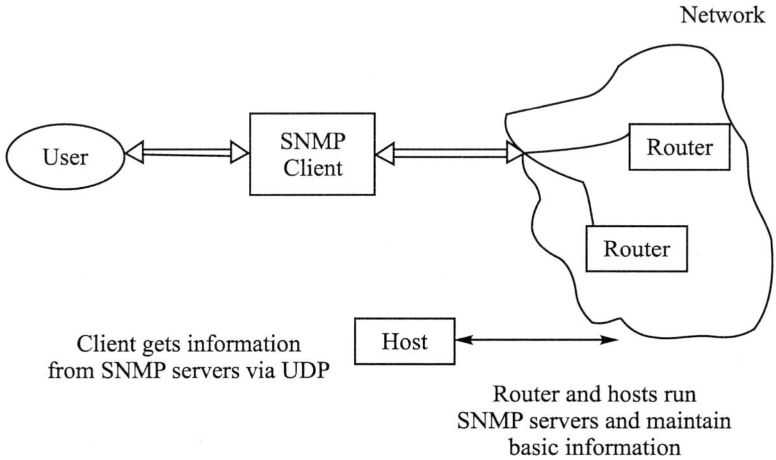

Figure 13.5 SNMP architecture.

communicates with the management server program at another site. Typically the server problems are run on remote hosts and especially network routers. Both management programs use commands defined by the SNMP protocol. Primarily the commands define how to request information from a server and send information to a server or client.

SNMP has several goals. The first is to simplicity SNMP function to reduce support costs and make SNMP easier to use. Second, it must be extensible to accommodate future updates in network operations and management. Third, the protocol must be independent of design, specifies of hosts or routers. The result is an application-layer protocol that interfaces with transport services.

Because SNMP is a management application it must know that process it is to manage and how to refer to them. The routers and hosts that SNMP manages are called objects. An object has a formed definition according to ASN.1 (Abstract Syntax Notation 1), a formal language designed expressly for the definition of PDU (Protocol Data Units) formats and objects.

Management Information Base (MIB)

Each object server maintains a database of information that describes its characteristics and activities. Because there are different object types, a standard defines precisely what should be maintained. This standard, the Management Information Base (MIB) was defined by group, that proposed SNMP. There are eight categories of information specified by MIB.

(a) *System:* Describes the host or router operating system and contains information such as when the server was booted, a description of the device it runs on, device location, and contact person.

(b) *Interface:* Describes each network interface and contains items such as MTU size (one of the problems the Internet Protocol faces is that different network architecture allow different maximum frame sizes, also called maximum transfer units or MTU), transmission rate, number of packets discarded for various reasons, number of octets transmitted and received number of interfaces, and an interface description.

(c) *Address translation:* Contains a table used to change as IP address into a network-specific one.

(d) *IP:* Describes information specific to the Internet Protocol. Examples of information maintained include default time-to-live value for IP packets, number of data grams eliminated for various reasons, number of data grams forwarded and delivered to the transport protocol and received from the data link protocol, number of fragments evaded, number of datagrams reassembled, and routing tables.

(e) *ICMP (Internet control message protocol):* Describes information specific to the ICMP protocol, primarily, it contains many counters tracking the number of each type of control message sent by ICMP.

(f) *TCP:* Among the items it contains are timeout lengths, number of connections, number of segments sent and received, maximum number of simultaneous connection, IP address of each entity using TCP and the IP address of the remote connection, and the number of failed connection attempts.

(g) *UDP (User datagram protocol):* Among the items it contains are the number of data grams delivered, discarded, or received and the IP addresses of entities using UDP.

(h) *EGP (Exterior gateway protocol):* This is a protocol to exchange routing information between two autonomous networks in an Internet. As with other categories, the MIB maintain counters tracking the number of EGP messages sent and received.

SNMP Commands

The management programs that use SNMP run asynchronously. That is, they send out requests but can do other things while waiting for responses. Generally the requests, or PDU, request information from a server, send information to a remote management program, or respond to special conditions. SNMP defines five PDU (Protocol Data Units) formats:

(a) *Get Request:* This command causes a Get Request PDU to be sent containing a command code, object name, and specification of an MIB variable. The receiving entity responds by sending a Get Response PDU containing values of the variable requested or an error code in the event of an error.

(b) *Get Next Request:* This command is similar to Get Request except that the request is for values of variables that "follow" the ones specified in the PDU. The notation of following is based on a lexicographic order determined by the MIB design. This is especially, useful for traversing tables maintained by the management server.

(c) *Get Response:* A PDU sent in response to a previously received Get Request PDU. It contains values requested or error codes.

(d) *Set Request:* This command allows the manager to update values of MIB variables maintained by remote management program and to remotely alter the characteristics of a particular object, which, in turn, can affect network operation the format does not violate any security measures that prevent unauthorized updates.

(e) *Trap:* The PDU is sent from a server to the manager when specific conditions or events have occurred. It allows the manager to stay abreast of changes in the operating environments. Some of the trap PDU's and their events are listed here:

- *Coldstart Trap:* The management program has been reinitialized with potential changes in the objects characteristics.
- *Warmstart Trap:* Reinitialization has occurred, but no characteristics have been altered.
- *Linkdown Trap:* A communication link has failed.
- *Linkup Trap:* A previously failed communication has been restored.
- *Neighbor Loss Trap:* The station has lost contract with an EGP peer neighbor.
- *Authentication Failure Trap:* An SNMP PDU that failed an authentication check has been received.

13.5.3 Simple Network Management Protocol Version 2 (SNMPv2)

In August 1988, the specification for SNMP was issued and rapidly became the dominant network management standard. A number of vendors offer standalone network management workstation based on SNMP. As the name suggests, SNMP is a simple tool for network management.

With its widespread use, the deficiencies of SNMP became increasingly apparent; these include both functional deficiencies and lack of security facility. As a result an enhanced version, known as SNMPv2, was issued in 1993, with a revised version issued in 1996.

SNMPv2 was designed to overcome some of the perceived weaknesses of SNMP. For example, one of the criticisms of SNMP is that, because of its simple command format, communication requires a large no. of packets, SNMPv2 provides more messaging options, thus, allowing the clients and hosts to communicate more efficiently. SNMPv2 also provides more security than the original SNMP through its implementation of message authentication and DES encryption. A third enhancement is increased flexibility to allow SNMPv2 to run on top of multiple protocols such as AppleTalk, 1PX, and OSI.

SNMPv2 does not provide network management at all. SNMPv2 instead provides a framework on which network management applications can be built. Those applications such as fault management, performance monitoring, accounting, and so on. Many of the functional deficiencies of SNMP were addressed in SNMPv2. To correct the security deficiencies of SNMPv1/v2, SNMPv3 was issued as a set of proposed standards in January 1998. This set of documents does not provide a complete SNMP capability but rather defines an overall SNMP architecture and set of security capabilities. These are intended to be used with the existing SNMPv2.

SNMPv3 provides three important services: authentication, privacy, and access control. The first two are parts of the *User-based Security* model and the last is defined in the *View-based Access Control Model.* Security services are governed by the identity of the user requesting the service; this identity is expressed as a principal, which may be an individual or an application or a group of individuals or applications.

REVIEW QUESTIONS

13.1 Define network management. Explain the importance of operation and maintenance in network management.

13.2 How is it possible to specify the goal of network management? Explain major groups, which comprises network management.

13.3 Make the diagram to represent the top-down view of network management.

13.4 Explain the network management functional groupings

13.5 What is importance of network operation group in management?

13.6 Explain OSI network management applications.

13.7 What is difference between performance management and goal management?

13.8 Explain network management standards.

13.9 Explain configuration management and its application in network management.

13.10 Explain accounting management and its application in network management.

13.11 Explain security management and its application in network management.

13.12 What is OSI management protocol?

13.13 What is common management information protocol?

13.14 What is simple network management protocol?

13.15 Discuss network management model and explain the importance of communication model in network management.

13.16 Define the terms, object, agent and management.

13.17 Discuss infrastructure for network management.

13.18 Explain SNMP architecture and discuss simple network management protocol.

13.19 Explain management information base.

13.20 What is difference between SNMP and SNMPv2?

CHAPTER 14

Security Management

Chapter Outline

As networks have extended, they have dramatically changed the nature of network security. The traditional security officer was a gatekeeper. Now, says one consultant, "there are many gates, and some one has to be in-charge of the gatekeepers". Security is no longer a single function. It is the responsibility of each department. The modern security manager is not a security czar, imposing and enforcing rules of access. The job now is to teach, motivate and support people who have taken charge of their own computing resources. These are not "users", in any sense of the word, and they certainly are not the enemy. They and their departments are clients and the purpose of computer security is to support them in doing their jobs.

The basic goals of a network security system are pretty much like the security goals for any kind of computer system.

- To protect information from accidental destruction or modification.
- To protect information from deliberate destination or modification.
- Make sure the data is available to authorized users, when they need it and in a form they can use.

Security management has always been important function within an organization. Now, with the ever-increasing risk associated with interconnections, the importance of good security management is paramount to an organization ability to manage risk effectively and reduce it whether possible. Internet, intranet and extranet connection all add complexity, which in turn add to the inherent risk. Security management, basically, is the process of managing and maintaining security within the organization. Both design and development are relatively easy compared with managing and maintaining the security from a logistic perspective. Although design and deployment both have more definitive starting and finishing points, managing security, on the other hand, is a journey that has no true end point.

The best technical security architecture can be designed and deployed, but without proper management and operations, it is of little use. Security management provides the necessary guidance and direction for the overall architecture and operations that govern the use of the architecture. This includes managing the policies and procedures, and managing the individual components within the architecture. Doing this enables the organization to stay on top of advances in technology that might affect how policy or procedures should be augmented.

14.1 SECURITY PLAN

A security plan identifies and organizes the security activities for a computing system. The plan is both a description of the current situation and a plan for improvement. Every security plan must address seven issues.

(i) **Policy:** Indicating the goals of a computer security efforts and the willingness of the people involved to work to achieve those goals.

(ii) **Current state:** Describing the states of security at the time of the plan.

(iii) **Requirements:** Recommending ways to meet the security goals.

(iv) **Recommended controls:** Mapping controls to the vulnerabilities identified in the policy and requirements.

(v) **Accountability:** Describing who is responsible for each security activity.

(vi) **Time table:** Identifying when different security functions are to be above.

(vii) **Continuing attention:** Specifying a structure for periodically updating the security plan.

There are many approaches to creating and updating a security plan. Some organizations have a formal, defined security planning process, much as they might have a defined and accepted development or maintenance process. Other look to security professionals for guidance on how to perform security planning.

14.2 SECURITY ANALYSIS

Who performs the security analysis, recommends a security program, and writes the security plan? As with any such comprehensive task, these activities are likely to be performed by the committee that represents all the interests involved. The size of the committee depends on the size and complexity of the computing organization and the degree of its commitment to security. Organizational behaviour studies suggest that the optimum size for a working committee is in between five and nine members. Sometimes large committee may serve as an oversight body to review and comment on the products of a smaller working committee. Alternatively, a large committee might designate subcommittees to address various sections of the plan.

Security in operating systems and networks requires the cooperation of the system administration staff. Program security measures can be understood and recommended by applications programmers. Physical security controls are implemented by those responsible for general physical security, both against human attacks and natural disasters. Finally, because control affects system users, the plan should incorporate user's views, especially with regard to usability and general desirability of controls.

Thus, no matter how it is organized, a security planning team should represent each of the following groups.

- Computer hardware group
- System administrators
- Systems programmers
- Applications programmers
- Data entry personnel
- Physical security personnel
- Representative users.

In some cases, a group can be adequately represented by someone who is consulted at appropriate times, rather than a committee member from each possible constituency being enlist.

After the plan is written, it must be accepted and its recommendations carried out. Acceptance by the organizations is key: a plan that has no organizational commitment is simply a plan that collects dust on the shelf. Commitment to the plan means that security functions will be implemented and security activities carried out. Three groups of people must contribute to make the plan a success.

- The planning team must be sensitive to the needs of each group affected by the plan.
- Those affected by the security recommendations must understand what the plan means for the way they will use the system and perform their business activities. In particular, they must see how what they do can affect other users and other systems.
- Management must be committed to using and enforcing the security aspects of the system.

14.3 CHANGE MANAGEMENT

Change management is the process of modifying equipment, systems, software, or procedures in a planned and authorized manner. This includes ensuring that a business purpose is behind the change request.

Change management procedures are one way to add structure and control to the development of large software systems as they move from development to operation. Change management refers to a standard methodology for performing and recording changes during software development and operation. The methodology defines steps that ensure that system changes are required by the organization, and are properly authorized, documented, tested and approved by management. The term change management is often applied to the management of changes in the business environment, typically as a result of business process reengineering or quality enhancement efforts.

Without change management, an organization can be a chaotic place to work. Human errors can result in a large number of system outages and downtime. With proper change management in place, many of these errors can be significantly reduced. Changes should follow a tightly controlled, repeatable process. Figure 14.1 shows the proper steps in the change management process. This process can be applied to all applications, networks, and systems as well as procedures within your corporation.

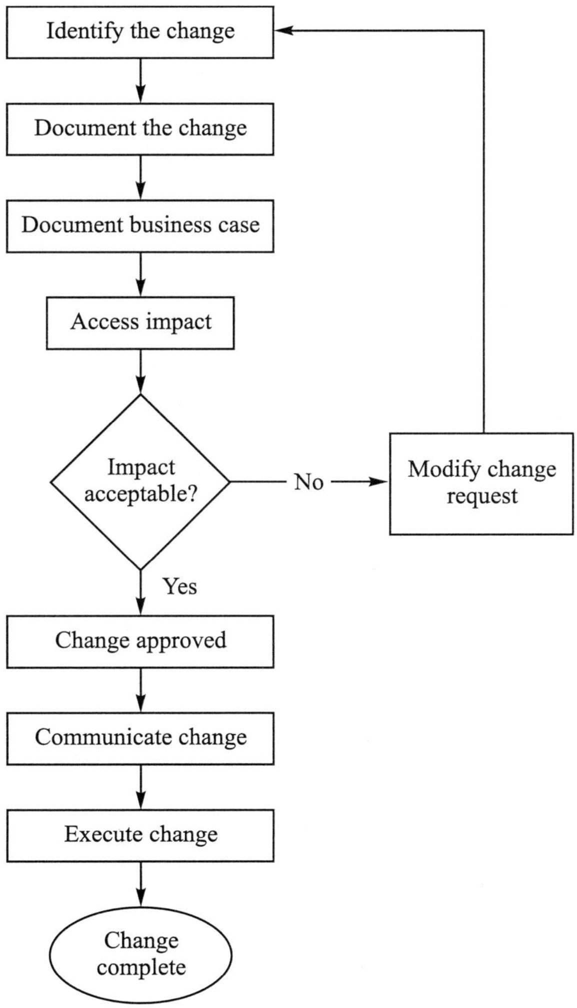

Figure 14.1 Change management process.

Following steps can be used to manage change control across the organization:

Identity and document the change: This step should include the type of equipment, system, or software to be modified. It should also include when the change will occur, how long the change will last, and who will perform the change.

Document the business reason, or driver, behind the change: Is this change in support of a new and critical business application, or is to upgrade code on a firewall to fix an existing problem?

Estimate the impact of the change and determine if the impact is acceptable: Is this change likely to bring down the Internet connection for an extended period, or is it a change that the users and applications should not notice?

Document accurate back-out procedures in the event that the change does not succeed: In this situation, the affected changes can be safely removed, enabling you to revert to your previous operational configuration.

Once the impact has been accessed and the change has been approved, the change should be communicated to all relevant parties: Only then should the change to be executed.

This may appear to be lengthy process, but it does provide many benefits to the organization. By forcing the implementers to document and access the impact of their changes, they think through the change more carefully. It also forces them to design and document a rollback plan ahead of time.

Process for implementing change management is as follows:

- A standardized process and a change control board provide management with proper oversight and control of the software development life cycle.
- A good change management process will exhibit good segregation of duties and have clearly defined roles, responsibilities and approvals.
- An effective change controls board facilities, good management oversight and coordination between projects.

14.3.1 The Capability Maturity Model

As an organization embarks upon implementing change management, an important concept to understand is the Capability Maternity Model (CMM) for software developed at Carnegie Mellon University's Software Engineering Institute (SEI). The CMM relies on configuration or change management as one of its fundamental concepts. It provides organization with the capability to improve their software processes by providing an evolutionary path from ad hoc processes to disciplined software management processes.

The SEI's web page defines the five maturity levels:

1. **Initial:** The software process is ad hoc.
2. **Repeatable:** The software process is structured enough that success with one project can be repeated for another similar project.

3. **Define:** The software process is standardized and documented.
4. **Managed:** Various aspects of the software process and products are measured and evaluated.
5. **Optimizing:** Key business processes and their supporting software projects are continuously improved based on measurements and testing new ideas.

Change management is a key process to implement the CMM in an organization. For example, if an organization is at CMM level 1, then it probably has no formal change management processes in place. At level 3, an organization has a defined change management process that is followed. At level 5, the change management process is a routine part of improving software products and implementing new ideas. In order for an organization to effectively manage software development, operations and maintenance, then it should be using the CMM and must have effective change management processes in place.

14.4 DISASTER RECOVERY

Many types of disasters, whether natural or caused by people, can disrupt your organization's operations for lengthy periods. Such disasters are unlike the previously discussed threats to your computer systems and networks because the events that cause the disruption are not specifically aimed at your organization. Regardless of source, there are many threats that may disrupt operations, including industrial espionage, hacking, attacks from disgruntled employers, and inside threats, which must all be considered important in planning for disaster recovery.

No matter what the event is that you are worried about whether natural or not targeted at your organization or not—there are certain preparations you can make to lessen the impact on your organization and the length of time that your organization will be out of operation. A Disaster Recovery Plan (DRP) is critical for effective disaster recovery efforts. A DRP defines the data and resources necessary and the steps to take in order to restore critical organizational process.

Put another way, what it, that is needed by your organization to perform its mission? Answer this question, and you have the beginning of a DRP, since you know what needs to be quickly restored. When speaking of the resources, don't forget to include both the physical resources (such as computer hardware and software) and the personnel (you need somebody who knows how to run the systems that process your critical data). A common way to begin creating your disaster recovery plan is to answer the following questions for all critical functions:

- Who is responsible for the operation of this function?
- What do these individuals need to perform the functions?
- When should this function be accomplished in relation to other functions?
- Where will this function be performed?
- How is this function performed (What is the process)?
- Why is this function so important or critical to the organization?

By answering these questions, you can create an initial draft of your organizations DRP. The name often used to describe the document created by addressing these questions is a Business Impact Assessment (BIA) or Business Impact Analysis. This DRP, of course will need be approved by management and it is essential that they buy into the plan otherwise, your efforts will more than likely fail. The old adage, "those who fail to plan, plan to fail certainly applied in this situation."

It is important in a good DRP to include the processes and procedures needed to restore your organization so that it is functioning again and to ensure continued operation. What specific step will be required to restore operations? These processes should be documented and, where possible and feasible, they should be reviewed and exercised on a periodic basis. Having a plan with step-by-step procedures that nobody knows how to follow, does nothing to ensure the continued operation of the organization. Exercising disaster provides you with the opportunity to discover flaws or weakness in the plan when there is still time to modify and correct them.

There are many types of disasters that can cause a disruption to an organization.

(i) A business impact analysis can be conducted to identify the most critical functions for an organization.

(ii) A disaster recovery plan is created to outline an organization's plans to recover in the event a disaster strikes.

(iii) A business continuity plan is created to outline the order that business functions will be restored so that the most critical functions are accomplished first.

(iv) One of the most critical elements of any disaster recovery plan is the creation and maintenance of system backups.

(v) Backup should include not only the organization's critical data but critical software as well.

(vi) Exercises can play an important role by allowing personnel to practice the procedures established by the organization in the event of a security incident.

14.4.1 Policies and Procedures

Disaster recovery and business continuity plans are designed to address the needs of an organization in the event of a disruption of operations. What, however, governs the organization's operations on a daily basis? Policies are high-level statements made by management laying out the organizations position on some issue. Policies are mandatory but are not specific in their details. Policies are focused on the result, not the methods for achieving that result.

Standards are accepted specifications providing specific details on how a policy is to be enforced. Procedures are generally step-by-step instructions that describe exactly how employees are expected to act in a given situation or to accomplish a specific task. While there are standard policies that can be described in general terms that will be applicable to all organizations, standards and procedures are often more organizational-specific and driven by specific organizational policies are:

(i) Security policies are high-level statements produced by senior management to outline what security means to the organization.
(ii) There are number of standard policies that most organizations create including acceptable use, Internet usage, and e-mail usage policies.
(iii) Human resource policies are important to ensure that unacceptable risks are not taken in the event of an employee separating or being terminated.
(iv) Incident response policies are critical in order to outline in advance the steps the organization will take to respond to a security incident.

14.5 SYSTEMS SECURITY MANAGEMENT

Communications and systems security management is fundamental to the protection of the confidentiality, integrity, availability, authenticity, and non-repudiation characteristics of information. It is also a key element in the implementation of security policy.

The formal validation of system security is achieved through a process of certification and accreditation. All systems that handle classified information, or are particularly critical to a department's operation, will require accreditation. The establishment of departmental computer security policy and the conduct of informal system reviews should provide sufficient assurance of security for other systems. Certification of an IT system is the confirmation that it meets all its stated security requirements. The certification process includes the development and maintenance of security documentation. It also involves confirmation by the system developers or administrators that the documentation is correct and complete and that the documented security architectures, mechanisms and processes have been implemented. Accreditation follows on from certification. It is the process of verifying the system's security and formally authorizing the system for operation. It involves an independent review of the certification documentation to ensure that the security measures meet the required level of security for the information and services managed by the system. It also involves site inspections to ensure that security has been implemented according to the documentation and appropriately for the environment. Once the verification process is complete, the accreditation authority will use the results to determine whether the system has approval to operate. The accreditation authority for a specific system is ultimately the Chief Executive of the department operating the system. However, the responsibility may be delegated to a member of the department's senior management group.

Configuration management or configuration control is a set of measures to keep system security, integrity and functionality from degrading when introducing new facilities or eliminating faults. An organizations security plan may not work against new threats or ongoing changes in system configuration. Configuration management is fundamental to the continued strength of system security.

14.5.1 Configuration Control Board

Organizations should consider setting up a Configuration Control Board (CCB) to co-ordinate and approve changes to a system's baseline configuration. The CCB should have representatives from the following areas:

- Security
- Systems support
- Applications development, and
- Users.

Procedures

All system changes require configuration management. These may include:

- Hardware changes.
- Software changes; for example, changes to operating systems, applications, programs, utilities, and packages such as e-mail or web applications.
- Documentation for hardware, software and system operations.

Software Control

Take care when changing operational software—seemingly minor changes may have significant, unexpected effects. Be especially careful to isolate "one-off" research-type programs, which can subvert the system if uncontrolled. Consider controlling:

- Software selection
- Software installation and tailoring
- Software development and test environments
- Vendor's distribution media
- Software documentation
- Version changes and upgrades
- System and software patches and hotfixes.

14.5.2 Management Procedures

System Monitoring

Organizations should set procedures to monitor system use, ensuring that users only perform authorized processes. Consider:

- A separate risk assessment to decide the appropriate level of monitoring.
- Audit trails, which record exceptions and other relevant events, kept for a defined period to assist in investigations and ongoing access-control monitoring.
- Recording successful as well as rejected attempts at system access.

Accurate computer system clocks ensure the accuracy of audit logs, which may be needed for investigations or as evidence in legal or disciplinary cases. Where a computer or communications device uses a real-time clock, it should be set to an agreed standard such as local standard time. Clocks should be regularly checked and corrected against any variation from the standard.

Intrusion and Misuse Detection

Despite appropriate security measures, attacks on systems occur and succeed. Intrusion-detection products are recommended to detect and warn of attacks. Intrusion-detection tools are like virus-detection products in that they must be regularly reviewed and kept up-to-date. Network-based intrusion-detection products can detect a range of suspicious network activity, including:

- Attempts to use services blocked by firewalls.
- Unexpected requests, especially from unfamiliar network addresses.
- Unexpected encryption, which may be used to conceal an attack.
- Excessive network traffic from an unfamiliar site.
- Notable changes from past network activity.
- Attempts to exploit known system bugs or vulnerabilities.

Host-based intrusion-detection tools may also use the audit features of the host-operating system to detect suspicious activity, including:

- Users logging in at strange times or from unexpected addresses.
- Failed login attempts with bad passwords.
- Unauthorized or suspicious use of administrator-level functions.
- Changes to critical system files.
- Notable changes in a particular user's activity.
- Attempts to exploit known system bugs or vulnerabilities.

Network and host-based intrusion-detection tools may overlap, detecting the same attacks. While intrusion-detection tools will not detect all attacks, and there may be false alarms, they significantly reduce the risk of undetected intrusions.

When an intrusion-detection tool detects a suspected attack, to prevent further attempts:

- The system administrator must be alerted, and may take specific actions
- The intrusion-detection product may disable or constrain network services.

Protection against Malicious Software

There are many ways to exploit the vulnerability of computer software. The following can make unauthorized changes:

- Computer viruses
- Network worms

- Trojan horses
- Logic bombs.

Organizations must know about and prevent the introduction of malicious software. Specific procedures might include:

- Prohibition on software not authorized by a Configuration Control Board.
- Mandated use of approved antivirus and software-change-detection software.

Network Management

Access to computers and networks should be closely managed to:

- optimize service to the business.

Consistently apply security measures across the information-systems infrastructure.

Procedural controls to achieve and maintain network security may include:

- Allocation and/or separation of responsibilities.
- Intrusion or misuse detection.
- Guidelines for managing devices such as routers and firewalls.
- Management of cryptographic keys and equipment.

Organizations may need to interconnect or share computers or networks beyond traditional boundaries. The risk of unauthorized access and security breaches is greater for information passed across such networks and their computer systems. Security policies for networks that span organizational boundaries should consider additional controls:

- Within networks, to segregate user groups
- Between networks, to protect information in transit.

14.6 PROTECTING STORAGE MEDIA

Organizations should develop and use procedures to protect all media, for example tapes, disks and system documentation. Media should be protected against:

- Damage
- Theft
- Loss
- Unauthorized access
- Virus or other software, or network, attacks
- Inappropriate sanitization and/or disposal

Classified information on media should be protected from unauthorized disclosure or modification during transport. Clearly defined procedures should be used to manage removable computer media, such as tapes and disks. All media should be marked and stored according to the most sensitive or highest-classified information it contains. Removable media, such as disks and back-up tapes, must be labelled clearly and distinctively, with the security classification on each item that contains material that is **Sensitive, Restricted** or above. All movements of media in and out of an organization should be recorded. Media should be checked:

- On arrival for classification, damage, and malicious software such as viruses.
- On departure for classified information and viruses.

Privately-owned media should be strictly controlled. As a general rule, private media should not enter systems in organizations. Organizations that process classified information should have a checking procedure, independent of the originator, to ensure that exported media contains only the information intended.

Adequate back-up facilities should be used so that all essential business data and software can be accessed or recovered after an incident. This may include a system failure, virus attacks, or a natural disaster. Back-up for each system should meet the requirements of the organization's business continuity plan. Organizations should have procedures in place for the emergency destruction of classified or sensitive information held in high-risk environments.

Sanitization is the process of erasing as far as possible the information from media or equipment. The process of sanitization does not automatically change the classification of the media or equipment. Note that sanitization does not involve destroying the media or equipment.

Considerable information can be retrieved from computing equipment and media that has failed or outlived its purpose. The only totally reliable method of removing all traces of information from memory devices and magnetic media is physical destruction. However, some sanitization methods can be a reliable alternative, in making the information too expensive to be worth recovering. Approved sanitization procedures can be used to cleanse a device or media for disposal or reuse.

Media or equipment retains the security classification of the highest-classified information it has ever held until appropriately sanitized or declassified.

Waste material that could contain official information must be disposed of securely as approved ways of disposing of information-systems media, such as magnetic media which include:

- Degaussing (or demagnetization)—for floppy disks and magnetic tape, though hard disks may also have tracking information destroyed this way.
- Overwriting with approved software—for hard disks, but not for floppy discs or magnetic tape.
- Destruction—mandatory for magnetic media that has held information classified TOP Secret.

14.7 PROTECTION OF SYSTEM DOCUMENTATION

System documentation may contain a range of sensitive information and should be protected from unauthorized access by:

1. Physically securing it.

2. Minimizing its distribution.
3. Disposing securely when it is superseded.

14.7.1 Security in Software Applications

Input data should be vetted in all key business systems. Processing errors or deliberate acts can corrupt data that has been correctly entered into an application system. Systems should have validation checks to detect any such corruption. The specific controls needed depend on the application and the assessed impact of any corruption.

14.7.2 Operating Systems and Package Maintenance

All changes to operating systems software must be managed through strong configuration management processes. Changes to original copies of systems software and standard commercial software should be discouraged. If necessary, changes should be made only to a clearly identified copy; the original software should be retained.

14.7.3 Protection of Development Suite and Test Data

Development and operational systems should be separated to reduce the risk of accidental changes or unauthorized access to operational software, processes and data. Developmental and operational software should be run in different operating environments. Source code and configuration files should be protected from unauthorized viewing and changing. They should be managed under strict version control, with clear separation between operational and development versions. Source code should not be stored on operational systems, nor should it be freely available to information systems support staff who do not need access.

Testing data should be completed before implementation. Test data should be protected and controlled. System and acceptance testing usually requires much test data that mimics live data. The use of live databases containing personal information should be avoided.

14.8 EXCHANGES OF INFORMATION AND SOFTWARE

Exchanges of information and software should be based on formal agreements, in line with any relevant legislation and licensing arrangements.

Procedures and standards should be set to protect information in transit, especially electronic data interchanges. One such mechanism is the Secure Electronic Environment (S.E.E.) for inter-organization communications classified up to **Sensitive**.

Organizations should consider the following security concerns in using leased lines or public networks to communicate between information systems that process classified information:

- Data interception
- Data modification

- User impersonation
- Unauthorized access into networks.
- Initial planning to use leased lines and public networks should incorporate security measures such as:
  - — Configuration management
  - — Security management
  - — Cryptography
  - — Border controls.

Organization networks connected to public networks must be protected by appropriate security measures, even if processing only unclassified information. The main public network, the Internet, has become a widely used business tool; electronic mail (e-mail) and access to the Worldwide Web are used more and more for business communications and transactions. The Internet is vulnerable to:

- Message interception.
- Unauthorized access to systems.
- Attacks which can modify, manipulate or destroy data and systems.
- Attacks which can hinder or disrupt services or systems.

Security policies should impose controls and processes to manage business or security risks from the Internet. These risks may include:

- Vulnerability of traffic to unauthorized interception or modification
- Vulnerability to error, for example, incorrect addressing or misdirection
- Lack of control over the reliability and availability of service
- Accessibility of official information in public directories.

Where the appropriate security measures are in place, connection to the Internet is permissible for networks handling official information classified up to **Restricted** or **Sensitive**. Systems that process information classified **Confidential** or above must not be connected to the Internet unless specific security measures are used such as encryption products.

No telephone conversation is free from the risk of interception:

- The telephone system is widely accessible by many people, such as maintenance technicians or switchboard operators, in the course of their normal duties.
- Authorized and unauthorized monitoring of telephones is possible at junctions and distribution points throughout the system.

Conversations classified **Confidential** or above must not be held over a telephone circuit unless it has end-to-end cryptographic protection. All staff should be briefed on the danger of using a telephone for classified conversations. Callers may try to get classified information by falsely representing themselves (social engineering). Staff should be reminded of the need to properly identify all callers before giving any information. Where a caller cannot be satisfactorily identified, they can be asked for a call-back number, which can be authenticated.

Security vulnerabilities of telephone systems include monitoring of room audio carried on telephone cables through built-in system features, or deliberate tampering with hardware or software, even when the telephone's handset is "on-hook".

Cellular phones (cellphones), both digital and analogue, should never be permitted in sensitive areas because:

- They can inadvertently transmit sensitive information.
- Some cellphones can be configured to ring silently and automatically answer an incoming call, and be used as an eavesdropping device to remotely monitor conversations.

Portable telephones (cellphones) and cordless telephones are generally vulnerable to intercept using inexpensive and readily available radio-scanning receivers.

Personal Electronic Devices (PEDs) such as Personal Digital Assistants (PDAs) have further vulnerabilities so that potential risks increase from using them in or around areas where classified information may be discussed or processed. Some issues of concern are:

Audio Recording Capabilities: Some PEDs are capable of recording up to six hours of audio. Additionally, microphones may be capable of picking up normal office conversations from a distance in excess of 50 feet.

IR Ports: Data from the IR port of a PED can be intercepted at (or exercised from) significant distances.

The following minimum precautions should be observed:

Microphones: Site policies should preclude the introduction of audio recording equipment including PEDs with microphones into controlled spaces.

IR Ports: Any IR Port on a PED should be covered with an IR opaque metallic tape.

Passwords: The use of strong device passwords should be mandated, as the password may be the only mechanism that prevents an attacker from loading malicious code onto a PED.

- Wireless-enabled personal electronic devices (WPEDs) such as e-mail or web-enabled cellphones, and wireless enabled palm-top computers, have the same set of vulnerabilities as Wireless LANs (WLANs) and must be handled accordingly.
- Information transmitted to a pager can be easily intercepted. Pagers must not be used to transmit classified information.
- Care should be taken when using answerphones in offices handling classified information to ensure that classified messages are not left on them.
- PABXs generally have a dial-in facility for remote maintenance. This might allow a person distant from a secure site to gain system access.The remote maintenance facility of PABXs should be disabled. However, if used it should be physically or electronically isolated when not in use.
- Dial in Subscriber Access (DISA) lines should be carefully managed.

- Commercial facsimile (fax) systems that transmit and receive information over open communications channels are not secure. They are as vulnerable as telephone systems.
- Additional security risks come from facsimile units that scan and print. They should not be connected simultaneously to both unclassified and classified systems.
- For occasional use within New Zealand, facsimile may be used without encryption to transmit information classified in **Confidence, Restricted** or **Sensitive**.
- Video-conferencing systems should be protected by encryption systems appropriate to the classification of material transmitted and to the transmission medium. Note that:
  —The auto-answer features should be disabled.
  —The Internet should not be used as a vehicle for sensitive video-conferencing at this time.

14.9 SECURITY REQUIREMENTS OF SYSTEMS

Systems security must consider:

- Infrastructure
- Applications, including user-developed applications
- Availability of adequate capacity and resources.

Security can depend on how a business process that supports an application or service is designed and implemented.

Before developing information systems, organizations should identify and agree on security needs. At the requirements phase of an information systems project, as part of the overall business case, all security needs including fallback arrangements should be:

- Identified
- Justified
- Agreed
- Documented.

For systems with information that requires confidentiality, authentication, integrity and protection in transit or on magnetic media, consider cryptography.

Cryptography or encryption is the process of transforming information into an unintelligible form to safeguard its security and integrity. It uses an encryption algorithm and a secret cryptographic key.

Cryptography also can ensure:

- Authentication: The identity of the respective parties can be confirmed.
- Integrity: Any change to the information while in transit can be detected.
- Non-repudiation: The sender cannot deny sending the information.

While encryption can be a powerful tool, used carelessly it can:

- Hinder virus and system-misuse detection.
- Cause information to be lost.
- Provide users with a false sense of security.

The policy for cryptographic systems and techniques should account for business needs within and between departments.

REVIEW QUESTIONS

14.1 What are the basic goals of network security system?

14.2 What is the role of security management?

14.3 What are the issues addressed by security plan?

14.4 Why security analysis is important? Who performs the security analysis?

14.5 What is change management? Explain its importance.

14.6 Describe change management process.

14.7 Explain capability maturity model.

14.8 What is CMM level 3?

14.9 Explain disaster recovery.

14.10 Why policies and procedures are important for disaster recovery?

14.11 What is importance of confidentiality, integrity, availability in security management?

14.12 Why protection of storage media is important for organization?

14.13 Why exchange of information and software should be based on formal agreements?

14.14 How to consider requirements to build security system?

CHAPTER 15

Risk Management and Incident Management

Chapter Outline

Risk is the underlying concept that forms the basis for what we call *security*. Risk is the potential for less that requires protection. If there is no risk, there is no need for security. And yet risk is a concept that is barely understood by many who work in the security industry.

Risk management can best be described as a decision-making process. In the simplest terms, when you manage risk, you determine what could happen to your business, you assess the impact if it were to happen, and you decide what you could do control that impact as much as you or your management deems necessary. You then decide to act or not to act and finally, evaluate the results. Best practices clearly indicate that an important aspect of effectively managing risk is to consider it an ongoing process. Effective risk management avoids costly oversights and unexpected problems. Security is only as effective as the response it generates. A structured response ensures that an incident is recognised early and dealt with in the most appropriate manner. An incident that is not responded to in a timely manner can expose an organization to many issues like disclosure of confidential information, exposure to legal cans from third party organizations impacted as a result of the incident, etc.

If you spend any time at all in the fields of network security or system administration, you will likely be involved in some sort of incident response or recovery effort. An "incident" can be anything from a hardware failure to a full-scale security breach, and while each one is handled in a slightly different manner, so it requires incident management.

15.1 WHAT IS RISK MANAGEMENT?

Three definitions related to risk management show why it is sometimes considered difficult to understand.

(i) The dictionary defines "Risk" as the possibility of suffering harm or loss.

(ii) Carnegie Mellon University's Software Engineering Institute (SEI) defines continuous risk management as, processes, methods and tools for managing risks in a project. It provides a disciplined environment for proactive decision-making to
   (a) assess continuously what could go wrong (risks),
   (b) determine which risks are important to deal with,
   (c) implement strategies to deal with those risks.

(iii) In modern business term, risk management is the process of identifying vulnerabilities and threats to an organization's resources and assets and deciding what countermeasures, if any, to take to reduce the level of risk to an acceptable level based on the value of the asset to the organization.

These three definitions show that risk management is based upon what can go wrong and what action should be taken, if any. Figure 15.1, provides a high-level view of how to manage risk.

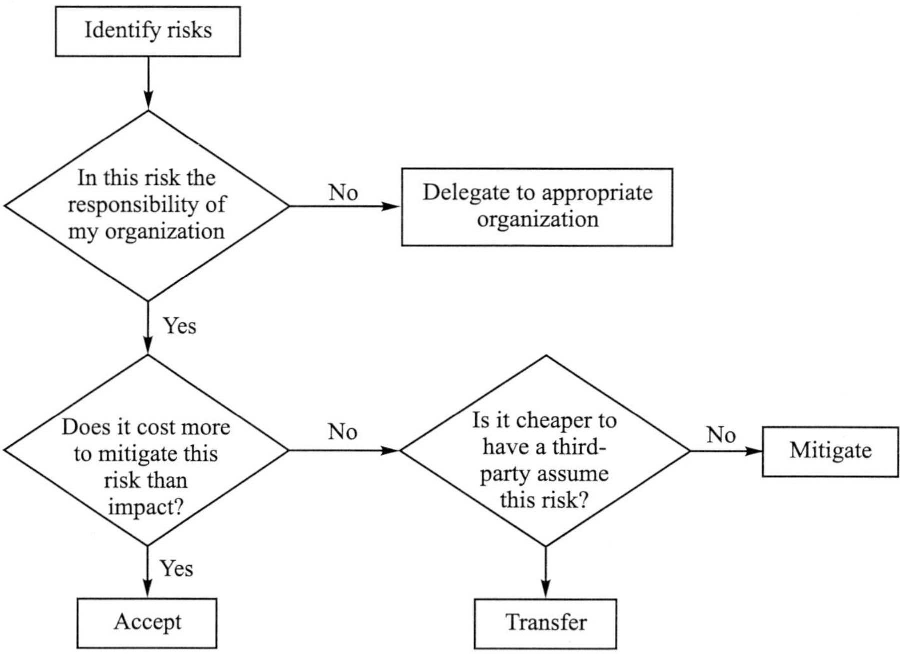

Figure 15.1 A planning decision flow chart for risk management.

15.2 AN OVERVIEW OF RISK MANAGEMENT

Risk management is the process of identifying, assessing, and mitigating risk. An organization has many individuals who are responsible for accepting the given risk for given applications. These individuals include the president, head of the business unit, and the information owner. The overall risk to an organization is dependent on the following attributes:

(i) The qualitative (effect of loss) and quantitative (monetary) value of the assets.
(ii) The likelihood of attack-based threats.
(iii) The business impact, if the threat is realized.

The ability to associate a cost with an asset's value or to determine the Return on Investment (ROI) is often difficult. The converse of that is to justify the cost of the protection mechanism. Classified national security information is valued as extremely sensitive. It is so sensitive that if it got in the wrong hands it could result in extreme damage to national security. The price the government is willing to spend to protect that information is typically much more than commercial-based organizations are willing to spend.

The direct quantitative costs include the replacement of damaged equipment, cost of restoring any backups, hard disks, and memory. The downtime suffered by the incident is measurable. Many financial trading systems have an associated cost of being offline. Productivity can also be lost; if the e-mail or voice mail servers are down, most organizations productivity will come to a standstill.

Qualitative costs can be more devastating to organization than quantitative costs. If retail web site was broken into by a hacker and all of the client credit card numbers were stolen, this would seriously affect the site's reputation. In all likelihood, the site would be out of business within a short time. If a state-run agency is operating an online business that requires a license (for example, life insurance) and the site shows a sign of negligence (no internet firewall), then the state could take away the site's license. This could potentially put it out of business.

Risks are assessed by examining the likelihood of a threat and vulnerability, and by considering the potential impact of an unwanted incident. The threat level is determined by the incentive of the individual (typically thrill-seeking, espionage, or revenge) and his or her ability. Most insiders are not capable to use automated hacker tools. They are, however, very familiar with the applications on the network. Typically, employees on their way out the door delete files or cause some physical damage. Some cases of logic bombs have been reported; there are software programs that once activated by a specific data, eat through files or reformat hard drives.

The vulnerability level is the inverse of the capability of the security architecture to protect an organization's assets (security controls). If the security controls are weak the exposure level will be high; this linked with opportunity can spell disaster. The likelihood of an exploit and vulnerability to the data/resource depend on the following attributes, which are difficult to predict:

- Assets value
- Attractiveness to adversaries
- The technology changes
- Network and processor speed
- Software exploits.

The best way to describe threats and vulnerabilities is in terms of the business impact. In addition, the impact assessed for a particular risk also has an associated uncertainty as the unwanted incident may not turn out as expected. This impact could be on the specific line of business or the organization at large; it all depends on the level of exposure. All these factors may have a large amount of uncertainty as to the accuracy of the predictions associated with them. Planning and the justification of security can be very difficult. Figure 15.2 provides risk assessment methodology.

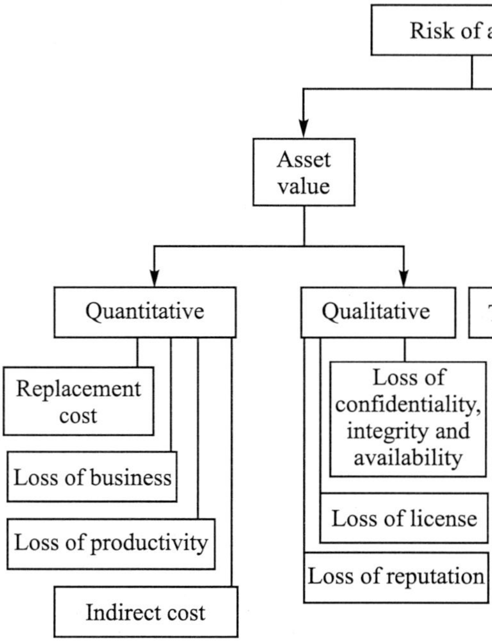

Figure 15.2 Risk assessment methodology.

Risk management is both a skill and a task that all managers do, either deliberately or intuitively. It can be simple or complex depending on the size of the project or business and the amount of risk inherent in an activity. Every manager, at all levels, must learn to manage risk. The required skills can be learned.

15.3 IDENTIFY THE RISK TO AN ORGANIZATION

The identification of risk is straightforward. All you need to do is to identify the vulnerabilities and the threats that you are exposed to. How do these identified risks relate to the actual risk to an organization? The short answer is: not very well. Once vulnerabilities, threats, and countermeasures are identified, we can identify specific risks to the organization.

When identifying specific vulnerabilities, begin by locating all the entry points to the organization. In other words, find all the access points to information (in both electronic and physical form) and systems within the organization. This means identifying the following:

- Internet connections
- Remote access points

- Connections to the other organizations
- Physical access to facilities
- User access points
- Wireless access points.

For each of these access points, identify the information and systems that are accessible. Then identify how the information and the systems may be accessed. Be sure to include in this list any known vulnerabilities in operating systems and applications.

Threat assessment is very detailed and in some cases, difficult task. Attempts to identify specific or targeted threats to an organization will often turn up obvious candidates such as competitors. However, true threats will attempt to remain hidden from view. True, targeted threats may not show themselves until an event has occurred.

A targeted threat is the combination of a known agent having known access with a known performing a known event against a known target. Thus, we may have a disgruntled employee (the agent) who desires knowledge of the latest designs an organization is working on (the motivation). This employee has access to the organizations information systems (access) and known where the information is located (knowledge). The employee is targeting the confidentiality of the new designs and may attempt to force his way into the files he wants (the events).

The identification of all targeted threats can be very time consuming and difficult. An alternative to identifying targeted threats is to assume a generic level of threat (we are not paranoid, somebody is out to get us). If it is assumed that there exists a generic level of threat in the world, this threat would be comprised of anyone with potential access to an organization's systems or information. The threat exists because a human (employee, customer, supplier and so on) must access the system and information used in the organization in order to be useful. However, we may not necessarily have knowledge of a directed or specific threat against some part of the organization.

If we assume a generic threat (somebody, probably has the access, knowledge and motivation to do something bad), we can examine the vulnerabilities within an organization that may allow the access to occur. Any such vulnerability than translates into a risk since we assume there is a threat that may exploit the vulnerability. Vulnerabilities cannot be examined in a vacuum. A potential avenue of attack must be examined in the context of the environment and compensating controls must be taken into account when determining if vulnerability truly exists.

Countermeasures include the following:

- Firewalls
- Antivirus software
- Access control
- Authentication systems
- Biometrics
- Guards

- Encryption
- Well-trained employees
- Intrusion detection systems
- Automated patch and policy management systems.

For each access point within an organization, countermeasures should be identified. For example, the organization has an Internet connection. This provides potential access to the organization's systems. This access point is protected by a firewall. Examination of the rule set on the firewall will identify the extent to which an external entity can actually access internal systems. Therefore, some of the vulnerabilities via this access point may not be available to an external attacker since the firewall prevents access to those vulnerabilities or systems in their entirety.

Once vulnerabilities, threats and countermeasures are identified, we can identify specific risk to the organizations. This question is now simple: Give the identified access point with the existing countermeasures, what could someone do to the organization through each access point? For the answer to this question, we take the likely threats for each process point (or a generic threat) and examine the potential targets (confidentiality, integrity, availability and accountability) through each access point. Based on the damage that can be done, each risk is then related high, medium or low. It should be noted that the same vulnerability, may pose different levels of risk based on the access point so there is no risk. However, internal employees have access to the system since they do not need to enter the network through firewall. That means any internal employee could exploit this vulnerability and gain access to the system. Employees are not considered a likely source of threat, so the risk is classified as a medium risk level. To complete this example, let's look at the physical access to the facility that houses the system in question. We find that the physical controls are weak and individual could walk in off the street and gain access to a system on the network. Controls on the network do not prevent an unauthorized system from plugging in and coming up on the internal network. In this case, we must assume that some individual with the motivation to do harm to this organization could gain physical access to the network and bring up an authorized system. This system would then be able to exploit the vulnerable mail system. The risk should now be classified a high risk. Physical countermeasures are lacking.

But high, medium, and low do not tell the whole story. A presentation to management about risk must show the damage an organization may sustain if vulnerability is exploited. How else can the organization identify how many resources to expand to reduce the risk?

15.4 RISK ANALYSIS

Good, effective security planning includes a careful risk analysis. A risk is a potential problem that the system or its users may experience. We distinguish a risk from other project events by looking for three things.

(i) **A loss associated with an event:** The event must generate effect: Compromised security, lost time, diminished quality, lost money, lost control, lost understanding, and so on. This loss is called the risk impact.

(ii) **The likelihood that the event will occur:** There is a probability of occurrence associated with each risk, measured from 0 (impossible) to 1 (certain). When the risk probability is 1, we say we have a problem.

(iii) **The degree to which we can change the outcome:** We must determine what, if anything, we can do to avoid the impact or at least reduce its effects. Risk control involves a set of actions to reduce or eliminate the risk. Many of the security control are examples of risk control.

We usually want to weigh the prons and cons of different actions we can take to address each risk. To that end, we can quantify the effects of a risk by multiplying the risk impact by the risk probability, yielding the risk exposure. For example, if the likelihood of virus attack is 0.3 and the cost to clean up the affected files is ₹ 10,000 then the risk exposure is ₹ 3,000. So, we may use a calculation like this, one to decide that a virus checker is worth an investment of ₹ 100, since it will prevent a much larger potential loss. Clearly, risk probabilities can change over time, so it is important to track them and plan for events accordingly.

In general, there are three strategies for risk reduction:

(a) Avoid the risk, by changing requirements for security or other system characteristics.

(b) Transferring the risk, by allocating the risk to other systems, people, organizations or assets; or by buying insurance to cover any financial loss should the risk become a reality.

(c) Assuming the risk, by accepting and controlling it with available resources, and preparing to deal with the loss if it occurs.

Thus, costs are associated not only with the risk's potential impact but also with reducing it. Risk leverage is the difference in risk exposure divided by the cost of reducing the risk. In other words, risk leverage is

$$\frac{\text{(Risk exposure before reduction)} - \text{(Risk exposure after reduction)}}{\text{(Cost of risk reduction)}}$$

If the leverage value of a proposed action is not high enough, then we look for alternative but less costly actions or more effective reduction techniques.

Risk analysis is the process of examining a system and its operational context to determine possible exposures and the potential harm they can cause. Thus, the first step in a risk analysis is to identify and list all exposures in the computing system of interest. Then for each exposure, we identify possible controls and their costs. The last step in a cost-benefit analysis: Does it cost less to implement a control or to accept the expected cost of the loss?

In our everyday lives, we take risks. In crossing the road, eating oysters or playing the lottery, we take the chance that our actions may result in some negative result—such as being injured, getting sick or losing money. Consciously or unconsciously, we weight the benefits of taking the action with the possible losses that might result. Just because there is a risk to a certain act we do not necessarily avoid it; we may look both ways before crossing the street, but we do cross it. In building and using computing systems, we must take a more organized and careful approach to assessing our risks. Many of the systems we build and use can have dramatic impact on life and health if they fail. For this reason, risk analysis is an essential part of security planning.

We cannot guarantee that our system will be risk-free, that is why our security plans must address action needed, should an unexpected risk become a problem. And some risks are simply part of doing business; for example as we have seen, we must steps to avoid disaster in first place. When we acknowledge that a significant problem cannot be prevented, we can use controls to reduce the seriousness of a threat. For example, you can backup files on your computer or a defense against the possible failure of a file storage device. But as our computing system become more complex and more distributed, complete risk analysis becomes more difficult and time consuming and more essential.

Risk analysis is performed in many different contexts, for example environmental and health risks are analyzed for activities such as building dams, disposing of nuclear waste or changing a manufacturing process. Risk analysis for security is adapted from more general management practices, paying special emphasis on the kinds of problems likely to arise from security issues. By following well-defined steps, we can analyze the security risks in computing system.

(i) Identify assets
(ii) Determine vulnerabilities
(iii) Estimate likelihood of exploitation
(iv) Compute expected annual loss
(v) Survey applicable controls and their costs
(vi) Project annual savings of control.

Different organizations take slightly different approaches, but the basic activities are still the same. For example, army used its operation security guidelines during the war. The guidelines involve five steps.

(i) Identify the critical information to be protected
(ii) Analyze the threats
(iii) Analyze the vulnerabilities
(iv) Assess the risks
(v) Apply countermeasures.

The steps are similar, but their details are always tailored to the particular situation at hand. For this reason, it is useful to use someone else's risk analysis process as a framework, but it is important to change it to match your own situation.

15.5 INCIDENT MANAGEMENT

Security is only as effective as the response it generates. A structured response ensures that an incident is recognized early and dealt with in the most appropriate manner. An incident that is not responded to in a timely manner can expose an organization to many issues including, but not necessarily limited to:

- Disclosure of confidential information
- Prolonged recovery times due to more extensive damage as a result of the ongoing incident.
- The inability to proceed with a criminal or civil case due to lack of evidence or inadequate evidence gathered.
- Negative impact to the organizations image in the eyes of shareholders, customers and/or partner organization.
- The organization may face potential legal and/or compliance issues depending on the regulatory and legal requirements.
- Exposure to legal cases from third party organizations impacted as result of the incident.
- Exposure to legal/libel cases from employees/individuals who may have been delt with unfairly by an inappropriate and/or cumbersome response.

An organization that has a structured and formalized response in place to internal and external IT security incidents demonstrates that it is taking its corporate and legal responsibilities seriously and has a positive security posture. This security posture ensures that the organization can deal with security incidents quickly, efficiently and effectively. This will result in:

(a) The rapid and accurate assessment of security incidents and the most appropriate response.
(b) Shortened recovery times to incidents and minimized business disruption.
(c) The confidence to proceed with a disciplinary, legal or civil case as a result of using proper procedures and processes to gather evidence in response to an incident.
(d) Ensures that the company complies with local legal, regulatory and industry requirements.
(e) A potential reduction in incidents as the organization is not considered a 'soft target'.
(f) Provides accurate reporting and statistics to continuously, improve the security of the organization.

15.5.1 Incident Notification/Identification

The notification or identification that an incident is occurring can happen in many different ways. Notification of an incident can happen:

- Automatically from specific security devices such as an alert from a firewall.
- Automatically from non-security devices such as a network monitoring systems that observes unusual network activity.
- From the manual review of system and security log files on network and/or security devices.

- Staff noticing unusual or suspicious activity on the computer system, or staff noticing content in breach of the company's security policy on a colleague's computer.
- From customers or the public who may have noticed corruption to their data, receiving a phishing e-mail or noticed defacement on the company's website.

A process should be in place to notify the relevant personnel that the incident has occurred and a response is required. This process should ensure that the following information is passed onto the response team:

(i) The date and time the incident occurred.
(ii) The date and time the incident was detected.
(iii) Who/what reported the incident.
(iv) Details of the incident including.
  - A description of the incident
  - Details of the systems involved
  - Corroborating information such as error messages, log files, etc.

Prior awareness to the possibility that an increase in the occurrence of certain incidents may happen can be improved as a result of known intelligence. Alerts from computer virus companies of a new computer virus will increase the awareness that an incident as a result of that virus could occur, alternatively hacking attempts are known to increase at the start of each autumn as students start university and try their new skills online.

15.5.2 Incident Classification

In order to ensure that incidents are responded to in a structured manner it is essential that incidents are classified into different levels so that high priority incidents can be responded to quicker than incidents of a lower nature. For example excessive traffic on port 80 on a firewall may indicate the start of a Denial of Service attack and would require a quick response to ensure minimal disruption to the network and therefore would be classified higher than, say a rejected access attempt to the personal directory of an employee.

The security of the incident does not alone impact the classification. The potential target also impacts the classification. A rejected access attempt to the organization's sensitive information will have a higher event classification than a rejected access attempt to unclassified information.

Classifying incidents will depend on many factors such as:

- The nature of the incident.
- The criticality of the systems being impacted.
- The number of systems impacted by the incident.
- The impact the incident can have an organization from a legal and/or public relations point of view.
- Legal and regulatory requirements for disclosure.

15.6 INCIDENT RESPONSE

In order to implement an appropriate incidence response, the proper people and processes need to be involved and the most appropriate response subsequently developed. Some incidents will simply require no response, others will require only an automated response, e.g. drop a connection to a blocked part on a firewall, whereas others will require a more complicated response involving personnel from various parts of the organization and different levels of management.

It is important to establish the appropriate levels of responses to an incident and also that the incident response has the necessary levels of authorization and autonomy. There is no point having senior management involved in a response to an incident that has minimal business impact.

All personnel involved in responding to an incident must be properly trained and versed in their responsibilities. If the skills are not available in house then they should be source-elsewhere. In addition all policies and procedures should be properly tested and reviewed on a regular basis to ensure their effectiveness and applicability. A review process should also be put in place to ensure that lessons are learnt from any incidents that require a response. Failure to take these steps could adversely impact business operations leading to loss of revenue or mission effectiveness, legal ramifications or a loss of public trust.

This incident response methodology will be dependent on the incident classification. The response team will also need to confirm that the incident has occurred and if so what the most appropriate response to the incident is. Once an incident has been confirmed and has initiated the appropriate incident response process, all care must be taken to preserve and record all information and potential evidence in the incident a legal or civil case ensues.

What response is required to an incident will depend on a mixure of business and technical drivers as the type of response can impact on employee, customer, and public relations and may even have legal ramifications. It is therefore essential that clear, concise and accurate processes and procedures that have been approved by senior management are in place for all personnel to follow.

As a large majorities of incidents may happen outside office hours or when key personnel are not immediately available, all staff must be given clear guidelines in how they report and respond to incidents.

Many incidents may simply require an automated response. For example a known computer virus detected in a file could be automatically deleted by the Anti-Virus software and not require a further response. However, an attack on the firewall will require a more measured response any many require the involvement of a senior management to decide whether to shut the firewall down to minimize the damage to the firewall or allow the attack to continue so further evidence may be gathered in the incident a legal case may be required.

An Incident Response Log should be kept where all actions and results of those actions are recorded accurately. Details as to who completed the actions, the time of the action and the outcome need to be maintained. This is to ensure that an accurate record of all action is taken in the event that the incident leads to a civil or criminal court case, or indeed these logs can be used to determine the effectiveness of the incident response procedures.

15.6.1 Incident Response Team

The Incident Response Team is responsible for managing the organization's response to an incident and how the organization interacts with third parties such as low enforcement agencies, regulatories bodies, customers, employees and the media.

The team should be made up of a number of people with knowledge and skills in different areas. It may be necessary to source certain skills externally to the organization. For example, forensic gathering skills are not commonplace and are often better sourced from vendors who specialize in the area. If this is the case then a formulated process should be in place to ensure that resource is available when required.

The Incident Response Team should also have the full backing and support of Senior Management. This should include giving the Incident Response Team the autonomy and authority to make decisions carry out actions in the absence senior management during a critical incident.

Typically an Incident Response Team will be made up of representatives of the following:

(i) ***IT security:*** The case team members will be those from the IT security team as they are the most knowledgeable with regards to managing and dealing with computer security incidents.

(ii) ***IT operations:*** As the operations team is very often the first line of defence/ detection of incidents either via monitoring tools or from reports to the support desk, it is essential that representation from this team is on the Incident Response Team.

(iii) ***Physical security:*** While IT security is arguably still in its infancy, the world of physical security has been around for a much longer time. A lot of experience and knowledge gained in the physical world can be applied to the virtual world. In addition, it may be necessary to involve the physical security team in the response to an incident where there has been physical access to compromised systems.

(iv) ***Human resources:*** It is essential that a representative from the Human Resource Team is involved in the Incident Response Team to ensure that processes and procedures comply with good Human Resource practice and do not impinge on industrial relations. The result of an incident response may be to discipline a staff member for breach of the organizations acceptable usage policy and this will require the Human Resource team's input to ensure due process.

(v) ***Legal department:*** As with the Human Resource Department, it is imperative that legal advice is taken both during the development of the processes and procedures and in the response to serious incidents.

(vi) ***Public relations:*** How information is communicated to the public, customers, partners, shareholders and press is a unique skill and one that is necessary to ensure the correct amount of information is disclosed at the right time to the right people.

(vii) ***External expertise:*** There will be times due to the nature of the information security incident external expertise will be required. For example, you may need external expertise in computer forensics or criminal investigations if those skills are not available in-house.

Note that depending on the seriousness and impact of an information security incident it may be necessary to mobilize all or only part of the Information Security Incident Response Team.

Once the Incident Response Team in place it should:

- Develop/review the processes and procedures that must be followed in response to an incident.
- Develop/review guidelines for incident classification. This should not be solely the responsibility of the Incident Response Team but must involve the business owners responsible for the systems and data being protected.
- Manage the response to an incident and ensure that all procedures are followed correctly.
- Review incidents to determine what lessons can be learnt and what process improvements may be required.
- Review changes in legal and regulatory requirements to ensure that all processes and procedures are valid.
- Review intelligence data such as information from log files, results from automated incident responses, third party websites and industry seminars to determine trends and changes in the IT security landscape and where future incidents could originate.
- Review and recommend technologies to manage and counteract incidents.
- Establish relationships with the local law Enforcement Agency and the appropriate government agencies.
- Relationships with the Incident Response Teams within key partners and key suppliers, such as the company's ISP, need also be established.

15.7 THE INCIDENT RESPONSE PROCESS

When an incident is reported the steps below should be followed:

15.7.1 Incident Recording

Details of the incident should be recorded accurately. The information gathered should include:

- The date and time the incident occurred.
- The date and time the incident was detected.
- Who/what reported the incident.
- Details of the incident including:

- A description of the incident
- Details of the systems involved
- Corroborating information such as error messages, log files, etc.

15.7.2 Incident Notification

In order to ensure an effective and appropriate response to a potential information security incident the Information Security Manager should be contacted immediately and given the details of incident.

The information security manager should then evaluate the incident and determine whether it should be treated as an Information Security incident or whether it should be referred to the support desk and handled as a normal service incident.

The information security manager should then escalate and notify the appropriate members of the team according to the classification of the incident.

15.7.3 Incident Classification

In order to ensure that incidents are responded to in a structured manner it is essential the Information Security Manager classifies incidents into the appropriate levels so that high priority incidents can be responded to quicker than incidents of a lower nature. It should be noted that based on additional information gathered during the response to an information security incident the classification of an incident can be changed appropriately.

The severity of the incident does not alone impact the classification. The potential target also impacts the classification. A rejected access attempt to sensitive data will have a higher event classification than a rejected access attempt to non-sensitive systems, for example unauthorized access to a staff member's home directory may be classified with a lower priority than unauthorized access to the payroll system.

Classifying information security incidents will depend on a number of factors such as:

- The nature of the incident.
- The criticality of the systems being impacted.
- The number of systems impacted by the incident.
- The impact the incident can have on the organization from a legal and/or public relations point of view.
- Legal and regulatory requirements.

Incident can be classified as shown in Table 15.1.

Table 15.1 Classification

Classification	*Explanation*	*Example*
High	An incident poses an immediate threat to all systems, the exposure of critical or sensitive systems, may result in criminal charges, regulatory fines or may result in undue bad publicity for the organization.	• Network wide virus/Worm outbreak • Active External/Internal unauthorized access to systems. • Compromise of information resulting in serious data disclosure. • Series breaches of the organization's acceptable usage policy.
Medium	An incident poses a threat to a limited number of systems, may compromise non-critical or non-sensitive systems involved time critical investigation investigation into a staff members activities.	• Inactive External/Internal unauthorized access to systems. • Localised Virus/Worm outbreak. • Breach of the organization's acceptable usage policy.
Low	An incident poses no immediate threat to systems.	• Failure to download anti-virus signatures. • Request to review security logs. • Minor breaches of the organization's acceptable useage policy.

15.7.4 Incident Tracking

Throughout the lifetime of the information security incident, it is important that accurate records are taken of each action taken and the consequences of each action. This is important from a number of points of view:

(i) To aid in the ongoing troubleshooting and diagnosis of the issues.

(ii) In the event the incident results in a criminal or civil case, the accurate recording of events may be submitted as evidence regarding the investigation.

(iii) In the event the incident results in a staff disciplinary case the accurate recording of events may be submitted as evidence regarding the investigation.

(iv) For post-mortem diagnosis of the incident to determine potential areas of improvement within the processes and procedures relating to information security incident response.

Once the information security incident has been classified, the method of tracking the issue needs to be carefully considered. If the network has been compromised it is likely that the attacker may have access to all systems within the organization and therefore could be alerted that a response is underway and take evasive, elusive and/or destructive action. Therefore thought should be given as to whether or not information security incidents classified as

"High" should be recorded within the normal help desk system or be tracked using alternative methods such as manual recording or using a standalone system not connected to the network.

During the information security incident, all actions should be documented, time recorded and signed. If not already notified, notify the support desk with details of the information security incident.

Depending on the scale, impact and duration of the information security incident consideration should be given as to whether additional resources may be required on the organizations support desk to deal with client queries. For example, a prolonged incident may result in the loss of business critical services which may result in a higher volume of calls to the support desk.

15.7.5 Response

The type of information security incident will determine the way that the information security response team will handle the incident. Standard operating procedures should be developed and tested by the Incident Response Team. These standard operating procedures should cover incident such as:

- Malware/Computer Virus infection.
- External unauthorized access to systems.
- Internal unauthorized access to systems.
- Theft of computer equipment and related data.
- Discovery of all illegal content on the organization's information processing systems.
- Series breach of the organization's acceptable usage policy.
- Minor breach of the organization's acceptable usage policy.
- Defacement of the organization's website.
- Denial-of-service attack on the organization's information processing systems, e.g. Internet connection.
- E-mail Flood Attack on the organization's information processing systems.
- Compromise of information processing services belonging to third party partners, e.g. ISP supplier and hosting provider.
- Disclosure of confidential information.

The above procedures should be constantly reviewed and tested for their efficiency and new standard operating procedures implemented when and where required. It should be noted that from time to time information security incidents may occur that fall outside the scope of the above standard operating procedures and as a result they will need to be managed in an ad hoc fashion.

Regardless as to whether an information security incident falls within the scope of existing standard operating procedures or not, the following are the main steps within the process;

Containment: Containment involves limiting the scope and impact of the information security incident. This is particularly applicable when responding to information security incidents as a results of malware such as a virus, due to the ability of such software to spread rapidly

The information security manager and/or the incident response team should decide on how best to contain an incident. This decision will need to be taken with the objectives of preventing further systems compromise, allowing adequate time and resources for investigating the incident, while at the same time restoring the systems to operational status as soon as possible.

The team should also have full authority to conduct whatever actions they deem necessary to contain the incident up to and including putting critical services and applications offline.

Eradication: Eradicating an incident entails identifying and removing the root cause of the information security incident. Simply restoring a system to operational status without identifying the root cause of the compromise may result in the information security incident reoccurring again at a later stage.

It is important to gather whatever evidence available in a forensically sound manner. This means ensuring all steps and actions are clearly documented with original media and log files digitally signed and stored securely to prevent tampering. All investigations should be conducted on verified copies of the original media and log files. It may be necessary to engage with external expertise to conduct the forensic investigation.

Recovery: Recovery means restoring a system's back to their normal operational status. This may require restoring systems from backups or reinstalling from known and certified original media. Part of the recovery process should ensure that the integrity of the backup being used for the restore operation has been thoroughly verified and that the restore operation was successful.

Communications: Throughout the information security incident, it is essential that appropriate communications are maintained. This includes communicating to the appropriate IT and business management levels on the impact and progress of the incident.

During an information security incident, it is essential that confidentiality is maintained throughout the incident lifecycle. In the event of a high priority incident no communication should occur over existing information systems, such as e-mail, as they may be compromised and alert the attacker to the investigation.

In addition, the nature of the incident may require confidentiality is maintained as it may involve a criminal case, the disciplining of a staff member or be publicly embarrassing to the organization.

Where possible, information on information security incidents should be shared on a strict need to know basis only. Ideally all updates from the Incident Response Team to those outside the team should come only from the Information Security Officer.

From time to time it may be necessary to communicate with external parties during or as a result of an information security incident. Following are the main contact points and how they should be handled;

(i) *Press enquiries:* All press and media enquiries should be strictly handled by the organization's Public Relation Department. No other members of staff should comment to media or press enquiries regarding any information security incident.

(ii) *Law enforcement:* It may be necessary to instigate criminal proceedings as a result of an information security incident. This could be due to criminal activity conducted by users within the organization or the requirement to prosecute a criminal case should be made by the Senior Management in Consultation with the legal department.

(iii) *Third party partners:* Depending on the nature of the information security incident, it may be necessary to contact third party partners and suppliers to alert them of the incident. This may be as a result of the investigations into the incident identifying the source of the incident being from one of those companies or requiring assistance from those companies to investigate or eradicate the incident.

For example, an attack on the organization's Internet connections may require the assistance of the providing ISP in dealing with the attack. In the main, these types of communications should be at an operational level and ideally relationships should be established previous to any incidents to ensure an effective response.

(iv) *Public:* Similar to press enquiries all public enquiries regarding an information security incident should be dealt with by the Press Officer.

Depending on where the organization conducts business, legal and/or regulatory requirements may require that affected customers are notified of the breach. The decision to contact customers should be made by the Senior Management in consultation with the legal department.

(v) *Staff:* It is important that appropriate levels of communication are maintained with staff during an incident not withstanding the requirements for maintaining confidentiality. This is particularly important when the incident involves the investigation of a staff member. In such a case it is extremely important that the suspected staff member's privacy and rights are maintained at all times. The Human Resource department will play a key role in this regard.

Information security incidents that impact directly on the availability of production systems will need to be managed in such a way to keep impacted staff updated as to when the systems may be likely to be restored while at the same time maintain any necessary confidentiality.

(vi) *Management:* Depending on the severity and the impact of the information security incident, senior management may need to be made aware and kept updated on the progress of the issues. Where possible the escalation tree for the information security incident should be the same as that used for all service issues.

(vii) *Legal:* Depending on the nature of the incident and whether it will involve a criminal prosecution or staff disciplinary proceedings, regular contact should be maintained with the legal expertise within the Incident Response Team to ensure that the most appropriate steps are taken.

Integration with other processes: Due to its nature, the information security Incident Response Process should be tightly integrated with other existing processes such as:

- Change Management Process
- Service Incident Management Process
- Disaster Recovery Management Process

Post information security incident review: Subsequent to any information security incident, a through review of the incident should occur. The purpose of this review is to ensure that the steps taken during the incident were appropriate and to identify any areas that may need to be improved. Any recommended changes to policies and/or procedures should be documented and implemented as soon as possible.

Reporting: In order to improve the Information Security Incident Response Process, it is essential that accurate records are kept of the change requests and reviewed accordingly. Monthly reports reflecting the following should be produced:

- Number of information security incidents submitted, broken down by priority.
- Number of information security incidents submitted, broken down by type.
- Number of information security incidents resulting in service requests.

REVIEW QUESTIONS

15.1 Explain risk. Justify that then is no risk, there is no need for security.

15.2 What is risk management? Explain with flow chart.

15.3 What are the attributes on which risk is dependent?

15.4 Write an overview of risk management.

15.5 Draw the planning decision flow chart for risk management.

15.6 Explain risk assessment methodology.

15.7 How to identify the risk for an organization?

15.8 How to identify threats and vulnerabilities?

15.9 How to perform risk analysis?

15.10 What are the strategies for risk reduction?

15.11 Write an overview on incident management.

15.12 What is the role of incident response in incident management?

15.13 Explain incident response process.

15.14 What is the important of post-information security incident review?

CHAPTER 16

Security and Law

Chapter Outline

Computer security is no different than any other subject in our society; as it changes our lives, laws will be enacted to enable desired behaviours and prohibit undesired behaviours. The one substantial difference between their aspect of our society and others is that the speed of advancement in the information systems world as driven by business, computer network connectivity, and the Internet is much greater than in the legal system of compromise and law-making. In some cases, laws have been overly restrictive, limiting business options, such as in the area of importing and exporting encryption technology. In other cases, legislation has been slow in coming and this fact has stymied business initiatives, such as digital signatures, and in some areas, it has been both too fast and too slow, as in the case of privacy laws. One thing is certain, you will never satisfy everyone with a law, but it does delineate the rules of the game.

One of the biggest legal challenges posed by the medium of the Internet is—"the source of jurisdiction of a court to decide and determine disputes that occur on or as a result of the use of Internet facilities". Ironically, because a page on the World Wide Web can reach web surfers in every state in the nation and perhaps every nation on the earth, there arises the issue of where exactly a person who has a cause of action, based upon a web transaction, can sue. The prospect that placing a page on the Internet can subject the web publisher to a law suit any where on earth can certainly have a chilling effect on perhaps the most powerful medium in the history of communication. Moreover, the Internet's decentred nature makes it likely that any given Internet transaction will involve parties from more than one jurisdiction.

Jurisdiction is the power of a court to hear and determine a case. Without jurisdiction a court's judgement is ineffective and impotent. For deciding whether a court has the jurisdiction, the concept of "territory" assumes great importance. For an off-line transaction/online human conduct, which results in litigation, the issue of jurisdiction of a court to decide the dispute/matter, would more or less be easy and settled, as for example, the court which has territorial jurisdiction over the local-area where the concerned contract took place, or where the injury was suffered, such a court will/can exercise its jurisdiction and will/can legally decide the dispute/matter that comes before it. However when it comes to an online transaction/online human conduct, the issue of jurisdiction can become the most complex issue, for the simple reason that the Internet, known as "Cyberspace" has no geographical location and territorial boundary. The issue of jurisdiction has, therefore, become the most important legal problem posed by the advent of the Internet. In fact, legal systems worldwide are still grapping with the search for answers to this vexed issue of "jurisdiction of courts" over online transaction/online human conduct. Till now, workable solutions remain elusive.

16.1 REGULATIONS IN INDIA

India has a detailed and well-defined legal system in place. The Indian legal system is based on English common law. The Indian judicial system has a unified structure, with the Supreme Court, the High Courts and the Lower Courts constituting a single judiciary.

Indian laws do not cover aspects related to the offshoring and the Internet, which has emerged recently. The arrival of the Internet resulted a new set of complex legal issues. This was followed by offshoring, which led to further complications. The Indian government has responded proactively in this sphere and has laid the foundations of the required legal framework. The first draft of the Information Technology (IT) Bill was introduced as early as 1999. The IT Act, which finally came into existence in 2000, includes laws and policies concerning data security and cyber crimes. Apart from the IT Act, the Indian Copyright Act of 1972 deals with copyright issues in computer programs.

At present, there are no data protection specific laws in India. However, in the absence of specific laws, the Indian Judicial System offers a few proxy laws and other indirect safeguards. In the following sections, we briefly discuss the IT Act and other laws, which companies can use to safeguard proprietary information.

16.2 INFORMATION TECHNOLOGY ACT, 2000

In May 2000, both the houses of the Indian Parliament passed the Information Technology Bill, which has subsequently become known as the Information Technology Act, 2000. The Act covers cyber and related information technology laws in India. The IT Act has made amendments to the Indian Penal Code of 1860, the Indian Evidence Act of 1872, the Bankers' Books Evidence Act of 1891 and the Reserve Bank of India Act of 1934, to update them with the provisions of the Act. The information security issues under the IT Act are the following:

Section 43

According to Section 43 of the IT Act, if a person without the permission of the person in charge of the computer system, accesses, downloads any data, introduces virus or causes denial of access, will be liable for a penalty of up to rupees 10 million.

Section 65: Tampering with Computer Source Code

Section 65 of the IT Act deals with the issue of tampering with computer science documents. According to Section 65, anyone who deliberate or purposely hides, destroys or alters any computer source code or induces someone else to do shall be punishable with imprisonment up to three years, or with fine, which may go up to two lakh rupees, or with both.

Section 66: Hacking

Section 66 of the IT Act deals with the issue of hacking. According to Section 65, hacking is committed if someone, with the intention of causing wrongful loss or damage (or with the knowledge that such damage or loss is likely to result) to the public/any person, destroys/ deletes/alters any information residing in a computer resource, diminishing its value or utility, or affects it injuriously by any means. If a person commits hacking, he/she is liable to be punished with imprisonment up to three years, or with a fine, which may go up to two lakh rupees, or with both.

Section 72: Breach of Confidentiality and Privacy

Section 72 of the Act relates to the disclosure of certain information by any person who has gained access to such information in pursuance of a power granted under the Information Technology Act. In case a person who has secured access to any electronic record, book register, correspondence, information, document, or other material discloses any of these to any other person, he will be punished with imprisonment for a term, which may extend to two years, or with a fine, which may go to ten lakh rupees, or with both.

The above provision does not apply to the disclosure of personal information regarding a person in a website or by his e-mail service provider, etc.

16.2.1 Cyber Crime and the IT Act, 2000

The Internet is fast becoming a way of life for millions of people. However, it is fast being transformed into a haven for criminals, and the crime rate on the net is increasing every week.

There have been various kinds of computer and Internet related crimes. The most common amongst these is the use of viruses to corrupt and/or destroy data stored in computer system. These viruses can be attached to e-mails, programmes, etc. Other forms of fraud, robbery, and forgery also exist. Bogus schemes on the Internet have already robbed many people of a vast amount of money. The Internet also makes defamation, assult on a person's character, etc, relatively easier and the possibilities of a person being caught and held liable are remote. In fact, the growth of crime on the Internet is directly proportional to the growth of the Internet itself, and so in the variety of crimes being committed or attempted.

Since the Internet is composed of computers, crimes occurring on the Internet are "computer crimes". But defining a "Computer crime" is difficult. A computer can be the subject of a crime by being stolen or damaged; it can be the site of a crime (such as fraud or copyright infringement); or it can be the instrument of the crime, such as when it is used to access other machines or store information illegally. These are all computer crimes in the sense that a computer is involved.

Since the Internet's strength and purpose is to facilitate communication, traditional crimes such as conspiracy, solicitation, securities fraud, and even espionage can be committed via the Internet. The problem, however, lies not in the fact that so many diverse kinds of crime can be committed via the Internet, but the fact the existing criminal law might be ill equipped to deal with this "upgradation" in the methods and media of committing crimes.

The Information Technology Act, 2000 neither defines "Cyber crime" nor uses this expression, but only provides the definition of, and punishment for, certain offences. In common parlance, there can be two definitions of 'cyber crime'. Narrowly defined, 'cyber crime' consists of only those offences provided in the Information Technology Act, 2000. As per this definition, cyber crimes would mainly be restricted to tampering with the computer source code, hacking and cyber pornography. Cyber proud, defamation, harassment, e-mail abuse and IPR (Intellectual Property Right) thefts etc. would not classify as cyber crimes. Broadly stated, 'cyber crime' can be said to be an act of commission or omission, committed on or through or with the help of or connected with, the Internet, whether directly or indirectly, which is prohibited by any law and for which punishment, monetary and/or corporal, is provided, Applying this definition, the IT Act, 2000 provides for and punishes only certain cyber offences and is not exhaustive of all cyber crimes. For example, if a person through the Internet threatens any person with causing death or grievous hurt, though he shall be liable for the offence or criminal intimidation under section 506 of the Indian Penal Code, 1860, and no offence under the IT Act, the offence would still be classified as a cyber crime as per the broad definition. Another example, which can be cited is when a person cheats another on the Internet, he shall be liable for cheating under section 420 I.P.C. and not under IT Act, 2000, but his act commonly called cyber fraud would nevertheless be classified as a cyber crime.

16.3 INDIAN CONTRACT ACT, 1872

It is necessary to understand certain important definitions and principles under the Indian Contract Act, 1872:

- When one person signifies to another his willingness to do or to abstain from doing anything, with a view to obtaining the assent of that other to such act or abstinence, he is said to make a proposal.

- When the person to whom the proposal is made signifies his assent thereto, the proposal is said to be accepted. A proposal, when accepted, becomes a promise.
- The person making the proposal is called the 'promisor and the person accepting the proposal is called the 'promisee'.
- When, at the desire of the promisor, the promisee or any other person has done or abstained from doing, or does or abstains from doing, or promises to do or to abstain from doing, something, such act or abstinence or promise is called a consideration for the promise.
- Every promise and every set of promises, forming the consideration for each other, is an agreement.
- Promises which form the consideration or part of the consideration for each other, are called reciprocal promises.
- An agreement not enforceable by law is said to be void.
- An agreement enforceable by law is a contract.
- An agreement which is enforceable by law at the option of one or more of the parties thereto, but not at the option of the other or others, is a voidable contract.
- A contract which ceases to be enforceable by law becomes void when it ceases to be enforceable.

A contract is a legally binding agreement between two or more persons. For example, purchasing goods, engaging a builder to carry out work, borrowing money, or ordering goods or machinery from a manufacturer are all contracts. The terms of a contract are for the parties to decide. The basic rule is that the contracting parties must perform as specified in the contract. Violation of the terms of the contract or non-performance of one's obligations under the contract amounts to a breach of contract. When a party to a contract commits a breach of the contract, the other party may resort to the following legal remedies.

Damages

The party, which suffers due to the breach of a contract, by the other party is entitled to received compensation for any loss or damage caused to it. However, the loss or damage must be shown to the court to have arisen in the usual course due to the breach. In other words, compensation is not to be given for any remote and indirect loss or damage sustained by reasons of the breach. Damages can also be recovered if it can be shown that it was known to the parties that a loss or damage resulting from the breach (at the time when the contract was made) is likely to result in a breach of the contract.

Where a sum has been named in the contract, to be paid in the case of a breach, or if the contract specifies a penalty, the party complaining of the breach is entitled (whether actual damage or loss is provided to have been caused) to receive a reasonable compensation not exceeding the amount agreed upon or, the stipulated penalty. A stipulation regarding an increased interested from the date of the default may be regarded as a penalty. The court is empowered to reduce it to an amount, it considers reasonable in the circumstances.

Specific Performance of the Contract

In certain special cases, the court may direct the "specific performance" of the contract against the party in default. In other words, the party may be directed to perform the very obligation, which he has undertaken, as per the terms of the contract. This remedy is discretionary and granted in exceptional cases.

The best way foreign can protect their data and intellectual property while offshoring work to India is through contracts. The Indian Contract Act, 1872 provides an adequate safeguards to foreign companies, provided both firms (Indian and Foreign) agree to the contract. The companies offshoring work need to ensure that they enter an exhaustive Service Level Agreement (SLA) with their vendor, which covers various aspects of data security and confidentiality. This will help companies safeguard themselves in the case of any fraud or misconduct.

As mentioned above, damages are the best remedy, but due to the lengthy timeliness of the Indian judicial system, companies should first try to obtain an injunction. It does not normally take more than a month to obtain an injunction, obtaining damages are quite a difficult task, and at times take several years.

16.4 INDIAN PENAL CODE

Section 406: Punishment for Criminal Breach of Trust

In case any person, who has been entrusted with property, or with any power over any property, dishonestly misappropriates the property, makes wrongful use of the property, dishonestly disposes off that property, or induces any other person to do so, such a person commits "criminal breach of trust". Under Section 406 of the Indian Penal Code, whoever commits criminal breach of trust shall be punished with imprisonment, which may extend to three years, or with a fine, or with both.

Section 420: Cheating and Dishonestly Inducing Delivery of Property

Section 420 of the Indian Penal Code (IPC) deals with cheating cases. Under the section, whoever cheats and consequently dishonestly induces a person to deliver any property (to any other person), or alter or destroy the whole or any part of a valuable security, shall be punished with imprisonment, which may extend to seven years, and shall also be liable to a fine.

16.5 INDIAN COPYRIGHT ACT

India has one of the most modern copyright protection laws in the world. A major development in the area of copyright was the amendment to the Copyright Act of 1957 in 1999, to make if fully compatible with the provisions of WTO's trade-related aspects of Intellectual Property Rights (TRIPS) Agreement. The Copyright (Amendment) Act, 1999, came into force on January 15, 2000.

The 1994 amendment of the Copyright Act of 1957 brought sectors such as satellite broadcasting, computer software and digital technology under Indian copyright protection.

The other important development during 1999 was the issuance of the International Copyright Order, 1999, which extended the provisions of the Copyright Act to nations of all World Trade Organization (WTO) member countries.

As per the provisions of the Indian Copyright Act, 1957 and as amended in 1994–95, any person who knowingly makes use of an illegal copy of a computer program shall be punishable. According to Section 63 B, copyright infringement attracts a minimum imprisonment of seven days. The Act further provides for fines, which shall not be less than fifty thousand rupees, but may go up to twenty lakh rupees, a jail term up to three years, or both.

Under Indian Law, computer programs have copyright protection but no patent protection. A software program is an algorithm and patent law does not protect algorithms per se. The term 'software' includes computer programs, databases, computer files, preparatory design material, and associated printed documentation such as users' manuals.

Source Code, Object Code and Copyright

The programs written by the programmer are known as the source code. When an assembler or a compiler converts it into machine code, it is known as the object code. This conversion is one way. It is not possible to convert object code into source code.

World Intellectual Property Organisation (WIPO) recommended in late 1970 that computer software (object code and subject code) should be protected under the Copyright Acts.

Article 10 of the TRIPS Agreement

Computer programmes, whether in source or object code, shall be protected as literary works under the Berne Convention. Compilations of data or other material, whether in machine readable or other form, which by reason of the selection or arrangement of their content constitute intellectual property and shall be protected as such.

Amendments in the Copyright Act

The position of amendment of computer databox/object code in India was similar to that of Australia. It was doubtful if the object code or the computer database was protected under the Intellectual Property Laws of India. The Indian response has been to amend to Copyright Act by two amending Acts namely Act No. 38 of 1994 with effect from 10th May 1995 and Act No. 49 of 1999 which came into force on 13th January 2000. By these amending Acts some new sub-sections to section 2, namely the interpretation clause, were added and section 2(o) of the Copyright Act was amended to change the definition of the word "literary work". It now includes computer programs as well as computer database. The result is that not only the computer programs (subject code as well as object code) are protected but computer database is also protected as a copyright. Section 14 of the Copyright Act defines "copyright". This section was also amended giving exclusive rights to the owners to do or authorizing the doing among the other things to reproduce, sell, or rent a computer database or a computer program.

16.6 CONSUMER PROTECTION ACT, 1986

Consumer Protection Act came into force on 15th April, 1986 to protect the consumers from exploitation and to save them from adulterated and substandard goods and deficient services. With regards to security, consumers can file a complaint with the court for "deficiency of service" such as disclosing proprietary information etc. without adequate authorization.

"Consumer" means any person who

- buys any goods for a consideration which has been paid or promised or partly paid and partly promised or under any system of deferred payment and includes any user of such goods other than the person who buys such goods for consideration paid or promised or partly paid or partly promised or under any system of deferred payment when such use is made with the approval of such person but does not include a person who obtains such goods for resale or for any commercial purpose or
- hires or avails of any services for a consideration which has been paid or promised or partly paid and partly promised or under any system of deferred payment and includes any beneficiary of such services other than the person who "hires or avails" of the services for consideration paid or promised, or partly paid and partly promised or under any system of deferred payment, when such services are availed of with the approval of the first mentioned person but does not include a person who avails of such services for any commercial purposes.

Who Can File a Complaint?

- A consumer
- Any voluntary consumer Association registered under Act 1956 or the Companies Act 1951 or any other law for the time being in force.
- The Central Government or any State Government.
- One or more consumers having the Same Interest.
- In case of death of consumer, his legal heir or representative

What Constitutes a Complaint?

- If you have suffered loss or damage as a result of any unfair/restrictive trade practices adopted by the trader.
- If the goods purchased suffers from any defect.
- If the services hired/availed or suffers from deficiencies in any respect.

- If you have been charged a price in excess of the price displayed or fixed by or under any law in force or agreed between the parties.
- If the goods purchased or services availed are hazardous to life and safety.

Relief Available to Consumers

- Removal of defects from the goods
- Replacement of the goods
- Refund of the price paid
- Award of compensation for the loss or injury suffered
- Removal of defects or deficiencies in the services
- Award for adequate costs
- To discontinue the unfair trade practice or restrictive trade practices
- To withdraw hazardous goods from being offered to sale
- To issue corrective advertisement to neutralize the effect of misleading advertisement

16.7 SPECIFIC RELIEF ACT, 1963

According to Section 39 of the Specific Relief Act, 1963, a person can claim temporary and permanent injunctions against unauthorized disclosure of a confidential information.

16.8 GOVERNMENT INITIATIVES

The Ministry of Information Technology in India has undertaken several initiatives to upgrade security standards. The following are some of them:

Standardization, Testing and Quality Certification (STQC) Directorate

Due to the international demand that Indian firms should have an international security standard accreditation, the Indian government has set up the Standardization, Testing and Quality Certification (STQC) Directorate (under the Department of Information Technology (DIT)). The Directorate has been able to set up to launch an independent third-party certification scheme for the Information Security Management System, as per BS 7799 Part 2, and has achieved Information recognition in the form of accreditation from RvA, Netherlands. The STQC Directorate provides services such as testing hardware and software products, product certification, and also training personnel in quality and security standards and processes.

Computer Emergency Response Team (CERT)

The Indian Computer Emergency Response Team (CERT-In) was established by the Department of Information Technology (DIT) to be part of the International CERT Community.

CERT was set up to protect India's IT assets against viruses and other security threats. It performs the following functions.

- It serves as central point, responding to computer security incidents and providing a reliable, trusted, 24-hour referral contact for emergencies.
- It disseminates best practices among System Administrators and Service Providers.
- It increases the awareness and understanding of information security and computer security issues among the Indian cyber user community.
- It alerts the community regarding the latest security threats in the form of advisories, vulnerability notes and incident notes.
- It serves as a coordinating centre among organizations, to solve computer security problems.
- It establishes linkages with similar organizations in the international arena.
- It performs research and development activities in collaboration with premier research and educational organizations regarding the security of existing systems and evolving cyber security problems.

Information Security Technology Development Council (ISTDC)

The ministry has recently set up the Information Security Technology Development Council (ISTDC). The main objective of this program is to facilitate, coordinate and promote technological advancements, and to respond to information security incidents, threats and attacks at the national level. ISTDC has been established for the following functions:

- To evaluate the cyber security project proposals received, and to provide recommendations for further processing by DIT.
- To review ongoing projects through monitoring committees and recommend any modification in scope, funding, duration, additional inputs, termination, transfer of technology, etc.
- To recommend follow-up action on completed projects—transfer of technology, initiation of next phase, etc.
- To form project review and steering groups of projects approved and funded by the DIT.

16.9 FUTURE TRENDS—THE LAW OF CONVERGENCE

Traditionally, communications media were separate. The print media, broadcasting, voice telephony and online services were completely distinct.

Each of these communications media operated on different networks and used different "platforms"—newsprint, TV sets, telephones and computers respectively;

Each of these communications media was regulated by different laws and different regulators, usually at national levels.

However, times have changed. We live in a digital age in which it is possible to have a much higher capacity of traditional and new services transported over the same networks and to use integrated consumer devices for purposes such as news, telephony, television or personal computing. All this has been made possible by one technological leap—"Convergence, or Converging Technologies".

Although it is difficult to precisely define what convergence means, it is most commonly expressed as "The ability of different network platforms to carry essentially similar kinds of services".

It is a fact that the Internet has had and will have a very big role to play in this transformation and development of technologies. By its very nature, the Internet promotes convergence. The net fosters a multimedia environment with sound, image, and text transmission, and at relatively low (and still declining) costs. This makes it much more versatile than any other contemporary media, which typically need to be combined with each other or with more traditional media to conclude many a transaction. The Internet could, through digitization (Digitization is technology that permits the conversion of text, sound, images, video, and other content into a common digital format. On digitization, these can be transmitted electronically with little difficulty or cost) achieve thing that traditional media, even all combined, struggled to do.

Convergence brings with it changing markets and changing consumer expectations. Many new products and services are being offered ; most of them are utilizing the dynamism of the Internet. Prime examples are:

(i) Home-banking and home-shopping over the Internet.

(ii) Voice over the Internet.

(iii) E-mail, data, World Wide Web access over a mobile phone network, and the use of wireless links to homes and business to connect them to the fixed telecommunication networks.

(iv) Data services over digital broadcasting platforms.

(v) Online services combined with television via systems such as Web-TV as well as delivery via digital satellites and cable modems.

(vi) Web casting of news, sports, concerts, and of other audiovisual services.

Convergence will certainly expand the overall information market and is likely to be the catalyst for the next stage in the integration of the world economy. If properly harnessed, convergence will be a powerful motor for growth even at the national level. By putting in place the right regulatory framework, the Government and policy makers can have a key role in ensuring a supportive environment exists in India. One of the ways is in promoting the use of the Internet, and also regulating it clearly. Even though converging technologies have arrived, the law is yet to take shape to even attempt to regulating these multidimensional technologies. The fact that nothing has been heard of the Convergence Bill, the draft of which was to be introduced in Parliament in 1999, speaks of the complexity of matters concerning convergence. But the day is not far away, when we would certainly have a defined law of convergence, simply because the era of convergence has already arrived and is adapting, growing and changing constantly, and having a deep influence on human transaction and interaction through the medium we know as "The Internet".

REVIEW QUESTIONS

16.1 Explain Information Technology Act, 2000.

16.2 Describe Indian Contract Act, 1872.

16.3 What is Indian Council Penal Code?

16.4 Explain Indian Copyright Act.

16.5 What is Consumer Protection Act and who can file a complaint?

16.6 What are the initiatives undertaken by government to upgrade security standards?

16.7 Describe cyber crime and the IT Act, 2000.

16.8 Explain Article 10 of the TRIPS Agreement.

16.9 Explain the Amendments in the Copyright Act.

16.10 What is importance of Law of Convergence?

CHAPTER 17

Internet Governance and Electronic Mail Policy

Chapter Outline

The potential of the Internet to transform the cultural, economic, and political contours of the world has been widely recognized. Increasing attention has been paid to the question of whether we need Internet governance and, if so, in what form. There has been a felt need for some form of central administration. The assignment of IP addresses represents one such widely recognized aspect. However, the decision-making, processes in matters related to the administration have always been debatable. There are many questions to be answered in all these matters. What is clear is that the decisions made today about the technical architecture of the Internet and the body which will administer that architecture will determine the course of development and impact of the Internet for several years to come.

The following major trends become serious concerns:

- Absence of competition in domain name registration leading to wide-spread dissatisfaction.
- Frequent conflicts between trademark holders and domain name holders.
- Mechanisms for resolving these conflicts have become expensive and cumbersome.
- Many commercial interests demanding a robust management of the Internet.
- Rapidly increasing percentage of the Internet users outside of the U.S.
- Those users outside of the U.S. are stakeholders in the growth of Internet.

- Internet names have high commercial value leaving no room for any ad hoc approaches in domain names.

The creation of the Internet Corporation for names and Number (ICANN) in November 1998 has given the debate on Internet governance a new focus. ICANN's mission is to administer the allocation of the IP address space and to manage the domain name system and the root server system functions ICANN represents the U.S. governments commitment to private sector, self-regulation of the Internet. ICANN was founded on stability of the Internet, fair competition amongst stakeholders, private-sector bottom-up co-ordination, and fair representation of Internet users.

The ARPANET Stanford Research Institute (SRI), Internet Assigned Names Authority (IANA), the agreement between National Science Foundation and Network Solutions Inc. (NSI) are all forerunners to ICANN. Each attempt taught valuable lessons on Internet Governance.

ICANN had to face serious controversies. Its decision making process has been described as sensitive and antidemocratic. Even the way the members of board were appointed became controversial.

The Working Group on Internet Governance (WGIG) was a United Nations multistakeholders working group set up after the 2003 World Summit on the Information Society (WSIS) first phase Summit in Geneva to agree on the future of Internet Governance. A report prepared by the WGIG provides the following definition.

"Internet governance is the development and application by Governments, the private sector and civil society, in their respective roles, of shared principles, norms, rules, decision-making procedures and programmes that shape the evaluation and use of the Internet".

The Internet Governance Forum (IGF), a forum for discussion has been set up by the United Nations to define the processes that enable free and fair Internet Governance.

Information and Communication Technologies (ICT) is a significant enables of successful e-governance projects, and can be new approach for touching the lives of the common man anywhere, and time. We need the technology and strategies for better e-governance initiatives that are benefiting the masses.

The Indian, central and various state governments are no strangers to the benefits of using ICT for e-governance. Many state governments and government based agencies have realized that ICT can add substantial value by surmounting the usual challenges of distance, slow speed of operations, and lack of accuracy of information.

17.1 INTERNET GOVERNANCE

Internet Governance means different things to different people. Telecommunication specialists see Internet Government through the prism of development of the technical infrastructure, computer specialists focus on the development of various standards and applications such as XML and Java. Communication specialists stress the facilitation of communication. Human Rights activists and Civil societies view Internet Governance from the perspective of the freedom of expression, whereas lawyers concentrate on jurisdiction, and dispute resolution.

Politicians worldwide focus on media and issues that play well with their electorate. The list of potentially conflicting professional perspectives on Internet Governance goes on. To simplify the things Governance of Internet can be categorized into four major areas.

17.1.1 The Infrastructure and Standardization

In order to enable the hetrogeneous technologies to work together, we need standardization of the infrastructure at the hardware level as well as at the software level. Telecommunication infrastructure, technical standards and services (Internet Infrastructure), Transport Control Protocol/Internet Protocol (TCP/IP), Root Server, Internet Service Providers (ISP), Internet Bandwidth Provider (IBP), Web standards, Internet Security, encryption, spam.

17.1.2 Legal

Legal aspects involve issues such as legislation, social norms (customs), self-regulation, jurisprudence, international regulation, jurisdiction, arbitration, trademark, copyright, patents, cyber crimes, digital signature, privacy rights, and data protection, Intellectual Property Rights (IPR).

17.1.3 Economic

Economic issues relate to e-commerce applications and are such as consumer protection, taxation, customs, e-payment, e-banking, and e-money.

17.1.4 Development

The development aspect of WSIS/World Summit on the Information Society) has been frequently repeated, beginning with UN General Assembly Resolution on WSIS, which stressed that WSIS should be "promoting development in particular with respect to access to transfer of Technology" the WSIS Geneva declaration plans and plan of Action highlighted development as a priority and linked it to the Millennium Resolution and its promotion of "access of all countries to information knowledge and communication technology for development". With the link of the Millennium Goals, WSIS is strongly positioned in the development context.

The Internet has grown for a long time without too much regulation. Defining protocols and standards had been for a long time the most developed regulatory activity. But as soon as business took its place the requirements changed. Standards and routing administration, encryption, digital signature, Internet Service Providers (ISP's) licensing, Intellectual Property Rights (IPR's), Computer crimes, etc. were questions raised as soon as commerce came to the forefront.

17.2 NETWORK SECURITY ASPECTS IN E-GOVERNANCE

Network and information security is a major concern involved in implementing e-governance projects. Problems in Information and Communication Technologies (ICT) like hacking, virus, spamming, invasion, and privacy issues can evolve from lack of security measures. Governments need to provide secure access to information, applications and services via networks. The network, applications and processes must be reliable to ensure availability and integrity of the e-government services.

We would like to describe e-governance as the use of Information and Communication Technology (ICT) to enhance information access and the delivery of government services for the benefit of citizens, business partners, organization and government functionaries.

e-governance, however, is not really the use of IT in governance but as a tool to ensure good governance; e-governance does not mean proliferation of computers and accessories; it is basically a political decision which calls for discipline, attitudinal change in officers and employees and massive government process re-engineering.

17.2.1 Why Securing e-Governance

As India adopts e-governance with a vengeance, the need for Network and Information Security measures to protect vital data will be a major part of e-governance framework.

To design an e-governance framework, security has become a key issue that needs to be addressed. Like any other online project, an e-governance project needs a network to execute, but the major difference is that in an e-governance project considerable amount of critical information could be involved. Hence, the need for security such information is must.

Security is critical in e-governance to safeguard the confidentiality of transactions and information on the network. Government documents and other important material such as birth and death registration, motor vehicle, license, land records, all of which have legal and legislative nuances have to be protected from unauthorized uses in case of e-governance projects. Hence, security is critical for their successful implementation.

17.2.2 Security Measures and Threats

Security measures are required wherever "authenticity", "validity", and "legal rights" of digital content have to be protected from repudiation. All digital content in form of applications that need protection from tampering, vandalism, decay and accident need security.

The role of network or information security is vital in every application, which collects or stores data, interacts with an outsider, carries some confidential information and other applications online and the best example of having most of such qualities and requirements are e-governance projects. In some online application we need transition of money, such as banking, shopping, gambling, and gaming. In e-governance framework central government can transfer a huge fund to state government online. With the Information Technology (IT) Act, 2000 coming into effect from 18th October, 2000, transaction on the Internet have got legal validity in India. This allows users to pay their bills for utilities on the web, at least on paper. All these applications handle money transactions whether it is transferring money through the online bank or using credit cards. Either way, they were interesting targets for criminals. It may be either through phishing scams, trying to fool the users to give away financial and personal information or it may be through Distributed-Denial-of-Service (DDoS) attacks. Either way, online transactions and their users are at higher risk of getting targeted by digital attacks.

The complex network and large size e-governance framework make it vulnerable for the virus, spam and Trojan attacks. A lot of intrusion attempts can be there to crack the security, in that network and information security is a greater challenge. Without having a proper security architecture the e-governance will face many security threats of a diverse nature.

In such a complex environment like e-governance project we need complete information security architecture. The architecture need to be further complemented with proper tools and solutions to keep itself away from any threat both at the network level and at the host level.

Once a virus attack is detected, everything comes to a standstill. Until the entire thing is cleaned up, work does not move further. When there was an intrusion at network or host level, it took a long time to cure and huge loss of money can be there. There were some inherent vulnerabilities like web defacements, stealing of information, etc.

17.3 SECURITY MONITORING TOOLS

If we look at the e-governance projects and the networks that are being rolled out for these, network or information security seems to be paramount. In an e-government project, a substantial amount of documentation is being done like maintenance of land records, police records, court judgements and so on. Each department functions independently and has its own set of transactions to undertake. Hence having security measures in each department is critical so that only authorized people get into the network and access the information.

The importance of security is high among industry and government, but the awareness is low. An understanding of the security technology and the need for its implementation is required for a safer and more secure IT environment in the country. Securing public data and ensuring security of the government websites are some applications where security solutions or monitoring tools are required. Some common processes of those tools are:

17.3.1 Vulnerability Assessment

Network and information security assessment services review all aspects of the data and voice networks and provide recommendations to maximize security, reliability and availability. Following can be deliverables:

- Identification of vulnerabilities that need to be immediately addressed.
- Verification of security products and features already in place.
- Prioritize security projects for future implementation.
- Assess the real-world threat to network assets.

17.3.2 Security Policy Development

Any security policy must satisfy working objectives as well as the technical aspects of securing e-governance information. Part of developing a secure network is crafting a set of organizational security policies. These policies establish the rules and guidelines that system and network engineers can use when deploying solutions. This policy would then guide how network engineers install and configure firewalls, intrusion detection systems and other network equipment. Developing a useful, practical, and feasible network security policy documents can be very time consuming, especially if you are unsure about all the possible technical and practical implications of certain decisions. Some automatic tools like Coleman Technologies, Inc. Managed Services tools can help any organization to develop and deploy a comprehensive security policy.

17.3.3 Wireless Network Analysis

Wireless networks are inexpensive, simple to deploy and very attractive for an increasingly mobile workforce and can be helpful to provide e-governance service in rural and remote areas. Unfortunately, wireless access points are designed for ease of use, not security. A through risk analysis provides an option for prioritizing and justifying future security expenditures. Depending on the scope of the risk analysis, the project may involve assessing sensitivity, criticality, threat, vulnerability, and susceptibility to penetration.

17.3.4 Successful Identity Authentication

Protecting access to electronic resources is not a simple process. Internet is a standard medium for conducting operations in e-governance framework, within and without organizations. At present, there is need for secured identity authentication, verification, and protection technology within all industries.

The information systems security research should be one of the visions of e-governance to concentrate in the next few years to develop security techniques, security technologies and products to be used for facing new challenges using open media for transactions pertaining to Government, Industry and Business covering commercial, financial and administrative aspects.

E-mail is a quick, cheap and easy means of communication. This makes e-mail a great business tool, but at the same time a potential threat for employers. E-mail threats such as confidentiality breaches, legal liability, lost productivity and damage to reputation cost companies crores of rupees each year. How can a company protect itself from these threats? The first step in securing your company is to create an e-mail usage policy. After you have created your e-mail policy you must make sure it is actually implemented. This can be done by giving regular trainings and by monitoring employees' e-mail using e-mail security software.

Any messaging system that depends on computing facilities to create, send, forward, reply to, transmit, store, hold, copy, download, display, view, read, or print computer records for purposes of asynchronous communication across computer network systems between or among individuals or groups, that is either explicitly denoted as a system for electronic mail or is implicitly used for such purposes, including services such as electronic bulletin boards, list servers, and newsgroups.

17.4 ELECTRONIC MAIL

One of the most popular services is electronic mail (e-mail). Originally, electronic mail was designed as a straightforward extension of the traditional office memo. That is, the original e-mail systems were built to allow a person to communicate with other people; an individual created a message and specified other individuals as recipients. The e-mail software transmitted a copy of the message to each recipient.

Electronic mail systems have evolved from the original design, and are automated to permit more complex interactions. In particular, because a computer program can answer an e-mail message and send a reply, e-mail can be used in a variety of ways. For example, a company can establish a computer program that responds automatically to requests for information that arrive in mail messages. A user sends an e-mail request to the program, and receives the desired information in a reply.

17.4.1 Electronic Mailboxes and Addresses

An e-mail system uses many of the terms and concepts from a traditional office environment. Before e-mail can be sent to an individual, the person must be assigned an electronic mailbox. The mailbox consists of a passive storage area (e.g., a file on disk). Like a conventional mailbox, an electronic mailbox is private—the permissions are set to allow the mail software to add an incoming message to an arbitrary mailbox, but to deny anyone except the owner the right to examine or remove messages. In most cases, an electronic mailbox is associated with a computer account. Thus, a person who has multiple computer accounts can have multiple mailboxes.

Each electronic mailbox is assigned a unique electronic mail address (e-mail address); when someone sends a memo, they use an electronic mail address to specify a recipient. A full e-mail address contains two parts; the second specifies a computer and the first specifies a mailbox on that computer. In the most widely used format, an "at sign" separates the two components:

mailbox@computer

Where the mailbox is a string that denotes a user's mailbox, and computer is a string that denotes the computer on which the mailbox is located (i.e., a domain name).

E-mail software on the sender's computer uses the second part to determine which computer to contact an e-mail software on the recipient's computer uses the first part of the address to select a particular mailbox into which the message should be placed. Thus, the first part of an address is interpreted locally; the string may not have meaning outside of a single computer system.

17.4.2 Mail Transfer

After a user composes an e-mail message and specifies recipients, e-mail software transfers a copy of the message to each recipient. In most systems, two separate pieces of software are required. A user interacts with an e-mail interface program when composing or reading messages. The underlying e-mail system contains a mail transfer program that handles the details of sending a copy of a message to remote computer. When a user finishes composing an outgoing message, the e-mail interface places the message in a queue that the mail transfer program handles.

The mail transfer program waits for a message to be placed on its queue, and then transfers a copy of the message to each recipient. Sending a copy of a message to a recipient on the local computer it is trivial because the transfer program can append the message to the user's mailbox. Sending a copy to a remote user is more complex. The mail transfer program becomes a client that contacts a server on the remote machine. The client sends the message to the server, which places a copy of the message in the recipient's mailbox. Figure 17.1 illustrates the interaction.

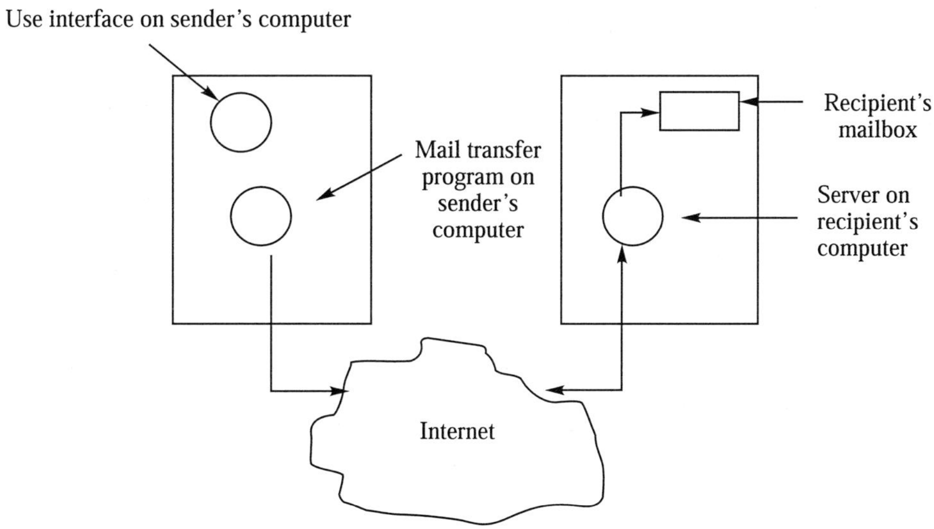

Figure 17.1 The path of an e-mail message. The mail transfer program on the sender's computer becomes a client of the remote mail server.

17.4.3 How Does E-mail Work?

Every Internet mail user has a unique Internet e-mail address. This e-mail address is in the format as:

username@domainname

To send e-mail to someone you need to know only his e-mail address. You do not need to know the hardware and software specification of the recipient. Figure 17.2 shows how mail messages move across the Internet.

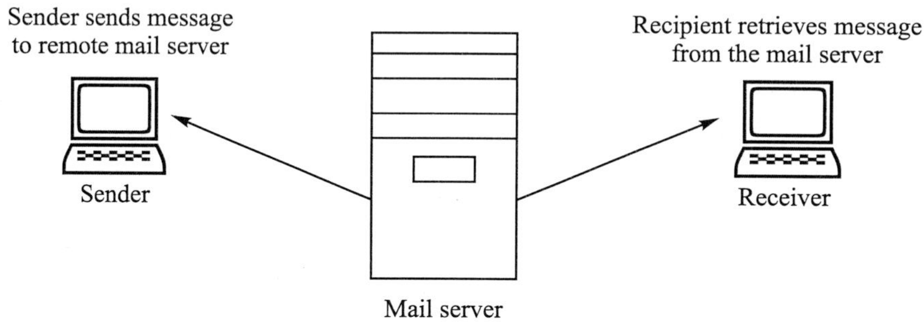

Figure 17.2 An e-mail system.

The above figure shows a very simplified model of an e-mail system. Following steps are involved in sending an e-mail message:

Step 1: The sender composes the mail message using his mail client software. A mail client allows a user to compose, edit and send the mail message. There are number of mail clients software—Netscape Mail, Outlook Express, Eudora, Pine, etc., are examples of mail clients.

Step 2: After composing the mail message the user sends it to the recipient's e-mail address. The message propagates across the Internet before it reaches the mail server of the recipient. The domain name in the recipient's e-mail address identifies his mail server and the username identifies the recipient on the server. For example, when you send mail to registrar@jp1.vsnl.net.in the address of the mail server is jp1.vsnl.net.in and the username is registrar.

Step 3: The recipient connects to his e-mail account on his mail server to read the messages sent to him.

The recipient also uses a mail client to receive, save and print mail messages. Figure 17.2 may give you an impression that the mail messages are directly sent to the recipients mail server. There is no direct link between the sender's computer and the recipient's mail server. A mail message propagates across several networks on the Internet before it reaches its destination.

17.4.4 Internet Mail Protocols

Internet e-mail is based on standards such as Simple Mail Transfer Protocol (SMTP), Post Office Protocol (POP), Internet Message Access Protocol (IMAP) and Multipurpose Internet Mail Extensions (MIME). These standards are known as mail protocols.

The SMTP specifies how messages are sent on the Internet. POP and IMAP define how mail clients can access messages on a mail server, and the MIME standard lets the mail client understand different types of data such as graphics, video, application files and text files.

An e-mail client based on these protocols can exchange messages with any other user on the Internet. These protocols are very important because there are a number of mail clients available in the market. Each of them provides a different set of features. The mail protocols help in standardizing the process of exchanging mail protocols, you need not know which mail client the recipient is using, what operating system he is using or what type of computer he is using. You just have to know his e-mail address to send message to him. The following are the mail protocols:

The Simple Mail Transfer Protocol (SMTP)

One of the most popular network services is electronic mail. The TCP/IP protocol that supports electronic mail on the Internet is called Simple Mail Transfer Protocol (SMTP).

When a mail transfer program contacts a server on a remote machine, it forms a TCP connection in place, the two programs follow the SMTP that allows the sender to identify itself, specify a recipient and transfer an e-mail message. SMTP provides for mail exchange between users on the same or different computers and supports:

- Sending a single message to one or more recipients.
- Sending messages that include text, voice or graphics.
- Sending messages to users on networks outside the Internet.

SMTP uses the ASCII character set for composing a message. An Internet mail message has two parts—a header and a body. The header of the message includes the address of the recipient, address of the sender, subject and other information about the message such as date and time when it was sent, type of mailing client the sender is using, etc. The body of the message contains the actual message.

Format of an E-mail Message

Mail header as follows:

Message-ID: <33D34795,5517@writeme.com
Date: Mon, 2 Oct 1998 : 17 : 30 : 10 + 0530
From: Boentika Singh boentika@writeme.com
X-Mailer: Mozilla 3.01 Gold (win 97 ; I)
MIME-Version: 1.0
To: registrar@jp1.vsnl.net.in
Subject: Request for extension of joining

Body of the mail message contains:

To,
Registrar

Sir,

With reference to your letter No. 2375/VIT, dated September 15, 1998, it is not possible to join immediately. I would like to join on November 10. Please extend the joining time.

Thanks,

Boentika

The SMTP protocol is used to transfer a message from the SMTP sender to the SMTP receiver over a TCP connection. SMTP attempts to provide reliable operation but does not guarantee to recover from lost messages. No end-to-end acknowledgement is returned to a message's originator that a message is successfully delivered to the message's recipient, and error indications are not guaranteed to be returned either. However, the SMTP-based mail system is generally considered reliable.

Post Office Protocol (POP)

SMTP expects the destination host, the mail server receiving the mail, to be on-line all the time; otherwise, a TCP connection cannot be established. For this reason, it is not practically to establish an SMTP session with a desktop computer because desktop computers are usually powered down at the end of the day.

In many organizations, mail is received by an SMTP server, that is always on-line. This SMTP server provides a mail drop service. The server receives the mail on behalf of every host in the organization. Workstations interact with the SMTP host to retrieve messages by using a client-server protocol such as Post Office Protocol (POP).

POP requires an additional server to run on the computer with the mailbox. The additional server uses the POP protocol. A user runs e-mail software that becomes a client of the POP server to access the contents of the mailbox. Figure 17.3 illustrates one way to use POP.

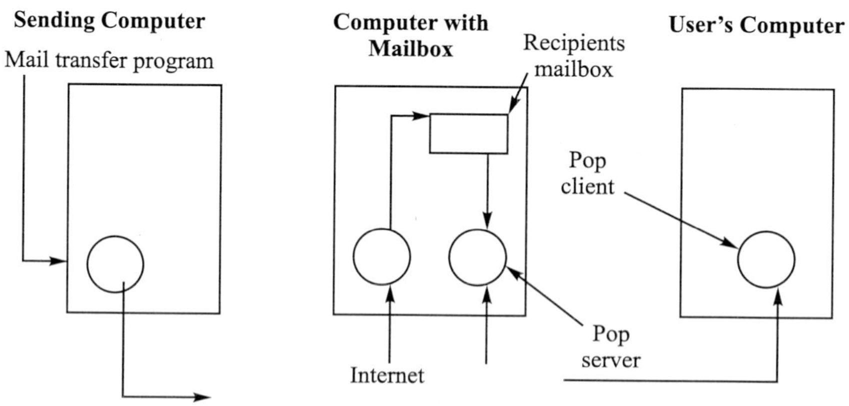

Figure 17.3 The path of e-mail when POP is used to access a mailbox. The mail can arrive from the sender's computer or mail gateway. To retrieve messages from the mailbox, a user runs a program that becomes a client of the POP server.

As the figure shows, a computer that has a mailbox must runs two servers. A conventional mail server accepts incoming e-mail and stores it in the appropriate mailbox. The mail can arrive either directly from the original sender or from a mail gateway. (A computer dedicated to processing electronic mail is often called a mail gateway). A POP server allows a user on a remote machine to access the mailbox.

Although both the e-mail server and POP server communicate across the Internet, there are several differences. First, the mail server uses the SMTP protocol, while the POP server uses the POP protocol. Second, the mail server accepts a message from an arbitrary sender, while the POP server only allows a user to access the mailbox after the user enters authentication information (e.g., password) messages. Third, the mail server can transfer only e-mail messages, while a POP server can provide information about the mailbox contents.

Although Figure 17.3 shows a client accessing the POP server across the Internet, POP is especially popular among users who rely on dialup telephone connections. In such cases a computer with the user's mailbox remains attached to the Internet as shown in figure. However, the user's computer does not need a permanent Internet connection. Instead, the computer can attach to a modem and use a telephone connection. To receive e-mail, the user forms a dialup connection either to the mailbox computer or to some other computer on the Internet. Once the user connects to a computer on the Internet, the user can run a POP client to contact the server and access e-mail.

The POP was developed for single user computers. There are three versions of this protocol: POP, POP2 and POP3.

Internet Message Access Protocol (IMAP)

Developed at Stanford University in 1986, the Internet Message Access Protocol is for retrieving e-mail messages. The latest version, IMAP4, is similar to POP3 but supports some additional features. For example, with IMAP4, you can search through your e-mail messages for keywords while the messages are still on mail server. You can then choose which messages to download to your machine. Like POP, IMAP uses SMTP for communication between the e-mail client and the server.

Multipurpose Internet Mail Extension (MIME)

The SMTP can be used to send only messages that are composed using ASCII character set. This restricts the utility of electronic mail. There is another protocol MIME that can be used to exchange e-mail messages containing non-textual data such as graphics, sound and other multimedia files.

Multipurpose Internet Mail Extension (MIME) offers a way to extend Internet standard mail so that users can interchange text in languages with different character sets and multimedia electronic mail among different computer systems that implemented Internet standard mail.

Whenever you want to send a nontext file such as a spreadsheet, program file, graphics file or a sound file, you can encode this file using MIME. The MIME encodes these files in a textual form, which can be sent using the SMTP. The recipient can then decode the MIME-encoded data to the original nontext file. Most e-mail clients such as Netscape automatically encode and decode the e-mail messages containing nontext data. However, there are some e-mail clients, which require you to encode data using an encoding utility such as Info-X-Fer.

17.5 WHAT ARE THE E-MAIL THREATS THAT ORGANIZATION'S FACE?

By using e-mail, organizations face several threats. These range from legal threats to network congestion:

17.5.1 Legal Liability

In most cases the employer is held responsible for all the information transmitted on or from their systems. As a result, inappropriate e-mails can result in multimillion dollar penalties. In the last few years there have been several high profile lawsuits such as the case against UK firm Norwich Union, who were forced to pay £450,000 in an out of court settlement after an employee sent an e-mail stating that their competitor Western Provident Association was in financial difficulties. In the US, Chevron settled a case filed by four female employees for $2.2 million. The employees alleged that sexually harassing e-mails sent through the organization e-mail system caused a threatening work environment. One of the sexually offensive messages was a 'joke' sheet titled '25 reasons why beer is better than women'. An organization can also be liable if one of its employees sends an e-mail containing a virus.

17.5.2 Confidentiality Breaches

Most confidentiality breaches occur from within the organization. These breaches can be accidental, for instance by selecting a wrong contact in the To: field. However, confidentiality breaches can also be intentional, as Borland International Inc. experienced first hand: A Borland employee used the organization's e-mail system to send out confidential information to competitor Symantec, his new employer. The trade secrets included product design specifications, sales data and information regarding a prospective contract for which both organizations were competing. The employee and recipient were both charged with trade secret theft. Whether it is by mistake or on purpose, the result of the loss of confidential data is the same.

17.5.3 Damage to Reputation

There is no doubt that the contents of corporate e-mails reflect on the business. A badly written e-mail, or an e-mail containing unprofessional remarks will cause the recipient to have a bad impression of the organization the sender is representing. UK law firm Norton Rose had to find this out the hard way when two of their employees originated the 'Claire Swire' e-mail, a sexually explicit e-mail that ended up being read by over 10 million people around the world. Especially since the organization in question was a law firm, and the employees were attorneys, this e-mail caused severe damage of reputation.

17.5.4 Lost Productivity

Lost productivity due to inappropriate use of an organization's e-mail system is becoming a growing area of concern. In the US, a survey revealed that 86 per cent of workers used their organization e-mail to send and receive personal e-mails. A recent study by the Gartner Group found that unproductive internal e-mails take up 30 per cent of employees' time spent in reading e-mail. It is concluded that banning e-mail which contains gossip, jokes, and other time-wasting content would save a considerable amount of employees' time. In addition to personal e-mails, unwanted spam messages are a huge time waster.

17.5.5 Network Congestion and Down Time

Spam and personal (mis) use of e-mail can cause organization's e-mail system to waste valuable bandwidth resources, not to mention employees' time. A Gartner Group Study held under 13,000 e-mail users, found that 90 per cent receive spam at least once a week, and almost 50 per cent get spammed more than 6 times a week. Personal e-mails cause network congestion since they are not only unnecessary, but tend to be mailed to a large list of recipients and often include large attachments such as mp3, executable or video files that users do not zip. Viruses are another important area of concern. If a virus hits the organization system this can cause network congestion or even down time.

17.5.6 E-mail Retrieval on Court Order

E-mail records are increasingly used in lawsuits since they tend to contain important evidence. For instance, if your company is faced with a wrongful termination lawsuit, chances are that you will be ordered to search all company e-mails for messages relating to that person. This is usually not just a matter of a quick keyword search. The retrieval often involves restoring thousands of e-mails on servers and result in slow and painful searches. Worse still, the court could even confiscate your computers as evidence. Not to mention the fact that the search might uncover some embarrassing evidence you never knew you were 'safekeeping'. If on the other hand you regularly delete e-mail as stipulated in corporate e-mail policy guidelines, the court might not force you to do an expensive search since it has enough reason to believe that it will not yield any result.

17.6 WHY DO YOU NEED AN E-MAIL POLICY?

By having a good e-mail policy in place you can secure your organization in several ways. Firstly, the e-mail policy helps prevent e-mail threats, since it makes your staff aware of the corporate rules and guidelines, which if followed will protect your organization.

Secondly, an e-mail policy can help stop any misconduct at an early stage by asking employees to come forward as soon as they receive an offensive e-mail. Keeping the incidents to a minimum can help avoid legal liability. For instance in the case of Morgan Stanley, a US investment bank that faced an employee's court case, the court ruled that a single e-mail communication (a racist joke, in this case) cannot create a hostile work environment and dismissed the case against them.

If an incident does occur, an e-mail policy can minimize the organization's liability for the employee's actions. Previous cases have proven that the existence of an e-mail policy can prove that the company has taken steps to prevent inappropriate use of the e-mail system, and therefore can be freed of liability. WorldCom Corp. for instance, faced a court case from two former employees for allowing four racially offensive jokes on its e-mail system. WorldCom successfully defended themselves because they had an e-mail policy that spelled out inappropriate content and because they took prompt remedial action against the coworker who sent the racially harassing e-mails.

Finally, if you are going to use e-mail filtering software to check the contents of your employee's e-mails, it is essential to have an e-mail policy that states the possibility of e-mail monitoring. If you do not have such policy you could be liable for privacy infringement.

17.7 HOW DO YOU CREATE AN E-MAIL POLICY?

Now that you know why you need an e-mail policy, the next step is to create one. Basically, an e-mail policy should include all the do's and don'ts concerning the organization's e-mail system:

17.7.1 E-mail Risks

The policy should list e-mail risks to make users aware of the potential harmful effects of their actions. Advise users that sending an e-mail is like sending a postcard: if you don't want it posted on a bulletin board, then don't send it.

17.7.2 Best Practices

This should include e-mail etiquette and writing rules in order to uphold the good reputation of the organization and to deliver quality customer service. Also include instructions on compressing attachments to save bandwidth.

17.7.3 Personal Usage

The policy should state whether personal e-mails are accepted and if so, to what extent. You can for instance set limits on the amount of personal e-mails sent each day, or you could require personal e-mails to be saved in a separate folder. You will probably want to prohibit the sending of chain letters and mass mailings and limit or eliminate certain e-mail attachments from being sent or received. In every case, include examples and clear measures taken when these rules are breached.

17.7.4 Wastage of Resources

Warn users that they are making use of the organization's e-mail system and that they should not engage in non-business activities that unnecessarily tie up network traffic. The policy must also cover the use of newsletters and newsgroups. For instance you can require a user to request permission before subscribing to a newsletter or newsgroup.

17.7.5 Prohibited Content

The policy should expressly state that the e-mail system is not to be used for the creation or distribution of any offensive, or disruptive messages, including messages containing offensive comments about race, gender, age, sexual orientation, pornography, religious or political beliefs, national origin or disability. State that employees who receive any e-mail with this content should report the matter to their supervisor immediately. Moreover, employees should not use e-mail to discuss competitors, potential acquisitions or mergers or to give their opinion about another firm. Unlawful messages, such as copyright infringing e-mails should also be prohibited. Include examples and clear measures taken when these rules are breached.

17.7.6 Document Retention Policy

Unless your organization is required to archive e-mail messages, which is the case for government, health care and financial institutions, it is best to create a policy rule that dictates deletion of e-mails after a certain amount of days. However, it is a good idea to provide an option to save certain e-mails in a different folder to avoid deletion. If you provide this option, spell out which e-mails may be saved and which must be deleted.

17.7.7 Treatment of Confidential Data

This includes rules and guidelines on how employees should deal with confidential information and trade secrets. Make employees encrypt any confidential information that is sent via e-mail and change passwords regularly. Also includes measures that will be taken if an employee is found to be sending out confidential information unlawfully.

17.7.8 E-mail Monitoring

If you are going to monitor your employees' e-mails, you must state this in your e-mail policy. Warn that employees should have no expectation of privacy in anything they create, store, send or receive on the organization's computer system and that the organization may, but is not obliged to monitor messages without prior notice. If you do not mention that the organization is not obliged to monitor messages, an employee could potentially sue the organization for failing to block a particular message.

17.8 PUBLISHING THE E-MAIL POLICY

The e-mail policy should be made available and easily accessible to all employees. The policy should be included in employee handbooks and organization intranets. It is best to include the e-mail policy, or a short statement regarding the policy, in employment contracts. In this way the employee must acknowledge in writing that he/she is aware of the e-mail policy and of the obligation to adhere to it. When the policy is updated a new copy can be circulated via e-mail as well as on paper. Preferably have each new update signed by employees.

17.9 UNIVERSITY E-MAIL POLICY

This policy clarifies the applicability of law and of other university policies to electronic mail. It also defines new policy and procedures where existing policies do not specifically address issues particular to the use of electronic mail.

The university recognizes that principles of academic freedom and shared governance, freedom of speech, and privacy of information hold important implications for electronic mail and electronic mail services. The university affords electronic mail privacy protections comparable to that which it traditionally affords paper mail and telephone communications. This policy reflects these firmly-held principles within the context of the university's legal and other obligations.

The university encourages the use of electronic mail and respects the privacy of users. It does not routinely inspect, monitor, or disclose electronic mail without the holder's consent. Nonetheless, subject to the requirements for authorization, notification, and other conditions specified in this policy, the university may deny access to its electronic mail services and may inspect, monitor, or disclose electronic mail (i) when required by and consistent with law, (ii) when there is substantiated reason to believe that violations of law or of university policies have taken place.

Some important definitions are given below:

Computing facilities: Computing resources, services, and network systems such as computers and computer time, data processing or storage functions, computer systems and services, servers, networks, input/output and connecting devices, and related computer records, programs, software, and documentation.

University e-mail systems or services: Electronic mail systems or services owned or operated by the university or any of its subunits.

E-mail record or e-mail: Any or several electronic computer records or messages created, sent, forwarded, replied to, transmitted, stored, held, copied, downloaded, displayed, viewed, read, or printed by one or several e-mail systems or services. This definition of e-mail records applies equally to the contents of such records and to transactional information associated with such records, such as headers, summaries, addresses, and addressees. This policy applies only to electronic mail in its electronic form. The policy does not apply to printed copies of electronic mail.

University record: Records held by students including e-mail are not university records unless such records are pursuant to an employment or agent relationship the student has or has had with the university. This exemption does not, however, exclude student e-mail from other aspects of this policy, regardless of whether such e-mail is a university record.

University e-mail record: A university record in the form of an e-mail record regardless of whether any of the computing facilities utilized to create, send, forward, reply to, transmit, store, hold, copy, download, display, view, read, or print the e-mail record are owned by the university.

Use of university or other e-mail services: To create, send, forward, reply to, transmit, store, hold, copy, download, display, view, read, or print e-mail (with the aid of university e-mail services). A (university) e-mail user is an individual who makes use of (university) e-mail services. Receipt of e-mail prior to actual viewing is excluded from this definition of "use" to the extent that the recipient does not have advance knowledge of the contents of the e-mail record.

Possession of e-mail: An individual is in "possession" of an e-mail record, whether the original record or a copy or modification of the original record, when that individual has effective control over the location of its storage. E-mail users are not responsible for e-mail in their possession when they have no knowledge of its existence or contents. An e-mail user who is in possession of a particular e-mail record, regardless of whether that e-mail user is the original creator or a recipient of the content of the record.

17.9.1 Purpose and Scope

The purpose of this policy is to assure that:

A. The university community is informed about the applicability of policies and laws to electronic mail.

B. Electronic mail services are used in compliance with those policies and laws.

C. Users of electronic mail services are informed about how concepts of privacy and security apply to electronic mail, and

D. Disruptions to university electronic mail and other services, and activities are minimized.

Scope of the policy is to apply to:

- All electronic mail systems and services provided or owned by the university; and
- All users, holders, and uses of university e-mail services; and
- All university e-mail records in the possession of university employees or other e-mail users of electronic mail services provided by the university.

17.9.2 Specific Provisions

Allowable Use

In general, use of university electronic mail services is governed by policies that apply to the use of all university facilities. In particular, use of university electronic mail services is encouraged and is allowable subject to the following conditions:

Purpose: Electronic mail services are to be provided by the university organizational units in support of teaching, research, and public service mission of the university, and the administrative functions that support this mission.

Users: Users of university electronic mail services are to be limited primarily to university students, faculty, and staff for purposes that conform to the requirements of this section.

Non-competition: University electronic mail services shall not be provided in competition with commercial services to individuals or organizations outside the university.

Restrictions: University electronic mail services may not be used for: unlawful activities; commercial purposes not under the auspices of the university, personal financial gain etc.

Representation: Electronic mail users shall not give the impression that they are representing, giving opinions, or otherwise making statements on behalf of the university.

False identity: University e-mail users shall not employ a false identity. E-mail may, however, be sent anonymously provided this does not violate any law or this or any other university policy, and does not unreasonably interfere with the administrative business of the university.

Interference: University e-mail services shall not be used for purposes that could reasonably be expected to cause, directly or indirectly, excessive strain on any computing facilities, or unwarranted or unsolicited interference with others' use of e-mail or e-mail systems. Such uses include, but are not limited to, the use of e-mail services to: (i) send or forward e-mail chain letters; (ii) "spam," that is to exploit listservers or similar broadcast systems for purposes beyond their intended scope to amplify the widespread distribution of unsolicited e-mail; and (iii) "letter-bomb," that is to resend the same e-mail repeatedly to one or more recipients to interfere with the recipient's use of e-mail.

Personal use: University electronic mail services may be used for incidental personal purposes provided that, in addition to the foregoing constraints and conditions, such use does not: (i) directly or indirectly interfere with the university operation of computing facilities or electronic mail services; (ii) burden the university with noticeable incremental cost; or (iii) interfere with the e-mail user's employment or other obligations to the University.

Security and Confidentiality

The confidentiality of electronic mail cannot be assured. Such confidentiality may be compromised by applicability of law or policy, including this policy, by unintended redistribution, or because of inadequacy of current technologies to protect against unauthorized access. Users, therefore, should exercise extreme caution in using e-mail to communicate confidential or sensitive matters.

The university attempts to provide secure and reliable e-mail services. Operators of university electronic mail services are expected to follow sound professional practices in providing for the security of electronic mail records, data, application programs, and system programs under their jurisdiction. Since such professional practices and protections are not foolproof, however, the security and confidentiality of electronic mail cannot be guaranteed. Furthermore, operators of e-mail services have no control over the security of e-mail that has been downloaded to a user's computer. As a deterrent to potential intruders and to misuse of e-mail, e-mail users should employ whatever protections (such as passwords) are available to them.

Users of electronic mail services should be aware that even though the sender and recipient have discarded their copies of an electronic mail record, there may be back-up copies that can be retrieved. Systems may be "backed-up" on a routine or occasional basis to protect system reliability and integrity, and to prevent potential loss of data. The back-up process results in the copying of data onto storage media that may be retained for periods of time and in locations unknown to the originator or recipient of electronic mail. The practice and frequency of back-ups and the retention of back-up copies of e-mail vary from system to system. Electronic mail users are encouraged to request information on the back-up practices followed by the operators of university electronic mail services, and such operators are required to provide such information upon request.

17.9.3 Campus Responsibilities and Discretion

Chancellor/Vice Chancellor shall develop, maintain, and publish specific procedures and practices that implement this policy and communicate its provisions to campus users of university electronic mail services. Violations of university policies governing the use of university electronic mail services may result in restriction of access to university information technology resources. In addition, disciplinary action, up to and including dismissal, may be applicable under other university policies, guidelines, implementing procedures, or collective bargaining agreements.

Chancellor/Vice Chancellor shall decide whether to publish students' electronic mail addresses as directory information.

Chancellor/Vice Chancellor shall establish guidelines as to who may use campus electronic mail services.

Chancellor/Vice Chancellor shall establish regulations and procedures on actions to be taken once an e-mail user's affiliation with the campus is terminated.

Campus shall establish appropriate notification procedures regarding this policy to all e-mail users. New users shall positively acknowledge receipt and understanding of the policy. Such notification and acknowledgment may be electronic to the extent that the e-mail user's identity can be assured. It is recognized that it may not be possible to phase in such procedures immediately, however, the lack of comprehensive procedures shall not, in the interim, invalidate the provisions and applicability of this policy.

17.10 ELECTRONIC MAIL SECURITY

E-mail is vital for today's commerce, as well as a convenient medium for communication among ordinary users. But, as we noted earlier, e-mail is very public; exposed at every point from the sender's work station to the recipient's screen. Just as you would not put sensitive or private thought on a postcard, you must also acknowledge that e-mail messages are exposed and available for others to read. Sometimes we would like e-mail to be more secure. If we were to make a list of the requirements for secure e-mail, our wish list would include the following protections.

- message confidentiality (the message is not exposed en route to the receiver)
- message integrity (what the receiver sees is what was sent)
- sender authentication (the receiver is confident who the sender was)
- nonrepudiation (the sender cannot deny having sent the message)

Not all of these qualities are needed for every message, but an ideal secure e-mail package would allow these capabilities to be invoked selectively.

PGP for Electronic Mail Security

PGP stands for Pretty Good Privacy. It was developed originally by Phil Zimmerman. However, in its incarnation as open PGP, it has now become an open standard. PGP is open-secure. Although PGP can be used for protecting data in long-term storage, it is used primarily for e-mail security.

PGP's operation consists of five services.

1. *Authentication service:* Sender authentication consists of the sender attaching his/her digital signature to the e-mail and the receiver verifying the signature using public-key cryptography. Here is an example of authentication operations carried out by the sender and the receiver:
   (a) At the sender's end, the SHA-1 hash function is used to create a 160-bit message digest of the outgoing e-mail message.
   (b) The message digest is encrypted with RSA using the sender's private key and the result prepended to the message. The composite message is transmitted to the recipient.
   (c) The receiver uses RSA with the sender's public key to decrypt the message digest.
   (d) The receiver compares the locally computed message digest with the receive message digest.

   The above description was based on using a RSA/SHA based digital signature. PGP also supports DSS/SHA based signatures. DSS stands for Digital Signature Standard. Additionally, the above description was based on attaching the signature to the message. PGP also supports detached signature to the message. PGP also supports detached signatures that can be sent separately to the receiver. Detached signatures are also useful when a document must be signed by multiple individuals.

2. *Confidentiality service:* This service can also be used for encrypting disk files. PGP uses symmetric-key encryption for confidentiality. The user has the choice of three different block-cipher algorithms for this purpose: CAST-128, IDEA or 3DES. With CAST-128 being the default choice. CAST-128 is a block cipher. The block size in CAST-128 is 64-bits and the key size varies between 40 and 128 bits. Depending on the key size, the number of rounds used in the Feistel structure is between 12 and 16.
   The steps for confidentiality are as given below:
   (a) The message and a random 128-bit number as a session key is created by the sender.
   (b) This message is encrypted using CAST-128 with the session key.
   (c) The RSA is, used for encryption of the session key using the receivers public key and is prepended to the message.
   (d) The receiver uses RSA for decryption and recovery of the session key. For this, he uses his private key.
   (e) This message is decrypted using the session key.

   PGP provides an option for the RSA. We can also use Diffie-Hellman for encryption.

   If confidentiality and sender authentication are needed simultaneously, a digital signature for the message is generated using the hash code of the message plaintext and appended to the e-mail message before it is encrypted with the session key (Previously shown PGP's authentication service).
3. *Compression service:* By default, PGP compresses the e-mail message after appending the signature but before encryption. This makes long-term storage of messages and their signatures more efficient. This also decouples the encryption algorithm from the message verification procedures. A compression is carried out with the ZIP algorithm.
4. *E-mail compatibility service:* Since encryption, even when it is limited to the signature, results in binary strings, and since network message transmission is character oriented, we must represent binary data with ASCII strings. PGP uses radix 64 encoding for this purpose.

Radix 64 encoding, also known as *Base-64 encoding*, has emerged as probably the most common way to transmit binary data over a network.

5. *Segmentation service:* For long e-mail messages (these are generally messages with attachments), many e-mail systems place restrictions on how much of the message will be transmitted as a unit. For example, some e-mail systems segment long e-mail messages into 50,000 byte segments and transmit each segment separately. PGP has built in facilities for such segmentation and re-assembly.

   PGP is designed to integrate into popular e-mail programs and operate on major operating systems such as Windows and Macintosh. It uses a graphical user interface(GUI) to simplify the encryption process. The actual operation of PGP consists of authentication, confidentiality, compression, e-mail compatibility and segmentation.

There are a number of reasons to use PGP for e-mail and file storage applications. These include the following:

- Available worldwide on a number of platforms
- Based on secure algorithm
- Works in a wide range of applicability
- Outside standards organizations and government control.

REVIEW QUESTIONS

17.1 What is Internet Governance? Is it possible to categorized the Governance of Internet?

17.2 What are the legal aspects in Internet Governance?

17.3 Describe network security aspects in e-governance.

17.4 Describe security monitoring tools.

17.5 Define electronic mail system.

17.6 What are the e-mail threats that organizations face?

17.7 How is it possible to damage the reputation of organization through e-mail?

17.8 How is it possible to reduce the productivity of organization through e-mail?

17.9 Why do you need an e-mail policy?

17.10 Explain, how do you create an e-mail policy for your organization?

17.11 Why e-mail monitoring should be legal?

17.12 Why e-mail policy of organization should be published?

17.13 What is the purpose of e-mail policy?

17.14 Who should be responsible in organization for development of e-mail policy?

17.15 What are the services provided by PGP?

17.16 Explain PGP for e-mail security.

CHAPTER 18

Security of Internet Banking System

Chapter Outline

The advent and popularity of the Internet presented the banking industry with both a challenge and an opportunity to utilize this medium. Although Internet banking offered customers the comfort of accessing their accounts from any place, there has been fear of exploitation of the inherent weakness in the technology. The opportunity was there to "take the bank to the customers' place" while the challenge lays in changing the mindset of the customers to begin to 'trust' and accept this system. The task was to ensure translation of the unquantifiable trust to a more palpable security to the system. This scenario, combined with the basic flow of the Internet banking system, has made us propose a holistic approach to security. Each layer of the Internet banking has its own risks that can be mitigated through the use of the suggested control mechanisms thereby enabling defence-in-depth, thus prompting the concept of a layered approach to security.

18.1 INTERNET BANKING SYSTEM

The early stages of the last decade heralded the arrival of the Internet as a public domain—as an avenue of information dissemination, a medium for interaction between people of geographic diversities and a worldwide broadcasting facility. The Internet was found to be easy to use and, slowly but surely, the world quickly lapped up all that it had to offer. The banking industry also found ample potential in the Internet and decided to leverage its business by utilizing the Internet as one of its delivery channels. In the initial stages of its inception, though it was fraught with some amount of risk, the banking industry wanted to utilize the reach and capabilities of the Internet.

Internet banking started in two modes—a nontransactional mode wherein the bank utilized the Internet as a medium of advertisement about its services and the transactional mode wherein the bank allowed its customers to use the Internet to check details pertaining to their account viz. account balance, statements, enquiries and even transfer of funds and payment of bills. Though both the modes are susceptible to risk, the transactional mode of Internet banking, referred to as online banking, was more prone to risk due to the heterogeneous architecture, the involvement of various components and the involvement of the finances of the bank and its customers.

18.2 SECURITY PROBLEM

The operational structure of the Internet banking system changed the way in which banking was traditionally done. With no requirement of any geographically stationary teller and a brick-and-mortar building in the Internet banking system, the 'trust' relationship that a customer enjoyed with the bank and its officials seemed lost. Moreover, the absence of inherent security in the Internet coupled with the growing threat to Internet from attackers, viruses etc. raised a valid doubt in the minds of the customers over the security of the Internet banking system.

18.3 METHODOLOGY FOR SECURITY PROBLEM

The central bank of our country, the Reserve Bank of India, had thrown open the doors to the various banks in the country to offer Internet banking, to its customers, circa 1999. With various private and tech-savvy banks taking the lead in this area, the legacy banks were now being virtually pushed to offer this service. These banks too realized that the 'trust' that their customers reposed in them through the traditional mode of banking would now change. The challenge lays in translating the palpable trust in the brick-and-mortar way of banking to a similar level of trust in the internet banking mode. All these factors, combined with our knowledge that not much work has been done in this area, have motivated us in endeavouring to create a similar level of trust in the Internet banking scenario. And we realized that to replicate the trust into the internet banking system we needed to create a sense of security in this delivery channel thereby enabling the customers to trust the system. To this end, the methodology that we decided to adopt was to utilize the various layers (components) of the Internet banking system and add security, by mitigating the risks involved, to each layer and hence create a holistically secure system. The driving force behind the choosing of this methodology was the working of the OSI 'layers' in ensuring a 'well-connected' network.

18.4 SCHEMATIC FLOW OF INTERNET BANKING

Schematic flow of Internet banking is shown in Figure 18.1.

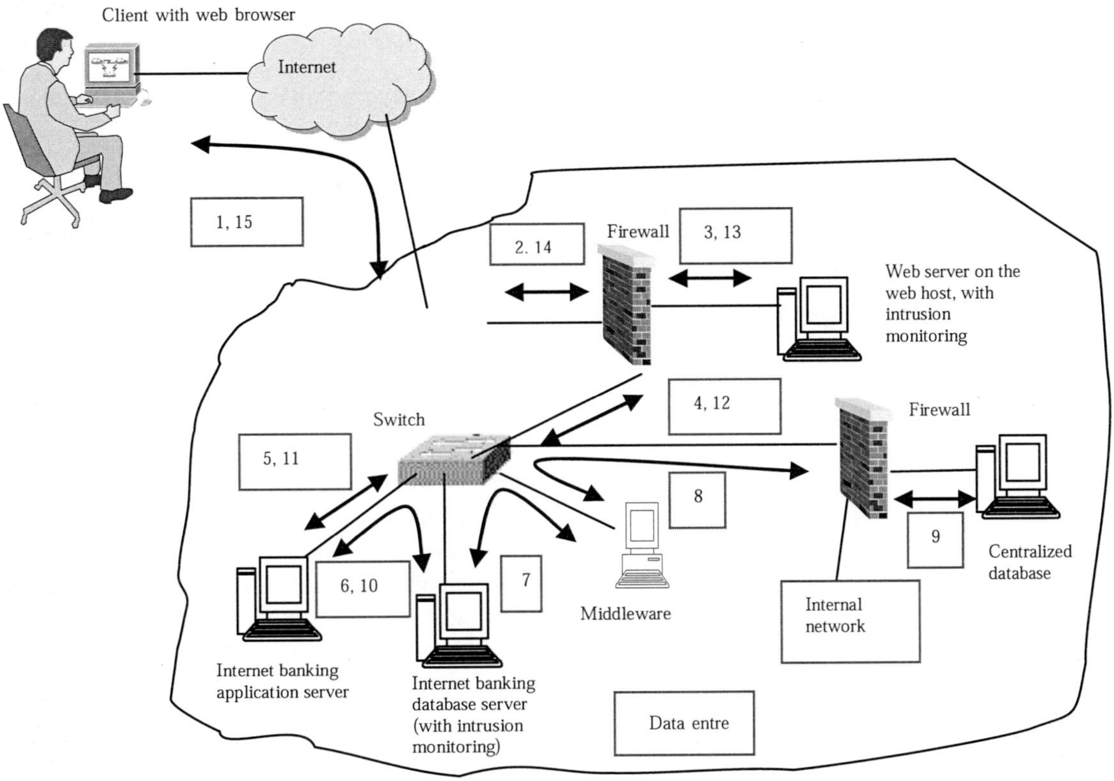

Figure 18.1 Schematic flow of Internet banking.

18.4.1 Steps

1. Client requesting for the web page of the bank offering Internet banking.

2. The request passes through the Internet to the firewall of the bank located in the data centre.

3. Depending upon the type of request and the configuration in the firewall, the request is passed on to the web server or the request is dropped.

4 and 5. The web server displays the web page containing the application interface and the control passes to the Internet banking application server.

6. The details entered by the customer are sent to the Internet banking database for verification and subsequent action.

7, 8 and 9. Data is transferred from the centralized database to the Internet banking database through the middleware.

10. The verification result and the transaction result are passed onto the Internet banking application server.

11, 12 and 13. The details are given to the web server to be displayed to the customer.

14 and 15. The web server displays the results of the transaction on the web browser of the customer.

Steps to be followed to complete one transaction, say, a balance enquiry, are:

1-2-3-4-5-6-10-11-12-13-14-15.

In case the transaction requires real-time connectivity, say, payment of bills, the control is transferred from the Internet banking database to the Central database. The steps to be followed to complete this transaction are:

1-2-3-4-5-6-7-8-9-10-11-12-13-14-15.

18.5 A LAYERED APPROACH TO SECURITY

The fact that each financial transaction has to traverse different layers of the Internet before it can reach its final conclusion, has prompted a layered approach to the security of such a transaction; wherein each layer adds a level of security and in this process also helps the succeeding layer determine the security mechanisms that it needs to incorporate to build a holistic secure system of Internet banking. Also the layers function as a complement to the other preceding and succeeding layers in providing a secure system—if one layer fails, then the next layer does a cover-up, i.e., if security is breached in one layer, then the other layers in the system can stop the attack and/or limit the damages that may occur. While this functioning of the layers in a complementary fashion aids in the security of the system, it should also be noted that total security in one layer does not guarantee the same level of security in its preceding or succeeding layers. Starting with the web browser at the client's end to the management of the bank offering this service, each layer is elaborated below, along with the risks associated with that particular layer and the control measures that need to be adopted to reduce the risk to a minimum.

It can be observed from the Figure 18.2, where the web browser is the starting point of the layers and can be said to be the tip of the security triangle with the management of the bank being the foundation.

18.5.1 Web Browser

The web browser is a software application located on the client system that is used to locate and display web pages.

Risks: The misuse of information provided by the end-user, active content (example: applets etc.) that can crash the system or breach the user's privacy, cookies that can cause annoyance.

Controls: Proper security settings in the browser based on the web content zone, non-disclosure of personal information unless warranted, robust-logon process and controlling cookies.

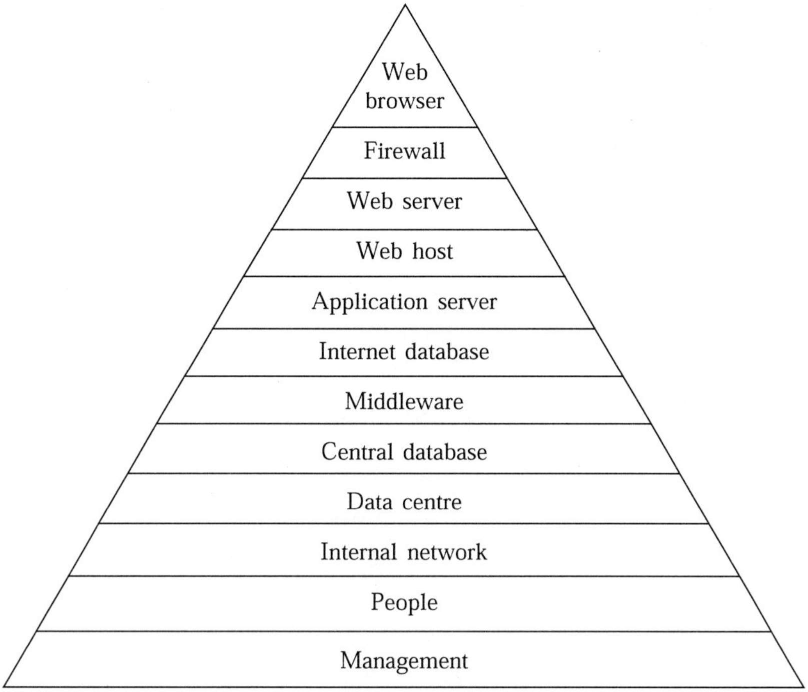

Figure 18.2 Layers of Internet banking.

18.5.2 Perimeter Access Control (Firewall)

A firewall is a system or group of systems that enforces an access control policy between a trusted network and an untrusted network.

Risks: The access control methodology—whether a firewall starts with a 'deny all' policy first or 'permit all' first, the attack on the firewall itself resulting in the failure or malfunction of the firewall and the inappropriate framing of the access control policy itself.

Controls: The primary control is to frame an access control policy that takes into consideration the various factors like the methodology to be used—use the 'deny all' first methodology to start with and later 'permit' based on requirement, the inbound and outbound access to be permitted, the type of firewall—use stateful inspection firewall; and the need for people with valid experience and expertize to configure the firewall. The firewall should be 'self-monitoring' and should prevent itself from being attacked; or in the least should be able to alert the administrator in any such event.

18.5.3 Web Server

The web server is a software application that is used to deliver web pages to a web browser, when requested for that particular web page.

Risks: Inherent weaknesses in the web server software itself, improper configuration, unnecessary open 'ports' and/or 'services', lack of authentication; and lack of access control.

Controls: A proper policy that specifies the requirement in terms of necessary services and ports; proper configuration of the web server in terms of the policy defined; removing unnecessary information and default pages from the web server; ensuring PKI-enabled server side certificate for authenticating itself to the customer; ensuring access control to each service, directory, the administrator password and the physical system per se; session encryption; appropriate utilization of the 'get' and 'post' operations; ensure content management and change management; ensure availability of the web server in terms of processors and memory; ensure proper 'patching' after due testing of patches; enabling auditing/logging and monitoring.

18.5.4 Web Host (with Intrusion Monitoring)

It is the system on which the web server software is loaded—the operating system. This web host is also loaded with intrusion monitoring software.

Risks: Unknown and unnecessary services in the operating system, access control of the system and the capacity planning of the web host.

Controls: Plan carefully to ensure sufficient amount of CPU, memory and disk storage for the expected usage; monitor system resources; ensure redundancy and availability of system resources; ensure physical and logical security; and ensure auditing/logging and monitoring. The intrusion monitoring software detects any attempts to attack the web host and/or web server and alerts the administrator to such attempts; to enable the administrator to take proper action on the alerts.

18.5.5 Internet Banking Application Server

It is a program, residing on a system, that handles all application (Internet banking, in this case) operations between the end-users and the back-end database.

Risks: Security of the operating system, access control for the server and the application, application-specific risks.

Controls: The application-specific risks need to be taken care of at the time of design of the application, while at the same time ensuring that it is properly configured in the server. All controls specified for the web host is valid in this case too. Ensure proper access control—both physical and logical for the system. Ensure sufficient redundancy and availability in terms of clustering and/or load-balancing.

18.5.6 Internet Banking Database (with Intrusion Monitoring)

It is the system on which all the details of the Internet banking customers are stored. It is also loaded with intrusion monitoring software to monitor the activity on the system and the database. This database gets its data from the centralized banking database through a middleware. All transactions which do not require online access to the central database are handled by this database server.

Risks: The customer details are classified as very sensitive and tampering with this database can cause a huge loss—quantitative and qualitative, to the bank; access control for the server and the database.

Controls: Apart from applying all the controls specified for the web host, ensure proper access control—both physical and logical for the system. Access to the database files should be allowed only through the application. Ensure sufficient redundancy and availability in terms of clustering and/or load-balancing.

18.5.7 Middleware

The middleware is software that connects otherwise separate applications. It is used to transfer data from the central database to the Internet banking database.

Risks: Availability is a major risk. If the middleware is not available, transfer cannot take place; also, a 'slow' middleware cannot guarantee availability. Access to the middleware is also a risk.

Controls: Apart from ensuring proper access control—both physical and logical for the system, there should also be sufficient redundancy built into the system to ensure availability of the resource.

18.5.8 Database (with Intrusion Monitoring)

It is the centralized location of data pertaining to all the customers of the bank and other data pertaining to the bank.

The risks and controls associated with the central database are similar to the Internet banking database. In addition to those controls, the bank should also ensure that proper back up of the database is taken; while also planning for contingencies like earthquake etc. by investing in a Disaster Recovery Site.

The data centre is the facility where the entire banking system viz. the servers, databases etc. are housed.

Risks: Physical security of the centre and the equipment it houses.

Controls: A physical security monitoring system should be in place to monitor all the entry/exit points. Access should be controlled through one/two factor mechanisms and backed up with logs/registers. Environmental conditions in the centre should be maintained as stipulated in the policies and procedures.

18.5.9 Data Centre

The data centre is the facility where the entire banking system viz. the servers, databases etc. are housed.

Risks: Physical security of the centre and the equipment it houses.

Controls: A physical security monitoring system should be in place to monitor all the entry/exit points. Access should be controlled through one/two factor mechanisms and backed up with logs/registers. Environmental conditions in the centre should be maintained as stipulated in the policies and procedures.

18.5.10 Internal Network

It is the network which hosts the systems used by the bank staff for the monitoring and maintenance of all the servers, databases and systems of the bank.

Risks: Improper network design for hosting each system can cause unwanted traffic; traffic to the systems for management purposes can eat up bandwidth.

Controls: The network should be properly designed so as to optimally utilize the bandwidth available—place the web server on a separate sub-network connected to the firewall, the database and application servers placed on a separate sub-network in the internal network. Also, the path between the internal systems and the servers and databases should be secure when doing content management.

18.5.11 People

This layer is basically the administrators and operators of each and every system, server or database.

Risks: Insufficient exposure to technology and their requirements during installation and maintenance; random application of patches and updates.

Controls: Ensuring the compliance to policies and procedures during administration and management; auditing of the people, processes and the systems; encouraging knowledge up-gradation activities and educating them on the evils of 'social engineering'. The most important control that we can suggest is '*to do the right things in the right way at the right time*'.

18.5.12 Management

This includes all the different types of management including the bank top management. The primary responsibility of the bank management is to lend support to the implementation of the Internet banking system as a delivery channel of the bank; support the framing, implementation and compliance to all the policies and the procedures relating to the entire Internet banking system.

When the control of a transaction traverses through the layers, it can be seen that the lacunae or weakness in one layer is made up for, by the next layer. For example, if the web server has some unnecessary service open and some attacker tries to enter the Internet banking system through that service, then the intrusion monitoring software in the web host will alert the administrator to some anomalous activity happening in the web host, enabling the administrator to take suitable corrective action thereby ensuring that the system remains secure. Also, total security in one layer will not guarantee the total security of the entire Internet banking system. For example, let the web server be totally secure. Now, this does not guarantee that the application server and the application is secure because any misconfiguration of the application could leave gaping holes through which the application server could be compromised thereby exposing the entire system to other threats. These lead us to the conclusion that a layered approach to security will give a secure credence to the Internet banking system and thus ensure the trust in this delivery channel that we had originally set out to achieve.

REVIEW QUESTIONS

18.1 Explain Internet banking system.

18.2 What are security threats to Internet banking system?

18.3 How Internet banking system can be made secure?

18.4 Explain flow of Internet banking.

18.5 Explain layered approach to security.

18.6 What is importance of web browser in Internet banking system?

18.7 What is importance of web server in Internet banking system?

18.8 Why web host should be loaded with intrusion monitoring software?

18.9 Why Internet banking database should be loaded with intrusion monitoring software?

18.10 What is the role of management in Internet banking system?

APPENDIX A

Internet Standards and the Internet Society

The Internet Society is the coordinating committee for Internet design, engineering and management. Areas covered include the operation of the Internet itself and the standardization of protocols used by end systems on the Internet for interoperability. Three organizations under the Internet Society are responsible for the actual work of standards development and publication:

- *Internet Architecture Board (IAB):* Responsible for defining the overall architecture of the Internet, providing guidance and broad direction to the IETF.
- *Internet Engineering Task Force (IETF):* The protocol engineering and development arm of the Internet.
- *Internet Engineering Steering Group (IESG):* Responsible for technical management of IETF activities and the Internet standards process.

Working groups chartered by the IETF carry out the actual development of new standards and protocols for the Internet. Membership in a working group is voluntary; any interested party may participate. During the development of a specification, a working group will make a draft version of the document available as an Internet Draft, which is placed in the IETF's "Internet Drafts" online directory. The document may remain as an Internet Draft for up to six months, and interested parties may review and comment on the draft. During that time, the IESG may approve review and comment on the drafts as an RFC (Request for comment). If the draft has not progressed to the status of an RFC during the six-month period, it is withdrawn from the directory. The working group may subsequently publish a revised version of the draft.

The IETF is responsible for publishing the RFCs, with approval of the IESG. The RFCs are the working notes of the Internet research and development community. A document in this series may be on essentially any topic related to computer communications and may be anything from a meeting report to the specification of a standard.

The work of the IETF is divided into eight areas, each with an area director and each composed of numerous working groups. Table A.1 shows the IETF areas and their focus.

Table A.1 IETF areas

IETF area	*Theme*	*Example of working groups*
General	IETF process and procedures	Policy framework process for organization of Internet standards
Application	Internet application	Web-related protocols (HTTP) EDI-Internet integration LDAP
Internet	Internet infrastructure	IPv6 PPP extension
Operations and management	Standards and definitions for network information	SNMPv3 Remote network monitoring
Routing	Protocols and management for routing information	Multicast routing OSPF QoS routing
Security	Security protocols and technologies	Kerberos IPSec X.509 S/MIME TLS
Transport	Transport-layer protocols	Differentiated services IP telephony NFS RSVP
User services	Methods to improve the quality of information available to users of the Internet	Responsible use of the Internet User services FYI documents

The Standardization Process

The decision of which RFCs become Internet standards is made by the IESG, on the recommendation of the IETF. To become a standard, a specification must meet the following criteria:

- Be stable and well-understood
- Be technically-competent
- Have multiple, independent, and interoperable implementations with substantial operational experience
- Enjoy significant public support
- Be recognizably-useful in some or all parts of the Internet.

Table A.2 shows the RFC numbers and their focus.

Table A.2 Internet RFCs

Number	*Title*	*Year*
RFC 822	Standard for the format of ARPA Internet text messages	1982
RFC 1510	The Kerberos Network Authentication Service (V5)	1993
RFC 1636	Security in the Internet Architecture	1994
RFC 1750	Randomness Recommendations for Security	1994
RFC 1928	SOCKS Protocol Version 5	1996
RFC 2026	The Internet Standards Process	1996
RFC 2040	The RC5, RC5-CBC, RC5-CBC-Pad, and RC5-CTS Algorithm	1996
RFC 2045	MIME Part One: Format of Internet Message Bodies	1996
RFC 2046	MIME Part Two: Media Types	1996
RFC 2047	MIME Part Three: Message Header Extensions for Non-ASCII Text	1996
RFC 2048	MIME Part Four: Registration Procedures	1996
RFC 2049	MIME Part Five: Conformance Criteria and Examples	1996
RFC 2104	HMAC: Keyed-Hashing for Message Authentication	1997
RFC 2119	Keywords for Use in RFCs to Indicate Requirement Levels	1997
RFC 2246	The TLS Protocol	1999
RFC 2401	Security Architecture for the Internet Protocol	1998
RFC 2402	IP Authentication Header	1998
RFC 2406	IP Encapsulating Security Payload (ESP)	1998
RFC 2408	Internet Security Association and Key Management Protocol	1998
RFC 2459	Internet X.509 Public Key Infrastructure Certificate and CRL Profile	1999
RFC 2630	Cryptographic Message Syntax	1999
RFC 2632	S/MIME Version 3 Certificate Handling	1999
RFC 2633	S/MIME Version 3 Message Specification	1999
RFC 2828	Internet Security Glossary	2000
RFC 3156	MIME Security with Open PGP	2001
RFC 3174	US Secure Hash Algorithm 1	2001
RFC 3302	Top Image File Format	2002
RFC 3949	File Format for Internet Fax	2005
RFC 4291	IP Version 6 Addressing Architecture	2006

WEB REFERENCES

Internet URLs sometimes change or become inactive, so it is possible that you may find a URL that no longer works. Is so, please use your web-search skills to locate the website you were seeking.

http://www.ietf.org

http://www.ieee.org

http://www.ansi.org

http://www.icir.org

http://www.cisco.org

http://www.unionway.com

http://www.cybertrace.com

http://www.cai.com

http://www.ipa.go.jp/STC/IDA/index.html

http://www.intrusion.com

http://www.short.org

http://buildsecurity.in.us.cert.gov/daisy/bsi/articles

http://www.aisto.com/roeder/dotnet

http://developer.apple.com/documentation/security

http://kpdus.tripod.com

http://msdn.microsoft.com

http://www.openssl.org/docs/ssl/ssl.html

http://www.signio.com

http://www.w3.org

http://pear.php.net/package/crypt-HMAC

http://www.securityfocus.com

http://www.perl.com

http://www.cert.org

http://www.owasp.org

http://www.foundstone.com

http://www.nist.gov

http://www.ibm.com

http://www.opennodes.org

http://www.ssc.com

http://www.atmfourm.com

http://www.sonet.com

http://www.rfc.editor.org

http://www.java.sun.com

http://www.internic.net

http://www.isoc.org

http://www.rsasecurity.com

http://www.pgp.com

http://www.fcc.gov

http://www.iso.org

http://www.otu.int

APPENDIX B

Abbreviations and Acronyms

AC	Access Control
AES	Advanced Encryption Standard
AH	Authentication Heads
ANSI	American National Standards Institute
ARPA	Advanced Research Project Agency
ASCII	American Standard Code for Information Interchange
ATM	Asynchronous Transfer Mode
BCD	Binary Coded Decimal
B-ISDN	Broadbased Integrated Services Digital Network
BSC	Binary Synchronous Communication
CBC	Cipher Block Chaining
CDC	Connected Device Configuration
CESG	Communications–Electronics Security Group
CFB	Cipher Feedback
CMIP	Common Management Information Protocol
CMIS	Common Management Information Service
CONS	Connection-Oriented Network Service
COTS	Connection-Oriented Transport Service
DARPA	Defence Advanced Research Project Agency
DES	Data Encryption Standard
DNS	Domain Name System
DSA	Digital Signature Algorithm
DSS	Digital Signature Standard
EIA	Electronic Industries Association
ECB	Electronic Code Book
ESP	Encapsulating Security Payload
FC	Frame Control
FDDI	Fiber Distributed Data Interface
FIPS	Federal Information Processing Standard
FTP	File Transfer Protocol
HDLC	High-Level Data Link Control

HTML	Hypertext Markup Language
HTTP	Hypertext Transfer Protocol
ICMP	Internet Control Message Protocol
IEC	International Electrotechnical Commission
IETF	Internet Engineering Task Force
IP	Internet Protocol
IPng	IP next generation
IPSec	IP Security
ISO	International Organization for Standardization
ITU	International Telecommunications Union
LAN	Local Area Network
LLC	Logical Link Control
LSL	Link Support Layer
MA	Multiple Access
MAC	Medium Access Control
MD5	Message Digest, Version 5
MIB	Management Information Base
MIC	Message Integrity Code
MIME	Multipurpose Internet Mail Extension
NBS	National Bureau of Standard
NIC	Network Interface Card
NIST	National Institute of Standards and Technology
NSA	National Security Agency
NSAP	Network Service Access Point
OFB	Output Feedback
OSI	Open System Interconnection
PDU	Protocol Data Unit
PGP	Pretty Good Privacy
RFC	Request for Comments
RSA	Rivest-Shamir-Adelman
SET	Secure Electronic Transaction
SHA	Secure Hash Algorithm
S/MIME	Secure MIME
SMTP	Simple Mail Transfer Protocol
SNMP	Simple Network Management Protocol
SSL	Secure Socket Layer
TCP	Transmission Control Protocol
TLS	Transport Layer Security
UDP	User Datagram Protocol
USM	User-based Security Model
WAN	Wide Area Network

APPENDIX C

Questions and Answers

1. **What is information security?**
The measures adopted to prevent the unauthorized use, misuse, modification, or denial of use of knowledge, facts, data or capabilities.

2. **What is computer security?**
Computer security is the process of preventing and detecting unauthorized use of your computer. Prevention measures help you to stop unauthorized users (also known as "intruders") from accessing any part of your computer system. Detection helps you to determine whether or not someone attempted to break into your system, if they were successful, and what they may have done.

3. **Why should I care about computer security?**
We use computers for everything from banking and investing to shopping and communicating with others through e-mail or chat programs. Although you may not consider your communications "top secret," you probably do not want strangers reading your e-mail, using your computer to attack other systems, sending forged e-mail from your computer, or examining personal information stored on your computer (such as financial statements).

4. **Who would want to break into my computer at home?**
Intruders (also referred to as hackers, attackers, or crackers) may not care about your identity. Often they want to gain control of your computer so they can use it to launch attacks on other computer systems.

   Having control of your computer gives them the ability to hide their true location as they launch attacks, often against high-profile computer systems such as government or financial systems. Even if you have a computer connected to the Internet only to play the latest games or to send e-mail to friends and family, your computer may be a target.

   Intruders may be able to watch all your actions on the computer, or cause damage to your computer by reformatting your hard drive or changing your data.

5. **How easy is it to break into my computer?**
Unfortunately, intruders are always discovering new vulnerabilities (informally called "holes") to exploit in computer software. The complexity of software makes it increasingly difficult to thoroughly test the security of computer systems.

When holes are discovered, computer vendors will usually develop patches to address the problem(s). However, it is up to you, the user, to obtain and install the patches, or correctly configure the software to operate more securely. Most of the incident reports of computer break-ins received at the CERT/CC could have been prevented if system administrators and users kept their computers up-to-date with patches and security fixes.

Also, some software applications have default settings that allow other users to access your computer unless you change the settings to be more secure. Examples include chat programs that let outsiders execute commands on your computer or web browsers that could allow someone to place harmful programs on your computer that run when you click on them.

6. **Identify the components of Information Security.**
   - Physical identity
   - Communication security
   - Emissions security
   - Computer security
   - Network security
7. **Why did computer security become necessary?**
   Because computers became multiuser.
8. **Why is security a process and not a product?**
   No one product will provide total security for an organization.
9. **What does the information policy define?**
   How information should be handled within the organization.
10. **What should the computer use policy define?**
    Who owns the computers, who owns the information acceptable use of the computers, and that there is no expectation of privacy.
11. **What is the purpose of the system administration procedure?**
    To define the procedures for normal system operation and maintenance.
12. **The user management procedures should include requirements for which individuals?**
    Requirements for employees, consultants and contractors.
13. **What three things can be used for authentication?**
    Something you know, something you have, or something you are.
14. **What is the weakest link in security?**
    In short, people.
15. **How secure am I likely to be after reviewing a system myself?**
    This depends partially on how much efforts you expand. In addition, you have to assume that you did not find all the holes. However, if you spend a reasonable amount of time, you have probably spotted the low-hanging fruit—the easy holes. This puts you ahead of the game. The script kiddies will be looking for the easy holes. Even if you become the target of a talented attacker, the attacker may try the easy holes, so you should have some way of burglar alarming them. Since you are likely to find something

when you lock, and you will probably publish your findings, everyone will know about the holes. Keep in mind that you are protected against the ones you know about, but not against the ones you don't know about. One way to help guard against this is to alarm the known holes when you fix them. This can be more of a challenge with closed-source software.

16. **Can an attack be a member of more than one attack class?**
Some attacks may fall into a number of attack classes, such as a denial of service that stems from a service crashing from invalid input.

17. **How can I prevent information leakage?**
A number of papers are available on this topic. Some types of leakage may be prevented by the alteration of things such as banners or default error messages. Other types of leakage, such as protocol-based leakage, will be stopped only by rewrite of the programs and the changing of standards.

18. **Is preventing information leakage "Security through obscurity"?**
Absolutely not, there is no logical reason for communicating credentials of a software package to users that should not be concerned with it. Stopping the flow of information makes it that much more resources–intensive for an attacker and increases the chances of the attacks being discovered.

19. **How can I protect my who is information?**
Currently, there is little that you can do. You can always lie when you registered your domain, but you might have problems later when you need to renew. Also should you ever get into a domain dispute, having false registration information won't be likely to help your case.

20. **Exactly which data should I filter and which is safe to not worry about?**
All incoming data should be filtered. No expectations. Do not assume that any incoming data is safe. Realistically, the small amount of code and processing time required to filter incoming data is so trivial that it's silly if you don't filter the data.

21. **Identify the five components of data communication system.**
Sender, receiver, medium, message and protocol.

22. **What are the three criteria necessary for an effective and efficient network?**
Performance, reliability, security.

23. **Is network monitoring legal?**
Although using sniffers for network diagnostics and management is legal, network monitoring of employee's activities by management has been highly debated. Commercial tools exist for exactly this purpose. In most countries (particularly the United States and United Kingdom), it is legal for employers to monitor any activity that traverses their own networks, including all employee activity.

24. **Name the four main categories of attack.**
Access modification, denial-of-service and repudiation.

25. **Access attacks require what type of access to paper records?**
Physical access.

26. **The use of nontechnical means to gain access to a system is the definition of what?**
Social engineering.

27. **In a buffer overflow attack, what portion of memory is the real target?**
The stack.

28. **What type of variable is targeted in a buffer overflow attack?**
String variables.

29. **If an employee opens a file in another employee's home directly, the employee is performing what type of attack?**
Snooping (part of access attack).

30. **Does a modification attack always include an access attack?**
No, an attacker could have authorized access to a file but not authorization to change the file.

31. **An employee overhearing confidential information from a boss's office is an example of what type of attack?**
An eavesdropping attack (part of access).

32. **Wireless networks are particularly vulnerable to what type of attack?**
Access attack, specifically eavesdropping.

33. **Changing an e-mail header is an example of what type of attack?**
Repudiation attack, specifically masquerading.

34. **What are the targets of denial-of-service attack?**
The availability of information, systems, communications and applications.

35. **What is a distributed denial-of-service (DDoS) attack?**
A distributed denial of service consists of launching a denial of service attack from a good number of sites against a single host. Such an attack is generally more effective to bring down huge corporate sites than DoS attacks. A typical DDoS attack consists of master, slave and victim—master being attacker, slave being the compromised systems and victim of course being the attacker's target. Once the attacker sends out a specific command to the slave or zombie systems, the attack is launched.

36. **What is a denial-of-service attack?**
A denial-of-service (DoS) attack is an attempt to prevent legitimate users of a service from accessing that service. DoS attacks usually make use of software bugs to crash or freeze a service, or bandwidth limits by making use of a flood attack to saturate all bandwidth.

37. **How do systems get hacked?**
Systems can get hacked when either of the following get compromised:

Physical security: An attacker will in this case obtain physical access to the machine. This can be done easily once the intruder gets past any physical security systems in place, for example by removing the disk drive and accessing it from home.

System security: An attacker will gain access to the system by gaining privileges on the system such as by obtaining access to a user account.

38. **Which of the following activities might be considered as a possible source of threat to a company's network?**

   (a) The daily courier service personnel who drop off and pick up packages.
   (b) Former employees who left the company because of downsizing.
   (c) An employee traveling on company business to a conference in another city.
   (d) The building management company where an organization has its offices has decided to install a fire sprinkler system to help reduce the spread of fire.

   All of the choices (a, b, c, d) could create the right conditions to threaten the network. The regular daily courier persons are familiar to employees, so they may not notice anything is wrong should a deliver person walk into the server room. Even with handsome severance packages and benefits, employees who lost their jobs due to downsizing may be disgruntled. An employee's traveling to another location may not create a threat, but if the employee has a laptop computer that contains private information or the web browser has saved passwords, if the laptop is stolen, a hacker has a powerful tool to access the network. Installing a sprinkler system to help reduce the spread of fire is a good idea. But, if the system ever went off and company's servers, computers, and other equipment were damaged by fire or water, the company might or might not be able to recover from the disaster.

39. **List six items that should be addressed by security policies.**
   The six items that all security policies should address are:

   - Authorization
   - Accountability
   - Data availability
   - Data integrity
   - Data confidentiality
   - Privacy.

40. **Describe a denial-of-service attack.**
   A denial-of-service (DoS) attack floods the network with so many unwanted packets that the affected systems are put out commission. The most common form of a DoS attack is the SYN attack. The attacker sends a flurry of SYN packets to a system, which then spends all of its time trying to satisfy all the requests to set up TCP connections it thinks are occurring.

41. **What service must be confidentiality service rely upon to provide complete protection of information?**
   Accountability.

42. **At what services are used to counter a modification attack?**
   Integrity and accountability.

43. **Access control can be used to provide what services?**
   Confidentiality and integrity.

44. **Should all commercial organization worry about traffic flow confidentiality?**
No, traffic flow confidentiality is used primarily in the military and only an issue occasionally in the commercial world.

45. **What is the primary mechanism for providing for the confidentiality and integrity of information while in transmission?**
Encryption.

46. **In order to prevent interception, encryption must be used with what security service?**
Proper accountability (specifically identification and authentication) is also necessary.

47. **Can availability be used to prevent denial-of-service attacks?**
No, nothing can prevent DoS attacks, availability can help detect and restore service after a DoS attack.

48. **What services are used to counter an access attack?**
Confidentiality and accountability.

49. **Why hardware hacking?**
Experimenting with and hacking hardware is important for a number of reasons. First, hardware hacking is not as prevalent as network or software hacking. Because of this, the doors are wide open for the discovery of hardware related security problems. Second, software cannot exist without hardware. Hardware is like the foundation of your house, which needs to exist before things are built on top of it. If the foundation is weak, it does not matter how strong the application is on top of it. This is especially of concern if there is security software (encryption, authentication or other data protection) running on the top of insecure, unprotected hardware. Third, many emergent technologies are based on both hardware and software (e.g. network appliances, wireless, smart cards). Hardware hacking serves as an important piece of the larger puzzle.

50. **What is vulnerability?**
A potential avenue of attack.

51. **When no threat exists, what is the level of risk?**
If there is no threat, there is no risk.

52. **In general public should be considered a threat to what sort of organization?**
The general public could be considered a threat for any organization.

53. **Should only malicious events be considered as part of threat?**
No, accidental events should also be considered.

54. **After vulnerabilities and threats are considered, what else should be examined in order to determine the risk to an organization?**
Countermeasures.

55. **Name the five areas to examine when measuring the risk to an organization.**
Money, time, resources, reputation and lost business.

56. What is the relationship between telecommunications and data communications? Is one a subset of the other? Give reasons for your answer.

Data communication is the data exchange between two or more devices; distance is irrelevant. Telecommunication is data communication between remote devices. Therefore, telecommunication is a subset of data communication.

57. What is the difference between a de facto standard and de jure standard?

A de jure standard is recognized by an officially recognized body. A de facto standard is established by a manufacturer seeking to define the functionality of a new product that has not been approved by an official body.

58. What is medium? Give three examples of a medium.

A medium is anything that conveys data from one place to another. Examples are coax, twisted pair of copper wire, fiber optics, radio wave, satellite transmission etc.

59. What does broadband mean?

"Broadband" is the general term used to refer to high-speed network connections. In this context, Internet connections via cable modem and Digital Subscriber Line (DSL) are frequently referred to as broadband Internet connections. "Bandwidth" is the term used to describe the relative speed of a network connection, for example, most current dial-up modems can support a bandwidth of 56 kbps (thousand bits per second). There is no set bandwidth threshold required for a connection to be referred to as "broadband", but it is typical for connections in excess of 1 Megabit per second (Mbps) to be so named.

60. What is cable modem access?

A cable modem allows a single computer (or network of computers) to connect to the Internet via the cable TV network. The cable modem usually has an Ethernet LAN (Local Area Network) connection to the computer, and is capable of speeds in excess of 5 Mbps.

Typical speeds tend to be lower than the maximum, however, since cable providers turn entire neighborhoods into LANs which share the same bandwidth. Because of this "shared-medium" topology, cable modem users may experience somewhat slower network access during periods of peak demand, and may be more susceptible to risks such as packet sniffing and unprotected windows shares than users with other types of connectivity.

61. What is DSL access?

DSL (Digital Subscriber Line) Internet connectivity, unlike cable modem-based service, provides the user with dedicated bandwidth. However, the maximum bandwidth available to DSL users is usually lower than the maximum cable modem rate because of differences in their respective network technologies. Also, the "dedicated bandwidth" is only dedicated between your home and the DSL provider's central office, the providers offer little or no guarantee of bandwidth all the way across the Internet.

DSL access is not as susceptible to packet sniffing as cable modem access, but many of the other security risks we will cover to apply both DSL and cable modem access.

62. How are broadband services different from traditional dial-up services?

Traditional dial-up Internet services are sometimes referred to as "dial-on-demand" services. That is, your computer only connects to the Internet when it has something to send, such as e-mail or a request to load a web page. Once there is no more data to be sent, or after a certain amount of idle time, the computer disconnects the call. Also, in most cases each call connects to a pool of modems at the ISP, and since the modem IP addresses are dynamically assigned, your computer is usually assigned a different IP address on each call. As a result, it is more difficult (not impossible, just difficult) for an attacker to take advantage of vulnerable network services to take control of your computer.

Broadband services are referred to as "always-on" services because there is no call set-up when your computer has something to send. The computer is always on the network, ready to send or receive data through its network interface card (NIC). Since the connection is always up, your computer's IP address will change less frequently (if at all), thus making it more of a fixed target for attack.

What's more, many broadband service providers use well-known IP addresses for home users. So while an attacker may not be able to single out your specific computer as belonging to you, they may at least be able to know that your service providers' broadband customers are within a certain address range, thereby making your computer a more likely target than it might have been otherwise.

The table below shows a brief comparison of traditional dial-up and broadband services.

	Dial-up	*Broadband*
Connection type	Dial on demand	Always on
IP address	Changes on each call	Static or infrequently changing
Relative connection speed	Low	High
Remote control potential	Computer must be dialed into control remotely	Computer is always connected, so remote control can occur anytime
ISP-provided security	Little or none	Little or none

63. How is broadband access different from the network I use at work?

Corporate and government networks are typically protected by many layers of security, ranging from network firewalls to encryption. In addition, they usually have support staff who maintain the security and availability of these network connections.

Although your ISP is responsible for maintaining the services they provide to you, you probably won't have dedicated staff on hand to manage and operate your home network. You are ultimately responsible for your own computers. As a result, it is up to you to take reasonable precautions to secure your computers from accidental or intentional misuse.

64. How to determine whether a communication system is LAN, MAN or WAN?

Communication system can be determined by size, distance covered by the network, structure and ownership.

65. **What is the significance of the data link layer of the OSI model?**
The data link layer provides the first level of software protocol that defines how nodes can communicate with each other.

66. **Which OSI layers are the network support layers?**
Physical, data link and network layers.

67. **Which OSI layers are the user support layers?**
Session, presentation and application layers.

68. **What is the difference between a service-point address, a logical address and a physical address?**
The physical address is the local address of a node. It is used by the data link layer to deliver data from one node to another within the same network. The logical address defines the sender and receiver at the network layer and is used to deliver messages across multiple networks. The service point address identifies the application process on the station.

69. **Which layer is responsible for decryption or encryption of data?**
Presentation layer.

70. **What does policy do?**
Policy defines the expected level of security or how security should be.

71. **Is security a process and not a set of steps that you go through once?**
Organization change, new projects come on line, new vulnerabilities, and new technology.

72. **Why are the information policy and security policy written first?**
Because they govern how the security awareness classes will be taught and how systems will be configured.

73. **Why might an organization attack lower-risk items first rather than high-risk items?**
Budget and resource constraints may not allow the highest risk items to be dealt with first.

74. **Identify four required security policies.**
Information policy, security policy, use policy and backup policy.

75. **Identify the six skills that all security departments should have.**
Security administration, policy development, architecture, research, assessment and audit.

76. **Who should have the responsibility for security within an organization?**
Ideally, there would be a chief information security officer. However, regardless of whether or not a CISO is present, the responsibility for information security should be an executive-level officer of the organization.

77. **What is meant by spoofing?**
Spoofing refers to the modification of packet's source address information so it appears that the packets were sent from another source.

78. In a public key cryptography system, a sender has encrypted a message with the recipient is public key. What key does the recipient use to decipher the message?
(a) The recipient's private key
(b) The recipient's public key
(c) The sender's private key
(d) The sender's public key

(a) When a message is encrypted with a public key, the only key that can decrypt the message is the private key of the same set. Thus, only the recipient can decrypt with his or her private key when the message has been encrypted with the recipients public key.

79. When a digital signature is created, which key is used to encrypt the signature?
In the case of digital signature, the message is encrypted with the sender's private key, and the recipient decrypts the message with the public key. Because only the sender has the private key, if the recipient can decrypt the message with the public key of the sender, then the recipient knows the sender is authentic.

80. What is a common authentication protocol used for digital signature?
A common authentication protocol used in digital signature implementation is Kerberos.

81. What is a protocol?
A protocol is a well-defined specification that allows computers to communicate across a network. In a way, protocols define the "grammar" that computers can use to "talk" to each other.

82. What is IP?
IP stands for "Internet Protocol". It can be thought of as the common language of computers on the Internet. There are a number of detailed descriptions of IP given elsewhere, so we won't cover it in detail in this document. However, it is important to know a few things about IP in order to understand how to secure your computer. Here we'll cover IP addresses, static vs dynamic addressing, NAT, and TCP and UDP Ports.

83. What is an IP address?
IP addresses are analogous to telephone numbers. When you want to call someone on the telephone, you must first know their telephone number. Similarly, when a computer on the Internet needs to send data to another computer, it must first know its IP address. IP addresses are typically shown as four numbers separated by decimal points, or "dots". For example, 210.214.254.3 and 192.168.62.231 are IP addresses.

If you need to make a telephone call but you only know the person's name, you can look them up in the telephone directory (or call directory services) to get their telephone number. On the Internet, that directory is called the Domain Name System, or DNS for short. If you know the name of a server, say www.cert.org, and you type this into your web browser, your computer will then go ask its DNS server what the numeric IP address is that is associated with that name.

Every computer on the Internet has an IP address associated with it that uniquely identifies it. However, that address may change over time, especially if the computer is

- dialing into an Internet Service Provider (ISP)
- connected behind a network firewall
- connected to a broadband service using dynamic IP addressing.

84. What are static and dynamic addressing?

Static IP addressing occurs when an ISP permanently assigns one or more IP addresses for each user. These addresses do not change over time. However, if a static address is assigned but not in use, it is effectively wasted. Since ISPs have a limited number of addresses allocated to them, they sometimes need to make more efficient use of their addresses.

Dynamic IP addressing allows the ISP to efficiently utilize their address space. Using dynamic IP addressing, the IP addresses of individual user computers may change over time. If a dynamic address is not in use, it can be automatically reassigned to another computer as needed.

85. What is NAT?

Network Address Translation (NAT) provides a way to hide the IP addresses of a private network from the Internet while still allowing computers on that network to access the Internet. NAT can be used in many different ways, but one method frequently used by home users is called "masquerading".

Using NAT masquerading, one or more devices on a LAN can be made to appear as a single IP address to the outside Internet. This allows for multiple computers in a home network to use a single cable modem or DSL connection without requiring the ISP to provide more than one IP address to the user. Using this method, the ISP-assigned IP address can be either static or dynamic. Most network firewalls support NAT masquerading.

86. What are TCP and UDP Ports?

TCP (Transmission Control Protocol) and UDP (User Datagram Protocol) are both protocols that use IP. Whereas IP allows two computers to talk to each other across the Internet, TCP and UDP allow individual applications (also known as "services") on those computers to talk to each other.

In the same way that a telephone number or physical mail box might be associated with more than one person, a computer might have multiple applications (e.g. e-mail, file services, web services) running on the same IP address. Ports allow a computer to differentiate services such as e-mail data from web data. A port is simply a number associated with each application that uniquely identifies that service on that computer. Both TCP and UDP use ports to identify services. Some common port numbers are 80 for web (HTTP), 25 for e-mail (SMTP), and 53 for Domain Name System (DNS).

87. What is meant by an application gateway?

Firewalls that provide upper OSI layers filtering are sometimes called application-layer gateways or proxies.

88. What does IPSec AH provide?

AH or IP authentication header provide access control, authentication, connectionless message integrity and replay protection.

89. What is replay attack?
A replay attack is one in which an attacker obtains a copy of an authenticated packet and later transmits it to the intended destination. The receipt of duplicate, authenticated IP packets may disrupt service in some way or may have some other undesired consequence.

90. What are the protocols which comprise SSL?
SSL handshake protocol;
SSL change cipher space protocol;
SSL alert protocol;
SSL record protocol.

91. What is the difference between SSL connection and SSL session?
Connection: A connection is a transport (in the OSI layering model definition) that provides a suitable relationships. The connections are transient. Every connection is associated with one session.
Session: An SSL session is an association between a client and a server. Sessions are created by the Handshake Protocol. Sessions define a set of cryptographic security parameters, which can be shared among multiple connections. Sessions are used to avoid the expensive negotiation of new security parameters for each connection.

92. What services are provided by the SSL Record Protocol?
Confidentiality: The Handshake Protocol defines a shared secret key that is used for conventional encryption of SSL payloads.
Message integrity: The Handshake Protocol also defines a shared secret key that is used to form a message authentication code (MAC).

93. Identify the fields in the IPv4 header that cannot be covered by the authentication header. What can be done to protect these fields?
The authentication header cannot cover those fields that are changed along the route of the packet, such as the header checksum, Time-to-live and fragment offset-assuming the packet didn't set the DF(don't fragment) flag. Tunnel mode or a node-to-node security association for encryption of these fields can be used to transfer the packets from one router to the next one all across the path.

94. Explain the benefits of authentication header in IPSec brings to the operation of a packet-filtering router.
The AH allows the packet-filtering router to ensure the identity of the sender is accurate. It also prevents the intruder from impersonating the identity of some other people by a forged packet.

95. Explain why a packet-filtering router should reassemble a packet that has been fragmented in the network and check its authentication header, instead of forwarding the fragments to the destination.
It is necessary for a packet-filtering router to reassemble a fragmented packet and check its authentication header because the authentication information is calculated over to

ensure IP packet including the IP header except the changeable fields. Therefore, it is required to reassemble the packet to ensure the identity of the packet before it is transmitted to the destination.

96. Explain how the use of cookies thwarts a denial-of-service attack in the Diffie-Hellman exchange.

The use of cookies allows each one of the two hosts to generate and exchange with the other host a pseudorandom number. The host associates this number with the expected receiving address. Every time the host receives a packet, it will first check the source address and the responder's cookie. If the cookie value does not agree with its own list, the packet will be ignored. This prevents from denial-of-service attack in Diffie-Hellman exchange because whenever a host receives an invalid cookie, it can simply ignore the packet to minimize the processing overhead.

97. What services are provided by IPSec?

Access control; connectionless integrity; data origin authentication; rejection of replayed packets (a form of partial sequence integrity); confidentiality (encryption); and limited traffic flow confidentiality.

98. Give examples of applications of IPSec.

Secure branch office connectivity over the Internet: A company can build a secure virtual private network over the Internet or over a public WAN. This enables a business to rely heavily on the Internet and reduce its need for private networks, saving costs and network management overhead.

Secure remote access over the Internet: An end user whose system is equipped with IP security protocols can make a local call to an Internet Service Provider (ISP) and gain secure access to a company network. This reduces the cost of toll charges for travelling employees and telecommuters.

Establishing extranet and internet connectivity with partners: IPSec can be used to secure communication with other organizations, ensuring authentication and confidentiality and providing a key exchange mechanism.

Enhancing electronic commerce security: Even though some web and electronic commerce applications have built-in security protocols, the use of IPSec enhances that security.

99. What does IPSec and ESP provide?

IP Encapsulating Security Payload (ESP) provides access control, authentication, connectionless message integrity, replay protection and confidentiality.

100. What is the purpose of firewall? Where are firewalls located?

Firewalls are used to prevent unauthorized access to files and web pages on the Internet. They are located at the client or host site.

101. Identify the two basic types of firewalls.

Application layer (proxy) and packet filtering.

102. List three design goals for a firewall.

(i) All traffic from inside to outside, and vice versa, must pass through the firewall. This is achieved by physically blocking all access to the local network except via the firewall. Various configurations are possible.

(ii) Only authorized traffic, as defined by the local security policy, will be allowed to pass. Various types of firewalls are used, which implement various types of security policies.

(iii) The firewall itself is immune to penetration. This implies that use of a trusted system with a secure operating system.

103. List four techniques used by firewalls to control access and enforce a security policy.

Service control: Determines the types of Internet services that can be accessed, inbound or outbound. The firewall may filter traffic on the basis of IP address and TCP port number; may provide proxy software that receives and interprets each service request before passing it on; or may host the server software itself, such as Web or mail service.

Direction control: Determines the direction in which particular service requests may be initiated and allowed to flow through the firewall.

User control: Controls access to a service according to which user is attempting to access it. This feature is typically applied to users inside the firewall perimeter (local users). It may also be applied to incoming traffic from external users; the latter requires some form of source authentication technology, such as is provided in IPSec.

Behaviour control: Controls how particular services are used. For example, the firewall may filter e-mail to eliminate spam, or it may enable external access to only a portion of the information on a local web server.

104. By default, firewalls do what to network traffic?

Prevent all traffic until certain traffic is specifically allowed.

105. What does an application layer firewall do to internal addresses by default?

Internal addresses are hidden behind the firewall's address by default when an application layer firewall is used.

106. What are some weaknesses of a packet-filtering router?

(i) Because packet filter firewall do not examine upper layer data, they cannot prevent attacks that employ application specific vulnerabilities or functions. For example, a packet filter firewall cannot block specific application commands; if a packet filter firewall allows a given application, all functions available within that application will be permitted.

(ii) Because of the limited information available to the firewall, the logging functionality present in a packet filter firewalls is limited. Packet filter logs normally contain the same information used to make access control decisions (source address, destination address, and traffic type).

(iii) Most packet filter firewalls do not support advanced user authentication schemes. Once again, this limitation is mostly due to the lack of upper layer functionality by the firewall.

(iv) They are generally vulnerable to attacks and exploits that take advantage of problems within the TCP/IP specifications and protocol stack, such as network layer address spoofing. Many packet filter firewalls cannot detect a network packet in which the as 1 layer 3 addressing information has been altered. Spoofing attacks are generally employed by intruders to bypass the security controls implemented in a firewall platform.

107. What is an application-level gateway?
An application-level gateway, also called a proxy server, acts as a relay of application-level traffic.

108. In what way is packet filtering firewall like a router?
Traffic is passed directly to the destination system rather than being terminated on the firewall.

109. Are firewalls only used on Internet connections?
Firewall should not be limited to use only for Internet connections. A firewall is a network access control device that can be used anywhere that access must be controlled. This includes internal networks that should be protected from other internal systems. Sensitive internal networks may include systems with extremely important information or functions or networks that conduct experiments on network equipment.

110. Name the two basic methods for securing Internet messages.
Authentication and cryptography.

111. What are the essential ingredients of a symmetric cipher?
Plaintext, encryption algorithm, secret key, ciphertext, decryption algorithm.

112. Explain the difference between symmetrical and an asymmetrical system.
A symmetrical key uses the same key for encrypting and decrypting messages. An asymmetrical key uses a different key for encrypting and decrypting.

113. What is the difference between public and private key?
A public key is maintained on a server and is used to encrypt messages. A private key is maintained by a user and is used to decrypt messages.

114. What is the relationship between plaintext and ciphertext?
The original message sent by the user is called the plaintext whereas the ciphertext is the result of encryption the plaintext.

115. Whats are the two basic functions used in encryption algorithms?
Permutation and substitution.

116. What are the two categories of encryption/decryption methods? What is the main difference between the categories?
Two main categories of encryption are conventional and public key. In conventional methods, the decryption algorithm is the inverse of the encryption algorithm; the same

secret key is used. Public key methods make their encryption key public, while the decryption key is known only to the receiver.

117. How many keys are required for two people to communicate via a cipher?
One key for symmetric ciphers and two keys for asymmetric ciphers.

118. What is difference between a block cipher and a stream cipher?
A stream cipher is one that encrypts a digital data stream one bit or one byte at a time. A block cipher is one in which a block of plaintext is treated as a whole and used to produce a ciphertext block of equal length.

119. For private key encryption, discuss the keys and their ownership.
In conventional (private key) encryption, the decryption algorithm uses the same key as the encryption algorithm, therefore, for security, the key is owned by and known only to the user.

120. List and briefly define types of cryptanalytic attacks based on what is known to the attacker.

Ciphertext only: One possible attack under these circumstances is the brute-force approaching of trying all possible keys. If the key space is very large, this becomes impractical. Thus, the opponent must relay on an analysis of the ciphertext itself, generally applying various statistical tests to it.

Known plaintext: The analyst may be able to capture one or more plaintext messages as well as their encryptions. With this knowledge, the analyst may be able to deduce the key on the basis of the way in which the known plaintext is transformed.

Chosen plaintext: If the analyst is able to choose the messages to encrypt, the analyst may be deliberately pick patterns that can be expected to reveal the structure of the key.

121. What is transposition cipher?
A transposition cipher involves a permutation of the plaintext litters.

122. What is steganography?
Steganography involves concealing the existence of a message.

123. For the public key encryption, discuss the keys and their ownership.
In public key methods, every user shares the same encryption algorithm and key. However, the decryption algorithm and key are kept secret so that only an authorized receiver can decrypt the information.

124. Why is authentication necessary in Internet communication?
Authentication is used in Internet communication to verify the identity of a sender.

125. What is product cipher?
In a product cipher, two or more basic ciphers are performed in sequence in such a way that the final result or product is cryptographically stronger than any of the component ciphers.

126. What is the difference between differential and linear cryptanalysis?
Differential cryptanalysis is a technique is which chosen plaintexts with particular XOR difference patterns are encrypted. The difference patterns of the resulting ciphertext

provide information that can be used to determine the encryption key. Linear cryptanalysis is based on finding linear approximations to describe the transformations performed in a block cipher.

127. What was the original set of criteria used by NIST to evaluate candidate AES ciphers?

Security—Actual security, randomness, soundness, other security factors.
Cost—Licensing requirements, computational efficiency, memory requirements.
Algorithm and implementation characteristics—Flexibility, hardware and software suitability, simplicity.

128. Explain how authentication thwarts the man in-the-middle attack.

A man in-the-middle attack has an intruder interpose itself between sender and receiver so that it can intercept and possibly modify messages in the exchange. The use of authentication between the sender and receiver prevents the intruder from modifying messages without being detected.

129. What are the three threats associated with user authentication over a network or the Internet?

(i) A user may gain access to a particular station and pretend to be another user operating from that workstation.
(ii) A user may alter the network address of a workstation so that the requests sent from the altered workstation appear to come from the impersonated workstation.
(iii) A user may eavesdrop on exchanges and use a reply attack to gain entrance to a server or to disrupt operations.

130. List three approaches to secure user authentication in a distributed environments.

(i) Rely on each individual client workstation to assure the identity of its user or users and rely on each server to enforce a security policy based on user identification (ID)
(ii) Require that client systems authenticate themselves to servers, but trust the client system concerning the identity of its user.
(iii) Require the user to prove identity for each service invoked. Also require that servers prove their identity to clients.

131. What are the five principal services provided by PGP?

(i) Authentication
(ii) Confidentiality
(iii) Compression
(iv) e-mail compatibility
(v) Segmentation.

132. What is the utility of a detached signature?

A detached signature is useful in several contexts. A user may wish to maintain a separate signature log of all messages sent or received. A detached signature of an executable program can detect subsequent virus infection. Finally, detached signatures can be used when more than one party must sign a document such as a legal-contract. Each person's signature is independent and therefore is applied only to document.

Otherwise, signatures would have to be nested, with the second signer signing both the document and the first signature, and so on.

133. Why does PGP generate a signature before applying compression?

(a) It is preferable to sign an uncompressed message so that one can store only the incompressed message together with the signature for future verification. If one signed a compressed document, then it would be necessary either to store a compressed version of the message for later verification or to recompress the message when verification is required.

(b) Even if one were willing to generate dynamically a recompressed message for verification, PGP's compression algorithm presents a difficulty. The algorithm is not deterministic, various implementations of the algorithm achieve different trade-off in running speed versus compression ratio and, as a result, produce different compressed forms. However, these different compression algorithms are interoperable because any version of the algorithm can correctly decompress the output of any other version. Applying the hash function and signature after compression would constrain all PGP implementations to the same version of the compression algorithm.

134. Why R 64 conversion useful for an e-mail application?

When PGP is used, at least part of the block to be transmitted is encrypted. If only the signature service is used, then the message digest is encrypted (with the sender's private key). If the confidentiality service is used, the message plus signature (if present) are encrypted (with a one-time symmetric key). Thus, part or all of the resulting block consists of a stream of arbitrary 8-bit octets. However, many electronic mail systems only permit the use of blocks consisting of ASCII text.

135. When is IPSec appropriate? When is SSL/TLS appropriate?

TLS and IPSec operate on different levels of the protocol stack. TLS runs over TCP and provides cryptographic protection for a single TCP session. On the other hand, IPSec is a security facility for the underlying IP protocol. With the current definition, IPSec is more appropriate for IPSec aware internet hosts and corporations that use VPN. In contrast, TLS is more appropriate for applications that require authentication and security on a per-user basis.

136. Suggest some SSL/TLS situations in which it is appropriate to authenticate the client.

It is appropriate for TLS to authenticate the client when the server is sending confidential information to the client and wants to ascertain the receiver's identity, for example, a banking statement sent to a customer (client) over the network. Telebanking and credit card purchases over the internet are other examples where authentication is required.

137. How does PGP use the concept of trust?

PGP includes a facility for assigning a level of trust to individual signers and to keys.

138. What is MIME?

MIME is an extension to the RFC 822 framework that is intended to address some of the problems and limitations of the use of SMTP (Simple Mail Transfer Protocol) or some other mail transfer protocol and RFC 822 for electronic mail.

139. What is S/MIME?

S/MIME (Security/Multipurpose Internet Mail Extension) is a security enhanced to the MIME Internet e-mail format standard, based on technology from RSA Data security.

140. What is the concept behind transpositional character-level encryption?

In transpositional character-level encryption characters retain their plaintext form but change position.

141. What is concept behind substitutional character-level encryption?

In substitutional character-level encryption, each character is replaced by another character from the set.

142. Why are conventional encryption/decryption methods not suitable for bank?

It would be impractical for a bank system to create millions of encryption/decryption algorithms with special secret keys for all of its users to be able to have private access to their accounts.

143. Suppose that a certain information source produces symbols from a ternary alphabet {A, B, C}. Suppose also that the source produces As three times as frequently as Bs and Bs twice as frequently as Cs. Can you break the following ciphertext?

(a) CBA (b) CBAACCBACBBCCCCBACC

A is three times as frequent as B and B is twice as frequent as C. Therefore, A should occur most frequently, followed by B and then C.

(a) There is not enough information in the ciphertext CBA to determine frequencies of the encrypted symbols.

(b) C appears 10 times; B appears 5 times; and A appears 4 times. C is likely to be the cipher for A. B is more likely to be the cipher for B than A, but there is not enough data conclude that this with reasonable certainty. Assuming that the cipher is, A => C, B=>B, and C => A., then

CBAACCBACBBCCCCBACC =>ABCCAABCABBAAAABCAA

144. Suppose that a certain information source produces symbols from a ternary alphabet {A, B, C}. Suppose that it is known that As always occur in pairs. Suppose that it is also known that an encryption scheme takes blocks of four symbols and permutes their order. Can you break the following ciphertext: BABACAABACACBAAB?

According to the transposition ciphers scheme, there are two possible ways to decode the ciphertext BABACAABACACBAAB :

Case 1 : 1st and 4th character swaps : AABBBAACCCAABAAB

Case 2 : 2nd and 3rd character swaps : BBAACAABAACCBAAB

145. In authentication using a secret key, consider the case where the transmitter is the intruder.

(a) What happens if the transmitter initiates the challenge?

(b) How secure is the system if the receiver changes the challenge value once every minute?

(c) How secure is the system if the receiver selects the challenge value from a set of 128 choices?

(a) If the transmitter (intruder) initiates the challenge, it will send an ordered list of numbers. The receiver responds to the intruder with an encrypted version of the listed numbers. The intruder receives the responses and stores them in a table of challenges. Once the table of challenges grows to a certain size, the intruder may be able to authenticate itself if the receiver sends a challenge value that is found in the intruder's table of challenges.

(b) The system is not very secure if the receiver changes the challenges value once every minute. This is because the intruder can use the same value to initiate a challenge within a minute and get the encrypted response from the receiver. Once the intruder receives the response, it can send the corresponding encrypted version of the receiver's challenge to authenticate itself. This time (one minute) is long enough for all this to happen.

(c) The system is not secure if the receiver selects the challenge value from a set of 128 choices. This is because the intruder can easily send the same set of 128 values and store them and their encrypted versions that it receives from the receiver in its table of challenges. Whenever the receiver starts a challenge with the intruder, it can look up the corresponding encrypted version of the value in its table of challenge for authentication.

146. Consider a system where a user is authenticated based on an ID and password that are supplied by the transmitter in plaintext. Does it make any difference if the password and ID are encrypted? If yes, explain why? If no, how would you improve the system?

If the system authenticates users based on IDs and passwords that are transmitted in plaintext, the system is very insecure. An eavesdropper can listen and record the authentication information over the network. This information can be replayed by the intruder when attempting to access the system. If the password and ID are encrypted, the system no more secure than in the plaintext case. The intruder can still record the encrypted ID and the corresponding encrypted password should be used only once so that it is not susceptible to the playback attack. The methods were the user identifies itself followed by a once challenge from the server uses this approach.

147. What is the difference between a message authentication code and a one-way hash function?

A hash function, by itself, does not provide message authentication. A secret key must be used in some fashion with the hash function to produce authentication. A MAC, by definition, used as a secrete key to calculate a code used for authentication.

148. What is the role of a compression function in a hash function?

A typical hash function uses a compression function as a basic building block, and involves repeated applications of the compression function.

149. List two disputes that can arise in the context of message authentication.

Suppose that Singh sends an authenticated message to Sharma. The following disputes that could arise;

(i) Sharma may forge a different message and claim that it came from Singh. Sharma would simply have to create a message and append an authentication code using the key that Singh and Sharma share.

(ii) Singh can deny sending the message. Because it is possible for Sharma to forge a message, there is no way to provide that Singh did in fact send the message.

150. What are the properties a digital signature should have?

(a) It must be able to verify the author and the date and time of the signature.

(b) It must be able to authenticate the contents at the time of the signature.

(c) The signature must be verifiable by third parties to resolve disputes.

151. What is the difference between direct and arbitrated digital signature?

A direct digital signature involves only the communicating parties (source, destination). It is assumed that the destination knows the public key of the source. A digital signature may be formed by encrypting the entire message with the sender's private key or by encrypting a hash code of the message with the sender's private key. An arbitrated digital signature operates as follows:

Every signed message from a sender X to a receiver Y goes first to an arbiter A, who subjects the message and its signature to a number of tests to check its origin and content. The message is then dated and sent to Y with an indication that it has been verified to the satisfaction of the arbiter.

152. What are some threats associated with a direct digital signature scheme?

(i) The validity of the scheme depends on the security of the sender's private key. If a sender later wishes to deny sending a particular message the sender can claim that the private key was lost or stolen and that someone else forged his or her signature.

(ii) Another threat is that some private key might actually be stolen from X at a time T. The opponent can then send a message signed with X's signature and stamped with a time before or equal to T.

153. What method is used to check the validity of a cryptographic key?

Brute force or plaintext attack.

154. What is brute force attack? What is it used for?

A brute force attack is a method to test cryptographic keys by testing various key combinations using several computers and mathematical algorithms.

155. For a user workstation in a typical business environment, list potential locations for confidentiality attacks.

LAN, dial-in communication server, Internet, wiring closet.

156. What is the difference between link and end-to-end encryption?
With link encryption, each vulnerable communications link is equipped on both ends with an encryption device. With end-to-end encryption, the encryption process is carried out at the two end systems. The source host or terminal encrypts the data; the data in encrypted forms are then transmitted unaltered across the network to the destination terminal or host.

157. What types of information might be derived from a traffic analysis attack?
Identifies partners: How frequently the partners are communicating. Message pattern, message length, or quantity of messages that suggest important information in being exchanged. The events that correlate with special conversations between particular partners.

158. What is the weakness of DES method? How does triple DES overcome this weakness?
DES has a small key size, which was cracked in 3 hours using a brute force attack. This weakness was resolved using triple DES that included a longer key code and three encoding processes.

159. Good encryption algorithms rely on the secrecy of what to protect the information?
Key.

160. List ways in which secret keys can be distributed to two communicating parties.
For two parties A and B, key distribution can be achieved in a number of ways as follows:

(i) A can select a key and physically deliver it to B.
(ii) A third party can select the key and physically deliver it to A and B.
(iii) If A and B have previously and recently used a key, one party can transmit the new key to the other, encrypted using the old key.
(iv) If A and B each has an encrypted connection to a third party C, C can deliver a key on the encrypted links to A and B.

161. What are the three ways of attack of an encryption scheme?
Through the algorithm, through brute force, and through the surrounding system.

162. What is the another name of private key encryption?
Symmetric key encryption.

163. How long are DES keys?
56 bits.

164. What is the size of triple DES keys?
112 bits.

165. What is the primary weakness of DES?
Its key is too short and thus brute force attacks are possible.

166. What is the difference between Rijndael and AES?
Rijndael allows for block lengths of 128, 192 or 256 bits. AES allows only a block length of 128 bits.

167. What is triple encryption?
With triple encryption, a plaintext block is encrypted by passing it through an encryption algorithm; the result is then passed through the same encryption algorithm again; the result of the second encryption is passed through the same encryption algorithm a third time. Typically, the second stage uses the decryption algorithm rather than the encryption algorithm.

168. How many keys are used in triple encryption?
Triple encryption can be used with three distinct keys for the three stages; alternatively, the same key can be used for the first and third stage.

169. Triple DES increases the security of DES at the expenses of what?
Speed.

170. What is the AES intended to do?
Replace DES.

171. Diffie-Hellman security is based on the difficulty of what problem?
The discrete logarithm problem.

172. What is the difference between a session key and a master key?
A session key is a temporary encryption key used between two principals. A master key is a long lasting key that is used between key distribution centre and a principal for the purpose of encoding the transmission of session keys. Typically, the master keys are distributed by noncryptographic means.

173. List four general categories of schemes for the distribution of public keys.
Public announcement, Public available directory, Public key authority, Public key certificates.

174. What is public-key certificates?
A public-key certificate contain a public key and other information, is created by a certificate authority, and is given to the participant with the matching private key. A participant conveys its key information to another by transmitting its certificate. Other participants can verify that the certificate was created by the authority.

175. Can Diffie-Hellman be used to encrypt traffic?
No, it can only be used to perform a key exchange.

176. Briefly explain Diffie-Hellman key exchange.
Two parties each create a public key, private key pair and communicate the public key to the other party. The keys are designed in such a way that both sides can calculate the same unique secrete key based on each side's private key and the other side's public key.

177. Why should user VPN's require strong authentication?
Because the user's system is not located on the internal network, and therefore, may be open to compromise.

178. Can encryption fully protect the data flowing over a VPN?
Encryption can protect the data from eavesdropping, but this assumes that the end points do not provide an easy avenue for an intruder to learn either the data or the key.

179. In order to secure a user VPN, what policy must be combined with?
Policy must be combined with technology in the form of antivirus software or personal firewalls.

180. Are site-to-site VPN's appropriate for use between organizations?
Yes.

181. Why is addressing a potential problem with site-to-site VPN's?
The remote site may be using the same internal address space.

182. What two criteria should be used for determining whether to use the firewall or a separate system as the VPN server?
Performance and capability.

183. If a separate VPN server is used, should it be placed in the Internal DMZ?
No, the VPN server should be placed in a separate DMZ dedicated to.

184. Why does the overall implementation of the VPN matter more than the choice of encryption algorithm?
Assuming that the algorithm is at least somewhat difficult to break, it is much easier to compromise a system weakness than the algorithm.

185. Which authentication mechanisms are best for a user VPN?
Something you know and something you have.

186. Describe why parity bits, checksums and CRS's do not provide security?
Parity bits, checksums and CRC's do not guarantee that the data arriving at the recipient has actually come from the reported sender. You cannot rely on these mechanisms for this type of data integrity because an unauthorized individual can capture the packets off the transmission media, modify the contents and the parity bits, checksum and/or CRC values, and place the modified packets back on the transmission media.

187. What is one major problem with substitution ciphers?
Substitution ciphers hide the actual character of the message, but they do not hide the frequency or patterns of characters in the message.

188. What does antivirus software do?
There are a variety of antivirus software packages that operate in many different ways, depending on how the vendor chose to implement their software. What they have in common, though, is that they all look for patterns in the files or memory of your computer that indicate the possible presence of a known virus. Antivirus packages know what to look for through the use of virus profiles (sometimes called "signatures") provided by the vendor.

New viruses are discovered daily. The effectiveness of antivirus software is dependent on having the latest virus profiles installed on your computer so that it can look for recently discovered viruses. It is important to keep these profiles up to date.

189. What is at risk?

Information security is concerned with three main areas:

- Confidentiality—information should be available only to those who rightfully have access to it.
- Integrity—information should be modified only by those who are authorized to do so.
- Availability—information should be accessible to those who need it when they need it.

These concepts apply to home Internet users just as much as they would apply to any corporate or government network. You probably wouldn't let a stranger look through your important documents. In the same way, you may want to keep the tasks you perform on your computer confidential, whether it's tracking your investments or sending e-mail messages to family and friends. Also, you should have some assurance that the information you enter into your computer remains intact and is available when you need it. Some security risks arise from the possibility of intentional misuse of your computer by intruders via the Internet. Others are risks that you would face even if you were not connected to the Internet (e.g., hard disk failures, theft, power outages).

190. What are the most common methods used by intruders to gain control of home computer?

(i) Trojan horse programs
(ii) Back door and remote administration programs
(iii) Denial of service
(iv) Being an intermediary for another attack
(v) Unprotected windows shares
(vi) Mobile code (Java, JavaScript, and ActiveX)
(vii) Cross-site scripting
(viii) E-mail spoofing
(ix) E-mail-borne viruses
(x) Hidden file extensions
(xi) Chat clients
(xii) Packet sniffing.

191. Explain Trojan horse programs.

Trojan horse programs are a common way for intruders to trick you (sometimes referred to as "social engineering") into installing "back door" programs. These can allow intruders easy access to your computer without your knowledge, change your system configurations, or infect your computer with a computer virus. ware/human entities.

192. Briefly describe RSA.

The basic concept behind DES is that the plaintext is substitution encrypted in blocks of 64-bits and is parameterized by a 64-bit key of which only 56-bits are actually used for the key.

193. Briefly describe RSA.

RSA typically uses a 512-bit key, which requires a lot more computational power than DES does. The security of RSA is based on the factoring of large numbers. Because of the necessary computational horsepower and time required to encrypt (and decrypt) with RSA, it is very hard to break.

194. How is the RSA algorithm used for privacy in practice?

In practice, the RSA system is often used together with a secret-key cryptosystem, such as DES, to encrypt a message by means of an RSA digital envelope.

Suppose, Alice wishes to send an encrypted message to Bob. She first encrypts the message with DES, using a randomly chosen DES key. Then she looks up Bob's public key and uses it to encrypt the DES key. The DES-encrypted message and the RSA-encrypted DES key together form the RSA digital envelope and are sent to Bob. Upon receiving the digital envelope, Bob decrypts the DES key with his private key, then uses the DES key to decrypt the message itself. This combines the high speed of DES with the key management convenience of the RSA system.

195. Is the RSA cryptosystem currently in use?

The RSA system is currently used in a wide variety of products, platforms, and industries around the world. It is found in many commercial software products and is planned to be in many more. The RSA algorithm is built into current operating systems by Microsoft, Apple, Sun, and Novell. In hardware, the RSA algorithm can be found in secure telephones, on Ethernet network cards, and on smart cards. In addition, the algorithm is incorporated into all of the major protocols for secure Internet communications, including S/MIME), SSL, and S/WAN. It is also used internally in many institutions, including branches of the US government, major corporations, national laboratories, and universities.

At the time of this publication, technology using the RSA algorithm is licensed by over 700 companies. The estimated installed base of RSA BSAFE encryption technologies is around 500 million. The majority of these implementations include use of the RSA algorithm, making it by far the most widely used public-key cryptosystem in the world.

This figure is expected to grow rapidly as the Internet and the Worldwide Web expand. For a list of RSA algorithm licensees, see http://www.rsasecurity.com/

196. Is the RSA system a de facto standard?

The RSA system is the most widely used public-key cryptosystem today and has often been called a de facto standard. Regardless of the official standards, the existence of a de facto standard is extremely important for the development of a digital economy. If one public-key system is used everywhere for authentication, then signed digital documents can be exchanged between users in different nations using different software on different platforms; this interoperability is necessary for a true digital economy to develop. Adoption of the RSA system has grown to the extent that standards are being written to accommodate it. When the leading vendors of U.S. financial industry were developing standards for digital signatures, they first developed ANSI X9.30 in 1997 to support the federal requirement of using the Digital Signature Standard. One year later they added ANSI X9.31, whose emphasis is on RSA digital signatures to support the de facto standard of financial institutions.

The lack of secure authentication has been a major obstacle in achieving the promise that computers would replace paper; paper is still necessary almost everywhere for contracts, checks, official letters, legal documents, and identification. With this core of necessary paper transaction, it has not been feasible to evolve completely into a society based on electronic transactions. A digital signature is the exact tool necessary to convert the most essential paper-based documents to digital electronic media. Digital signatures make it possible for passports, college transcripts, wills, leases, checks and voter registration forms to exist in the electronic form; any paper version would just be a "copy" of the electronic original. The accepted standard for digital signatures has enabled all of this to happen.

197. What are hackers and crackers?

An intruder is also referred to as hacker or a cracker. A hacker is basically someone who hacks a system he could do this because he finds it interesting or because he wants to access your system. In the latter case he would be cracker.

In any case, hacker and crackers are both intruders and can be classified as external or internal intruders (outsiders or insiders).

External/outsiders: Intruders from outside your network. They attack your web servers, e-mail servers and may also attempt to go bypass the firewall to attack machines on the internal network. Outside intruders may come from the Internet, dial-up lines, physical break-ins, or from a partner (vendor, customer, reseller, etc.) network that is linked to your corporate network.

Internal/insiders: Intruders that are using your internal network legitimately. These include users who misuse privileges or who attempt to get higher rights or use another user privileges. Internal intruders are often overlooked. Most security breaches (80%) are done by insiders.

198. What is the advantage of using digital signatures and public key cryptography together?

By combining digital signatures and public key cryptography, you can deliver messages that are confidential and verify that the sender is authentic.

199. What is a dual signature and what is its purpose?

A dual signature is used to sign two concatenated documents each with its own hash code. The purpose of the dual signature is to link two messages that are intended for two different recipients. In this case, the customer wants to send the order information to the merchant and payment information to the bank. The merchant does not need to know the customer's credit card member, and the bank does not need to know the details of the customer's order.

200. List and briefly define three classes of intruders?

Masquerader: An individual who is not authorized to use the computer and who penetrates a system's access controls to exploit a legitimate user's account.

Misfeasor: A legitimate user who accesses data, programs, or resources for which such access is not authorized or who is authorized for such access but misuse his or her privileges.

Clandestine user: An individual who seizes supervisory control of the system and uses this control to evade auditing and access controls or to suppress audit collection.

201. Briefly describe how a Virtual Private Network (VPN) functions.

Virtual Private Network is software that is run by both organizations on the devices that are used to connect to each other across the Internet. The VPN software acts like a packet filter in that it allows data to travel only from one VPN device to the VPN device that the VPN software is configured for. The second task VPN performs is encryption of the data before it is transmitted across the VPN link.

202. What is meant by intrusion detection?

The identification of attempts to penetrate a security barrier.

203. Name the two primary types of IDS.

Host-based and network-based.

204. What are the two common techniques used to protect a password file?

One way encryption: The system stores only an encrypted form of the user's password. When the user presents a password, the system encrypts that password and compares it with the stored value. In practice, the system usually performs a one-way transformation (not reversible) in which the password is used to generate a key for the encryption function and in which a fixed length output is produced.

Access control: Access to the password file is limited to one or a very few accounts.

205. What are the three benefits that can be provided by an IDS (intrusion detection system)?

(i) If an intrusion is detected quickly enough, the intruder can be identified and ejected from the system before any damage is done or any data compromised. Even if the detection is not sufficiently timely to preempt the intruder, the sooner that the intrusion is detected, the less the amount of damage and the more quickly that recovery can be achieved.

(ii) An effective intrusion detection system can serve as a deterrent, so acting to prevent intrusions.

(iii) Intrusion detection enables the collection of information about intrusion techniques that can be used to strengthen the intrusion prevention facility.

206. Can a host-based IDS always determine if an attack attempt was successful?

In most cases, the answer is yes if the information about the results of the attack are logged or the indication exists (files changed, for example).

207. Can a host-based IDS prevent an attack?

Yes, specifically, system call analyzers and application behaviour analyzers can prevent an attack from taking place.

208. Compare the level of security provided by a server that stores a table of IDs and associated passwords as follows:
   (a) Name and password stored unencrypted.
   (b) Name and password stored in encrypted form.
   (c) Hash of name and password stored.

(a) The security level is low because an attacker can access the server and obtain the unencrypted name and password database over the network.
(b) The security level is better than in part(a) because an attacker must have the decryption algorithm and secret key to decrypt the name and password file before it is useful. The security problem is converted into the security of the encryption algorithm.
(c) The security level is the best among the three alternatives. Having the hash of a password does not allow the intruder to access the system. However, if the intruder gets a hold of the table of hashes of user passwords, it can try a dictionary attack where it guesses passwords and computes the corresponding hash until it finds matches in the stolen table.

209. Explain why the processing required to provide privacy service is more complex than the processing required for authentication and integrity.

Authentication and integrity involve binary outcomes: either the user passes the authentication or not; either the message has been tampered with or not. The processing involved is designed to provide one of the two outcomes only. Thus information can be "boiled down" to a relatively small number of bits (as in a hash computation). Privacy requires mapping the entire message into another message that is of the same size (assuming redundancy has been removed from the original message via compression. Every bit in the message must be secured and every bit must be recoverable by the receiver. The associated processing is generally much higher than for authentication or integrity.

210. Consider the following hashing algorithm. A binary block of length M is divided into subblocks of length 128 bits, and the last block is padded with zeros to a length of 128. The hash consists of the XOR of the resulting 128-bit vectors. Explain why this hashing algorithm is not appropriate for cryptographic purposes.

The purpose of the hash algorithm is to map a set of messages to a smaller set of distinct hash codes. The mapping must be one-way in the sense that it must be difficult to find two messages that map to the same hash code. This particular algorithm (the hash code only depending on the XOR of the 128-bit vectors) fails this requirement; it is not hard to find a message that generates a particular hash code. Furthermore, the same hash code can have many messages map to it. In other words, it is very easy to break this hash code.

211. Consider the operation of the key distribution centre: the KDC sends $E_{KA}(K_{AB})$ and $E_{KB}(K_{AB})$ to host A; host A in turn sends the "ticket" $E_{KB}(K_{AB})$ to host B. Explain why the term ticket is appropriate in this situation.

In order for the two hosts A and B to be able to communicate they need to have a common secret key. A initiates the connection by contacting the key distribution centre and obtaining $E_{KA}(K_{AB})$ and $E_{KB}(K_{AB})$. A then extracts the secret key K_{AB} and sends $E_{KB}(K_{AB})$ to B such that B can also extract and possess the secret key K_{AB}. The term ticket for $E_{KB}(K_{AB})$ implies that host B needs the secret key much like a ticket to communicate with host A.

212. Identify the five steps to implement an IDS.
Identify the goal of the IDS, choose what to monitor, choose the response, set thresholds, and implement the system.

213. Is identifying user actions a good choice for an IDS goal?
Generally, no. Tracking user actions would be better performed by examining audit logs.

214. Can a network-based IDS prevent attacks from reaching the target?
Not unless the IDS is in the path of the traffic.

215. What are whitehats and blackhats?
Hackers are often categorized as either whitehate or blackhat. Both whitehats and blackhats have knowledge of how to penetrate a system but their motives are different. A whitehat's aim is to know a system's loopholes to secure the system. On the other hand, blackhats make use of this knowledge for personal gain and other selfish and unethical purposes.
Some computer security consultants are described as whitehat, while "script kiddies" are also sometimes described as blackhat. Script kiddies are known to be less sophisticated hackers who launch attacks against computer systems such as port scanning, defacing a website or launching a denial-of-service attack.

216. How do intruders get password?
Intruders get passwords in various ways. These are some of the most popular methods being used by the hackers nowadays:

Sniffing: Data passing on Ethernet or Wireless networks can usually be intercepted. This is done by making use of protocol analyzer, which sets the network card to promiscuous mode—meaning that it is able to pass all data on the network to the operating system without filtering. Passwords are typically "sniffed" off clear text protocols. Such protocols include POP3, FTP and Telnet. In these cases, passwords flow through the network without making use of any encryption. Many new protocols now make use of encryption. Although encryption makes the task of sniffing passwords more difficult, it is still possible to get the passwords from the encryption data by making use of dictionary and Brute force attacks. Sniffing is very effective method for hackers and attackers since it is usually a passive, and therefore more stealthy and more difficult to detect.

Replay attack: In some cases, intruders do not need to decrypt the passwords. They can use the encrypted form instead in order to login to systems. Tools are also available to make this kind of attack easier. This kind of attack is very popular against web applications.

Passwords file stealing: System passwords are usually stored in files or in the windows registry. On Windows NT 2000 and XP, the passwords are stored in encrypted form on the SAM file. On UNIX systems the password is usually stored in the /etc/password/etc/ shadow. Once an attacker gets his hand on the password file he can launch a dictionary or brute force attack against the encrypted passwords.

Social engineering: Many successful hackers and attackers make use of human weakness-one such well-known hacker is Kevin Mitnick. A common (successful) technique is simply call the user and say," Hi, this is Tom from some company. We have problems within the network and they appear to be coming from your machine. Can you give me your password?" Many users will happily supply this sensitive information without thinking twice.

Default passwords: Sometimes it is not even required to guess the passwords, science the system would have default passwords put in by the system vendor. A lot of network devices such as switches and hardware routers will have default passwords allowing an attacker to easily gain access.

217. What are the limitations of Network-based IDS?

A network-based IDS (Intrusion Detection System) has two big limitations:

Switched network: A network-based IDS must be able to see all network traffic of the network that it is protecting. If a network uses a switch (most do nowadays) a sniffer will not be able to see all the network traffic. This usually means that you would deploy a network-based IDS at the gateway only, i.e. on your interconnection. However, this does not protect you from internal attacks.

High speed: Modern networks are so fast, that an intrusion detection system has a hard time keeping up.

218. How do I collect enough evidence about the hacker?

An interesting field of IDS is collecting enough information about the incident to identify the hacker. This can be very hard because truly elite hackers will be bouncing their attacks from another compromised system. Hackers will also often employ IP address spoofing, which may appear as if attacks are coming from machines that are not even turned on.

As far as I can tell, the best technique is to collect as much information as you can. For example, I have put a packet sniffer capturing to trace file on our T-1 line saving to files on a 16-gigabyte disk (any sniffing program on most platforms can do this). You may not think it fun, but I enjoy perusing these files. It's amazing how many TCP/UDP scans and other probes I see on regular basis. Likewise, you should make sure you have full auditing and logging enabled on any/all systems exposed to the Internet. These will help you figure out what happened when you were hacked.

219. Briefly describe Packet Filtering.

The main process by which packet filtering works in the firewall examines the header information in the packets. Firewalls can examine the source and destination IP addresses and if the numbers or networks are on the permitted lists, the packets can pass through the firewall. Packet filtering of IP addresses operates at the network layers of OSI model.

220. What are the three primary features and functions of IPSec?
IPSec provides three main features and functions.

(i) Modularity: The security administrators can choose an encryption algorithm and security protocols.

(ii) Security services: There are number of security services the administrators can choose. These include access control, message integrity, authentication, replay protection so packets cannot be resent from an unauthorized parity and privacy.

(iii) Level of detail of security services applications: Administrators can choose to place a restriction on all packets meeting a specific criteria or on a subset of those packets based on other factors.

221. What are the four features provided by Pretty Good Privacy (PGP)?
Pretty Good Privacy (PGP) provides the following features:

- Privacy
- Authentication
- Digital signature
- Compression

222. Briefly describe the Privacy Enhanced E-mail (PEM) process.
The Privacy Enhanced E-mail (PEM) message is first converted to a canonical form so that all the messages have the same format for white spaces, carriage returns and line feeds. MD5 or MD2 is used to generate a hash of the message. The original message and hash are concatenated and encrypted by using DES. The encrypted message is encoded with Base64 coding and sent to the recipient as a MIME format e-mail message.

223. What is the approximate range of 802.11x WLANs indoors and outdoors?
Indoors is 150 feet. Outdoors is 1500 feet.

224. Name the three services that WEP provides.
Authentication, confidentiality and integrity.

225. Describe the cryptographic authentication mechanism in WEP.
The AP sends a random number as a challenge to the workstation. The workstation encrypts the challenge with the shared secret and sends it back to the AP. If the AP can decrypt the response with the shared secret and get the original challenge, workstation is authenticated.

226. Suppose a directory that stores certificates is broken into, and the certificates in the directory are replaced by bogus certificates, explain why users will still be able to identify these certificates as bogus.
The users will be able to identify a bogus certificate because each certificate contains a signed message. The signed message is used to authenticate and ensure its integrity. When a user receives a certificate, he/she verifies the integrity based on the signed message. If the computed checksum does not agree with the message, the certificate is invalid.

227. Consider a firewall consisting of packet-filtering router.

(a) Explain how this firewall could be set-up to allow in only HTTP requests to a specific server.

(b) Suppose an outside intruder attempts to send packets with forged internal addresses, which presumably are allowed access to certain systems. Explain how a packet-filtering router can detect these forged packets.

(c) Explain how packets from a given remote host can be kept out.

(d) Explain how inbound mail to specific mail servers is allowed in.

(e) Explain how inbound Telnet service can be blocked.

(a) The firewall examines the packet's IP and TCP header and only forwards the packet with the destined HTTP server address and TCP port 80.

(b) The firewall examines the actual interface the packet is coming from. If the packet with a forged internal address is coming from an interface that is not connected to the internal network, the router will know the packet is a forged packet and can be discarded.

(c) The firewall can keep out all the packets with the source IP address of the given host. However, intruders can use IP spoofing where they modify their IP packets so that they are sent with false IP addresses.

(d) To allow inbound mail to specific mail servers, the firewall can forward packets destined to the specific mail server's IP address with an appropriate TCP port for accessing the mail system.

(e) The firewall can block any Telnet service by blocking any IP packets with a TCP/UDP port set to port number 23. This will avoid any inbound Telnet service.

228. The ICMP "Most Unreachable" error message is sent by a router to the original sender when the router receives a datagram that it cannot deliver or forward. Suppose that the router in question is a packet-filtering router. Discuss the pros and cons of having the router return an ICMP message from the following viewpoints: processor load on the router, traffic load in the network, susceptibility to denial-of-service attacks, and disclosure of filtering operation to intruders.

Processor load on the router: Preparing and sending the ICMP message requires processing, so simply discarding packets and not sending the "Host Unreachable" message can conserve processing bandwidth.

Traffic load in the network: Not sending the "Host Unreachable" message reduces the traffic occupied by such message type. However, the point of sending the "Host Unreachable" message is to fix a problem with misrouting. On balance, sending the message may result in better efficiency in the network.

Susceptibility to denial-of-service attacks: Responding with "Host Unreachable" messages uses processing and hence makes the server more susceptible to denial-of-service attacks.

Disclosure of filtering operation to intruders: If the server responds to "Host Unreachable" messages under some circumstances, then an intruder can send a set of packets to the firewall to try to determine which packet gets the host unreachable message and thus determine the filtering policy used by the router.

229. Compare the following two approaches to operation of a packet-filtering router: discard everything that is not expressly permitted versus forward everything that is not expressly prohibited.

(a) Which policy is more conservative?
(b) Which policy is more visible to the users?
(c) Which policy is easier to implement?

(a) Discard everything that is not expressly permitted is more conservative.
(b) Discard everything that is not expressly permitted is more visible to the users because only a small set of packets are forwarded. The users can easily identify the policy definition in this type of router.
(c) Forward everything that is not expressly prohibited is easier to implement. The router only needs to examine the packet header and determine whether the information matches the prohibited table.

230. What algorithm is used by WEP to provide confidentiality?
RC4.

231. What algorithm is used by WEP to provide integrity?
CRC-32.

232. Identify two targets of active attacks on a WLAN.
Active attacks may be directed at an organization, internal systems or they may be directed at other organizations.

233. If sensitive information is involved in a transaction, what the best location is to use to store session information.
In the back-end database.

234. What type of system is best to identify configuration control problems?
Cryptographic checksums that check files or change.

235. Can availability be completely assured by redundant equipment?
No, as some events are outside the control of the organization.

236. Why is ICMP important to network?

ICMP messages provide valuable information about how the network is functioning.

237. From a security perspective, how should system accessed via partner networks differ from systems accessed from the Internet?
There really is no difference between systems accessed via a partner network and systems accessed via the Internet as they should both be considered semi-trusted systems.

238. Define smart card.
A smart card is used to electronically-authenticate user.

239. What are the factors that influence security policy?
The factors that influences security policy are:
Mission of organization, management support, risk assessment, level of security needed, cost-effectiveness, personnel security responsibilities and accountability, and social factors.

240. Discuss hash function.

A function that maps a variable-length data block or message into a fixed-length value called a hash code. The function is designed in such a way that when protected, it provides an authenticator to the data or message.

241. Explain logic bomb.

Logic embedded in a computer program that checks for a certain set of condition to be present on the system. When these conditions are met, it executes some functions resulting in unauthorized actions.

242. What is fault management?

Detection and isolation of a problem causing a failure in the network.

243. What is integrated local management interface?

A management interface between two ATM interface management entities. It provides a view of configuration and fault parameters across the user network interface.

244. Discuss management information base (MIB).

A management information object holds a unique position and ID in the MIB. The portion of the MIB that a network element permits an SNMP agent to access is called the MIB view.

245. What is management information tree?

A hierarchical tree structure used to organize managed objects and object classes. It is called MIB in SNMP and naming tree or containment tree in OSI.

246. Explain network management system.

A platform that houses the network manager components from a centralized operation.

247. What is network operation centre?

A centralized operation to monitor and manage the network using network management tools and systems.

248. Explain security management.

Provides for legal access to the network resources and protects the data from modification of information, masquerade, message stream modification of information, and disclosure during data transfer. It is one of the OSI systems management functions.

249. Explain structure of management information.

A set of definitions for the structure of management information. It defines management objects and their characteristics as well as the relationship between the objects.

250. What is performance management?

The monitoring and management of performance parameters of a network and the network components.

251. Define network management.

Network management can be defined as operations, administration, maintenance and provisioning of network and services.

Appendix D

Glossary

Access control: A technique used to permit or deny use of data or information system resources to specific users, programs, processes or, other systems based on previously granted authorization to those resources.

Access point: A layer two connectivity device that interfaces wired and wireless networks and controls the networking parameters of its wireless LAN.

Accountability: The ability to trace activities on information resources to unique individuals who accept responsibility for their activities on the network.

Active IDS: An intrusion detection system (IDS) that can react to the traffic it is analyzing. Reactions can be simple, such as running a script or sending a TCP reset, or complex, such as forcibly logging off offending users and terminating their processes.

Active scanning: A method by which client devices discover wireless networks. Active scanning involves a client device broadcasting a probe request frame and receiving a probe response frame containing the parameters of the responding network.

Ad hoc network: A wireless LAN composed of wireless stations without an access point. Also referred to as an independent network or independent basic service set (IBSS).

Address Resolution Protocol (ARP): The protocol used to convert IP addresses into MAC addresses.

AES (Advanced Encryption Standard): A new encryption algorithm chosen by the United States as a replacement for DES (data encryption standard), the official government encryption standard.

Anomaly detection: An IDS model that detects threats by modelling known good network behaviour and characteristics and altering on exceptional differences. *See also* intrusion–detection system.

Asset: Resources or information an organization needs to conduct its business.

Asymmetric encryption: A form of cryptosystem in which encryption and decryption are performed using two different keys, one of which is referred to as the public key and one of which is referred to as the private key. Also known as public-key encryption.

Attacker: A person or computer program that intentionally attempts to gain unauthorized access to information resources, or that attempts to prevent legitimate access to those resources.

Auditing: The name given to any actions or processes used to verify the assigned privileges and rights of a user, as well as any capabilities used to create and maintain a record showing who accessed a particular system and what actions they performed.

Authentication: Verification of who a person or information resources claims to be that sufficiently convinces the authenticator that the identity claim is true. This is followed by an evaluation of whether that entity should be granted access to resources.

Authentication Header (AH): A portion of the IPSec security protocol that provides authentication services and replay–detection ability. AH can be used either by itself or with Encapsulating Security Payload (ESP).

Authenticator: Additional information appended to a message to enable the receiver to verify that the message should be accepted as authentic. The authenticator may be functionally independent of the content of the message itself (e.g. a nonce or a source identifier) or it may be a function of the message contents (e.g. a hash value or a cryptographic checksum).

Authorization: A determination, based on prior authentication, of what rights a person or information resource has, and what elements they should be granted access to.

Availability: Requirement for information to be accessible when it is in need.

Back door: A means of bypassing established authentication, authorization, and access controls protecting an information resource. Back doors are usually left in place intentionally by the original developers to allow them unauthorized access by circumventing security controls. Also called a trap door.

Bacteria: Program that consumes system resources by replicating itself.

Biometrics: An access control mechanism in which a physical characteristic, such as a fingerprint or the geometry of an individual's hand, is used to uniquely identify users.

Block chaining: A procedure used during symmetric block encryption that makes an output block dependent not only on the current plaintext input block and key, but also on earlier input and/or output. The effect of block chaining is that two instances of the same plaintext input block will produce different ciphertext blocks, making cryptanalysis more difficult.

Block cipher: A cryptographic algorithm that operates on a block of bits at a time.

Bluetooth: A wireless technology designed as a short range (approximately ten meters) Personal Area Network (PAN) cable replacement technology that may be built into a variety of devices such as mobile phones, and laptop computers.

Boot virus: A computer virus that infects a hard drive or floppy disk boot sector.

Brute-force attack: A method used for breaking encryption systems. Brute-force methodology entails trying all the possible keys until the proper one is found.

Bus topology: The network topology where all network devices are connected to the same cable or media, called the bus.

Certificate authority: An entity that is responsible for issuing and revoking certificates. CAs are typically third parties, although they exist for internal company use as well. This term is also applied to server software that provides these services.

Certificate repository: A centralized storage location to maintain copies of digital certificates for use by authorized entities.

Challenge Handshake Authentication Protocol (CHAP): Used to provide authentication across point-to-point links the Point-to-Point Protocol.

Cipher: An encoded message.

Ciphertext: The output of an encryption algorithm; the encrypted form of a message or data.

Common Gateway Interface (CGI): The original method of having a web server execute a program outside the web server process, yet on the same server.

Confidential information: Information that requires special handling and protection because it is not intended to be viewed, modified, or discarded by everyone.

Confidentiality: Sharing information among a select group of recipients while protecting it from access by everyone else. Confidentiality is different from privacy in which information is kept a secret known only to the originators of that information.

Configuration auditing: The process of verifying that configuration items are built and maintained according to requirements, standards, or contractual agreement.

Configuration control: The process of controlling changes to items that have been baselined.

Configuration identification: The process of identifying which assets need to be managed and controlled.

Configuration item: Assets identified during configuration identification which need to be managed or controlled.

Conventional encryption: Symmetric encryption

Cookie: Information stored on a user's computer by a web server to maintain the state of the connection to the web server. Used primarily, so preferences or previously used information can be recalled or future requests to the server.

Cracker: A hacker who attempts to break into computer. *See also* hacker.

Cryptanalysis: The branch of cryptology dealing with the breaking of a cipher to recover information or forging encrypted information that will be accepted as authentic.

Cryptographic checksum: An authenticator that is a cryptographic function of both the data to be authenticated and a secret key. Also referred to as a message authentication code (MAC).

Cryptography: The branch of cryptology dealing with the design of algorithms for encryption and decryption, intended to ensure the secrecy and/or authenticity of messages.

Cryptology: The study of secure communications, which encompasses both cryptography and cryptanalysis.

Database auditing: Recording specific actions that are performed on a database server. Auditing can be specified at the level of the database server or on specific database objects.

Database permissions: Permission placed on objects within a database. Database permissions specify which actions a database user can perform on tables, views, stored procedures, and other objects.

Datagram: The name sometimes given to packets in an IP network.

Decryption: The translation of encrypted text or data (called ciphertext) into original text or data (called plaintext).

Denial-of-Service (DoS): Causing an information resource to be partially or completely unable to process requests. This is usually accomplished by flooding the resource with more requests than it can handle, thereby rendering it incapable of providing normal levels of service.

Detection: Protective measures intended to reduce the likelihood of a successful compromise of information resources by recognizing that an attack has occurred or is occurring. An IDS system is a detection measure.

Digital certificate: A digital document that establishes an association between a user and his public key.

Digital Rights Management (DRM): The use of encryption and access control technologies is an attempt to limit access to authorized users. DRM is typically built into software programs and the data files they manipulate.

Digital signature: An authentication mechanism that enables the creator of a message to attach a code that acts as a signature. The signature guarantees the source and integrity of the message.

Digital Subscriber Line (DSL): A local phone circuit designed to directly carry digital communications.

Direct Sequence-Spread Spectrum (DSSS): One of the two approaches to spread spectrum radio signal transmission. In DSSS, the stream of transmitted data is divided into small pieces each of which is allocated across a wide frequency channel. A data signal at the point of transmission is combined with a higher-data-rate bit sequence that divides the data according to a spreading ratio.

Directory attack: An attack against encrypted ciphertext in which a dictionary, or word list, is used. Each word on the list is encrypted in the same manner that a user password is, and then they are compared to the stored, encrypted passwords. If a match is found, the password in cracked. *See also* brute-force attack.

Disaster recovery plan: A written plan developed to address how an organization will react to a natural or man-made disaster in order to ensure business continuity. Related to the concept of a business continuity plan.

Domain Name System (DNS): The service that translates domain and system names, such as www.cnn.com, to IP addresses.

Encoding: Data conversion techniques used to obscure plaintext characters.

Encryption: The conversion of plaintext or data into unintelligible form by means of a reversible translation, based on translation table or algorithm. Also called enciphering.

Extranet: A network that is outside the control of the company. Extranets are usually connections to outside companies, service providers, customers, and business partners.

Fault tolerance: A method to ensure high availability is accomplished through the mirroring of data and systems. Should a "fault" occur, causing disruption in a device, the mirrored system provides the requested data with no apparent interruption in service.

Federal Communications Commission (FCC): An independent U.S. government agency directly responsible to congress. The FCC regulates all forms of interstate and U.S. international communications.

File Transfer Protocol (FTP): File Transfer Protocol is an application level protocol used to transfer files over a network connection.

Finger printing: Using software techniques to discover the identity (version, patch level, or operating system) of remote software or hardware. Finger printing is often used by malicious hackers in preparation for an attack.

Firewall: A network access control system that uses rules to block or allow connections and data transmission between a private network and an untrusted network, such as the Internet.

Forensics: The preservation, identification, documentation, and interpretation of computer data for use in legal proceedings.

Frequency-Hopping Spread Spectrum (FHSS): One of the two approaches to spread spectrum radio signal transmission. FHSS is characterized by a carrier signal that hops pseudo-randomly from frequency to frequency over a defined wide band.

Hacker: Either a person who explores computers and networks to discover their capabilities, or a malicious intruder who tries to discover information by gaining unauthorized access and who may make changes or commit hostile acts.

Harsh function: A function that maps a variable-length data block or message into a fixed-length value called a hash code. The function is designed in such a way that, when protected, it provides an authenticator to the data or message. Also referred to as a message digest.

Heuristic attack: An attack, usually against a password, which attempts to apply knowledge of how users commonly create passwords. It exploits the common ways people think. For example, when asked to add numbers to passwords, users commonly add them to the end of the password. The heuristic attack looks for numbers in the last two digits before looking for characters there. Another example is the use of capital letters. Users commonly capitalize the first character. An example of a seemingly complex password which will be cracked fairly quickly by a heuristic attack is Kopper 2.

Honey pot: A host-based IDS where the entire system is created solely to monitor, detect, and capture security threats against it. *See also* intrusion-detection system.

Host-based IDS: An IDS used to monitor a single host. Usually a host-based IDS is software that is installed on the host it protects. *See also* intrusion-detection system.

Information security: The practice of protecting information in all its forms, whether written, spoken, electronic, graphical, or using other methods of communication.

Information warfare: Warfare conducted against the information and information processing equipment used by an adversary.

Injection attack: A hacker attack where malicious commands are sent in response to host requests solely for the purpose of exploiting the host.

Integrity: Validation, verification that information exists in the form it is supposed to, that it has not been modified, and that it is completely intact.

Internet Control Message Protocol (ICMP): The protocol designed to carry error, network control availability, and traffic flow messages.

Intruder: An individual who gains, or attempts to gain, unauthorized access to a computer system or to gain unauthorized privileges on that system.

Intrusion-Detection System (IDS): A hardware appliance or software designed to detect, alert on, and report malicious attacks and unauthorized misuse on a network or host. An IDS does not do anything about the attack, it simply raises and alert.

Intrusion-Prevention System (IPS): Either an inline device that examines network activity passing through it, dropping any communications that are identified as malicious, or software that resides on a computer system that blocks activity identified as inappropriate (such as buffer overflow, memory allocation violation, and so on). Unlike an IDS, the IPS responds to an attack with some action. The IDS simply reports it.

IPSec: IP Security, a protocol used to secure IP packets during transmission across a network. IPSec offers authentication, integrity, confidentiality services. It uses Authentication Headers (AHs) and Encapsulating Security Payload (ESP) to accomplish this functionality.

Kerberos: The name given to Project Athena's code authentication service.

Key space: The number and range of keys that can be used in a cryptographic algorithm.

Logic bomb: Logic embedded in a computer program that checks for a certain set of conditions to be present on the system. When these conditions are met, it executes some function resulting in unauthorized actions.

Malware: Also known as malicious code, this refers to software that has been designed for some nefarious purposes.

Mandatory access control: A means of restricting access to objects based on fixed security attributes assigned to users and to files and other objects. The controls are mandatory in the sense that they cannot be modified by users or their programs.

Misuse: Any activity that is unauthorized, and which may or may not include specially crafted code or techniques.

Mitigate: Action taken to reduce the likelihood of a threat occurring.

Monoalphabetic algorithms: Encryption algorithms that use a single alphabet.

Multilevel security: A capability that enforces access control across multiple levels of classification of data.

Multiple encryption: Repeated use of an encryption function, with different keys to produce a more complex mapping from plaintext to ciphertext.

Mutual authentication: In this process, not only does the client authenticate to the server, but the server also proves its identity to the client.

Netware: Novell's network operating system.

Network-based IDS: A hardware or software system designed to detect malicious threats by capturing and analyzing network packets.

Non-repudiation: A characteristic of a message or a system that prevents the sender from being able to deny sending the message (in practice, this is very difficult to achieve).

Object-level security: Security-permissions that are applied to specific database objects. For example, a database administrator might allow certain users to update name and address information within the "Employee" database table.

One-time password system: A system in which passwords are used once only, each time the user authentications.

Open system authentication: The default 802.11 authentication method of exchanging

Packet: A small chunk of data transmitted from one device to another.

Password: A character string used to authenticate in Identity. Knowledge of the password and its associated user ID is considered proof of authorization to use the capabilities associated with that user ID.

Plaintext: Text that has not been encrypted

Port scan: The systematic scanning of ports on a specific system to determine which ports currently are active/open with an application listening on it/responding to connection requests.

Pretty Good Privacy (PGP): A popular encryption program. It has the ability to encrypt and digitally sign e-mail and files.

Privacy: Keeping information as a secret, known only to the originators of that information. This contrasts with confidentiality, in which information is shared among a select group of recipients.

Private key: One of the two keys used in an asymmetric encryption system. For secure communication, the private key should only be known to its creator.

Protocol anomaly detection: Anomaly detection done by analyzing network packet headers only.

Public Key Infrastructure (PKI): Infrastructure for binding a public key to a known user through a trusted intermediary, typically a certificate authority.

Public key: One of the two keys used in an asymmetric encryption system. The public key is made public, to be used in conjunction with a corresponding private key.

Quality of service: Network technology that enables network administrators to manage bandwidth and give priority to desired types of application traffic as it traverses the network.

Redundancy: The assurance of availability by providing duplicate systems or alternative processes.

Reliable: Describes a network protocol that will automatically confirm that sent packets are received by the destination host and will retransmit unconfirmed packets.

Replay attacks: An attack in which a service already authorized and completed is forged by another "duplicate request" in an attempt to repeat authorized commands.

Risk elimination: Processing a risk by preventing the risk from occurring by eliminating a vulnerability, eliminating all threats, reducing the cost of a realized threat to zero, or increasing the effectiveness of security measures to 100 per cent.

Risk management: Controlling vulnerabilities, threats, likelihood, loss, or impact with the use of security measures.

Risk mitigation: Processing a risk by controlling its likelihood, its cost, or its threats, through the use of security measures designed to provide these controls.

Risk: The consequences of a realized threat.

Role-based security: The practice of authorizing access to a resource on the basis of the user's identity.

Rule-based authorization: Users rules that stipulate what a specific user can do on a system.

Secret key: The key used in a symmetric encryption system. Both participants must share the same key, and this key must remain secret to protect the communication.

Secure Sockets Layer (SSL): SSL is an encrypting layer between the session and transport layer of the OSI model designed to encrypt above the transport layer, enabling secure sessions between hosts.

Security: The practice of protecting assets. This is fundamental level of the security hierarchy, of which information security, data security, and network security are branches.

Security control: Any technique, technology, activity or practice that is intended to protect assets.

Security policy: The set of decisions that govern security controls.

Security strategy: The proactive plan of action governing the implementation of a security infrastructure.

Signature-detection IDS: An IDS system that works by comparing captured traffic against databases of known bad patterns. Also known as misuse detection.

Sniffing: The capturing of network packets not intended for the host doing the capturing. This can be used maliciously to discover unauthorized information. Also known as packet capturing or protocol analyzing.

Spam: E-mail that is not requested by the recipient and is typically of a commercial nature. Also a known as unsolicited commercial e-mail.

Sticky honey pot: A honey pot built to attack malicious threats and to keep them and slow them down from attacking other legitimate hosts.

Stream cipher: A symmetric encryption algorithm in which ciphertext output is produced bit-by-bit or byte-by-byte from a stream of plaintext input.

Strong security: Security controls that approach being completely effective.

Symmetric encryption: A form of crypto system in which encryption and decryption are performed using the same key.

Threat: An event, action, or object that may cause harm.

Transport Layer Security (TLS): A newer form of SSL being proposed as an Internet standard.

Transposition cipher: A cipher where the same letters are used but the order has been changed.

Trap door: Secret undocumented entry point into a program, used to grant access without normal methods of access authentication.

Trojan horse: A computer program with an apparently or actually useful function that contained additional (hidden) functions that surreptitiously exploit the legitimate authorizations of the invoking process to the detriment of security.

Or

An apparently useful and innocent program containing additional hidden code that allows the unauthorized collection, exploitation, falsification, or destruction of data. A Trojan horse is often received from a familiar e-mail address or URL or in the form of a familar attachment.

Trusted system: A computer and operating system that can be verified to implement a given security policy.

Trustworthy: Having reliable, appropriate, and validated levels of security.

Virtual Local Area Network (VLAN): A logical grouping of two or more nodes that are not necessarily on the same physical network segment but that share the same IP network number. This is often associated with switched Ethernet.

Virtual Private Network (VPN): An encrypted network connection across another network, offering a private communication channel across a public medium.

Virus: Code embedded within a program that causes a copy of itself to be inserted in one or more other programs. In addition to propagation, the virus usually performs some unwanted function.

Vulnerability: A characteristic that leads to exposure, and that may be exploited by a threat to cause harm. Vulnerabilities are most commonly a result of a software flow or misconfiguration.

Weak security: Security controls that are significantly less than completely effective.

Wireless Application Protocol (WAP): A protocol for transmitting data to small handheld devices like cellular phones.

Wireless Transport Layer Security (WTLS): The encryption protocol that is used on WAP networks.

Worm: Program that can replicate itself and send copies from computer to computer across network connections. Upon arrival, the worm may be activated to replicate and propagate again. In addition to propagation, the worm usually performs some unwanted function.

Virtual Local Area Network (VLAN): A logical grouping of two or more nodes that are not necessarily on the same physical network segment but that share the same IP network number. This is often associated with switched Ethernet.

Virus: Code embedded within a program that causes a copy of itself to be inserted in one or more other programs. In addition to propagation, the virus usually performs some unwanted function.

Vulnerability: A characteristic that leads to exposure, and that may be exploited by a threat to cause harm. Vulnerabilities are most commonly a result of a software flow or misconfiguration.

Weak security: Security controls that are significantly less than completely effective.

Worm: Program that can replicate itself and send copies from computer to computer across network connections. Upon arrival, the worm may be activated to replicate and propagate again. In addition to propagation, the worm usually performs some unwanted function.

X.509 standard: The standard format for digital certificates.

Bibliography

Abadi, M. and Needham, R. "Prudent engineering practice for cryptographic protocols", *Proc. IEEE Symp. on Security and Privacy*, 1994, 122–136.

Adam, J. "Threats and countermeasures", *IEEE Spectrum*, vol. 29, August 1992, 21–28.

Adam, N. and Wortman, J. "Security control methods for statistical databases: A study." *ACM Computing Survey*, vol. 21, December 1989, 515–556.

Adam. J. "Cryptography—Privacy", *IEEE Spectrum*, vol. 29, August 1992, 29–35.

Akl, S. "Digital signatures: A tutorial survey", *IEEE Computer*, vol. 16, February 1983, 15–26.

Allen. J., et. al. "State of the practice of intrusion-detection technologies", *Software Engineering Institute Technical Report*, CMU/SEI-99-TR-D28, 1999.

Ames, S., et. al. "Security kevnel design and implementation: An introduction", *IEEE Computers*, vol. 16, July 1983, 14–23.

Anderson, J. "A unification of computer and network security concepts", *Proc. IEEE Symp. on Security and Privacy*, 1997, 65–71.

Beck, L. "A security mechanism for statistical databases", *ACM Transaction on Database Systems*, vol. 5, September 1980, 316–338.

Bell, D. "Security computer systems: A retrospective", *Proc. IEEE Symp. on Security and Privacy*, 1983, 161–162.

Bell, T. "Technology 1996: Communications", *IEEE Spectrum*, vol. 33, January 1996, 30–31.

Bellare, M., Canetti, R., et. al. "Keying hash functions for message authentication", *Proceedings, 'CRYPTO' 96*, August 1996.

Bellovin, S. "Security problems in the TCP/IP protocol suite", *Computer Communication Review*, vol. 19, April 1989, 32–48.

Bellovin, S. and Cheswick, W. "Network firewalls", *IEEE Communication Magazine*, September 1994.

Bellovin, S. and Merritt, M., "Encrypted key exchange", *Proc. IEEE Symp. on Security and Privacy*, 1992, 72–84.

Bennett, C. "Experimental quantum cryptography", *Journal of Cryptography*, vol. 5, 1992, 50–57.

Biham, E. and Shamir, A. "Differential cryptanalysis of the full 16-round DES", *Proceedings CRYPTO Conf.*, 1993, 487–496.

Bishop Matt, *Computer Security*, Pearson Education, 2003.

Bluementhal, U., Hien, N., et. al. "Key derivation for network management applications", *IEEE Network*, May/June 1997.

Boer, B. and Bosselaers, A. "Collisions for the compression function of MD5. *Proceedings Eurocrypt Conf.*, 1993, 293–304.

Bollinger, T. and McGrowan, C. "A critical look at software capability evaluations", *IEEE Software,* vol. 8, July 1991, 25–41.

Booth, K. "Authentication of signatures using public key encryption", *Commn. of the ACM*, vol. 24, November 1981, 772–774.

Bowler, J. and Pelaez, C. "Bad code", *IEEE Spectrum*, vol. 29, August 1992, 36–40.

Brauchle, R. "Hidden risks in web code", *Software Testing and Quality Engineering Magazine*, vol. 4, March/April 2002, 12–13.

Brewin, B. "Retailers defined low-level security on wireless LANs", *Computer World*, 31 May 2002.

Caloyannides, M. "Encryption wars: Early battles", *IEEE Spectrum*, vol. 37, April 2000, 37–43.

Charles, P., Pfleeger, et al., *Security in Computing,* Prentice-Hall of India, 2006.

Chaun, D. "Security without identification: Transaction systems", *Commn. of the ACM*, vol. 28, October 1985, 1030–1044.

Cheng, P., et. al. "A security architecture for the internet protocol", *IBM System Journal*, No. 1, 1998.

Chess, D. "Computer viruses and related threats to computer and network security", *Computer Networks and ISDN Systems*, vol. 17, 1989, 141–147.

Cheswick, W. and Bellovin, S. *Firewall and Internet Security*, Addison-Wesley, 2002.

Chiou, Cr. and Chen, W. "Secure broadcasting using the secure lock", *IEEE Trans. on Software Engineering*, vol. 15, August 1989, 929–934.

Christopher, M. King, Curties E., et. al. *Security Architecture,* Tata McGraw-Hill, 2001.

Clark, D. and Wilson, D. "A comparison of commercial and military computer security policies", *Proc. IEEE Symp. on Security and Privacy*, 1987, 184–194.

Cohen, F. "Computer viruses", *Computer Security: A Global Challenge*, Elsevier Press, 1984, 143–158.

Commer, D. *Internetworking with TCP/IP*, Prentice Hall, 1988.

Davida, G. "Database security", *IEEE Trans. on Software Engineering*, vol. 4, November 1978, 531–533.

Davies, D. "Applying the RSA digital signature to electronic mail", *IEEE Computer*, vol. 16, February 1983, 55–62.

Davies, R., et. al. "A new view of intellectual property and software", *Commn. of the ACM*, vol. 39, March 1996, 21–30.

DeMillo, R. and Merritt, M. "Protocols for data security", *IEEE Computer*, vol. 16, February 1983, 39–54.

Denning, D. "An intrusion-detection model", *IEEE Transaction on Software Engineering*, February 1987.

———. "Protecting public keys and signature keys", *IEEE Computer*, vol. 16, February 1983, 17–35.

———. "Views for multilevel database security", *IEEE Trans. on Software Engineering*, vol. 13, February 1987, 129–140.

Denning, D. and Denning, P. "Certification of programs for secure information flow", *Commn. of the ACM*, vol. 20, July 1977, 504–513.

Denning, D. et. al. "The trackers: a threat to statistical database security", *ACM Trans. on Database System*, vol. 4, March 1979, 76–96.

Dhanjani Nitesh and Clarke Justin, *Network Security Tools*, Shroff Publishers, 2005.

Durst, R., et. al. "Testing and evaluating compuer intrusion detection systems". *Commn. of the ACM*, vol. 42, July 1999, 53–61.

Endorf Carl, Schultz, et. al., *Intrusion Detection* and *Prevention*, Tata Mcgraw-Hill, 2006.

Ehrsam, W., et. al. "A cryptographic key management scheme for implementing the DES", *IBM System Journal*, vol. 17, 1978, 106–125.

El Coamal, A. "A public key cryptosystem and signature scheme based on discrete logarithms", *Proc. Crypo. Conf.*, 1984, 10–18.

Evans, A., et. al. "Comparing information without leaking IT", *Commn. of the ACM*, vol. 39, May 1996, 77–85.

Ford, W. "Advances in public key certificate standards", *ACM SIGSAC Review*, July 1995.

Garvey, T. and Lunt, T. "Model-based intrusion detection", *Proc. National Computer Security Conf.*, 1991.

Gasser, M. and McDermott, E. "An architecture for practical delegation of distributed systems". *Proc. IEEE Symp. on Security and Privacy*, 1990, 20–30.

Gifford, D. "Cryptographic sealing for information secrecy/authenticity", *Commn. of the ACM*, vol. 25, April 1982, 274–285.

Gilgor, V., et. al. "Logics for cryptographic protocols—virtues and limitations", *Proc. IEEE Computer Security Foundation Workshop*, 1991, 219–226.

Goan, T. "Collecting and appraising intrusion evidence", *Commn. of the ACM*, vol. 42, July 1999, 46–52.

Goguen, J. and Mesegure, J. "Security policies and security models", *Proc. IEEE Symp. on Security and Privacy*, 1982, 11–20.

Graubert, R. and Kramer, S. "The integrity lock approach to secure database management", *Proc. IEEE Symp. on Security and Privacy*, 1984.

Hellman, M. "An overview of public key cryptography", *IEEE Communications Society Magazine*, vol. 16, November 1978, 24–32.

———. "DES will be totally insecure within ten years", *IEEE Spectrum*, vol. 16, July 1979, 32–39.

Hoarg, C. "Monitors, an operating system structuring concept", *Commn. of the ACM*, vol. 17, October 1974, 548–557.

Hoffman, L. "Risk analysis and computer security: bridging the cultural gap", *Proc. National Computer Security Conference*, 1986.

Houle, K. and Weaver, G. "Trends in denial of service attack technology", *CERT Coordination Centre Report*, 2001.

Householder, A., et. al. "Computer attack trends challenge internet security", *IEEE Computer and Privacy 2002 Supplement*, April 2002.

Humphrey, W. "Characterizing the software process: a maturity framework", *IEEE Software*, vol. 5, March 1988, 73–79.

I'Anson, C. and Mitchell, C. "Security defects in CCITT recommendation x. 509—the directory authentication framework", *Computer Communication Review*, April 1990.

ISA (Internet Security Alliance), "Internet risk impact summary for March 26, 2002 through June 24, *ISS Report*, 2002.

ITSEC Working Group ITSEC, "Information technology security evaluation criteria, 10 January 1991.

Joner, A. and Lipton R., "The enforcement of security policies for computation", *Journal of Computer and System Science*, vol. 17, August 1978, 35–55.

Joshi, J., et. al. "Security models for web-based applications", *Comm. of the ACM*, vol. 44, February 2001, 38–44.

Juenerman, R. "Electronic document authentication", *IEEE Network*, vol. 1, April 1987, 17–23.

Juenerman, R., et. al. "Authentication with manipulation detection code", *Proc. IEEE Symp. on Security and Privacy*, 1983, 33–34.

Karger, P. "Implementing commercial data integrity with secure capabilities", *Proc. IEEE Symp. on Security and Privacy*, 1988, 130–139.

Karger, P., et. al. "A retrospective on the VAX VMM security kernel", *IEEE Trans. on Software Engineering*, vol. 17, November 1991, 1147–1165.

Kaufman Charlie, Perlman Radia, and Specines Mike, *Network Security*, Pearson Education, 2006.

Kemmerer, R. and Vigna, G. "Intrusion detection: a brief history and overview", *IEEE Computer Security and Privacy, 2002 Supplement*, April 2002, 27–30.

Kent, S. "On the trail of intrusion into systems", *IEEE Spectrum*, vol. 37, December 2000, 52–56.

Kieburtz, R. and Silberschantz, A. "Capability managers", *IEEE Trans. on Software Engineering*, vol. 4, November 1978, 467–477.

Kohl, J. "The use of encryption in kerberos for network authentication", *Proceedings, Crypto* '89, published by Springer–Verlag.

Lamport, L. "Password authentication with insecure communication", *Comm. of the ACM*, vol. 24, November 1981, 770–771.

Lamport, L., et. al. "The byzantine generals problem", *ACM Trans. on Programming Languages and Systems*, vol. 4, July 1982, 382–401.

Landwehr, E., et. al. "The best technologies for computer security", *IEEE Computers*, vol. 16, July 1983, 86–100.

Landwehr, C., et. al. "A security model for military message systems", *ACM Trans. Computing Systems*, vol. 2, August 1984, 198–222.

Laudon, K. "Ethical concepts and information technology", *Comm. of the ACM*, vol. 38, December 1995, 33–39.

Laudon, C. Kenneth, Jane P. Laudon, *Management Information Systems,* Prentice-Hall of India, 2006.

Lawton, G. "Open source security: Opportunity of oxymoron", *IEEE Computer*, vol. 35, March 2002, 18–21.

Lechter, M. "Protecting software and firmware devices", *IEEE Computer,* vol. 16, August 1983, 73–82.

Lee, T. "Using mandatory integrity to enforce commercial security", *Proc. IEEE Symp. on Security and Privacy*, 1988, 140–146.

Lenstra, A. and Verheul, E. "Selecting cryptographic key sizes", *Journal of Cryptography*, vol. 14, 2001, 255–293.

Liepens, G. and Vaccaro, H. "Intrusion detection: Its role and validation", *Computers and Security*, vol. 11, 1992, 347–355.

———. "Anomaly detection: Purpose and framework," *Proc. National Computer Security Conf.*, 1989, 495–504.

Lu, W. and Sundereshan, M. "Secure communication in internet environment", *IEEE Trans. on Communications*, vol. 37, October 1989, 1014–1023.

Lunt, J., et. al. "The seaview security model", *IEEE Trans. on Software Engineering*, vol. 16, June 1990.

Lunt, T. "A survey of intrusion detection techniques", *Computers and Security*", vol. 12, June 1993, 405–418.

Lynch, D. *Internet Systems Handbook*, Addison-Wesley, 1992.

Mason, R. "Ethics to information technology issues", *Commn. of the ACM*, vol. 38, December 1995, 55–57.

McDermid, John A. "Safety-critical software: a vignette", *IEE Software Engineering Journal*, vol. 8, 1993, 2–3.

McLean, J. "Security models and information flow", *Proc. IEEE Symp. on Security and Privacy,* 1986, 134–137.

Merkle, R. and Hellman, M. "On the security of multiple encryption", *Comm. of the ACM,* vol. 24, July 1981, 465.

Merkle, R. "Protocols for public key cryptosystems", *Proc. IEEE Symp. on Security and Privacy,* 1980, 122–133.

Milberg, S., et. al. "Values, personal information, privacy, and regulatory approaches", *Comm. of the ACM,* vol. 38, December 1995, 65–74.

Millen, J., et. al. "The interrogator: Protocol security analysis", *IEEE Trans. on Software Engineering,* vol. 13, February 1987, 274–288.

Millen, J. "A resource allocation model for denial of service", *Proc. IEEE Symp. on Security and Privacy,* 1992, 137–147.

Moffet, J. and Sloman, M. "The source of authority for commercial access control", *IEEE Computer,* vol. 21, February 1988, 59–69.

Morris, R. and Thompson, K. "Password security: A case history," *Comm. of the ACM,* vol. 39, May 2002, 40–45.

Needham, R. "Denial of service: an example" *Comm. of the ACM,* vol. 37, November 1994, 42–47.

Nessett, D. "Factors affecting distributing system security", *IEEE Trans. on Software Engineering,* vol. 13, February 1987.

NIST (National Institute of Standards and Technology). "The digital signature standard, proposal and discussion". *Comm. of the ACM,* vol. 35, July 1992, 36–54.

Palmer, C. "Ethical hacking", *IBM Systems Journal,* vol. 40, 2001, 769–780.

Parker, D. and Nycum, S. "Computer crime", *Comm. of the ACM,* vol. 27, April 1984, 313–321.

Paulk, M. "How ISO 9001 compares with CMM", *IEEE Software,* vol. 12, January 1995, 74–82.

Paulk, M., et. al. "Capability maturity model, version 1.1", *IEEE Software,* vol. 10, July 1993, 18–27.

PCSG (Public Cryptography Study Group). "Report of the public cryptography study group", *Comm. of the ACM,* vol. 24, July 1981, 834–450.

Pfleeger, C. and Pfleeger, S. "A transaction flow approach to software security certification", *Computer and Security,* vol. 7, 1988, 495–502.

Pfleeger, S. "A framework for security requirements", *Computers and Security,* vol. 10, 1991, 515–523.

Pfleeger, C. "The fundamentals of information security", *IEEE Software,* vol. 14, January 1997, 15–16.

Pless, V. "Encryption schemes for computational confidentiality", *IEEE Trans. on Computers,* vol. 26, November 1977, 1133–1136.

Purdy, G., et. al. "A software protection scheme", *Proc. IEEE Symp. on Security and Privacy,* 1982, 99–103.

Rivest, R., et. al. "Method for obtaining digital signature and public-key cryptosystems", *Comm. of the ACM,* vol. 21, February 1978, 120–126.

Rivest, R. "The MD4 message digest algorithm", *Proc. Crypto. Conf.,* 1991, 303–311.

Robert Bragg, et. al. *Network Security: The Complete Reference,* Tata McGraw-Hill, 2006.

Rubin, A. and Geer, D. "Mobile code security", *IEEE, Internet Computing,* November–December 1998.

Rushby. J.M. and Randell, B. "A distributed secure system", *IEEE Computer,* vol. 16, July 1983, 55–67.

Schaefuer, M. "Symbol security condition considered harmful", *Proc. IEEE Symp. on Security and Privacy,* 1989, 20–46.

Schaumueller-Bich and Piller, E. "A method of software protection based on the use of smart cards", *Proc. Euro. Crypt. Conf.* 1984, 446–454.

Shamir, A. "How to share a secret", *Comm. of the ACM,* vol. 22, November 1979, 612–613.

Shamir, A. and Zippel, R. "On the security of the Merkle-Hellman cryptographic scheme", *IEEE Trans. on Information Theory,* vol. 26, May 1980, 339–340.

Simmons, G. "Cryptanalysis and failures", *Commn. of the ACM,* vol. 37, November 1994, 56–64.

———. "Symmetric and asymmetric encryption", *Computing Surveys,* vol. 11, December 1979, 305–330.

Stallings William, *Cryptography and Network Security,* Pearson Education, 2006.

Singh, Brijendra, *Data Communications and Computer Networks*, Prentice-Hall of India, 2004.

———. "Network reliability evaluation by decomposition", *Microelectronics and Reliability,* vol. 34, 1994.

———. "Procedure for generating sums of dispoint products", *Microelectronics and Reliability,* vol. 33, 1993.

———. "Research methodology in information technology", *Proceedings of UGC Refresher Course,* 11–30, November 2002.

———. "Distributed computing network reliability", *Proceedings of 13th National Convention of Computer Engineers,* IIT Roorkee, December 1988, 22–24.

———. "Security of information system", *Proceedings of the International Symposium of Information Technology: Emerging Trends,* IIT Allahabad, 19–21, September 2003.

———. Network Security and Management, IEEE *International Conference on Computational Intelligence* and *Computing Research,* 28–29 December 2010.

Singh, Brijendra and Jaisankar, N. "A network intrusion detection system framework using mobile agents", *International Conf. on Reliability and Safety Engineering,* IIT Kharagpur, 21–23, December, 2005, 185–194.

Singh, Brijendra, P. Dhanavanthan, and Mani, T. "SEYS: Statistical Expert Systems for Information Management", *IETE, Technical Review*, March–April 2004.

Singh, Brijendra and Hemant Kumar Singh, Web Data Mining Research: A Survey, *IEEE International Conference on Computational Intelligence* and *Computing Research*, 28–29 December 2010.

Singh, Brijendra and Pooja Agarwal, "Algorithm for web server security", IETE Journal of Research, Vol. 57, No. 5, Sept–October 2011.

———. Study of Security Measures in Indian Websites, *National Conference on Reserach & Development Trends in ICT*, 12–13 February 2010, Lucknow.

Singh, Brijendra and S.P. Kannojia, Development of High Quality Software, *National Conference on Research* and *Development Trends in ICT*, 12–13 February 2010, Lucknow.

Smith, G. "Modelling security—Relevant data semantics", *IEEE Trans. on Software Engineering*, vol. 17, November 1991, 1195–1203.

Stillerman, M., et. al. "Intrusion detection for distributed applications", *Comm. of the ACM*, vol. 42, July 1999, 62–69.

Stoll, C. "Stalking the wily Hacker", *Comm. of the ACM*, vol. 31, May 1998, 484–497.

Turn, R. "Private sector needs for trusted/secure computer systems", *Proc. AFIPS National Computer Conf.*, 1982, 449–460.

Vigna, G. and Kemmerer, R. "NetSTAT: A network-based intrusion-detection system", *Proc. Annual Computer Security Application Conf.*, December 1988.

———. "NetSTAT: A network-based intrusion-detection system, *Journal of Computer Society*", vol. 7, 1999.

Voydock, V. and Kent, S. "Security mechanisms in high-level network protocols", *Computing Surveys*, vol. 15, June 1983, 135–171.

Walker, S. "Network security overview", *Proc. IEEE Symp. on Security and Privacy*, 1985, 62–76.

Ware, W. "Information system security and privacy", *Comm. of the ACM*, vol. 27, April 1984, 316–321.

Weisband, S. and Reining, B. "Managing user perceptions of e-mail privacy", *Comm. of the ACM*, vol. 38, December 1995, 140–47.

Whitehorn-Umphers, D. "Hackers, hot roads, and the information drag strip", *IEEE Spectrum*, vol. 38, October 2001, 14–17.

Wm. Arthur Conklin, et. al. *Principles of Computer Security*, McGraw-Hill, 2004.

Zimmerman, P. "A proposed standard format for RSA cryptosystems", *IEEE Computer*, vol. 19, September 1986, 21–34.

Index